Forage Plants and Their Culture

M.S. CHARLES V. PIPER

The Rural Text-Book Series

MANN, BEGINNINGS IN AGRICULTURE.

WARREN, ELEMENTS OF AGRICULTURE.

WARREN, FARM MANAGEMENT.

LYON AND FIPPIN, SOIL MANAGEMENT.

J. F. DUGGAR, SOUTHERN FIELD CROPS.

B. M. DUGGAR, PLANT PHYSIOLOGY.

HARPER, ANIMAL HUSBANDRY FOR SCHOOLS.

MONTGOMERY, CORN CROPS.

WHEELER, MANURES AND FERTILIZERS.

LIVINGSTON, FIELD CROP PRODUCTION.

WIDTSOE, IRRIGATION PRACTICE.

PIPER, FORAGE PLANTS AND THEIR CULTURE.

Others in preparation.

FORAGE PLANTS AND THEIR CULTURE

BY

CHARLES V. PIPER, M.S.

AGROSTOLOGIST IN CHARGE OF FORAGE CROP INVESTIGATIONS
BUREAU OF PLANT INDUSTRY, UNITED STATES
DEPARTMENT OF AGRICULTURE

New York
THE MACMILLAN COMPANY
1914

Norwood Press
J. S. Cushing Co. — Berwick & Smith Co.
Norwood, Mass., U.S.A.

PREFACE

The exceedingly diversified climatic conditions in North America have led to the cultivation of an unusually large number of plant species for forage production. Some of these are successful or important over but a comparatively small area, and not one is capable of profitable cultivation over the whole region. The climatic conditions of some parts of North America, especially the dry regions and the southernmost states, are not closely duplicated in any part of Europe. This fact has necessitated the introduction of numerous grasses and legumes from other regions to secure forage plants capable of profitable cultivation. The success of these endeavors has resulted in the utilization of many forage crops practically unknown in Europe, such as numerous varieties of sorghum, cowpeas, soybeans, Japan clover, Florida beggarweed, velvet bean, Bermuda-grass, Rhodes-grass, and many others. In some sections, there is still need of better adapted or more productive forage crops. Extensive experimental investigations have been conducted with only a few forage crops in America, so that there yet remains much to be learned concerning most of the others.

The aim of the author has been to present as concisely as practicable the present state of our knowledge with reference to each forage crop grown in America, and it is hoped that no important contributions to the subject have been omitted.

The illustrations are mostly those which have been used in various publications of the United States Department of

Agriculture, the seed illustrations being reproductions of the unequalled drawings of Professor F. H. Hillman.

The bringing together of the scattered results of American research with some references to those of Europe will, it is hoped, reveal to students the phases of the subject which need further investigation.

In preparing this volume the author wishes to acknowledge the aid he has received from his colleagues, R. A. Oakley, J. M. Westgate, H. N. Vinall, W. J. Morse, M. W. Evans, H. L. Westover, and Katherine S. Bort.

CHARLES V. PIPER.

Washington, D.C.,
January, 1914.

CONTENTS

vii

LIST OF ILLUSTRATIONS

xvii

LIST OF PLATES

FORAGE PLANTS AND THEIR CULTURE

CHAPTER I

INTRODUCTION

Domestic animals are an indispensable part of a good agriculture, even though they may have no place in the business of some of the high-class specialty farmers. To rear animals necessitates forage; and the more important the animal production, the greater is the necessity that the forage be grown as a crop and be made a part of the farm scheme. The forage crops are now of many kinds, and they are taking their places in the regular farm-management plans of the forward farmer. These crops also have their own value as marketable products, constituting one of the important cash incomes of the farm.

1. Definitions. — Forage includes any vegetable matter, fresh or cured, eaten by herbivorous animals, such as grain, hay, pasturage, green feed, roots and silage. The term *feed* is synonymous with forage, although sometimes restricted to grain. Fodder and stover are also identical in original meaning, but in the United States are used with special significations.

Forage crops include only those plants grown primarily for feed and of which animals consume all or much of the vegetative parts; that is, herbage, or roots. Most cereal crops are also grown for hay, pasturage or silage, and when thus grown may be considered forage crops. Several plants cultivated in other regions as cereals are in the United States grown mainly or wholly for forage. Among these are the grain sorghums, penicillaria, foxtail millet and proso or broom-corn millet. The distinction between cereals and forage crops in such cases is arbitrary. Such a plant is a cereal when grown primarily for the grain, and a forage when grown primarily for the herbage.

Fodder (German *futter*) really means the same as feed. In the United States the term is used mainly in reference to corn cut before the plant is fully mature, and from which the ears are not removed. The stems and leaves when dried and after the ears are removed is called *stover*. In the Southern States the term *fodder* is applied to the dried leaves and tops of the corn plant, removed while green, and before the ears are fully mature.

The terms *fodder* and *stover* are also used in connection with the sorghums and similar coarse grasses.

Hay consists of the entire dried herbage of comparatively fine-stemmed grasses or other forage plants. It is commonly dried or cured in the sun, but artificial drying apparatus has been used. The process of curing is not merely one of drying, as grass dried quickly with artificial heat is quite different from that cured with relative slowness. Under the latter conditions fermentative changes take place, due mainly to enzymes, which give freshly cured hay a characteristic aroma varying with the plant used. This odor is much less evident in plants quickly dried.

Brown hay is prepared by stacking grass or clover when only half cured, on account of which it undergoes fermentation with heating. The product is brown and compact. Brown hay is commonly prepared in regions where on account of climatic conditions dry curing is difficult. It is somewhat intermediate between hay and silage in quality.

Soiling is a term used to denote feeding with green plants, when the plants are cut and carried to the animals. Next to pasturing, this is the most primitive way of feeding animals. It is practically the only way that cut herbage is used in half-civilized countries.

Silage is prepared by compacting green herbage in an air-tight receptacle in which it undergoes fermentation. In America the principal crop used for silage is corn, and this, after cutting in small pieces so that it will pack closely, is placed in a specially constructed *silo* to insure fermentation under nearly anaërobic conditions. The material is *ensilaged* in the silo.

Straw is a term applied to the dried remnants of a crop from which the seed has been thrashed. The term is used most commonly in reference to the small grains, wheat, oats, rye and barley, but is properly applied also to thrashed flax, cowpeas, millets, etc.

Root crops is applied to forage crops whose principal value lies in the subterranean portion, whether true roots or tubers. They are extensively grown for forage only in countries where they can be produced more cheaply than grain feeds. Their culture is therefore extensive in northern Europe, but has thus far received very little attention in America except in Canada, the Northeastern States and in the humid belt along the Pacific coast, all being regions not well adapted to the culture of corn. Root crops require a considerable amount of hand labor and, partly on this account and partly because of their greater cost, are not popular where plants like corn, sorghum or similar crops can be grown.

Feeds are conveniently distinguished according to nutritive value into *concentrates* with high feeding value and *roughage*, or *roughness*, with relatively low feeding value. Concentrates include grains, or products thereof, oil meal, and for hogs tankage and similar products. Roughage includes hay, fodder, straw, silage, roots, pasturage.

Roughages have been considered to be made up of two or three general classes. Very commonly two such classes are recognized, one composed of the grass hays, roots, silage and stover, which are low in protein; the other composed of the legumes and also grass in the form of pasturage and rowen, which differ in having a higher protein content.

Another classification recognizes three groups; namely, 1. legumes; 2. mixed legumes and grasses; 3. grasses (including corn). Perhaps a fourth group should be added; namely, the straws, which, however, are very variable in value.

A meadow on a farm is a field planted to grasses or legumes or both for hay. Commonly the term implies perennial meadows, but the phrase "annual meadows" is occasionally used. In northern regions the word meadow is also used for natural grass areas, especially if wet.

The second growth of most grasses, especially those which bloom but once a season is called *aftermath* or *rowen*.

Grass. — Besides its use in a purely botanical sense, the word grass is often used in agriculture to mean any plant growing for hay or pasture. The crop in a rotation is thus called grass even if it be clover or alfalfa.

A pasture is a field in which animals graze on herbaceous plants. Any crop thus utilized is spoken of as a pasture crop. Permanent pastures are such as can be grazed upon for several years and contain perennial plants or a succession of annuals, or both.

Browsing is sometimes used as synonymous with grazing, but usually the word browse is restricted to shrubs of which animals eat the leaves or twigs.

Wild pastures, whether wooded or prairie, are often called *ranges* or *range lands*, especially in the West.

2. Knowledge of forage crops compared with other crops. — A critical survey of the present state of agronomic knowledge concerning forage crops as revealed both in literature and in practice makes clear the fact that there is not nearly as much accurate information about these crops as there is concerning others such as cereals, cotton, tobacco, etc. The reasons for this are not far to seek. *First*, forage crops are only rarely grown as money crops, and the farmer seldom knows with any degree of accuracy what yields he obtains. His forage crops are, therefore, not brought into yearly comparison with those of his neighbors, so that no definite criterion becomes established as to what are good and what poor yields. Consequently, there is lacking the spur for better effort brought about by the knowledge of the yields, and especially the money returns secured by neighboring farmers. *Second*, there is a larger variety of plants grown for forage, no one of which is cultivated over so wide an area as any of the important cereal crops. There is, consequently, a smaller amount of information about each of the many forage crops than there is concerning any one of the few cereal crops.

The purely agronomic knowledge available, — that is, that relating to yield as affected by environmental, cultural or other factors, namely, climate, soil, fertilizers, culture, irrigation, variety, rate of seeding, rotation, — is partly the result of definite experiments, but largely the experience of farmers. Experimental results, where available, are more enlightening than those based on farm returns, but a vastly greater amount of experimental data is necessary for a better understanding of the com-

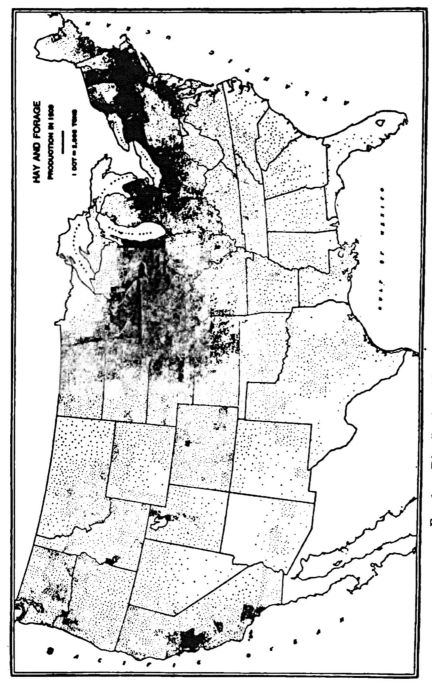

FIG. 1. — Distribution of hay and forage in the United States.

plex factors which affect yield. To the critical student, the relative paucity of accurate knowledge concerning yield relations will be apparent as the data concerning each crop is studied.

3. Forage crops and civilization. — The culture of crops grown purely as feed for herbivorous animals is mainly a product of European civilization. Even yet such crops are seldom grown except in regions settled or governed by Europeans. Less civilized peoples have depended for the sustenance of their flocks wholly or mainly on natural pasturage; or, where the population is dense, as in India and China, have utilized as forage only the refuse or surplus of crops grown for human food, supplemented by any pasturage available. To a slight extent, it is true, alfalfa was cultivated in ancient Persia, and perhaps red clover also, but this exception only emphasizes the fact that the culture of most forage crops originated and developed in Europe.

In America the relative importance of forage to other staple crops has been still more developed. This is easily seen in a comparison of the forage crops with the total value of all field crops in India, Europe and America: —

TABLE SHOWING THE ACREAGES OF ALL CROPS, OF FORAGE AND THE NUMBER OF CATTLE AND HORSES IN THE UNITED STATES, CANADA, EUROPE AND INDIA.

COUNTRY	ALL CROPS	FORAGE	CATTLE AND HORSES	YEAR
	Acres	Acres		
United States	301,325,598	72,280,776	85,952,446	1909
Canada . .	33,047,783	9,156,573	9,353,000	1911
Europe . .	792,644,963	92,789,168	181,989,750	1906–11
India . . .	225,892,425	4,881,742	103,677,987	1910

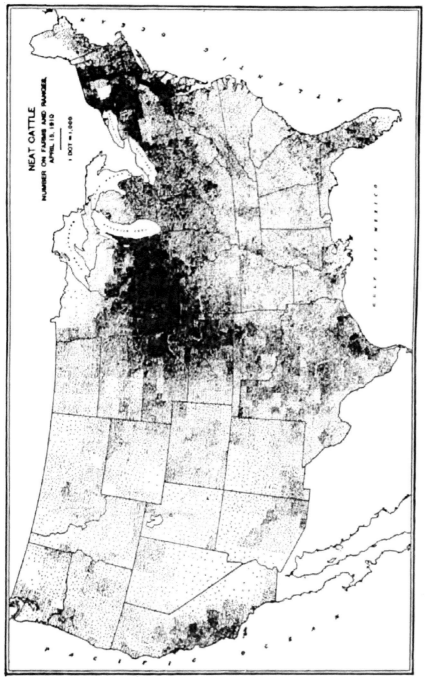

FIG. 2. — Distribution of cattle in the United States. 1 dot equals 1000 head. Compare distribution with that of forage in Fig. 1.

The actual value of the forage grown is, of course, far greater than the hay and forage of the census returns. To these figures need to be added the value of pasturage and of the straw of various crops. It is probable that each one of the 103,000,000 of cattle in India consumes about as much feed as does each of the 86,000,000 in the United States, but in India practically all of the forage is either straw or wild grass. While the growing of crops purely to feed animals is partly based on sentimental grounds, its justification lies in the fact that it is sound economy.

4. Forage crops in Europe and in America. — In comparing the forage crops grown in America and in Europe, it must be borne in mind that there are great differences in the climate and some in the soil which in large measure account for the relative importance of particular forage plants in the two continents. So far as climate is concerned, only California corresponds closely with the countries of southern Europe; only the northwest Pacific coast region is at all comparable with England and northern Germany; and the eastern portion of the Great Plains is not very different from eastern Russia. On the other hand, the northeastern portion of the United States and adjacent Canada differs from any portion of Europe in having hot humid summers, and the winters too are colder than those of western Europe; the Southern States, especially the cotton region, are still more different in climate from any portion of Europe.

Almost without exception the plants of southern Europe succeed well in California, those of middle western Europe on the north Pacific coast, and those of eastern Russia on the Great Plains.

In marked contrast, but very few European forage plants are well adapted to the Southern States, the most important being primarily winter crops; namely, vetch, bur clover, white clover and redtop.

Likewise, in the Northern States and Canada, many important European forages have found but little place, but four of them have on account of their marked adaptation for the region attained relatively a much higher importance than they have in Europe. These four are timothy, red clover, Kentucky blue-grass and redtop. The utilization of these over much of the eastern United States to the practical exclusion of many of the other perennial grasses and legumes much used in Europe is striking. Over the area in question at least 50 per cent of the hay crop is made up of timothy and red clover alone, and probably 70 per cent of the improved pastures of Kentucky blue-grass and redtop.

Some European plants, like sainfoin, are not grown in America because there are no chalky soils; others, like the lupines and serradella, seem poorly adapted to withstand summer heat; and many of the perennial grasses do not hold their own in pastures and meadows in competition with the more aggressive, better adapted species.

5. Perennial hay plants in Europe and America compared. — In Europe eleven perennial grasses — namely, perennial rye-grass, Italian rye-grass, orchard-grass, meadow foxtail, meadow fescue, tall oat-grass, yellow oat-grass, velvet-grass, timothy, redtop and sweet vernal grass, — and five perennial legumes — namely, red, white and alsike clovers, alfalfa and sainfoin, — may be considered as of prime importance.

In North America, if we except alfalfa, these European grasses are well adapted only to the area north of latitude 36°, after excluding much of the semi-arid region. South of this latitude few of them are worth cultivating.

The general practice in Europe is to sow both meadows and pastures to complex mixtures of grasses. In marked contrast the American practice is to sow pure cultures or very simple mixtures.

Of the above list only seven can be said to be much cultivated in America; namely, timothy, redtop and orchard-grass, alfalfa, and red, white and alsike clovers. The remainder are relatively much neglected, though most of them have distinct value, at least in special areas. Neglect of their greater use is perhaps due to the ascendancy which timothy has in American favor and to an actual lack of knowledge concerning their merits.

6. Botany of forage crops. — The greater numbers of forage crops are either grasses (*Gramineæ*) or legumes (*Leguminosæ*). There are definite reasons why this is the case. On prairie or meadow lands in all parts of the world, grasses make up a large percentage of the herbage. This is particularly true in areas where wild herbivorous animals existed in large numbers, as on our western prairies and in south Africa. The two facts are correlated. Without the grasses the abundant herds of animals could not have existed, and with the abundant herds few plants are so well adapted as the grasses to withstand heavy grazing and trampling. The reason for this lies in the fact that the growing part of a grass leaf is near its base and so is not injured when the upper part is bitten off, while with most other plants the growing point is terminal and therefore easily destroyed by grazing animals. Furthermore, many grasses are amply provided with vegetative means of spreading and reproducing, so that even if continuously cropped short, they nevertheless survive. The other plants most like the grasses — namely, the rushes and sedges — are, with a few exceptions, not

8. Characteristics of grasses. — Botanically the grasses form a sharply defined family characterized by having jointed, usually hollow, stems, with cross partitions at the nodes; two-ranked, parallel-veined leaves, the basal portion or *sheath* inclosing the stem, and bearing where it joins the *blade* a peculiar appendage, the *ligule* (Fig. 3); flowers very small, mostly perfect, but sometimes unisexual, consisting of 3 stamens, rarely 1, 2 or 6; one pistil with two papillate or plumose stigmas; and 2,

Fig. 3. — Ligule of a grass leaf.

Fig. 4.—Spikelet of orchard-grass.

Fig. 5. — A single floret of orchard-grass.

rarely 3, small perianth segments, the *lodicules* at the base of the ovary; flowers always in spikelets, with 2-ranked bracts or scales, arranged on an axis, the *rachilla*. The two lower bracts are called *glumes*, and each succeeding one is a *lemma*. Above and opposite the lemma is the 2-nerved palea, which incloses the floret. The florets are usually as numerous as the lemmas, but the upper ones are often sterile.

The fruit is a caryopsis or grain, with small lateral embryo and relatively large starchy endosperm. For the most part grass flowers are wind pollinated, but some on which the stamens do not become exserted are self-pollinated, as in the case of wheat.

Agricultural grasses are either annuals or perennials.

The annuals are mostly grown as cereals in some part of the world at least, but several are grown in America primarily as forage, such as millets and sorghums.

The perennials may be distinguished as bunch grasses, like orchard-grass and timothy, and creeping grasses, like Kentucky blue-grass and Bermuda. In the former the new shoots are *intravaginal;* that is, the new shoots do not break through the lowest sheath but grow erect within it; in the creeping grasses the shoots are *extravaginal;* that is, they pierce the lowest sheath and for a longer or shorter distance develop as rhizomes below ground, or stolons above ground. In a few grasses, like various-leaved fescue, both types of shoots are formed.

The roots of all grasses are very slender and but little branched. Even in perennial grasses the roots usually live but one season and then new ones are formed.

To possess high agricultural value, a grass must be palatable and healthful; it must yield well; and above all, it must have good seed habits, so that the seed can be harvested cheaply. Even in the best of the perennial grasses the seed is relatively inferior in viability, as compared with other crop plants.

9. Legumes. — Legumes or pulses are distinguished botanically by having the leaves alternate, with stipules and mostly compound; flowers usually papilionaceous — that is, like a pea flower; pistil simple, becoming in fruit a legume; embryo usually completely filling the seed.

Biologically, most leguminous plants are remarkable for their ability to use free atmospheric nitrogen, by the aid of certain bacteria that form nodules on the roots.

Most of the cultivated legumes thrive best in soil containing a high content of lime, but others, like trefoil and white clover, are indifferent to lime. A few, like lupines and serradella, are injuriously affected if lime be added to the soil. Perennial legumes have as a rule stout roots which serve partly as storage organs for reserve food. Partly on this account, they are cut for hay in early bloom, as after this stage reserve stuff is deposited in the roots.

10. Root nodules. — On the roots of most legumes and a few other plants occur nodules or tubercles. Woronin in 1866 discovered that these contained bacteria-like organisms, but their importance was not realized until Hellriegel in 1887 demonstrated that leguminous plants can utilize atmospheric nitrogen by the aid of these nodule bacteria. When the root nodules are absent, legumes, like most other plants, must depend on combined nitrogen in the soil.

It was known to the Romans in Pliny's time that certain legumes helped succeeding crops, and indeed legumes mixed or in rotation with other crops have been used in India and China probably since prehistoric times. The importance of leguminous crops is, however, more clearly recognized since their rôle as nitrogen conservors has been discovered.

11. The nodule organism. — The organism causing the nodules in legumes is now called *Pseudomonas radicicola*. Apparently it is but one and the same species that causes the nodules on legumes and on such plants as *Alnus*, *Shepherdia*, *Podocarpus*, *Ceanothus* and others. The organism occurs in different physiological forms, for it is not possible, except in a few cases, to inoculate a legume of one genus directly with the nodule bacteria from another. The only definitely proved case of this is Melilotus and Medicago, alfalfa being readily inoculated by sweet clover. It is probable, also, that the bacteria of garden peas inoculate vetch and *vice versa*, but this lacks proof, as does Nobbe's contention that Pisum will inoculate Phaseolus.

12. Forms of root nodules. — The root nodules on different legumes vary greatly in size, shape and abundance. To a certain extent they are characteristic for each genus. The nodule is morphologically a modified rootlet. In many legumes it is always simple, but in others is more or less branched, sometimes into a coral-like mass. In the common cultivated clovers the nodules on the younger roots are small and globose, becoming club-shaped and often bilobed. On older roots they become more branched or lobed.

Alfalfa produces nodules much like red clover, but usually longer and more branched.

On Canada peas and the vetches the nodules are still more branched and fan-shaped in form. Clusters of these often form globose masses.

In the cowpea, peanut and most beans, the nodules are irregularly globose and solid. These are frequently as large as a pea seed. On the soybean, the nodules are also globose but marked on the surface with raised ridges.

The velvet bean produces perhaps the largest nodules of any legume. These are sometimes as large as a baseball. Such are really clusters of branched nodules but packed together very densely.

13. Natural inoculation. — Any legumes may easily be inoculated on new land by scattering soil from an old field where the same legume has previously produced nodules, as is nearly always the case when a legume crop is successful. This method was used in Europe before its significance was discovered. In thus inoculating new land, from 100 to 500 pounds of old soil should be used to the acre. It may be scattered in any convenient way,

c

but preferably with a drill or on a cloudy day. Sunlight is destructive to the bacteria, so the inoculating soil should be harrowed in unless sown with a drill.

The use of the naturally inoculated soil is open to the objection that it may serve to spread weeds, insects and plant diseases, especially if brought from a distance.

In some cases, the nodule bacteria are undoubtedly carried on the surface of the seeds, especially where these are trampled out by animals. Thus plots of guar (*Cyamopsis tetragonoloba*), an East Indian legume, were well inoculated when grown for the first time at Chillicothe, Texas, although no closely related legume occurs in North America. In this case it seems practically certain that the bacteria were carried on the seeds.

Inoculation of the soil for a new legume is sometimes secured by sowing a little of the seed in mixtures, as alfalfa with grass. Frequently some of the plants survive, and when this happens generally to scattered plants throughout a field, it is safe to conclude that the soil is sufficiently well inoculated.

14. Artificial inoculation. — The first artificial cultures of *Pseudomonas radicicola* were made by Beyerinck in 1888. In 1896 Nobbe introduced commercial cultures under the name of nitragin. Commercial cultures have been prepared in various forms; namely, in liquids, upon agar jelly, in dry powders and on cotton. Moore in 1904 prepared cultures grown on media poor in nitrogen under the idea that this would select the strains most efficient in fixing free nitrogen, and that these cultures would, therefore, prove beneficial even on soils already inoculated for any particular legume by providing a superior strain. Attempts have also been made to prepare cultures adapted to each soil by growing the bacteria in media prepared from a solution of the particular soil to be inoculated. Whatever method is employed, it is necessary to prepare the cultures from nodules of the same species of plant for which the culture is intended.

Beginning with the introduction of nitragin, many hundreds of inoculation experiments have been performed. There can be no question of the importance of nodules to the plants, as the difference between inoculated and uninoculated plants is often markedly apparent. Any superiority of artificial cultures over natural inoculation has thus far not been realized. Artificial inoculation for reasons not ascertained is less certain than natural soil inoculation. Artificial cultures have the advantage of cheapness and convenience, but thus far the uncertainty attending their use on uninoculated soil has more than counterbalanced these advantages.

From theoretical considerations, there is abundant reason to believe that methods will yet be perfected to secure reliable inoculation by artificial cultures of especially efficient strains of the nodule bacteria.

15. Dependence of legumes on root nodules. — Many legumes will grow normally in a fertile soil without root nodules. In this case, however, the plant is less rich in nitrogen. Thus, Hopkins analyzed cowpeas grown at the Illinois Experiment Station, comparing plants with and without nodules. The former were three times as large and contained 3.9 per cent nitrogen and the latter but 2.2 per cent. At Amarillo, Texas, in 1908, plots of cowpeas of several varieties planted in fertile virgin soil were entirely devoid of nodules, although their growth was apparently perfectly normal.

On the other hand, alfalfa seems to be dependent under some conditions on root nodules for existence. In Maryland and Virginia, numerous experimental fields of alfalfa planted in 1907 failed to survive where inoculation was not secured.   This was the case even in well-fertilized soils. The plants grew to a height of about four inches and then gradually turned yellow and died.   Under the conditions of these experiments alfalfa seems absolutely dependent on root nodules for successful growth.   In contrast to this, alfalfa is said to have succeeded well in Kansas from its first introduction in that state, but no observations are recorded in regard to nodulation.

According to Kirchner, no nodules had been observed on soybeans grown in Europe up to 1895, although this plant had been successfully cultivated since 1877.

CHAPTER II

PRESERVATION OF FORAGE

THE principles and methods of preserving forage are quite different from those employed with other crops. This is necessitated largely by the bulky nature of forage crops and the comparatively low value of the product. One method of preservation — silage — is perfected to a degree which makes it comparable with a factory process. The making of hay, however, is still dependent almost wholly on favorable weather conditions, and in the absence of this condition the crop is often lost or greatly damaged.

16. Preservation of forage crops. — Herbage may be preserved as forage in one of three ways, hay, brown hay and silage. The form in which it is preserved depends partly on the particular crop, partly on climatic conditions and partly on the special purpose for which it is required. Grasses and legumes with fine stems are mostly harvested as hay. Under adverse climatic conditions, however, such crops are often saved as brown hay, but never if bright hay can be cured. Coarse fodders, like corn and sorghum, are more and more being preserved as silage, as this avoids both the difficulties of curing and the loss from leaching if left unprotected, and besides, furnishes a succulent feed. The finer grasses and legumes may also be preserved as silage, but this is seldom done, except when weather conditions prevent drying, and a silo is available.

17. Time of cutting. — There are five different criteria which may be considered in determining the stage at which to cut a crop of forage : —

1. When the plants can be most satisfactorily cured either as hay or silage.

2. When there is the least injury to the succeeding cutting.

3. When the greatest total yield can be obtained.

4. When the degree of digestibility is greatest, especially of the proteids.

5. When the greatest total amount of digestible nutrients is obtained.

The first criterion is of importance only in regions where the climatic conditions can be predicted with some certainty. For example, in most of the Southern States the weather in fall is quite likely to be more satisfactory for curing hay than is midsummer. On this account the cutting of some crops, like lespedeza and Bermuda grass, is commonly postponed till then, while others, as cowpeas, are planted so that they will mature at this time.

The second consideration has some bearing on crops that yield two or more cuttings. As a rule, the later the first cutting is made, the smaller the second one will be.

The third criterion would postpone the cutting of most grasses until the seed is mature, and most legumes until the leaves begin to fall off, as the total weight increases until maturity except as there is loss from defoliation or leaching. At this stage, however, most plants become more woody and less palatable.

The fourth criterion is unimportant from the fact that in nearly all forage crops the digestibility is greatest when the plants are young, and cutting at this time is at the expense of a greatly reduced yield and greater difficulty in curing.

The fifth criterion would apparently, from a theoretical consideration, be the most satisfactory basis to use. In grasses the percentage of digestibility varies but slightly from full bloom till when the seeds are nearly ripe, but in clovers it begins to fall off even before blooming. From this, it would appear that grasses may be cut at any time from full bloom until nearly ripe, excepting where the stems become decidedly woody; while perennial legumes should be cut not later than full bloom.

18. Haymaking in dry weather. — Under favorable climatic conditions, haymaking is a simple process. The curing will then often take place in the windrows into which it is raked when well wilted, so that it can be stacked or housed the day following without further handling, though it is usually desirable to turn the windrows an hour or more before loading. This method is often pursued in dry climates. The only objection to this system is that more bleaching from the sun takes place than if the hay is put into cocks or shocks as soon as dry enough. With such rapid curing, however, the bleaching is not sufficient to justify the additional labor required in cocking. Some loss, however, will result, especially in legumes, from the leaves becoming too dry and brittle so that they break off in subsequent handling.

Even with perfect haying weather, the best hay is secured by raking into windrows as soon as well wilted, and afterwards piling into small cocks before any of the leaves become brittle. At this stage the leaves are drier than the stems, but in the cocks this is partly equalized by the leaves absorbing moisture from the stems. When thus cured, there is less bleaching from the sun, or sun and dew combined, few leaves are lost by becoming brittle and a higher degree of aroma is engendered. By thoroughly curing in the cocks, any danger of subsequent heating in the stack or mow is largely removed. Under the best conditions hay may be stacked or housed the same day that it is cut, but this is seldom done until the second or third day.

19. Curing of hay. — In curing hay under ideal conditions, three different processes take place; namely, (1) a reduction in water content from about 70 per cent (60 per cent to 85 per cent) in the green plant to about 15 per cent (7 per cent to 25 per cent) when dried; (2) enzymatic changes in the composition of the hay, usually with the development of a characteristic aroma; (3) bleaching, due to destruction of the chlorophyll by the sunlight which is increased by the action of the dew.

The conditions sought in prime hay are bright color, that is, as green as possible; good aroma; retention of leaves (in legumes); and freedom from " dust " or mold spores.

20. Haymaking under humid conditions. — While haymaking in favorable weather is simple, it becomes greatly complicated by cloudiness, rain and heavy dews. Rain is injurious both because it delays drying and because it leaches out soluble nutrients. If long continued, especially in warm weather, it induces the growth of various molds and other fungi, and the hay becomes " dusty."

Two processes to facilitate curing of hay under uncertain conditions are commonly employed. The first of these is designed to hasten drying by turning the grass over as soon as the top is dried, using pitchforks if done by hand, or a tedder if by horse power. Where the crop is very heavy, this is done while the hay is in the swath, but usually it is first raked into windrows. The second process is to pile into cocks after partially curing in windrows. The object here is mainly to reduce the surface exposed to moisture that may fall on the half-cured hay either as dew or rain. Where the drying is long protracted, much additional labor is entailed by spreading the cocks each favorable morning and recocking in the evening until cured.

While the difficulty of thus curing grass hay is great, it is far less than in the case of legumes. Grasses have slender, usually hollow stems, and persistent leaves, while most legumes have solid stalks that are relatively thicker, and consequently dry much more slowly. Furthermore, the leaflets of legumes dry first and fall off easily when the hay is half cured, so that if much handled a large portion of the leaves may be lost. In addition, legume hays do not shed rain water as well as do grass hays, the latter indeed often being put on the top of shocks of legume hay to shed moisture.

Cut hay should never be handled while wet. If the surface hay was best cured before the rain, as would be the case in the swath, it is in the most favorable position to dry promptly. If in the windrow, the stirring of the hay while the surface is wet brings this moisture in contact with the drier hay beneath, by which it is readily absorbed.

Unfavorable weather greatly increases the cost of haymaking, both in requiring more labor and in causing greater loss of leaves from the more frequent handling necessitated.

Continuous rains do but little more damage to freshly cut hay plants than to the uncut plants, at least during the first three or four days after cutting. Cured or partially cured hay, however, loses by leaching. Headden, at the Colorado Experiment Station, compared alfalfa hay exposed to warm humid weather for fifteen days, during which time 1.76 inches of rain fell in three showers, with a sample cut at the same time and immediately dried in an oven. The former contained but 11.01 per cent of protein against 18.71 per cent for the latter.

Corn stover exposed two months to weather at the Wisconsin Experiment Station lost from 12.76 per cent to 22.83 per cent of the total dry matter and 59.6 per cent to 71.55 per cent of the total protein. At the Colorado Experiment Station, corn stover spread on the ground in small shocks and in large shocks lost, respectively, 55, 43 and 31 per cent of the dry matter. In these cases, however, the loss is partly due to fermentation and to molds.

Westgate sprinkled perfectly cured crimson clover hay with water to imitate rain for one hour each on three successive days. On analysis it was found in comparison with a sample unsprinkled to have lost about three-fourths of its sugar, one-ninth of its protein and three-fourths of its ash constituents.

Kellner in Germany analyzed two lots of alfalfa hay, one very carefully dried, the other exposed during drying to one heavy thunder storm and one light shower. The latter was poorer than the former in protein 2.1 per cent; in fiber, 2.2 per cent; in carbohydrate, .4 per cent and in fat, .5 per cent.

21. Special devices to facilitate hay curing. — Where weather injury is frequently experienced in curing hay, certain devices are often used that are helpful.

Most common perhaps is the *perch*, which in its simplest form is a stake about six feet long with cross arms two to three feet long. This is driven into the ground and the green or half-dried plants are hung upon it so as to make a tall, slender cock. Perches are much used in curing peanut vines and are also very useful for cowpeas and similar viny plants.

A less simple, but more effective device is the *pyramid*, which permits of making larger cocks with an open air space in the interior. Numerous forms of pyramids have been devised, even metal ones being used in Europe. They consist essentially of three or four legs jointed at the top and sometimes sharpened below so that they can be pushed firmly into the ground. Cross pieces joining the legs are also useful. The legs are commonly 6 to 8 feet long. A form devised at the Tennessee Experiment Station is so joined at the top that the three legs come together when the pyramid is not in use.

Still more elaborate frames are sometimes used for cowpeas, combining the characteristics of a pyramid and of a permanent stack. It is a common practice in stacking cowpea hay not completely cured to make alternate layers of hay and of wooden rails. The rails prevent the hay from matting and facilitate curing by permitting the circulation of the air. Such a stack is greatly improved by supporting the rails at each end, so that the air may more easily circulate between the layers of hay.

Hay caps are also very desirable to protect cocks from rain. The form most commonly used consists of a piece of canvas about one yard square with a weight at each corner. By the use of a hay cap the hay cock is protected from the rain that falls directly upon it.

If hay be stacked on low, wet ground, the bottom portion becomes ruined by the absorption of moisture. This may be prevented by building the stack on a raised stage. Where hay is annually cut on wet meadows which become overflowed, permanent hay stages built on a level above high water mark are often employed.

In Europe, another method of curing hay which involves much hand labor is employed. This consists in tying the grass in sheaves after it has wilted one or two days. The sheaves are bound near the top so that when the cut ends are spread, they will stand alone. As these are often blown down by the wind, it involves an excessive amount of labor. Sometimes a number of sheaves are tied together so as to form a hollow cone, or many may thus be placed to form a rectangle with sloping sides and open ends. Such structures do not blow down so readily, but require much labor to set up. The sheaves are dried out principally by the circulation of the air.

In semi-arid regions immature wheat, barley and other cereals are sometimes cut with a binder, and the bound sheaves cure readily without further handling.

22. Completion of curing. — The stage at which curing is complete enough to make it safe to stack or house the hay is not easily determined. Where damage from weather is feared, it is important to get the crop in as soon as possible, especially in the case of legumes. A common rule is to consider legumes safe to put in large cocks or stacks when moisture can no longer be made to exude from the stems by twisting them tightly. When hay is stacked before thoroughly dry, it undergoes a process of heating or sweating. Legumes heat much more than grasses. Even when put in the mow at the stage indicated, alfalfa and crimson clover may become about as hot as the hand can bear.

It is a common practice to sprinkle salt or lime over each layer of hay which is thought to be insufficiently cured. To what extent this may modify sweating and subsequent moldiness is not well ascertained.

Hay is safe to place in the barn when the moisture

content is reduced to 20 per cent. It is rarely practicable, however, to make moisture determinations. Among empirical rules used to determine when curing is so far completed to make housing safe are (1) when the hay breaks if a wisp is tightly twisted in the hand; (2) when it is dry enough to rattle if gently shaken; and (3) when it no longer feels cool if pressed to the cheek.

23. Shrinkage of stored hay. — Hay when stored contains a varying amount of water, depending on the thoroughness of the curing. Even in very dry climates it is seldom less than 10 per cent and in moist climates or under unfavorable conditions is commonly as high as 25 per cent. In the West hay is often stacked when the moisture content exceeds 25 per cent, and instances are reported where it contained as high as 38 per cent and yet kept well. The average moisture content of cured hay ranges from 15 to 20 per cent.

Shrinkage is mainly due to loss of water; in rare cases where the hay is put in the mow when very dry, there may be gain in water content. Shrinkage due to loss of moisture varies according to the water content when stored and the humidity of the air.

Besides the shrinkage due to evaporation of moisture, there is a varying amount of loss due to oxidation. Even in well cured hay the enzymatic changes which go on cause a small loss by oxidation. In poorly cured hay the loss may be much greater, not only from the high degree of heat engendered by the preliminary fermentation, but also by the growth of destructive molds and other organisms.

The actual shrinkage which takes place in stored or stacked hay has been determined at several experiment stations.

At the Rhode Island Experiment Station, hay removed from the barn in February, 1902, contained 12.21 per cent of moisture. The shrinkage of hay from three plots differently fertilized was determined as follows on this basis of water content: —

	PLOT 17 WITHOUT NITROGEN	PLOT 19 NITRATE OF SODA, 138 LB.	PLOT 21 NITRATE OF SODA, 414 LB.
Percentage loss during barn curing in 1901	14.9	15.7	19.6
Percentage loss during barn curing in 1902	13.3	15.8	16.0

From these results it would appear that hay from land fertilized with nitrogen shrinks more than that from unfertilized.

The Maine Experiment Station reports that two lots of timothy cut respectively July 9 and July 24 and put in a barn when dry, showed a shrinkage on November 24 of 12.2 per cent for the early and 13.3 per cent for the later cutting.   In another test the loss in storing field-cured hay for 10 months was 16.6 per cent in early-cut hay and 18.1 per cent in late-cut hay.

The Pennsylvania Experiment Station reports that timothy hay cut in bloom showed an average shrinkage in weight in the barn after 5 or 6 months of 25.7 per cent, while hay cut two weeks later shrunk in weight on the average 18.8 per cent.   Three mowings of red clover cut respectively when in bloom, " some heads dead," and " heads all dead," showed a shrinkage after several months' storage in the barn of 42.4 per cent, 44.2 per cent and 25.7 per cent in the order named.

The Michigan Experiment Station reports that timothy hay stored in a barn lost in one case 7 per cent in 6 months; in three other cases the losses were respectively 13.8, 15.0 and 21.7 per cent. Red clover hay lost 9 per cent by November in one case and 3.6 per cent in another; the loss from July to February was 11.2 per cent.

At the Utah Experiment Station one ton of timothy placed in the center of a mow July 15 contained 1790.8 pounds dry matter, the moisture content being 10.46 per cent. The following May it contained 1557.4 pounds of dry matter and 14.61 per cent moisture. The loss in dry matter was 14.9 per cent.

Twenty-nine pounds of timothy hay suspended in a gunny bag for the same length of time increased in moisture content from 12.3 to 14.52 per cent. There was no loss in dry matter.

At the Kansas Experiment Station moisture determinations were made for several kinds of hay when stored in summer and again December 15. The results indicate that when curing is complete the moisture content of all hays is much the same under the same conditions:—

MOISTURE CONTENT OF HAYS AT KANSAS EXPERIMENT STATION

KIND OF HAY	PER CENT MOISTURE WHEN STORED IN SUMMER	PER CENT MOISTURE DECEMBER 15	PER CENT LOSS OR GAIN IN WEIGHT
Orchard-grass, blue-grass and clover	15.65	10.54	5.71 loss
Blue-grass	19.59	10.60	10.05 loss
Orchard-grass and clover	19.75	11.80	9.01 loss
Clover	9.08	11.87	3.17 gain
Prairie hay	14.00	10.61	3.39 loss
Millet	21.86	8.89	14.25 loss

24. Loss of hay or fodder in the field. — Hay in stacks
or fodder in shocks loses much more substance than when
stored in barns. This is especially true in humid regions.
The additional loss is largely due to leaching by rains,
but the bleaching effect of sunlight and the larger loss
by molds and other fungi is also important.

Short at the Wisconsin Experiment Station compared
the loss in corn fodder both when stored and when exposed to the weather. His results are shown in the following table : —

		Fresh	Weath- ered	Loss	Loss
		lb.	lb.	lb.	per cent
Sample I	Weight	27.00	11.25	18.75	——
	Dry matter	7.84	6.84	1.00	12.76
	Protein	.663	.22	.343	59.56
	Date . .	Sept. 21	Nov. 14		
Sample II	Weight	28.50	10.25	18.25	——
	Dry matter	8.45	6.52	1.93	22.83
	Protein	.485	.138	.347	71.55
	Date . .	Sept. 21	Nov. 14		

25. Relation of green weight to dry weight. — There is
no fixed ratio between the green weight and the dry
weight of any plant. This varies, obviously, with the
water content of the plant, which is never constant. It
also varies with the conditions under which the plant was
grown, a rapid succulent growth making a relatively
smaller amount of dry matter than a slow retarded growth.

For these reasons, as well as the variable amount of
moisture in hay, there is a wide variation in the ratio
of green weight and hay weight, not only for different hay
plants but even in different cuttings from the same plot.

The actual water content of a plant is easily determined by laboratory methods, care being taken to weigh the green plant under conditions that do not permit of loss by evaporation before weighing. The hay yield can be approximated from the water-free weight by arbitrarily adding 20 per cent. Such estimates are more nearly accurate than those obtained in the field by obtaining first the green weight and later the hay weight, as the moisture content of both vary greatly under field conditions. The discrepancies that thus occur in field weights, green and dry, are sometimes very large.

The relation between dry weights and green weights of 29 varieties of red clover grown at the Ontario Agricultural College, show an average ratio of 1 : 6. The widest ratio of any variety is 1 : 8.1 and the narrowest, 1 : 4.8.

Jordan at the Maine Experiment Station found that timothy cut when the heads were beginning to appear lost, on an average, 75 per cent of water in curing into hay; when beginning to bloom, the loss was 66 per cent; when past bloom, 57 per cent.

At the same station the green and air-dried yield of 29 strains of clover in duplicate plots was weighed. The shrinkage in drying ranged from 68 per cent in one plot of Bohemian red clover to 82 per cent in a strain from Denmark. The average shrinkage was 73 to 75 per cent. Very leafy plants shrink more than those less leafy.

The following relations appear between green weight and dry weight, in pounds per acre, of various crops grown at the Pennsylvania Experiment Station. As will be noticed, the water contents of the crops reported upon differ greatly. The low water content of spring vetch in contrast with that of sand vetch is especially surprising : —

D

	Green	Dry	Ratio
Canada peas	20,142	3,937	1 : 5
Spring vetch	8,832	5,934	1 : 1.5
Sand vetch	6,756	2,492	1 : 2.4
Red clover	17,760	4,808	1 : 3.7
White clover	20,250	4,133	1 : 4.9
Alsike clover	15,960	3,956	1 : 5
Crimson clover	12,492	3,402	1 : 3.7
Timothy	7,920	3,344	1 : 2.4

26. Loss of substance from growing plants. — Studies of the chemistry of plants at different stages have in many cases shown that the total amount of such substances as nitrogen, phosphoric acid, potash and soda was smaller at maturity than some time previously. The same fact has also been shown in field investigations where the total weight of hay produced per unit of area was less at maturity than at an earlier stage.

Three general explanations of the phenomenon have been advanced, namely : —

1. The backward flow of the salts of the plant through the stem and roots into the soil.

2. The mechanical loss of material from the leaves by decay, drying, etc.

3. The leaching effects of rain and dew.

The subject has recently been studied by LeClerc and Brezeale. From their investigations it is demonstrated that all growing plants exude salts upon the surface of the leaves which are washed off by rains. No evidence was found that salts migrate downward, as the lower part of the stem is always poorer in phosphorus, potash and nitrogen than the upper part and leaves. Wheat plants were grown in the greenhouse and watered only at the roots so as not to wet the foliage. Some of these plants blighted so that the whole plant slowly died, or else the tips of the leaves were killed. Analyses of the dead leaf tips showed that they were always poorer in nitrogen and potash than the living basal portions. Other analyses of these dying plants showed that the lower nodes of the stem, whether dead or alive, were always poorer in nitrogen, phosphoric acid and potash than the upper ones, which would not be the case if the movement were downward. From these observations, the conclusion is drawn that on ripening the salts held in the sap of the plants have a tendency to migrate from the dying to the living tissue; and that the migration is upward and not downward.

In another series of experiments, a whole barley plant at the heading stage was soaked in a dish of distilled water for several minutes and lost 1.6 per cent of its nitrogen content, 36 per cent of its phosphoric acid and 65 per cent of its potash. A pot of rice plants before the heads were mature was tilted over a dish and the tops sprayed with about $2\frac{1}{2}$ quarts of water, imitating somewhat the action of rain. Analyses made both of the ash of the plant and of the leachings showed that the artificial rain had removed salts from the plant.

Wheat plants in bloom and fully ripe were washed in distilled water five to ten minutes, and both the plants and the water analyzed. The percentage losses of mineral substances were as follows:—

	Nitrogen	Phosphoric Acid	Potash	Soda	Lime	Magnesia	Chlorine
In bloom	1.4	0	4.4	12.7	0	10.3	7.6
Fully ripe	7.0	33.0	54.0	41.0	34.0	46.0	60.0

Similar losses were also found when wheat plants grown in the greenhouse to ripeness were exposed to four rainfalls in such a way that the rain after falling on the plant was caught in a tray. Oat plants were also subjected to a test of this sort with comparable results.

From these experiments the conclusion is drawn that plants exude salts upon their surfaces and the rain then washes these salts back to the soil.

27. Hay stacks. — In the absence of barn room, hay is frequently stacked in the field, especially in dry regions. The shape of stacks varies greatly. If circular at base, they may be conical or thimble-shaped in form, not infrequently being built so that they are largest above the middle, as this will shed water from the base. In the west, they are most commonly rectangular in outline, higher than broad, and with the top ridge-like or less commonly rounded.

Well-built stacks are compact and the hay so laid that it sheds water both on the top and sides. This is difficult to accomplish with legume hays, so that stacks of these are frequently covered with grass hay or straw.

To build a good stack requires both knowledge and experience.

28. Spontaneous combustion. — Under certain conditions hay, especially of legumes, if put in a mow or stack while still moist, engenders great heat, and in some cases destructive fires have resulted. Several instances have been recorded where the center of a mow or stack has been found entirely charred when opened. Apparently the only reason that prevented ignition was the absence of air. There have, however, been a number of well-authenticated cases where barns have been burned by spontaneous combustion from alfalfa and from crimson clover hay.

Conditions which cause spontaneous combustion are not sufficiently well known to warrant any definite statement as to just when hay is sufficiently cured to be safe. There is apparently always risk unless the hay is thoroughly cured.

The problem has been specifically studied by Hoffmann, in Germany, who experimented especially with red clover hay. He finds that the heat is generated through a process of fermentation, probably enzymatic, in which oxygen is taken from the air and the organic matter is transformed into carbon dioxide and water. From this additional moisture a secondary fermentation due to bacteria takes place. If the hay has external moisture when first stored, the fermentation is more rapid. The preliminary fermentation causes a temperature of 56° C. This temperature causes a second and more violent oxidation to take place and the temperature rises to about 90° C. In further fermentation processes the heat slowly rises to as high as 130° C., at which temperatures the hay is charred. From theoretical consideration Hoffmann figures that the temperature may rise to 190° C. In the presence of oxygen ignition will take place at 150° C. or higher. If, however, oxygen be excluded, ignition will not occur, but the hay will be converted into a mass of charcoal.

29. Statistics of hay yields. — Yields of forage crops per acre are much less accurately known than those of grain crops. Reliable data of hay yields are available mainly in connection with definite experiments. Estimates of farmers upon which statistical and census data are based are probably too large. It is a difficult matter to estimate closely a yield of hay, and there is little chance to become proficient, as hay yields are so seldom weighed. On the other hand, the farmer sells his wheat, barley, or other small grain crop, and puts his corn into bins or cribs, so that he has every year an approximately accurate measure to compare with his estimates..

Another factor that leads to exaggeration is the large unit of measurement employed; namely, the ton of 2000 pounds. The smallest fraction ever used in estimates is ¼ of a ton.

The farmers' actual estimates are commonly based on the wagon load, usually considered as being one ton, but it is probable that the average wagon load is nearer three-fourths of a ton.

Only where hay is baled can the yield figures be considered reliable. Even in this case some allowance for moisture needs to be made. Well-cured timothy hay contains about 14 per cent of moisture, but as baled in the field, the water content is usually higher.

Experiment station yields are usually higher than those obtained by farmers, as experimental plots are as a rule small, and secure better treatment than farmers' fields.

30. Brown hay. — When climatic conditions interfere with the curing of bright hay, the crop may be preserved as brown hay. In this process the hay is cured largely by the aid of the heat engendered in fermentation. After cutting, the grass is made into cocks, trampling each layer to make it as dense as practicable. In these cocks, the heat engendered by fermentation may reach the boiling point of water. The second or third day after cocking, the piles are opened so as to permit the escape of the vapor, after which the product may be safely housed.

A more common process is to dry the hay as much as possible in the air and then pile into compact stacks, where it is permitted to remain until fed. The final product varies in color from dark brown to nearly black.

31. Silage. — Silage is made by the natural fermentation of green fodder in receptacles from which the access of air is excluded. In some form this process has been employed over a century. Originally pits in the earth either lined or unlined were used, and such are still employed, but in recent times specially constructed buildings called *silos* have become common. These may be built of wood, brick, tile, concrete, or steel. Most commonly they are cylindrical in form, and much taller than broad. (Silage is sometimes called *ensilage;* but this word is properly a verb meaning *to place material in the silo*, or *to make silage*, as *to ensilage corn*. The verb is sometimes shortened, in the vernacular, to *ensile*.)

The proper fermentation requires only the exclusion of air, but practically this is best secured by close packing. Usually this is promoted by cutting the fodder fine and often by trampling and the use of weights. The cut fodder also has the advantage of being more easily removed from the silo when used. The volume decreases as fermentation proceeds, so provision must be made for even settling.

The fermentation results in the formation of various acids and the loss of some substance as gas. While fermenting, a considerable degree of heat is engendered. The fermentation is complete in from two to eight weeks, but corn silage is as a rule ready for use in four weeks. In contact with air silage decays, due to the attacks of fungi and aërobic bacteria.

To provide the necessary conditions silos are constructed with air-tight walls smooth on the inside, and the fodder is cut small so as to pack closely and settle evenly. In filling a silo, the top should not be left exposed more than a day or two, as decay then ensues.

When filled, the top should be covered to exclude air. This was formerly done with a foot or so of earth, the weight of which assisted the settling. Usually, however, the top portion is allowed to decay, and it thus makes a nearly air-tight layer, but sometimes a layer of straw, chaff or green grass is used to exclude the air so as to preserve all the silage.

This name " summer silage " has been given to silage prepared in late spring or early summer to feed after the corn silage of the previous season is exhausted. Among crops that have been thus used are rye, wheat, oats and red clover. The principal precaution to be taken is to have the silo small enough so that at least 4 inches is removed a day, as during hot weather silage spoils more quickly. It is claimed that the use of summer silage is far more economical than soiling and just as satisfactory, but few data have as yet been published.

In using silage, the material is generally removed from the top. About 2 inches per day should be removed, as otherwise considerable loss occurs from mold.

Silage is sometimes made simply by piling the green plants in large compact stacks. This method has been used with sorghum and is sometimes employed by canneries to preserve green pea vines from which the peas have been separated. Such silage stacks are not economical unless they are very large, as there is always considerable loss on the surface.

32. The nature of silage fermentation. — The investigations at the Wisconsin Experiment Station by Babcock, Russell and King lead to the conclusion that the fermentation of silage under proper conditions is not due to bacteria or other organisms, as has generally been held. Among the facts that are significant are the following : —

1. Silage may reach its maximum temperature within twenty-four hours, a period much briefer than occurs with bacterial fermentation.

2. When silage is fully cured, the further evolution of gas is small and mainly stationary. If now the silage be exposed to air, a new fermentation by bacteria and molds will ensue and cause a rise in temperature far above the previous anaërobic fermentation.

3. Freshly cut corn in air-tight receptacles treated with chloroform, ether or benzol to suppress bacteria, nevertheless ferments into silage, though with lower acid content.

4. Freshly cut corn in air-tight receptacles filled with an inert gas like hydrogen or nitrogen, ferments into silage more slowly and the final product is more acid.

5. Corn killed by frost will not produce silage, but untreated, decays into an ill-smelling mass, due to bacteria. Treated with ether to destroy the bacteria, the frozen corn retains all the characteristics of green corn.

6. The gas given off during silage fermentation is mainly carbon dioxide, but in the case of clover silage, also contains hydrogen. Nitrogen is apparently given off in small quantities in all silage fermentation.

From the above facts, silage fermentation is ascribed to respiration of the green tissues — probably of an enzymatic nature — and not at all due to bacteria or fungi. In silage exposed to the air fermentation by the latter will occur, but it is always undesirable and destructive.

33. Advantages of silage. — The preservation of forage as silage possesses a number of advantages, especially with coarse plants like corn and sorghum. Among these advantages are : —

1. Silage preservation saves all of the forage in edible form. The loss both in preserving and feeding is very small.

2. Silage is more palatable than dry fodder, and animals will eat a larger quantity.

3. Silage preservation is not dependent on favorable weather conditions.

4. Silage requires less space for storage than an equivalent amount of hay or fodder.

5. When corn and especially grain sorghums are preserved as silage, the seeds are softened so that they are thoroughly digested.

While silage is undoubtedly the best way to preserve corn, sorghum and similar coarse plants, it has not proven very satisfactory with legumes or hay grasses, perhaps because proper methods of ensiling these plants have not been developed. Legumes mixed with corn or sorghum are very satisfactory, but when ensiled alone, the product seems frequently to be ill-smelling and unpalatable. A more satisfactory method of ensiling grasses and clovers is a desideratum for regions where hay curing is difficult.

34. Crops adapted to ensiling. — Corn is the principal American crop preserved as silage, and constitutes probably more than 90 per cent of the total amount. The sorghums, both saccharine and non-saccharine, are also very satisfactory, and apparently not inferior to corn. Japanese sugar cane has given excellent results at the Florida Experiment Station.

Meadow grasses and small grains are not much used for silage in America. They are, however, thus preserved in western Oregon and western Washington as well as in Europe. Georgeson reports the successful ensiling of beach lyme grass (*Elymus mollis*) at the Alaska Experiment Station. The silage kept well and made satisfactory feed for oxen. Millets have been preserved satisfactorily as silage at several experiment stations.

Legumes alone have not proven altogether satisfactory as silage. Red clover in some experiments has yielded a palatable product, in others rank flavored and not relished by cattle. At the Colorado Experiment Station alfalfa yielded a silage that was readily eaten by dairy cattle. Cowpeas made good silage at the Georgia and Delaware Experiment Stations; while both hairy vetch and soybeans produced well-flavored and aromatic silage at the Vermont Experiment Station. Soybeans alone made good silage at the New Jersey Experiment Station. Lloyd reports that in Ohio sweet clover has been used with good results. One reason for failures with ensilaged legumes is probably their higher water content, as pointed out by several investigators. On this account such crops should be allowed to become as mature as practicable before ensiling.

Mixtures of corn and legumes such as cowpeas or soybeans make excellent silage. In Ontario sunflower heads are often mixed in corn silage. The Vermont Experiment Station tested the Robertson silage mixture; namely, corn, horse beans and sunflower heads, but the cows did not eat it quite as readily as pure corn silage.

Peas and oats and vetch and oats both proved very satisfactory at the Vermont Experiment Station.

Sugar beet pulp, a refuse from beet sugar factories, also makes a palatable silage.

35. Soiling or soilage. — Soiling is stall feeding with green fodder. This method of feeding is far more common in Europe than in America. It obviates the necessity of curing much of the forage, and the loss that accompanies the process. For dairy cows, at least, it gives better returns than the feeding of an equivalent amount of dry hay. On the other hand, it has certain disadvantages,

particularly the cutting and hauling of small areas of green feed every day, regardless of weather conditions, — in this way not being economical in the use of labor and machinery.

Soiling is well adapted mainly to the feeding of dairy cows, and is practically the only way to utilize certain crops, such as thousand-headed kale and spineless cactus. For short periods of time — especially in the absence or scarcity of other feed — soiling is often utilized by dairymen.

In the tropics, soiling is the common method of feeding roughage, not only to cattle, but to city horses. This is especially the case where labor is cheap, and humid conditions prevent the curing of hay. Grasses of various kinds are cut green, tied into bundles and thus marketed fresh each day. Among the grasses thus commonly used for horses are Guinea-grass, Para-grass, and Bermuda-grass. In the Philippine Islands, Bareet grass (*Homalocenchrus hexandrus*) is extensively cultivated about the towns for this purpose.

Soiling such crops as millet, kale, sorghum, etc., is usually preferable to pasturing, at least for cattle. The latter method occasions much loss by trampling, and expense for temporary or permanent fences. On the other hand, soiling involves the expense of cutting and hauling green feed daily, and the planning of a succession of crops so that each will be ready when needed in ample quantity. On these accounts soiling is seldom used in America except to tide over a temporary shortage of feed. Instead of soiling, the practice is growing of feeding silage the whole year, thus securing a succulent feed and avoiding the difficulties involved in soiling.

36. Soiling systems. — A succession of crops to provide green feed for a season or for a portion of a season is called a *soiling system*. To plan such a succession of crops requires accurate knowledge of the time required for each crop to reach its growth, the length of time it may be fed and also the average yield to be expected, so that the proper area to be planted can be accurately determined.

Annuals are more convenient to use in soiling systems than perennials because plantings of the same crop can be made at successive dates, and its feeding period thus extended over several weeks' time. Furthermore, the land becomes at once available for other plantings. While perennials are often utilized in soiling systems, such are seldom planted for this purpose alone, as it is rarely economy to plant them in an area as small as would be required.

Soiling systems for the whole growing season have been devised at several experiment stations, a few examples of which are here given : —

SOILING SYSTEM RECOMMENDED BY PHELPS FOR CONNECTICUT

CROP	TIME OF SEEDING	TIME OF FEEDING
Rye	Sept. 1	May 10 –20
Wheat	Sept. 5–10	May 20–June 5
Red clover	July 20–30	June 5– 15
Grass		June 15– 25
Oats and peas . . .	April 10	June 25–July 10
Oats and peas . . .	April 20	July 10– 20
Oats and peas . . .	April 30	July 20–Aug. 1
Clover rowen . . .		Aug. 1– 10
Hungarian millet . .	June 10	Aug. 10– 20
Cowpeas	June 5–10	Sept. 5– 20
Grass rowen . . .		Sept. 20– 30
Barley and peas . .	Aug. 5–10	Oct. 1– 30

At the Pennsylvania Experiment Station the following data were secured on the date of planting and yields of various soiling crops : —

CROP	DATE OF SOWING	DATE OF HARVESTING	YIELD PER ACRE	
			Green substance	Air-dried substance
Flat peas . .		June 17–June 28	10,004	1861
Peas and oats	May 5	June 29–July 11	27,671	3929
Peas and oats	May 16	July 12–July 22	18,137	2938
Peas and oats	May 21	July 22–July 25	22,773	3120
Peas and barley	May 21	July 26–Aug. 2	19,415	3436
Flat peas . .		Aug. 3–Aug. 12	11,782	2344
Clover silage .				
Cowpeas and milo maize	June 11–29	Aug. 29–Sept. 6	18,083	3707
Black cowpeas	June 25	Sept. 7–Sept. 22	18,251	3705
Red Ripper cowpeas . . .	June 25	Sept. 22–Sept. 25	11,117	2590

The flat peas are, however, not recommended on account of difficulty of establishing the crop, unpalatability and possible danger of tainting the milk. Rape, too, is not recommended because not very palatable and likely to taint the milk.

On the basis of these and other data the station suggests the following soiling system : —

SOILING SYSTEM FOR TEN COWS

Based on Data obtained at the Pennsylvania Experiment Station

CROP	AREA	WHEN TO BE FED
Rye	½ acre	May 15–June 1
Alfalfa	2 acres	June 1–June 12
Clover and timothy	¾ acre	June 12–June 24
Peas and oats	1 acre	June 24–July 15
Alfalfa (2d crop)	2 acres	July 15–Aug. 11
Sorghum and cowpeas (after rye)	½ acre	Aug. 11–Aug. 28
Cowpeas (after peas and oats) .	1 acre	Aug. 28–Sept. 30

CHAPTER III

CHOICE OF FORAGE CROPS

The number of species of plants which the domesticated animals or their wild ancestors devour for food is very large. While comparatively few of these meet the needs of profitable agriculture, yet over 100 species are more or less utilized, while many others have been tested in an experimental way. There is thus presented to the agriculturist the problem of determining which of many possible forage plants is the most satisfactory to grow under given conditions.

37. What determines the choice of a forage crop. — The extent to which a forage crop is grown in any particular region or for any particular purpose is correlated with a number of considerations. Among these the following are important : —

1. Purpose for which grown; namely, hay, fodder, silage or soiling.

2. Adaptation to the conditions of climate, soil and culture in rotations.

3. Yield.

4. Cost of seeding per acre.

5. Ease of harvesting and curing.

6. Time of harvesting.

7. Feeding value.

8. Demands or prejudices of the user.

47

If the forage is grown to sell, the last consideration is often the controlling factor. It is usually easy to determine the characteristics of several forage crops as regards each point compared. It is sometimes, however, difficult to ascertain why, on the whole, one crop is preferred to another closely comparable.

38. Special purposes for which forage crops are grown. — Forage crops may thus be classified, as regards the purposes for which they are grown : —

1. Long-lived meadows, for hay; such as timothy, alfalfa, brome-grass, redtop, etc.

2. Annual hay crops; such as crimson clover, millet, cowpeas, rye, etc., often sown as " catch " crops.

3. Coarse grasses for silage or fodder; such as corn, sorghum, pearl millet and Japanese sugar-cane.

4. Permanent pastures, for which are used Kentucky blue-grass, white clover, Bermuda-grass and various more or less complex mixtures.

5. Temporary pastures, using such plants as rye, wheat, crimson clover, cowpeas, Italian rye-grass and others.

6. Soiling crops, often planted in succession so as to give green feeds during definite periods.

It is obvious that most forage crops utilized for one of the above purposes are usually not well fitted for other purposes.

39. Adaptation to conditions. — Different forage crops are adapted to widely different conditions of climate, and this factor usually closely limits the area in which each can be profitably grown. Sometimes market considerations lead to the growing of a crop under conditions which are not very favorable, as timothy in the South and alfalfa on unsuitable soil types in the East. While alfalfa and red clover both do well in some places, the latter is much better fitted for use in short rotations.

40. Yields per acre. — The yielding capacities of various hay grasses and other closely comparable forage crops have been tested at various experiment stations. In comparatively few places, however, have such experiments been adequate to reach clear conclusions. Some of the experiment station results are shown in the accompanying table. Usually yield per acre is the most important single characteristic upon which the popularity of a good forage crop depends. In some areas, and under certain conditions, a particular forage crop will so far outyield all others that there is practically no choice. Thus alfalfa is by far the heaviest yielding hay crop for the irrigated lands of the West, and sorghum usually gives far larger returns than any other comparable crop on much of the dry land area.

European yields that are commonly quoted are often based on very small plots, necessitating multiplication by a large factor to secure the acre yield. Thus the English yields reported by Sinclair were usually based on weighing the grass and hay from an area two feet square; and those of Vianne in France on areas little if any larger.

Some yields reported by American experiment stations are also based on very small plots. While these as a rule give results that can hardly be secured on larger plantings, yet they do give comparable values. In the accompanying table, the hay grasses are arranged in the approximate order of their importance. It will be noticed that this order is in many cases not consistent with their yielding capacities. It is questionable, however, if the results at any one experiment station are sufficiently exhaustive to admit of a definite conclusion : —

E

YIELDS OF HAY IN POUNDS PER ACRE OF DIFFERENT GRASSES AND LEGUMES AT VARIOUS EXPERIMENT STATIONS

Crop	Ohio Experiment Station ⅕ A. Plots	Kansas Experiment Station ¼ A. Plots	Illinois Experiment Station	Virginia, Arlington Farm ⅕ A. Plot	Michigan, Copper Peninsula Experiment Station 1 year	Ontario Agricultural College 7 Year Av. 1 Cutting	Pennsylvania Experiment Station 1 year	North Carolina Experiment Station 1 year	North Dakota Dickinson	Utah Experiment Station 2 Year Av.
Timothy	6994. 6 yr.	5528. 4 yr.	4400. 2 yr.	3600	3466	6940	3344	2136	1856. 3 yr.	2349
Redtop	5634. 6 yr.	3399. 2 yr.	3600. 1 yr.	3200	3493	3560		2940		1685
Orchard-grass	4394. 6 yr.	2809. 4 yr.	2800. 2 yr.	2880	2080	5100		1554		
Tall oat-grass	4494. 6 yr.	2453. 4 yr.	5480. 1 yr.	3720	5680	5520		2994		1786
Perennial rye-grass	3644. 6 yr.	1050. 2 yr.		2800		2500		3229		
Italian rye-grass	5120. 1 yr.	2341. 2 yr.	3775. 1 yr.	3200				5557		
Meadow fescue	4200. 6 yr.	2155. 4 yr.	3135. 1 yr.	3080	6720	4460				
Tall fescue	4870. 6 yr.									3690
Brome	2900. 1 yr. 5760. 1 yr.	3008. 4 yr.			4295	4320			2149. 3 yr.	2245
Kentucky blue-grass	4374. 1 yr.	1830. 2 yr.			3280	3160				
Western wheat-grass		2378. 1 yr.			5440					
Slender wheat-grass					5440	8720			2267. 3 yr.	
Erect brome		1782. 2 yr.			3706					
Meadow foxtail					2906					
Johnson-grass						3100				
Alfalfa		7345. 4 yr.						5139		10787
Sanfoin										2400—1 yr.
Mammoth clover		4456. 2 yr.								
Red clover		7580. 2 yr.	4200. 2 yr.		5146		4808	3965	2211. 2 yr.	9420
Alsike		3110. 2 yr.	2400. 2 yr.		6800		3956			4960
White clover							4133			
Crimson clover							3402			
Hairy vetch							2492			
Common vetch							5934			
Canada peas							3937		1780.	

YIELD OF HAY OF DIFFERENT CROPS WITH DIFFERENT QUANTITIES OF WATER

Utah Experiment Station

Amount of Water in Inches	Timothy		Orchard-Grass		Brome-Grass		Italian Rye-Grass		Alfalfa	
	Total	Yield per Inch of Water	Total Yield	Yield per Inch of Water	Total Yield	Yield per Inch of Water	Total Yield	Yield per Inch of Water	Total Yield	Yield per Inch of Water
In.	Lb.	Lb.	Lb.	Lb.	Lb.	Lb.	Lb.	Lb.	Lb.	Lb.
5	—	—	2526	505	—	—	—	—	—	—
7.5	—	—	—	—	—	—	2357	314	—	—
10.	3982	531	2829	283	4480	597	—	—	9884	988
15.	3844	256	2685	179	4957	496	2218	148	7546	503
20.	6054	202	—	—	3821	255	—	—	9097	455
25.	—	—	—	—	—	—	—	—	9354	374
30.	—	—	—	—	—	—	—	—	8840	295
40.	—	—	4042	102	4757	119	—	—	—	—
45.	—	—	—	—	—	—	3201	71	10813	241
50.	—	—	—	—	—	—	—	—	—	—
60.	8406	140	5270	87	—	—	—	—	—	—
100.	2214	22	1192	13	3068	31	2357	23	—	—

41. Yields under irrigation. — Under irrigation in the Western States no other hay plant will produce such high yields as alfalfa. The most extensive investigations comparing different hay crops under irrigation have been conducted at the Utah Experiment Station. Up to a certain maximum, the yields tend to increase with the amount of water applied, but the highest return per inch of water is secured with the smallest applications. See table, p. 51.

42. Cost of seeding. — The cost of seeding per acre is in some cases a reason for preference where choice is possible, as is shown in the following table. The prices given are New York wholesale prices in January, 1914: —

COST OF SEED PER ACRE, USING AVERAGE AMOUNT

PLANT	RATE OF SEEDING	COST OF SEED PER POUND	COST OF SEED PER ACRE
	Pounds	Cents	$
Timothy	15	6½	.975
Orchard-grass	20	15	3.00
Redtop	10	10	1.00
Brome-grass	20	10	2.00
Kentucky blue-grass . .	25	14	3.50
Italian rye-grass	30	5	1.50
Perennial rye-grass	30	5	1.50
Tall oat-grass	30	14	4.20
Tall fescue	20	18	3.60
Meadow fescue	20	11	2.20
Red clover	8	17	1.36
Alsike clover	12	20	2.40
Alfalfa	20	15	3.00
Sweet clover	25	20	5.00

The cost of some of these seeds would be much reduced if the demand for them were greater.

In the case of many grasses the high cost of the seeds is more due to small demand than to high cost of production.

43. Time of harvesting. — The time of harvesting some hay plants is much earlier than that of others. Furthermore, some hay plants must be promptly harvested at a certain stage, or otherwise the crop deteriorates, and in some cases the subsequent growth is affected. It is obviously unsatisfactory to have the haying season come at a time when other farm work is pressing. It is even more so if the crop is one that must be cut during a very brief period, as both unfavorable weather and press of other work may interfere. Timothy remains in good condition to cut much longer than most grasses. Alfalfa with its frequent cuttings often comes into conflict with other farm operations.

44. Ease of harvesting and curing. — This factor is important mainly in determining the choice between forages of approximately equal yields. Corn is preferred to sorghum partly because it deteriorates less easily, partly because sorghums are considered "hard on the land." Timothy is preferred over other similar grasses partly because its mowing season extends over a period of two or three weeks, thus permitting a better chance of good curing weather. Alfalfa is handicapped in humid regions by the necessity of prompt cutting when mature, and the difficulty of curing. Cowpeas are notoriously difficult to harvest and cure, and partly for this reason soybeans are becoming more popular.

45. Demands or prejudices of the user. — Where hay is grown to market, the demand or prejudice of the user is frequently the principal factor that determines the crop to be grown. Such market prejudices are the result of long-established experience or custom, and even where erroneous, are changed only with great difficulty.

In most American cities, the market is strongly prejudiced in favor of timothy hay as horse feed, so that any other sort of grass hay commands a smaller price. In Europe, on the contrary, Italian rye-grass furnishes the popular market hay, though timothy apparently grows quite as well in Europe as in America.

Cattle feeders in the West favor alfalfa greatly, and are willing to pay considerably more for alfalfa hay than for any other.

In the region where Kentucky blue-grass does well it is almost the only grass sown for permanent pastures. European farmers do not regard it nearly so highly, and in their practice usually plant more or less complex mixtures of grass seeds for pasture.

46. Feeding values. — The problem of determining the relative values of roughages for feeding purposes is involved and difficult. Three general methods have been employed, namely : —

1. Direct feeding experiments in which the value of the compared feeds is determined by the results secured, whether in milk, flesh, wool, labor, etc.

2. Determination by chemical analyses of the nutrient substances contained in the feed, and the proportion digested by the animal, the latter constituting the digestible nutrients.

3. Determination of the net energy of a feed; namely, that available to the production of milk, flesh and the like.

47. Feeding experiments. — Simple feeding experiments may be planned so that two single feeds may be directly compared with each other or both may be compared to a third taken as a standard. To secure reliable results in feeding experiments, both care and skill are required. Broadly speaking, the reliability of the results will depend upon the uniformity of the animals as to size, sex, age, used in the experiment; upon the number of individuals used; and upon the length of time the experiment continues.

But few experiments in which two roughages have been compared fulfill the above requirements, but the results secured in American experiments with grass or legume hays are cited in connection with the feeding value of each particular hay.

Perhaps the most extensive data from direct feeding trials are those secured in Denmark and Sweden in connection with the feeding of dairy cows. In these trials the standard of value or *feed unit* is one pound of dry matter in corn, wheat, barley, palm-nut meal or roots, with which the value of other feeds as determined by actual feeding is compared.

The results thus far reached lead to the conclusion that for milk production there is required to equal 1 feed unit 2 to 3 (average 2.5) pounds hay; 6 to 10 (average 8) pounds silage, green clover or mixed green grasses; 8 to 12 (average 10) pounds mangels, rutabagas and carrots; 10 to 15 (average 12.5) pounds turnips; 12 to 18 (average 15) pounds beet leaves.

Woll has determined *tentatively* that the following amounts of American feeds probably equal 1 feed unit; namely, 1.5 to 3 (average 2) pounds alfalfa or mixed hay, oat hay, oat and pea hay, barley and pea hay or redtop hay; 2.5 to 3.5 (average 3) pounds timothy hay, prairie hay or sorghum hay; 3.5 to 6 (average 4.2) pounds corn stover, stalks or fodder, marsh hay or cut straw.

It by no means follows that the relative value of these feeds for dairy cows represents their respective value for

other animals, for which separate feeding trials would
need to be conducted.

48. Chemical analyses. — Chemical analyses of feeds
usually consider the dry matter as made up of *crude
protein*, that is, the nitrogen multiplied by 6.25; *ether
extract*, sometimes called *fat*, the materials soluble in ether
and consisting of fats, resins, chlorophyll and other
substances; *ash*, the mineral matters that remain after
incineration of a sample; *crude fiber*, the portion that
remains undissolved after boiling successively in a weak
acid and a weak alkali under standard conditions; and
nitrogen-free extract, the remaining matter after the above
are subtracted, and consisting mainly of starches and
sugars. In recent years part of the nitrogen-free extract
has been determined as *pentosans*, while the remainder
has been called *undetermined*.

Chemical analyses of the same plant species may vary
greatly, depending on the soil in which the plant grew,
the stage when cut, the amount of irrigation water applied
or the presence of fungous disease. Indeed, any factor
which affects the growth of the plant also affects its
composition.

In different American analyses of timothy hay the
protein content varies from 3.75 to 9.69 per cent, and in
European analyses from 4.7 to 10.8 per cent; the ether
extract from .97 to 3.98 per cent in American and 1.1 to
3.8 per cent in European analyses.

Chemical analyses can in no sense replace feeding experiments in determining feeding values. With a new
forage plant a chemical analysis can throw no light on
palatability, digestibility or physiological effect.

**49. Chemical composition as affected by soil fertility
and by fertilizers.** — Extensive experiments on the effect

of fertilizers on the protein content of grasses were conducted at the Connecticut (Storrs) Experiment Station. In every case the protein content of the grass was greater when nitrogen was applied in fertilizers than when it was not. In general, the protein content of the grass increased with the amount of nitrogen applied as fertilizer. The results of 73 experiments are summarized in the following table : —

TABLE SHOWING PERCENTAGE OF PROTEIN IN TIMOTHY AND OTHER GRASSES AS RELATED TO FERTILIZERS APPLIED

RESULTS OF ANALYSES SHOWING RELATION BETWEEN NITROGEN APPLIED IN FERTILIZERS AND PROTEIN (N. × 6.25) FOUND IN RESULTING CROPS

	No. of experiments	Phos. acid and potash (mixed minerals)	Mixed minerals and 25 lb. nitrogen per acre	Mixed minerals and 50 lb. nitrogen per acre	Mixed minerals and 75 lb. nitrogen per acre
		%	%	%	%
Mixed grasses	5	7.6 [1]	7.6	8.8	9.8
Orchard-grass	2	8.9	10.2	—	12.6
Timothy . .	2	7.7	8.1	—	10.6
Redtop . .	3	—	8.3	—	11.7
7 other pure grasses . .	7	—	10.2	—	12.1

At the New York Experiment Station in 1887, fertilizing plots of timothy and Italian rye-grass did not indicate any definite effect upon the protein composition, apparently because there was already ample nitrogen in the soil. The experiment was repeated in 1888, and in every case where nitrogen fertilizers were added the proteid content of the timothy was increased.

Similar work has been conducted at other experiment

[1] Included more clover than other plots.

stations and much along the same line in Europe. There remains no doubt that the chemical content of plants is directly influenced by the soil, and that other things being equal the richest feed, especially of grasses, is that grown on the most fertile soil.

50. Chemical composition as affected by stage of maturity. — The variation in chemical composition depending on stage of development has been studied in many plants by many investigators.

The results secured in 1890 by Stone at the New Hampshire Experiment Station are here cited : —

TIMOTHY — CHEMICAL COMPOSITION AS AFFECTED BY TIME OF HARVESTING

	WATER	ASH	PROTEIN	FIBER	N.-FREE EXTRACT	FAT
Average height of plants 8 inches . .	4.33	5.16	11.54	19.23	54.64	5.10
Heads appearing . .	5.85	6.19	9.14	24.28	50.71	3.83
Heads beginning to bloom	5.35	5.47	7.00	26.09	53.66	2.43
Heads in full bloom .	6.37	5.81	6.81	26.60	51.88	2.53
Seed forming . . .	7.37	5.03	5.81	26.86	52.23	2.70
Seed becoming hard	7.51	5.03	6.25	26.10	52.85	2.26

51. Variation in chemical composition from unascertained causes. — In any series of chemical analyses of a hay plant such as timothy there is a wide variation shown in the amount of each constituent.

The following table shows the average and extremes for each constituent in the 68 American analyses of timothy compiled by Jenkins and Winton and 29 European analyses compiled by Stebler and Volkart : —

ANALYSES OF TIMOTHY HAY

CHEMICAL ANALYSES	No. of ANAL-YSES	PERCENTAGE COMPOSITION					
		Water	Ash	Protein	Fiber	N.-free Extract	Fat
American : —							
Average . .	68	13.18	4.37	5.87	29.03	45.08	2.47
Minimum . .		6.12	2.50	3.75	22.20	34.27	0.97
Maximum . .		28.88	6.34	9.69	38.46	58.52	3.98
European : —							
Average . .	29	14.3	5.0	6.9	26.2	45.0	2.6
Minimum . .			3.2	4.7	13.6	36.4	1.1
Maximum . .			7.3	10.8	37.5	50.6	3.8

52. Digestible nutrients. — To determine the digestible nutrients of a feed, it is fed to an animal under test conditions and the voided matter in the feces is then analyzed. The difference is the digestible portion, which is usually expressed as a percentage of the whole, and is called the *coefficient of digestibility*. The coefficient of digestibility varies considerably. It is affected more or less —

1. By the kind of animal employed, especially the horse as compared to ruminants ;

2. By the individuality of the animal ;

3. By the stage of development of the plant when cut, young plants being more digestible ;

4. By the age of the feed, fresh being better than old ;

5. By fine cutting of the feed in some cases ;

6. Sometimes by other feeds in the ration ;

Digestibility is not appreciably affected by drying, moistening or cooking.

In thus comparing the different feeds it is assumed that the digestible portions of the protein, carbohydrates, fats, and fiber in different plants are each of equal nutritive value, although they differ considerably in actual composition, and as is now known, in actual feeding value. The method of digestible nutrients requires much less time and expense than the direct method of actual feeding, but the results are less reliable. In the absence of actual feeding experiments, however, it furnishes an approximation of the feeding value of the substance in question.

The feeding value of a substance of which only a chemical analysis is available may be conjectured by assuming that the coefficient of digestibility is the same as that of some similar feed.

In the accompanying table is shown the amount of digestible nutrients in four grass hays, four legume hays, and two concentrates : —

TABLE SHOWING POUNDS OF DIGESTIBLE NUTRIENTS IN
100 POUNDS DRY MATTER. (HENRY)

KIND OF FEED	PROTEIN	CARBO-HYDRATES	ETHER EXTRACT
Johnson-grass	2.9	45.6	0.8
Timothy	2.8	42.4	1.3
Redtop	4.8	46.9	1.0
Bermuda	6.4	44.9	1.6
Red clover	7.1	37.8	1.8
Crimson clover	10.5	34.9	1.2
Sweet clover	11.9	36.7	0.5
Alfalfa	11.4	40.0	0.8
Bran	11.9	42.0	2.5
Shelled corn	7.8	66.8	4.3

Attempts have often been made to determine the relative value of a feed in a single term by assigning a definite value per pound to the protein, the fat, the carbohydrates and the fiber digested. No matter what value is assigned to each of these constituents, the results secured vary considerably from the market prices. Nevertheless, the price of protein feeds is based to some extent on their protein content.

TABLE SHOWING THE RELATIVE MONEY VALUE OF VARIOUS FEEDS, DETERMINED BY ASSUMING VALUES TO EACH DIGESTIBLE NUTRIENT

KIND OF FEED	PROTEIN $.037 CARBOHY. .014 FAT .032	- - - $.04 - - - - .01 - - - .02	- - - $.04 - - - .0125 - - - .02	- - - $.025 - - - .01 - - - .0225	- - - $.03 - - - .01 - - - .02
Grass hay : —					
Johnson-grass .	$15.04	$11.76	$14.04	$10.93	$11.18
Timothy . . .	14.89	11.24	13.36	10.49	10.70
Redtop. . . .	17.51	13.42	15.76	12.19	12.66
Bermuda . . .	18.59	14.74	16.98	12.90	13.46
Average value per ton . .	16.53	12.79	15.04	11.63	12.00
Legume hay : —					
Red clover . .	19.27	13.96	15.86	11.92	12.54
Crimson clover .	18.31	15.86	17.66	12.77	13.76
Sweet clover . .	19.88	17.06	18.90	13.52	14.68
Alfalfa	19.99	16.94	18.90	13.64	14.72
Average value per ton . .	19.36	15.96	17.83	12.76	13.93
Concentrates : —					
Bran	22.65	18.92	21.02	15.48	16.54
Shelled corn . .	27.54	21.32	24.68	19.35	19.76
Gluten feed . .	35.31	30.76	33.40	21.42	26.50
Cottonseed meal	41.46	35.74	35.82	27.54	27.22
Average value per ton . .	31.74	26.64	25.73	20.95	22.51

In the above table the values of various feeds has been figured in terms of money by determining the average values of the digestible proteins, carbohydrates and fat a pound in timothy taken at $15 a ton, bran at $27.60 a ton, gluten feed at $30 a ton, cottonseed meal at $32 a ton, and alfalfa at $20 a ton.   By comparing timothy with each of the others in order the value of the carbohydrates is determined respectively as $.012, $.015, $.014 and $.014 a pound, an average of $.014. The respective values for the protein are $.066, $.025, $.025 and $.041 a pound,—an average of $.039.   The average value of the fat similarly determined is $.032 a pound.

In the other four columns of the table arbitrary values are given to the nutrients for comparison.

In a general way the figures show correspondence to market value.   How nearly they may represent the true relative values of the feeds does not appear in the light of present knowledge.

53. Net energy values. — The *energy value* of a feed is determined by an instrument called a calorimeter, and is measured in *therms* of 1000 *calories*.   A calorie is the amount of heat required to raise 1 kilogram of water 1 degree Centigrade.

The *net energy* value of a feed is that which remains after deducting from its total energy value that lost in the feces, in the urine, in gases and in the work of mastication, digestion and assimilation.   The loss in gases and in the labor of assimilating the feed is measured by keeping the animal in a special apparatus — the *respiration calorimeter*.

From investigations conducted at the Pennsylvania Experiment Station, Dr. H. P. Armsby has determined the net energy values for a number of roughages as well as concentrates.   The energy values of the roughage feeds are shown in the following table: —

ENERGY VALUE OF ROUGHAGE IN 100 POUNDS

FEEDING STUFF	TOTAL DRY MATTER	DIGESTIBLE TRUE PROTEIN	NET ENERGY VALUE
	Pounds	Pounds	Therms
Green fodder and silage : —			
Alfalfa	28.2	2.50	12.45
Clover, crimson	19.1	2.19	11.30
Clover, red	29.2	2.21	16.17
Corn fodder, green . . .	20.7	.41	12.44
Corn silage	25.6	.88	16.56
Hungarian grass	28.9	1.33	14.76
Rape	14.3	2.16	11.43
Rye	23.4	1.44	11.63
Timothy	38.4	1.04	19.08
Hay and dry coarse fodders : —			
Alfalfa hay	91.6	6.93	34.41
Clover hay, red	84.7	5.41	34.74
Corn forage, field cured .	57.8	2.13	30.53
Corn stover	59.5	1.80	26.53
Cowpea hay	89.3	8.57	40.76
Hungarian hay	92.3	3.00	44.03
Oat hay	84.0	2.59	26.97
Soybean hay	88.7	7.68	38.65
Timothy hay	86.8	2.05	33.56
Straws : —			
Oat straw	90.8	1.09	21.21
Rye straw	92.9	.63	20.87
Wheat straw	90.4	.37	16.56
Roots and tubers : —			
Carrots	11.4	.37	7.82
Mangel-wurzels	9.1	.14	4.62
Potatoes	21.1	.45	18.05
Rutabagas	11.4	.88	8.00
Turnips	9.4	.22	5.74

These values have been secured wholly from experiments on fattening cattle.

"Even for this purpose many of them are confessedly approximate estimates, and still less can they be regarded as strictly accurate for other kinds of animals and other purposes of feeding. Nevertheless, there seems to be reason for believing that they also represent fairly well the relative values of feeding stuffs for sheep at least, and probably for horses, and for growth and milk production as well as for fattening. At any rate, there can be little doubt that they are decidedly more accurate than the figures which have been commonly used, and we are quite justified in using them tentatively and subject to correction by the results of later experiments.

"As regards swine, the matter is far less certain, and it may perhaps be questioned whether the values given in the table are any more satisfactory for this animal than the older ones."

54. Starch values. — The unit of this system proposed by Kellner is one pound of digestible starch for beef production. Kellner found that one pound of digestible starch in excess to a maintenance ration would form approximately one-fourth pound of fat. On this basis 1 pound of digestible protein is equal to .94 pound of digestible starch, and 1 pound of oil in seeds equals 2.41 pounds of digestible starch in fattening value.

These values are in excess of what the animal actually gets from the feed, so that arbitrary deductions have to be made to compensate for the work of mastication and digestion.

55. Comparison of feeding values. — Woll has endeavored to reduce to a common basis the relative values of various feeds as determined by the feed unit system, by Kellner's starch values and by Armsby's therms. The average of the net energy values of corn, wheat, rye, barley and wheat middlings is approximately 80 therms, which is considered equal to 1 feed unit. By the same method 83 starch values is equivalent to 1 feed unit. In general, the corresponding values by the three methods are close, but there are some marked exceptions : —

TABLE SHOWING COMPARISON OF THERMS, STARCH VALUES
AND FEED UNITS

	THERMS (ARMSBY)		STARCH VALUES (KELLNER)	FEED UNITS	
				Average	Range
Corn	88.8 ⎫	Ratio	.74 ⎫		
Wheat	82.6		.85		
Rye	81.7 ⎬ 80[1] = 1.00		.85 ⎬ .83[1]	1.0	———
Barley	80.8		.89		
Wheat middlings	77.7 ⎭		.83 ⎭		
Cottonseed meal .	84.2	.95	.83	.8	———
Oil meal . . .	78.9	1.01	.84	.9	———
Distillers' grains	79.2	1.0	.9	.9	———
Gluten feed . .	79.3	1.0	.9	.9	———
Dried brewers' grains . . .	60.0	1.3	1.1	1.0	———
Peas	71.8	1.1	.9	1.0	———
Malt sprouts .	46.3	1.7	1.6	1.1	———
Oats	66.3	1.2	1.0	1.1	———
Wheat bran . .	48.2	1.7	1.25	1.1	———
Sugar beet pulp, dried . . .	60.1	1.3	1.2	1.1	———
Alfalfa hay . .	34.4	2.3	1.9	2.0	1.5–3.0
Timothy hay . .	33.6	2.4	2.6	3.0	2.5–3.5
Corn stover . .	26.5	3.0	3.0	4.0	3.0–6.0
Oat straw . .	21.2	3.8	3.6	4.0	4.0–5.0
Green alfalfa . .	12.5	6.4	7.2	7.0	6–8
Green corn . .	12.4	6.5	8.3	8.0	6–10
Corn silage . .	16.6	4.8	7.7	6.0	5–7
Potatoes . . .	18.1	4.4	3.2	6.0	4–6
Carrot . . .	7.8	10.3	7.0	8.0	———
Turnips . . .	5.7	14.1	12.6	12.5	11–15
Rutabagas . .	8.0	10.0	10.4	9.0	9–10

In figuring the values of the feeds according to the
digestible nutrients, redtop, johnson-grass and Bermuda

[1] Assumed average figures.

are apparently all more valuable than timothy; and sweet clover fully as valuable as alfalfa.

If measured by therms, cowpea hay is superior to alfalfa, and Hungarian-grass to either; while corn stover is practically as valuable as oat hay.

It may be that the relative values assigned to roughage based on experience and reflected in market values are as erroneous as the above data would indicate.   It is apparent that much further work is necessary before there can be agreement as to the comparative feeding values of roughage for different purposes.

CHAPTER IV

SEEDS AND SEEDING

Nothing is more important than the seeds, as to quality and name, in the growing of a crop. The best of land and preparation and the best effort in tillage may bring small return if the seed is not good, clean and true to name.

56. Quality. — The quality of seeds depends on various characteristics, especially genuineness, purity and viability. Other points of more or less importance are age, size, plumpness, color, weight per bushel, source of seed and in some cases freedom from insects and such diseases as smut. Among the legumes the percentage of hard seeds is also to be considered.

The determination of the actual quality of the seed requires special knowledge and experience. In the first place the sample must be representative of the bulk. The other seeds present either as impurities or adulterants should be identified to prevent fraud and to avoid introducing noxious weeds. Finally, many forage seeds — especially grasses — require much care and special apparatus to secure a fair test of germination.

For these reasons, most forage crop seeds should be purchased under guarantee, or a sample secured first, to be referred to a seed laboratory.

57. Genuineness. — By this term is meant the trueness of the seed to name. As most forage crops do not contain special varieties, this is readily determined by comparison with authentic samples.   In other crops, however, special varieties are often indistinguishable by their seeds, so that one must depend upon the reliability or the guarantee of the seedsmen.   Among forage crops, mammoth and medium red clover, and Grimm and ordinary alfalfa are examples of varieties indistinguishable by their seeds.

58. Purity. — By the purity of seed is meant its freedom from foreign matter, whether trash, chaff, weed seeds or adulterants.   With the exception of perhaps the last-mentioned, impurities are far more common in forage crop seeds than in any others.   This is due partly to the fact that most grasses and many legumes are grown broadcasted, and it is rarely possible to keep the fields free from weeds.   Furthermore, grass seeds as a rule are light in weight, so that it is difficult to remove chaff, small pieces of straw and the like.

The impurities that usually occur in each region where seed is largely grown are well known, so that if any others are present, it is strong evidence of adulteration.

59. Viability. — The viability of seed or capacity for germination depends upon many factors, among which are the conditions of the season when grown, the care exercised in harvesting and curing, the manner in which it has been stored, and the age of the seed.

Viability is tested in laboratories by means of special germinators in which the temperature, moisture, ventilation and light can be controlled.   The best temperature varies somewhat for the different species.   For most grasses the temperatures between 68 degrees and 86 degrees Fahrenheit are considered best, and it is found advantageous to use the higher temperature 6 hours and the lower 18 hours each day.

Most kinds of farm seeds may, however, be tested in

very simple germinators, such as in a box of sand, or between two moist cloths in a covered dish. Grass seeds are, however, more exacting in the conditions they require than most other farm seeds, so that misleading results may easily be secured.

The length of time required by different seeds to germinate also varies widely. With most sorts ten days is sufficient time to allow, but many grasses require twice this amount of time.

60. Actual value of seed. — The real or actual value of seed for sowing can be determined only when its purity and viability are known. It is the product of the purity multiplied by the viability, both expressed as percentages. Thus, if the purity be 90 per cent and the viability 80 per cent, the actual value or percentage of good germinable seeds is 90 times 80, or 72 per cent. One reason why rates of seeding recommended by different authorities vary so widely is due to the difference in the actual value of the seeds used.

61. Superiority of local seed. — Numerous European experiments with grasses and clovers show as a rule that locally grown seeds give superior yields to those brought from a distance. In the United States this phenomenon is well known in the case of highly bred crops like corn, but has obtained little recognition in the case of grasses and clovers. Results with these crops are particularly instructive, as they have not been subject to artificial breeding, and hence the differences they show may fairly be considered due to natural selection or local adaptation. With most other crops, the factor of difference in variety enters the problem.

The amount of evidence on this subject is insufficient for final conclusions, but it tends to uphold the generalization that seeds grown locally produce superior crops to those brought from a distance. Theoretically this has been ascribed to adaptation or acclimatization, usually with the idea that superiority is attained by the elimination more or less gradually of the inferior individuals. Much more experimental data are needed on this subject, which indeed has been but little investigated in the United States.

62. Standards of purity and germination. — Attempts have been made to establish standards of purity and germination for all farm seeds. There is, however, a considerable variation in the purity of many forage crop seeds, depending on the place grown, the season and the care exercised. Furthermore, it is not so much the amount of the impurity as the character of it which is most important. Thus, alfalfa seed containing 1 per cent of dodder seed is less desirable than that containing no dodder but a larger percentage of other weed seeds. A few seeds of dangerous weeds like Canada thistle are far more serious than many seeds of ordinary weeds.

The viability of seed varies not only with its age, but with the care in handling, and with the season, especially at harvest time. In some seeds, indeed, the viability is less when fresh than when one year old. On the whole there is little choice between 100 pounds of forage seed germinating 90 per cent and 120 pounds germinating 75 per cent.

While fixed standards of purity and germination are scarcely practicable, it is well to know what degrees of purity and germination are found in high grade commercial seed. The average purity and germination found in the trade is of less consequence, as this is influenced by the efficiency of legislation and inspection : —

TABLE SHOWING PURITY AND GERMINATION OF FORAGE SEEDS
OF HIGH QUALITY

NAME OF SEED	PURITY	GERMINATION
	Per cent	Per cent
Kentucky blue-grass	75–85	70–85
Timothy	95–99	95–99
Orchard-grass	90–98	90–95
Meadow fescue	95–99	95–98
Perennial rye-grass	95	85–90
Italian rye-grass	95	80–85
Brome-grass	98–99	90–95
Redtop	95–98	95–98
Tall oat-grass	80	80
Velvet-grass	70	70
Meadow foxtail	75	70
Millets	99	95
Red clover	96–99	90–99
White clover	95–99	90–99
Alsike clover	96–99	90–99
Alfalfa	98–99	90–99
Sainfoin	98	75–80
Crimson clover	99	95–99
Hairy vetch	98–99	95–98
Common vetch	98–99	95–98

63. Adulteration and misbranding. — Seeds are not infrequently adulterated by the admixture of similar-looking cheaper seeds. Whenever such inferior seeds are found present in considerable quantities, it may reasonably be considered to be due to adulteration. Sometimes one kind of seed is sold for another which it closely resembles, as trefoil for alfalfa, or Canada blue-grass for Kentucky blue-grass. Such are usually willful cases of misbranding.

Adulteration and misbranding of seeds was formerly much more common, but the practice is by no means obsolete. At one time in Europe particles of quartz were prepared and colored especially to adulterate clover seed. In England there was a regular business in the collecting and killing of weed seeds to be used as adulterants.

Among the seeds that are still often adulterated are red clover, alfalfa, alsike, Kentucky blue-grass, orchard-grass, redtop, meadow fescue and brome-grass.

64. Color and plumpness of seeds. — Depending on the conditions under which it was grown, there is much difference in seeds as to brightness of color and degree of plumpness.

Shriveled seeds make weak seedlings, but no field experiments where shriveled were compared with plump seeds seem to be recorded.

Discolored seed is evidence that the seed is old, or has been badly stored, or more usually that it was harvested under unfavorable conditions.

65. Age of seed. — Seeds vary greatly in the length of time they will retain their germinating power. In general, the seeds of legumes are much longer lived than those of grasses. Old seeds make weaker seedlings than fresh seeds, and this probably has its effect on the resultant yield.

In red clover and other legumes the germination of fresh seeds is usually less than that of seeds one year old, owing to the presence of " hard " seeds.   (§ 71.)

Cowpea seeds, at least some varieties, also refuse to germinate when fresh unless the testa is broken or scratched with sand. Apparently there is a waterproof coating that for a time prevents the absorption of water.

The results obtained during many years at the Zürich, Switzerland, Seed Control Station, show that few forage seeds are worth planting when three years old.

If, however, seeds be stored in small quantities under very favorable conditions, the viability is retained much longer than in seed warehouses. Thus Samek secured the following results : —

VIABILITY OF VARIOUS FORAGE SEEDS STORED IN PAPER BAGS IN A DRY AIRY ROOM DURING 11 YEARS. — J. SAMEK

KIND OF SEED	PERCENTAGE OF VITALITY										
	1 yr.	2 yr.	3 yr.	4 yr.	5 yr.	6 yr.	7 yr.	8 yr.	9 yr.	10 yr.	11 yr.
Red clover	90	90	88	84	74	68	44	16	10	3	2
White clover	74	72	63	52	50	50	35	31	26	23	22
Alsike clover	73	64	51	37	15	7	6	5	3	3	3
Sainfoin	92	92	78	61	54	52	19	18	13	9	*
Serradella	36	32	33	22	14	11	9	6	2	0	0
Alfalfa	94	91	87	75	72	71	68	66	63	59	54
Tall oat-grass	70	66	59	43	24	12	10	2	1	0	0
Italian rye-grass	67	62	61	55	43	39	29	15	8	4	1
English rye-grass	72	70	66	60	42	28	22	9	5	1	0
Tall fescue	83	80	72	68	48	42	35	18	9	1	0
Sweet vernal-grass	70	62	57	46	43	37	31	13	9	8	4
Meadow foxtail	13	11	9	7	7	5	3	1	1	0	0
Timothy	95	90	90	88	86	79	66	39	15	1	0
Orchard-grass	46	47	44	44	39	29	21	12	8	5	*
Blue-grass	28	17	17	17	16	11	8	5	2	0	0
Crested dogstail	46	39	33	29	20	12	6	3	2	1	0
Fiorin	66	61	46	43	37	35	34	31	22	20	*
Sheep fescue	68	67	68	42	21	18	10	4	3	0	0
Hair-grass	37	27	21	17	7	3	0	0	0	0	0
Spurry	85	70	68	59	46	42	37	25	21	8	2

* No seeds for examination, all having been used up in previous years.

66. Source of seeds. — The place in which seed is grown may have an important effect upon the resulting plant. This is particularly true in the case of highly bred plants like corn, but it is also true of crops which have never been improved by artificial selection. As a general rule, locally grown seed is likely to be most satisfactory, but this is by no means always the case. The reasons for this phenomenon are not clear, but it is commonly believed that all plants become better adapted to the conditions of culture, or the climate and soil of the region in which they are grown a long time, by the gradual elimination of such individuals as do not thrive.

In North America the seeds of most forage crops are grown in the same general region in which they · are cultivated, but the exceptions occur to this in case of alfalfa, vetches and many grasses of minor importance. In Europe, on the contrary, there is a relatively much greater importation of grass and legume seeds from foreign sources, so that much experimentation has been devoted to determining their relative crop-bearing capacities.

It is usually possible to determine the origin of any lot of forage crop seed by the presence of characteristic weed seeds. Thus, if orchard-grass is found to contain seeds of *Lepidium virginicum*, *Panicum dichotomum* or *Carex cephalophora*, it certainly was grown in North America; if it contains *Danthonia pilosa*, *Danthonia semiannularis*, *Sporobolus indicus*, *Hypochœris radicata* and others, it indicates New Zealand origin. If alfalfa seed contains that of *Grindelia squarrosa*, it is probably from the western United States; while *Argemone alba* indicates an Argentine origin, and *Centaurea picris* that it is from Turkestan.

67. Seed inspection. — In recent times the adulteration and misbranding of seeds is becoming less common, mainly due to legislation and the official examination of seeds at special central stations or laboratories. The first of these was established in 1867 at Tharand, Saxony, by Nobbe. At the present time such stations are supported by nearly all of the countries of Europe, there being over 40 in Germany alone.

The first work of this sort in America was inaugurated by Jenkins at the Connecticut Experiment Station in 1877. The Seed Laboratory of the United States Department of Agriculture was established in 1894, and similar work has been carried on by the Canada Department of Agriculture since 1903.

At the present time there are legislative provisions in many states for preventing the adulteration and mis-branding of seeds.

68. Sampling. — To secure a fair sample from a bag of seed a small amount should be taken from different parts of the bag, including the top and the bottom. There is a tendency for the smaller and heavier seeds to rattle to the bottom in handling, and for the lighter and larger seeds to rise toward the top. By mixing the smaller samples thus contained, a fair sample of the contents of the bag is obtained.

69. Guaranteed seeds. — The practice of guaranteeing the purity and germination of seeds has been adopted by several firms, and is likely to become more general. This is the fairest and most satisfactory method for the buyer. In lieu of guarantees, large users of field seeds frequently purchase on the basis that the delivery shall be equal in quality to a sample previously submitted. No matter how stringent future control laws may become, seeds will continue to vary in quality. In a perfectly fair transaction both the buyer and the seller should know the quality of the goods.

70. Fungous diseases. — A few grasses are more or less subject to the attacks of smut fungi that infect the ovary, which, when ripe, is converted into a mass of black spores.

In thrashing, these spores are scattered over the seeds, and thus the young plants become infected. Among the forage grasses thus subject to smut are the sorghums and tall oat-grass. Treating the seeds by various different methods will destroy the spores or prevent them from germinating in time to infect the young seedlings. Such methods are commonly used to prevent smut in such grain crops as wheat, oats and sorghum, and probably would be found efficient in such forage grasses as may be similarly affected.

71. Hard seeds. — In many legumes some of the seeds will not absorb water and germinate but remain hard. The percentage of hard seeds varies with the seasonal or other conditions under which it was grown. In the same lot of seed the percentage of hard seed will gradually diminish with age. Owing to the presence of such seeds, red clover often shows a higher percentage of viability when one year old than when fresh.

American seed laboratories usually state the percentage of hard seeds present in a sample. In Europe the practice has been to consider a certain per cent of the hard seed to be viable; namely, that which it is believed will germinate in the soil under favorable conditions.

The actual value of hard seed when sown in the field needs to be determined for each species. It is certain that some of it remains unsprouted in the ground at least a year.

Duvel buried " hard " seeds of red clover in porous earthenware pots at depths of 6–8, 18–22 and 36–42 inches. At the end of 11 months the seeds germinated respectively 10.5, 15.5 and 14.5 per cent. The hard seed was selected by soaking seeds one year old in water for 18 hours and then for 20 hours, saving only those that

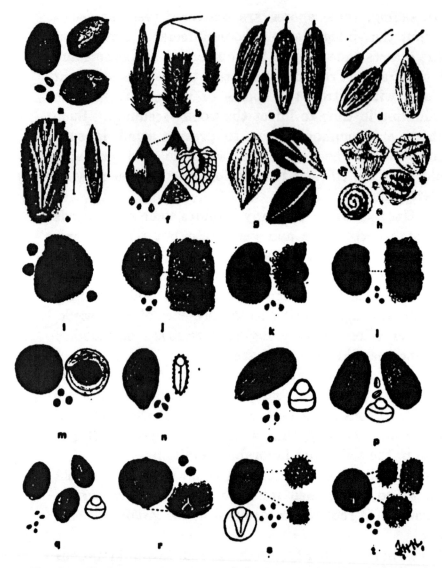

FIG. 6. — Noxious weed seeds found in farm seeds (No. 1): a, Sand bur; b, wild oat; c, chess; d, darnel; e, quack-grass; f, dock; g, black bindweed; h, Russian thistle; i, corn cockle; j, white campion; k, bladder campion; l, night-flowering catchfly; m, cow cockle; n, pennycress; o, field peppergrass; p, large-fruited false flax; q, small-fruited false flax; r, ball mustard; s, black mustard; t, English charlock.

remained hard, which was 51.5 per cent of the whole. In another series of samples from this lot, the percentages which germinated after 11 months were respectively 4.5, 5 and 6 per cent for the different depths.

If hard seed be scratched so that water can be absorbed by the embryo, prompt germination results. Recently machines have been devised for this purpose, but as their capacity is small, they have been used only in experimental work.

Another method of making hard seed viable is to soak the seed in commercial sulfuric acid [1] for thirty minutes, and then wash with water to remove the acid. Running water should be used, if possible, as the mixing of the acid with water engenders much heat, and if only a small proportion of water is used, the seeds may be injured by the heat. The seed, after washing, should be spread out to dry. The acid corrodes the seed coat sufficiently so that it no longer is impervious to water.

72. Most dangerous weed seeds. — The percentage of weed seeds present as impurities, unless very large, is of less concern than the presence of really dangerous weeds, even if in very small amount. Among the most dangerous weed seeds are the dodders, which occur in red clover, alfalfa, lespedeza and rarely in other forage seeds; Canada thistle, which is not infrequent in many sorts of seeds; and quack-grass, which may be present in other grass seeds. In cases where these weeds cannot be removed by recleaning, it is usually not advisable to plant the seeds.

73. Weight of seeds. — The weight of seeds to the bushel varies considerably with the same species, depending

---

[1] Cornell Agr. Exp. Sta. Bul. No. 312.

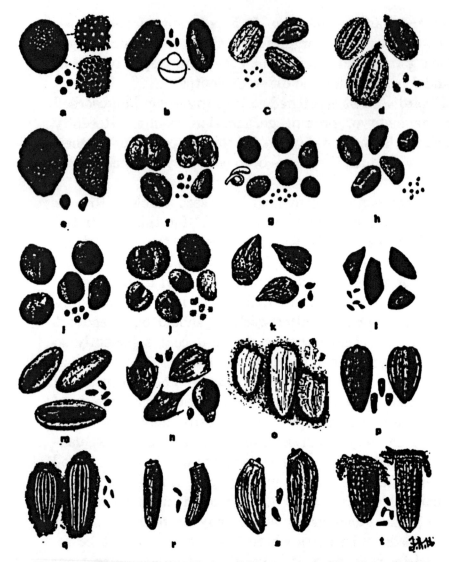

Fig. 7. — Noxious weed seeds found in farm seeds (No. 2) : **a,** Indian mustard; **b,** hare's-ear mustard; **c,** tumbling mustard; **d,** wild carrot; **e,** field bindweed; **f,** flax dodder; **g,** clover dodder; **h,** small-seeded alfalfa dodder; **i,** field dodder; **j,** large-seeded alfalfa dodder; **k,** corn gromwell; **l,** rat-tail plantain; **m,** buckhorn; **n,** ragweed; **o,** gumweed; **p,** wild sunflower; **q,** oxeye-daisy; **r,** Canada thistle; **s,** bull thistle; **t,** wild chicory.

on the conditions of the season or of the locality in which the seed was grown, and with the amount of chaff or other impurities which it may contain. In most states a legal weight to the bushel has been established for each important kind of seed.

The influence of weight of seed upon resultant yields is still an open question. With cereals where the same volume of heavy, light and unseparated seeds have been sown, the resulting differences obtained have usually been too small to be significant.

Few experiments of this sort have been carried out with grasses or clovers. Hunt secured better yields of timothy at the Cornell Experiment Station with heavy seed, both when the same weight and the same number of seeds were sown. At the Utah Experiment Station heavy and light timothy seeds were separated by means of a salt solution, but no difference was obtained in the yield of plots planted to each.

74. Number of seeds in one pound. — The number of seeds in one pound of different kinds of field seeds has been determined by several investigators. The figures of different authorities often show wide variation for the same kind of seed. This may be due in part to the quality of the seed used, as the weight of a bushel from different sources or in different seasons may vary greatly. The subject is not one of much agronomic value, and mainly on this account has received but little attention. In some crops like the cowpea, soybean and field pea, the size of the seeds and the number in a pound vary greatly according to variety. In this case it is often preferable to use the small-seeded varieties for forage production, as less seed is required to the acre, and the price of the small-seeded sorts is usually just as cheap.

TABLE SHOWING WEIGHTS OF SEED IN A BUSHEL

NAME OF SEED	LEGAL WEIGHT MOST COMMONLY ADOPTED	EXTREMES IN LEGAL WEIGHTS ADOPTED	AVERAGE WEIGHT OF ONE BUSHEL	EXTREME WEIGHTS OF ONE BUSHEL
	Pounds	*Pounds*	*Pounds*	*Pounds*
Alfalfa	60			63
Red clover	60			64
Alsike clover	60			66
White clover	60			63
Crimson clover	60			
Kidney vetch				60–64
Hairy vetch	60		60	
Common vetch	60		60	
Yellow trefoil				64–66
Bird's foot trefoil			60	
Field peas	60			52–68
Cowpeas	60			
Soybeans	60			
Velvet beans			60	
Timothy	45	42–60		50
Orchard-grass	14		14	12–22
Redtop	14	12–14	14	12–40
Kentucky blue-grass	14		18	6–28
Canada blue-grass				14–24
Meadow fescue				20–30
Smooth brome			13	12–20
Bermuda				35–36
Tall oat-grass			10	10–16
Perennial rye-grass			20	10–30
Italian rye-grass	20		16	12–24
Creeping bent			16	8–32
Foxtail	48–50	48–50		40–55
Millet				
Sorghum	56	30–57		
Johnson-grass	28			25–28
Yellow oat-grass			5	12–14
Meadow foxtail			6–8	12–14
Velvet-grass	7		6½	6–7
Reed canary-grass				44–48
Sheep's fescue			12	10–30
Red fescue			13	10–15
Erect brome				14–15
Crested dogstail			26	20–38
Sweet vernal				16

G

TABLE SHOWING NUMBER OF SEEDS IN ONE POUND OF VARIOUS FORAGE CROPS

Name of Plant	Authority				
	Stebler & Schröter	Werner	Hunter	Hunt	Misc.
Alfalfa	{ 182,000 237,000 }	178,000	224,000	{ 200,000 240,000 }	
Red clover	279,000	258,000	232,000	200,000 550,000	
Alsike clover	707,000	643,000	718,000	700,000	
White clover	740,000	682,000	732,000	800,000	
Crimson clover		121,000	118,000	{ 125,000 150,000 }	
Kidney vetch	{ 126,000 182,000 }	176,000	193,000		
Yellow trefoil		270,000	319,000	325,000	
Sainfoin	22,500	22,300		22,500	
Bird's foot trefoil	375,000	313,000	412,000		
Cowpea				{ 75,000 250,000 }	
Burnet			54,000		
Chicory			325,000		
Yarrow			3,510,000		
Goat's rue	62,000				
Timothy	1,170,500	948,000	1,320,000		
Redtop	603,000	4,000,000		7,800,000	{ 4,135,900 Ill. Exp. Sta. 6,400,000 N. C. Exp. Sta.
Creeping bent				8,000,000	
Orchard-grass	579,500	400,000	426,000	{ 400,000 480,000 }	
Kentucky blue-grass	2,400,000	2,400,000	1,860,000	3,888,000	2,185,000 Ill. Exp. Sta.
Meadow foxtail	907,000	465,000	490,000	1,216,000	
Italian rye-grass	285,000	260,000	270,000	285,000	
Perennial rye-grass	336,800	223,000	223,000	336,000	
Meadow fescue	{ 318,200 226,400 }	240,000	236,000	300,000	
Tall fescue			246,000		
Sheep's fescue	680,000	923,000			
Hard fescue			578,000		
Fine-leaved fescue		1,056,000	1,561,000		
Tall oat-grass	159,000	147,000	138,000	159,000	
Wood meadow-grass		2,000,000	2,325,000		
Rough-stalked meadow-grass	{ 2,500,000 4,000,000 }	2,000,000	2,235,000		
Sweet vernal	924,000	760,000	738,000	924,000	
Yellow oat-grass	2,045,000	1,175,000	1,400,000		
Crested dogstail	1,127,000	678,000	886,000		
Velvet-grass	1,304,000	1,195,000		1,304,000	
Reed canary	660,000	577,000		660,000	
Various-leaved fescue	{ 350,000 545,000 }				
Red fescue	{ 364,000 820,000 }	400,000			
Erect brome	114,000	127,000			
Brome	137,000				
Bermuda-grass				1,800,000	
Foxtail millet		240,000		{ 175,000 250,000 }	

75. Seed production of forage crops, United States, 1909. — The census statistics for the production of grass seeds including grasses, clovers, millet and alfalfa are given only in production, as the acreage is wholly or mainly included under hay and forage. In the case of peas and beans, however, the acreage and production are both given, though much of the field peas, cowpeas and sorghums are cut for hay.

" Grass seed," including timothy, clovers, millet and alfalfa, is most largely produced by the following states, the numbers referring to acres harvested: Illinois, 1,289,-996; Iowa, 1,118,044; Minnesota, 945,666; Kentucky, 612,406; South Dakota, 424,623; Kansas, 324,321; Ohio, 288,605; Missouri, 257,872; Indiana, 165,488; Michigan, 151,567; Oregon, 151,016.

Field pea seed is mostly produced in Michigan and Wisconsin, but much more is grown in Canada.

Cowpea seed is produced in all the Southern States, especially Georgia, North Carolina and South Carolina.

Sorghum seed is produced most largely by Kansas, followed by Nebraska, Texas and Oklahoma.

76. Seeding in practice. — In actual practice three systems of sowing grass seeds may be distinguished; namely : (1) seeding on especially prepared land ; (2) seeding with another broadcasted or drilled crop, usually a small grain either simultaneously or in some cases in spring on fall-sown grain ; and (3) seeding in the rows of a cultivated crop. In some regions, all three of these systems prevail. The first system unquestionably gives the best results as regards the grass crop, but requires additional labor in preparing the land. Where difficulty is experienced in securing a good stand of grass, or where perennial weeds are troublesome, this method should always be employed. The second system is the common one employed in the sowing of timothy and clover, as well as other mixtures, the " nurse " crop being some small grain. Most commonly the timothy is sown with fall wheat and the clover is broadcasted over the field in early spring as soon as the frost is out of the ground. In the northernmost states and in Canada, the grass seeds are sown with a spring crop of small grain.

The " nurse crop " system has the advantage of economy of labor. In fertile farm lands, especially in the north, it is as a rule very satisfactory. It needs to be clearly recognized that the grasses succeed not by the help of, but in spite of, the " nurse crop." After the grain is harvested, the slender grass plants which have developed in the shade of the cereal are then subjected to the heat of midsummer, and sometimes to drought as well. This often results in damage to the grass, more serious as a rule to spring-sown than to fall-sown.

The third system, — namely, sowing the grass seed in between the rows of a cultivated crop, — is not widely employed. Crimson clover is, however, very commonly sown in corn at the time of the last cultivation, and this same method has been used successfully with red clover, alfalfa and with mixed grasses. It has all the advantages of a small cereal nurse crop without certain disadvantages. The young grass thrives better because it is less crowded and less shaded, and practically no injury can accrue from lodging. In rotation systems, however, it is desirable to follow grass with a cultivated crop, and this is usually corn. For this reason, small grain crops necessarily follow corn, if employed in the rotation, as is usually the case. It is mainly due to the requirements of rotation systems that grasses are so seldom sown in cultivated crops.

77. Rate of seeding. — In the accompanying table is given the ordinary rate of seeding broadcasted forage crops, with calculations showing the number of seeds sown on each square foot. It will be noticed that the number is large and that it varies greatly with different plants. Were such plants allowed to develop undisturbed by weeds, only a small portion of the seed would be required to give a satisfactory stand. It is difficult to determine what constitutes a perfect stand, but the numbers given are based on the room necessary for the full development of a young plant.

The rates of seeding ordinarily used are purely empirical — the result of experience or of experimental field trials. The effect of the heavy seeding is to secure a dense stand of young plants, which in a measure restrains weeds, and which further insures that in competition with the weeds a majority of the survivors will be the plant desired. This dense stand is especially necessary in perennial grasses where the seedlings are slender and in their early stages grow but slowly, and thus are relatively inefficient against broad-leaved, vigorous weeds.

It is scarcely possible to seed perennial grasses and clovers so heavily that the resultant yield is seriously affected. With annuals, however, too dense seeding reduces the size of the individuals so much that the yield to the acre is also diminished.

In general the rate of seeding is least in regions where the crop is best adapted; that is, where the individual plants are most vigorous and the natural mortality therefore least. The weediness of the soil is also an important factor.

Where seed can be drilled the amount necessary to secure a good stand is about 25 per cent less than when broadcasted. The reasons are evident; namely, the covering of the seed uniformly to the most favorable depths as well as its more even distribution : —

TABLE SHOWING THE GENERAL RELATIONS BETWEEN NUMBER
OF SEEDS SOWN AND FINAL STAND

NAME OF PLANT	AVERAGE RATE OF SEEDING TO THE ACRE POUNDS	NUMBER OF SEEDS TO THE POUND	NUMBER OF SEEDS TO THE SQUARE FOOT	AVERAGE NUMBER OF PLANTS TO THE SQUARE FOOT FOR A PERFECT STAND
Red clover	8	250,000	47	15
Crimson clover . . .	15	130,000	45	15
Alsike clover . . .	8	700,000	130	15
Alfalfa	20	200,000	93	15
Sweet clover	25	235,000	140	7
Timothy	15	1,100,000	350	90
Kentucky blue-grass .	25	2,400,000	1400	130
Orchard-grass . . .	20	4,500,000	210	90
Brome-grass	20	137,000	65	90
Redtop	10	4,000,000	930	140
Meadow fescue . . .	20	250,000	115	90
Italian rye-grass . .	30	270,000	215	90
Perennial rye-grass . .	30	270,000	215	90
Tall oat-grass . . .	40	150,000	140	90

78. Time of seeding. — There are certain general principles involved in determining the best time to seed any particular forage crop. These principles refer partly to the climate, but more to the inherent habits of the crop in question, since these determine almost absolutely the time when the seed must be sown. The principles involved will be more clear by classifying forage crops into summer annuals, winter annuals, biennials and perennials.

Summer annuals include such forage crop as millets,

sorghums and cowpeas, which like maize require a continuous, rather high temperature for their best development. They are all plants of tropical origin carried by agriculture into temperate regions. All are characterized by rather rapid and uniform growth from germination to maturity. At their northern limits they succeed best if planting is delayed until the latest time which safely permits of their maturing, as their growth is seriously checked by cool weather. Where the season is longer plantings may be timed according to weather and soil conditions; or better, late varieties which can utilize the longer season may be grown. A few summer annuals like the soybean will withstand cool weather, even light frosts, both in spring and fall, but most of them are intolerant of cold.

Winter annuals include wheat, rye, oats, barley, Canada peas, common vetch, crimson clover and others. Naturally, they are plants which germinate in the fall and mature in spring or summer in regions of mild, often frostless, winters. They differ from summer annuals in being intolerant of high temperatures during growth, and in undergoing more or less dormancy during winter. Where the winters are too severe they must be planted in spring, but in such cases often suffer from summer heat, as commonly occurs with Canada peas and common vetch. Where both fall and spring sowings are possible, as wheat in some regions, the former usually produce better crops, owing partly to better root development, and partly to the longer growing season in spring which fall planting insures. To a slight degree winter annuals show a dual period of development like biennials.

Biennial plants like the carrot, beet and rutabagas are especially instructive, in that their development during the two seasons is in sharp contrast. Ordinarily they are planted in spring. The first season they produce above ground only a rosette of leaves, but below ground a great root development. During the second season there is a large growth of flowering stems, in part due to the stored food in the roots. The growth of the first season constitutes the crop, unless seed is the object, but the amount of herbage above ground is far greater the second season. This sharp contrast between the growth of the two seasons occurs regardless of whether the seed is sown in the spring or in the fall so long as the plants survive the winter.

Herbaceous perennials are much like biennials in that the first season is devoted mainly to root development. The rosette habit is not so conspicuous, and with many species a few flowering shoots are produced if the seed is sown in spring. The second season, abundant top growth is produced, and this is regardless of whether the seed was sown in the spring or fall, as it is only during the first season that the rosette habit predominates. There is seldom any gain by sowing a perennial grass or legume in spring, as the yield during that season is usually negligible and the crop must compete with numerous summer weeds during the period when it produces but little top growth. It is a safe general rule, therefore, that perennials should be sown in the fall, but early enough that good root growth be established by winter. Spring seeding of such crops is desirable only where moisture conditions compel it or winter injury by cold is likely to be excessive.

79. Depth of planting. — The depth to which seeds of a particular species should be planted cannot be stated arbitrarily nor based on any definite theory. Under natural conditions seeds fall on the surface of the ground and most of them germinate on or very near the surface. The percentage of mortality of such seeds is, however, very high, much greater than it is necessary to provide against in agriculture.

The principal objects desired are to plant the seed deeply enough to germinate under average climatic conditions at the place, and not too deeply, to prevent the seedlings from reaching the surface.

In general, small seeds must be planted shallow and large seeds may be planted deep. Some large seeds, like peas, may be planted as deep as 8 inches, but this is due to the fact that the young shoot does not carry the cotyledons with it. In the case of equally large bean seeds, where the cotyledons are raised out of the ground, such deep planting would be fatal.

In sandy soils planting may be twice as deep as in clay soils, both to secure the necessary moisture, and because such soils offer less resistance to the developing seedling.

80. Experimental results. — The best method of sowing any hay crop in any particular place can be determined only by direct trials. This involves experiments in rate of seeding, depth of planting, time of sowing, use of nurse crop, etc. The best method depends quite as much on the adaptations of the plant itself as upon local conditions. Thus, some grasses and legumes do not well endure shade, consequently the seeding of these with a nurse crop is inadvisable.

The following experiments conducted at the Ontario Agricultural College illustrate how greatly different methods of seeding may affect the yield of the same and of different species of grasses and clovers.

Two distinct experiments were performed, one from the

autumn of 1896 and the spring of 1897 to the autumn of 1898; the other from the autumn of 1899 and the spring of 1900 to the autumn of 1901.

The table shows the *average of the two experiments,* of the yields obtained at *one* cutting, *the second summer after seeding :*—

Crops	Tons of Hay to the Acre			
	Fall Sowing		Spring Sowing	
	With Winter Wheat	No Nurse Crop	With Oats	No Nurse Crop
	Tons	Tons	Tons	Tons
Orchard-grass	3.49	4.20	4.44	3.73
Meadow fescue . . .	2.12	2.86	3.66	3.64
Timothy	2.94	3.44	3.27	4.28
Common red clover . .	3.07	1.09	3.61	4.18
Alsike clover	2.66	.91	2.47	2.79
Lucerne	3.65	1.42	4.03	4.17
Average 3 grasses . .	2.85	3.50	3.79	3.89
Average 3 clovers .	3.13	1.14	3.37	3.71

81. Nurse crops. — In sowing grass or clover seeds, it is a very common practice to sow them with a crop of small grain or, as is usually the case, with red clover, to sow the seed in spring on a field of fall-sown grain. When grass seed is thus sown with a grain crop, the latter is spoken of as a nurse crop.

The advantages of a nurse crop are :—

1. To secure a greater return from the land the first year.

2. To economize labor by making one seed bed answer for two crops.

3. To check weeds from developing.

4. To hold snow to prevent washing of the land.

The disadvantages of a nurse crop, as far as the grass is concerned, are : —

1. Weakening the grass by shading.

2. Injuring the young grass when soil moisture is not sufficient for both.

3. Requiring a higher rate of seeding of the grass.

Wheat, rye, barley and oats are desirable as nurse crops, probably in the order named, but there are few comparative experimental data available. Oats shade the ground more than barley, and barley more than wheat or rye. The time of harvesting the nurse crop is also of some importance to the grass crop, as sudden exposure of the latter to heat and drought is very harmful. The water requirement of each of the four nurse crops is least for wheat, followed in order by barley, oats and rye.

CHAPTER V

MEADOWS AND PASTURES

Success in the profitable rearing of herbivorous animals is nearly always conditioned on good grass. This applies almost as truly to the most specialized forms of animal husbandry as to the primitive wandering herdsman. The highest type of agriculture is in those regions where grass culture is most developed. Meadows usually supply the most economical feed that can be preserved. Pastures, whether temporary or permanent, furnish the cheapest means for maintaining farm animals that can be grown, and permit the utilization of land too poor or too rough to use for other farm crops.

82. Meadow mixtures. — The practice of growing mixtures of grasses or legumes or both, is an old one antedating in agriculture the sowing of pure cultures. Originally grass seeds were gathered from mixed meadows, and hence pure sowings could not be made. In oriental countries, especially India, where labor is very cheap, all sorts of crops are still grown in mixtures, and the belief prevails generally that a larger total return is thus secured. The cost of harvesting each separately is so great that such mixed plantings are seldom made in Europe or America, and only where all of the plants in the mixture can be harvested at the same time, or where the harvesting of the one does not interfere with the further development of the other.

92

So far as hay plants are concerned, experience and experiments both show that as a rule larger yields are secured from mixtures than from pure cultures. Exceptions are, however, found in such crops as alfalfa and sometimes Italian rye-grass, mainly because no other plants will coincide with either of these in producing several cuttings.

Among the reasons why mixtures yield better as a rule than pure cultures are the following : —

1. The diverse root habits of the different crops make their distribution through the soil more thorough.

2. Their differing requirements do not make them direct competitors, but enable them more thoroughly to utilize the soluble substances of the soil.

3. The average annual return can be made more nearly even over a longer period by including both short-lived, quick-growing plants, and long-lived plants.

4. The loss by insects or disease is lessened, as most of these attack but a single plant species. Thus, pure cultures furnish far better opportunities for their increase and spread than do mixed cultures. In mixtures, such losses are often confined to but a single species in the mixture ; and as this leaves more room for the others to develop, there is at least a partial compensation for the damage. Practically the same facts hold true if any of the species in the mixture are destroyed or injured by drought or other adverse weather conditions.

5. The leaves and shoots of different grasses and legumes vary greatly in habit and in light requirement. Some low-growing species do well in the shade of taller species, and thus the total quantity of herbage is increased. Low-growing plants form the so-called " bottom grass " in contrast to the " top grass " of tall species. A mixture

of the two is good practice and apparently good theory. Among the common " bottom " hay plants are blue-grass, redtop, sheep's fescue and the clovers; typical " top grasses " are orchard-grass, tall oat-grass and timothy.

6. Legumes probably aid the growth and increase the protein content of the non-legumes in the mixture.

Besides the reasons which apparently affect the yield, mixtures afford a more varied and usually better feed, and mixtures of grasses and legumes are more easily cured than legumes alone.

Data from various experiment stations showing the relative returns from mixtures and pure sowings are given in the accompanying table : —

TABLE SHOWING HAY YIELDS IN POUNDS TO THE ACRE OF MIXED GRASSES COMPARED TO THE BEST SINGLE GRASS

GRASS OR MIXTURE	ILLINOIS EXPERIMENT STATION	ONTARIO AGRICULTU- RAL COLLEGE	KANSAS EXPERIMENT STATION	MINNESOTA N. E. EXPERI- MENT STATION
Timothy	4400 — 2 yr.	6940 — 7 yr.	4779 — 4 yr.	4340 — 1 yr.
Red clover	4200 — 2 yr.	6620 — 6 yr.	5490 — 4 yr.	8000 — 1 yr.
Tall oat-grass	5480 — 1 yr.	5520 — 7 yr.	1707 — 4 yr.	———
Alfalfa	———	———	7345 — 4 yr.	———
Redtop	3600 — 1 yr.	3580 — 7 yr.	3399 — 2 yr.	5260 — 1 yr.
Timothy and mammoth clover	5400 — 2 yr.	———		
Timothy and medium red clover	5200 — 2 yr.	———	5490 — 4 yr.	7820 — 1 yr.
Tall oat and alfalfa . .		8820 — 2 yr.		
Timothy and alfalfa .		8000 — 2 yr.		
Tall oat and mammoth clover		7160 — 2 yr.		
Timothy and mammoth clover		7140 — 2 yr.		
Brome and red clover			4133 — 4 yr.	
Brome and alfalfa . .			5473 — 4 yr.	
Brome, orchard-grass and red clover . . .			3825 — 4 yr.	
Brome-grass, timothy and red clover . . .			3560 — 4 yr.	8480 — 1 yr.
Brome and timothy .				5160 — 1 yr.
Timothy and redtop .				8740 — 1 yr.

83. Composition of meadow mixtures. — Innumerable meadow mixtures have been recommended by writers, based partly on observation and partly on theoretical considerations. European authorities advise as a rule complex mixtures. They also advise a heavier rate of seeding where several or many grasses are mixed. Such complex mixtures have not found much favor in America as yet, either at the hands of experimenters or farmers.

The principal objects desired in mixtures are to secure plants of varying habit adapted to the conditions under which they are to be grown, and to have them mature at about the same time.

Important mixtures which are based both on sound experiment and abundant observations include the following : —

1. Timothy and red clover, the standard mixture for the timothy region on well-drained soils. Where red clover fails, it may be replaced with alsike, or both clovers may be used. Frequently redtop is added to the mixture.

2. Redtop and alsike clover for low wet lands in the timothy region. If the land is not too wet, timothy may be added. Fowl meadow-grass is also well adapted to such soils.

3. Orchard-grass, tall oat-grass and alsike clover. This mixture is especially desirable where timothy and red clover do not succeed well. Italian rye-grass may be added to this mixture to increase the yield of the first crop.

4. For semi-humid regions brome and timothy or brome- and orchard-grass.

5. Where alfalfa thrives, it makes good mixtures with timothy, tall oat, slender wheat or brome-grass.

A complex mixture that has been recommended at the Ontario Agricultural College, particularly for pasturage, but also for hay, contains the following seeds in the amounts needed to the acre : —

Alfalfa	5 pounds
Alsike clover	2 pounds
White clover	1 pound
Trefoil	1 pound
Orchard-grass	4 pounds
Meadow fescue	4 pounds
Tall oat-grass	3 pounds
Timothy	2 pounds
Meadow foxtail	2 pounds
Total	24 pounds

84. Treatment of hay meadows. — Hay meadows may be distinguished as temporary meadows where the lay is for 1 or 2 years and permanent meadows where the lay is for 3 years or an indefinite longer period.

The yield on permanent meadows may usually be increased (1) by plowing or harrowing; (2) by occasional reseedings; and (3) by the use of fertilizers.

85. Scarifying old meadows. — The scarifying of an old meadow by harrowing in early spring with a disk or other harrow usually encourages a larger growth of grass. In some sections it must be done with judgment as otherwise the increased growth may be largely weeds.

In the case of certain grasses with rootstocks like Bermuda- and Johnson-grass the field may be plowed and harrowed, the effect being a greatly increased crop of grass. The same method can be used with brome-grass, but more care must be used, as brome is more easily destroyed than the other two grasses.

86. Reseeding old meadows. — It is rarely good practice to keep meadows for a long period of years even if fertilized annually. In time the proportion of weeds increases and often mosses and lichens become abundant.

The latter are supposed to indicate a lack of lime, but they often remain in spite of liming.

At the Massachusetts Experiment Station it was found that the yield on certain plots was greatly increased by replowing and reseeding without changing the amount of fertilizer applied. Thus on a plot fertilized annually with 5805 pounds of wood ashes to the acre the portion plowed and reseeded yielded 8546 pounds hay to the acre while that portion not replowed nor reseeded yielded but 6243 pounds. On a plot fertilized annually with 8 tons of barnyard manure the part plowed and reseeded produced 10,002 pounds hay to the acre in comparison with 5642 pounds on the portion not reseeded. The only difference in the fertilizer application was that the manure was harrowed in the plowed portion and top-dressed in the undisturbed part.

Another method is sometimes used by farmers, especially on land difficult to plow; namely, that of scattering a little new seed over the meadow each year, especially of such grasses and clovers which tend to disappear.

87. Fertilizers for hay crops. — Most of the hay grown in the northeastern fourth of the United States and adjacent Canada is timothy and red clover, with a much smaller proportion of redtop, alsike and other plants. At least three-fourths of the total yield in this region is produced from a two years' lay grown in the five-course rotation of corn, oats, wheat, clover, timothy or some essentially similar rotation. In this rotation fertilizer is rarely applied to the hay crop, which can therefore obtain only the residues of fertilizers applied to the grain crops. With this system of agriculture the average yield of hay an acre for the region mentioned is according to census figures about 1.3 tons an acre. In this area a yield to be

H

considered good should reach at least 1.5 tons an acre and to be large 2 to 2.5 tons an acre. With heavy fertilizing yields of 5 to 6 tons an acre or even more have been secured. As a rule, the timothy region has ample rainfall; so that the principal factor in limiting the hay yield is the fertility of the land.

While larger hay yields can be obtained by the use of heavy applications of fertilizers, the practice of selling hay as a money crop has almost universally been condemned by agricultural writers because a bulky crop contains so much nitrogen, phosphorus and potassium, which is usually considered as selling that much of the fertility of the land. This conclusion is, however, based more on theoretical considerations than on any adequate basis of empirical data.

The results of the long-continued rotation experiments at the Ohio Experiment Station show that the residues of fertilizers from the cereal crops will give as a rule a good increase in the crops of both clover and timothy, as compared to unfertilized plots.

From the results secured with fertilizers applied to grasses it is an open question whether it would not be more profitable to apply the fertilizers to this crop than to the hoed or small grain crops. Lyon and Morgan in discussing this problem advance the following reasons why it would apparently be better to apply the fertilizers ` to the hay crop in New York : —

" (1) Fertilizers applied to grass increase not only the growth of that part of the crop cut for hay, but also the roots and sod which are plowed under the soil and in decomposing add to the soil productiveness. It seems, therefore, that anything that aids the growth of timothy would help the grain, while the reverse is not true in the same sense.

" (2) The hay crop is generally the crop which in a rotation with grain brings the largest financial returns in New York State. If a certain application of manures increases in the same ratio the yields of hay and grain, the value of the increase in the former crop would be greater than that of the latter. It should pay best to increase the crop that is worth the most, provided the cost of the increase is the same in both cases.

" (3) Grass is peculiarly sensitive to readily available nitrogen in fertilizers. Grain crops are not benefited to the same extent by this form of nutrient. As most commercial fertilizers contain some more or less readily available nitrogen, much of which may be carried off in the drainage water and thus be lost to crops after the year it is applied, it would seem to be advisable to add this to the crop that it will benefit most. On the other hand, the phosphorus and potassium contained in the fertilizer are not removed in large amounts by the drainage water and the unused parts remain in the soil to benefit the succeeding grain crops."

Whether or not it is best to apply the fertilizers to the hay crop or elsewhere in the rotation, there can be no doubt that the judicious fertilizing of hay crops is often very profitable, especially where fertilizers can be obtained cheaply and where the good city markets for the hay are convenient.

Well-rotted barnyard manure invariably increases the crop of hay greatly, but in the absence of this material comparable results may be secured with commercial fertilizers.

The results of many fertilizer trials on mixed grasses and legumes, both in Europe and in America, lead to the general conclusion that nitrogenous fertilizers tend to increase the proportion of grass herbage, while phosphate and potash fertilizers stimulate the growth of legumes particularly. Lime is far more pronounced in its effect on legumes than on non-legumes.

At the Massachusetts Experiment Station it has been observed that a top dressing of muriate of potash to a mixed plot of timothy, redtop and clover caused a remarkable increase in the proportion of clover. The further work at this station showed that sulfate of potash was far more efficient in this respect than the muriate.

For very heavy yields of grass a larger application annually of a complete fertilizer is necessary. Thus Wheeler at the Rhode Island Experiment Station was able to secure yields of hay averaging over 4 tons per acre for 3 years by using the following amount of fertilizers to the acre : —

350 pounds nitrate of soda.

500 pounds acid phosphate.

200 pounds muriate of potash.

It is questionable whether such heavy applications are most profitable in the long run, especially as in seasons of insufficient moisture the full benefit of the fertilizer cannot be secured.

On the basis of the Rhode Island work Wheeler recommends an annual application to each acre of : —

400 to 500 pounds acid phosphate.

300 to 350 pounds muriate of potash.

300 to 350 pounds nitrate of soda.

From the results secured at the Massachusetts Experiment Station, Brooks suggests that the hay crop in rotations be top-dressed about May 1 with the following mixture of fertilizer to the acre : —

Nitrate of soda	175 to 200 pounds
Acid phosphate	50 to 100 pounds
High grade sulfate of potash	50 to 100 pounds

If a high percentage of clover is desired in the hay the nitrate of soda should be omitted, and the following applied to the acre : —

Acid phosphate	100 pounds
Basic slag meal	400 pounds
High grade sulfate of potash	150 to 200 pounds

For permanent meadows producing market hay composed largely of grass, Brooks recommends with much confidence the use to the acre of the following amounts of fertilizer : —

Nitrate of soda	150 to 250 pounds
Basic slag meal	300 to 400 pounds
High grade sulfate of potash	75 to 100 pounds

Top-dressings of nitrate of soda alone are not considered desirable for a longer period than two years.

On peat marsh soils in Wisconsin the yield of hay from a mixture of timothy and alsike yielded without treatment 2727 pounds hay an acre. An application of 275 pounds acid phosphate an acre increased the yields on two plots to 5015 and 5158 pounds respectively. Sulfate of potash, 100 pounds to the acre, increased the yields on two plots to 4588 and 4781 pounds respectively. When both fertilizers were used together in the amounts above indicated the results were not as good as the phosphate alone.

At the West Virginia Experiment Station the application of both barnyard manure and commercial fertilizers greatly increased the yields of timothy. On the larger part of a 4-acre field that yielded 1 ton hay or less a year the average application for 6 years of 17 loads of manure brought up the yield to the acre from 3775 pounds the first year to 11,315 pounds the sixth year, or an average of 8044 pounds annually for the 6 years. Commercial fertilizer composed of nitrate of soda, acid phosphate and sulfate of potash gave an average yield of 6380 pounds hay per acre, the average annual cost of the fertilizer per acre being $11.76. In both cases the increased yield gave a large profit.

88. Top-dressing for aftermath or rowen. — Fertilizing meadows to secure a larger aftermath or rowen is seldom practiced. From experiments at the Massachusetts Experiment Station Brooks considers that fertilizing grass meadows with 150 to 200 pounds nitrate of soda immediately after the first crop is removed is profitable.

89. Acreage of improved pasture in the United States. — Statistics and other data relative to American pasture crops are very unsatisfactory. According to the thirteenth United States census, the crops where acreage was reported occupied 68.3 per cent of the improved land. The improved land not occupied by crops included pasture land, fallow land, land in orchards whose acreage was not reported and land in house yards and barnyards.

As both fallow lands and the stubble and aftermath of various crops furnishes considerable temporary pasturage, it is conservative to consider 30 per cent of the improved land as pasture, but probably not much over 20 per cent of the improved land is permanent or long lay pasture. If this be true, the acreage of permanent improved pastures is one-third greater than that devoted to " hay and forage " and one-half as great as that of corn.

90. Area of wild pasture in the United States. — From the census figures of 1909 the following table is compiled, assuming that 20 per cent of the improved farm land area is pasture and that half of the unimproved land is pasturable. According to these estimates the area of unimproved pasture lands is about 4 times as large as the improved pastures : —

CLASS OF LAND	PER CENT OF TOTAL AREA
Farm land	46.2
Improved farm land	25.1
Improved pastures	9.2
Non-farm lands	53.8
Unimproved pasture land	37.4

91. Most important tame pasture plants. — The most important grazing plants on improved American pastures are Kentucky blue-grass, redtop, white clover and Bermuda. Of less importance are timothy, orchard-grass, Canada blue-grass, red clover, alfalfa, alsike, lespedeza and crab-grass.

As to the relative value of these, there are no data available to make accurate estimates. Kentucky blue-grass is by far the most valuable pasture grass in the North and Bermuda-grass in the South. White clover and redtop are of importance over most of North America except the semi-arid regions and the extreme South.

Scaling the principal tame permanent pasture grasses on a basis of 100, the following estimate is made of their relative importance in America : —

Kentucky blue-grass . .	40	Alsike clover	3
Redtop	10	Canada blue-grass . . .	3
White clover	8	Orchard-grass	2
Bermuda-grass	8	Johnson-grass	2
Timothy	8	Lespedeza	2
Red clover	4	Crab-grass	2
Alfalfa	4	All others	4

These are but rough estimates, and probably minimize rather than exaggerate the relative importance of the first five.

92. Palatability of pasture grasses. — One method by . which the relative palatability of pasture grasses may be ascertained is to permit animals to have free access to plots of different grasses and then to note their preferences.

At the Washington Experiment Station horses preferred brome-grass to orchard and red clover mixed, to tall oat-grass and to a mixture of 11 standard grasses.

At the Idaho Experiment Station sheep showed the following order of choice : 1. orchard-grass; 2. meadow fescue; 3. brome; 4. perennial rye-grass; 5. tall oat-grass.

In tests at Cornell Experiment Station cattle exhibited the following order of preference: brome, Kentucky blue-grass, meadow fescue, timothy, orchard-grass, red-top.

The marked preference of cattle for brome was also shown at the Ottawa, Canada, Experimental Farm, where cattle grazed brome close to the ground, while scarcely touching mixed timothy and red clover.

93. Pasture yield as determined by number of cuttings. — At the Michigan Experiment Station a plot of orchard-grass cut 7 times with a lawn mower yielded 29 pounds of dry hay and a similar plot cut 4 times 60.9 pounds. A third plot not cut until in bloom gives 112 pounds of hay.

In a similar experiment with timothy the yield for 8 cuttings was 15.76 pounds, and for a single cutting where in bloom, 172 pounds.

Extensive investigations of this sort have been conducted by Zavitz at the Ontario Agricultural College from whose data the following table is compiled. The significance of figures thus obtained is not very clear. The total yield is invariably less than if the crop be cut 1 to 3 times. This can only be interpreted as indicating that the yield of pastures is less than that of meadows, but what relation the yield from 6 or more clippings is to that eaten by animals on pasture continuously is not evident : —

TONS OF GREEN HERBAGE TO THE ACRE AT EACH OF SIX CUTTINGS PER ANNUM. AVERAGE OF FOUR YEARS FOR GRASSES, THREE YEARS FOR LEGUMES

CROP	FIRST CUTTING	SECOND CUTTING	THIRD CUTTING	FOURTH CUTTING	FIFTH CUTTING	SIXTH CUTTING	TOTAL PER ANNUM
	Tons	Tons	Tons	Tons	Tons	Tons	Tons
Tall oat-grass .	5.93	.83	1.59	1.23	1.33	.87	11.8
Orchard-grass .	4.34	1.71	.92	1.30	1.05	1.40	10.7
Meadow fescue	4.60	1.72	.69	1.09	.84	.61	9.6
Timothy . . .	4.87	1.71	.58	1.11	.62	.49	9.4
Perennial rye	4.10	1.49	.61	.78	.90	.80	8.7
Kentucky blue .	3.76	1.04	.73	.58	.58	.58	7.5
Redtop . . .	2.71	1.03	.62	.67	.44	.34	5.8
Alfalfa . . .	8.73	3.06	2.70	3.62	1.56	1.27	20.9
Red clover . .	10.88	1.10	2.37	3.39	1.52	1.15	20.4
White clover .	7.35	2.35	1.95	1.91	2.08	1.63	17.3
Alsike	8.22	.28	3.06	1.41	2.56	.93	16.5

94. Pasture mixtures. — There is only one safe rule to follow in regard to grasses and clovers to be planted for permanent pastures ; namely, use those which experience has shown hold the ground most tenaciously. It is desirable to use in addition, however, one or more quick growing grasses to furnish pasturage while the slower growing ones are developing.

In England excellent results have been obtained by planting complex mixtures containing long and short-lived, and shallow and deep-rooted plants. No such mixtures have, as yet, proved profitable in America.

For the humid portions of America the best permanent pasture grasses come in, for the most part, spontaneously. These are, in the timothy region: 1. Kentucky blue-grass and white clover for fertile, moist soils; 2. redtop for low, wet soils; 3. Canada blue-grass, redtop and white clover for upland soils; in the cotton region: 4. Bermuda-grass, lespedeza and bur clover for clayey lands; 5. carpet-grass for sandy coastal lands.

The lines of division indicated are by no means absolute, but the pasture mixtures proposed by various investigators generally recognize the fundamental importance of most of the ten species named. As more or less temporary elements; other seeds should be included in seeding new pasture, as follows: —

Where the soil and the region are adapted to Kentucky blue-grass, add white clover, timothy and either Italian or perennial rye-grass. Meadow fescue is also desirable in many places.

Where the soil is wet and the region adapted to redtop, add white clover and alsike clover.

Where the soil is poor upland in the north, use redtop, Canada blue-grass and white clover.

Where Bermuda-grass thrives, add lespedeza, white clover, bur clover and Italian rye-grass.

Where carpet-grass predominates, Italian rye-grass may prove valuable for temporary pasture in winter.

In addition to the grasses mentioned, orchard-grass is always desirable because it furnishes the earliest pasturage, and southward tall oat-grass is very useful. On the sandy lands along the coast northward, sheep's fescue will often grow to the practical exclusion of other grasses.

Attempts to establish permanent pastures of other grasses in places where one or more of those mentioned above are aggressive have rarely been successful.

95. Treatment of permanent pastures. — The treatment of pastures to secure the maximum return is a subject upon which much writing has been done, but in America at least but little experimentation.

The first comprehensive experiment of this kind is that being carried on at the Virginia Experiment Station, but no results of which have yet been published. The object of these experiments is to determine the relative merits of different treatments : —

1. Continuous light grazing.
2. Continuous heavy grazing.
3. Alternate light grazing, without harrowing.
4. Alternate light grazing, with harrowing.
5. Alternate heavy grazing, without harrowing.
6. Alternate heavy grazing, with harrowing.

It is only by such experiments that quantitative results can be obtained that will definitely determine the best methods of treating permanent pastures.

From observations there is strong reason to believe that heavy grazing, but not overgrazing, is preferable to light grazing. In any pasture, unless overgrazed, it may be observed that the animals keep the grass closely grazed in definite areas and neglect the remainder. The animals prefer the short, fresh growth and avoid the older leaves and stems, unless driven by hunger. Farmers usually prefer to graze their pastures lightly so as to have a surplus in case of emergency — such as periods of drought — but it would seem wiser to utilize the pastures more fully and provide against emergencies by having a reserve of other feed.

Among methods that have been recommended to improve pastures are : —

1. Sowing a little seed each year.
2. Light harrowing, especially with a chain drag.
3. Mowing the weeds in time to prevent their seeding.
4. Top-dressing with manure or other fertilizers.

On account of the relatively small return from pastures, the amount that can be spent profitably in improving them is small, often not more than one dollar an acre a year. With this limitation in mind, the first three methods of improvement are with little doubt sound, but fertilizers can usually be applied more profitably elsewhere than in pastures. Seeding on pastures where the turf is dense and the weeds few is not advisable. As may easily be observed, the sod in early spring on most pastures does not make a complete cover, but the vacant spaces often occupy one-fourth to one-half the ground. Where this is the case, it is probable that a light scattering of seed in very early spring is desirable.

96. Pasturing meadows. — The aftermath or rowen of grass meadows is very commonly used for pasturage in the fall. If the grazing be light, the probabilities are that the succeeding year's crop is not injuriously affected, but no critical experiments on this subject have been reported.

Pasturing meadows in early spring is, however, generally considered to be harmful to the succeeding hay crop.

97. Carrying capacity. — The carrying capacity of a pasture is the number of animals of a particular kind that a unit of area will support for a definite period. On permanent pastures and on range lands this is usually stated in terms of animals to the acre for the grazing season. Thus, the carrying capacity of much of the western range lands is 1 steer to 100 acres. The carrying capacity of the best blue-grass pasture is 1 steer to about 2.5 acres, and for the best Bermuda and lespedeza pasture in the South 2 steers to 1 acre. In the last two examples the period is understood to be that of the growing season, but on range lands the period is sometimes meant to cover the whole year.

98. Temporary pastures. — A temporary pasture is one designed to carry stock for only a short period. Temporary pastures are usually sown to annual plants. Sometimes such sowings are arranged so as to have a succession of temporary pastures. This is often desirable in raising hogs, but is also used with sheep and dairy cows.

In pasturing such crops, there is less waste by trampling if the area to be grazed each day is inclosed by hurdles or other temporary fencing. This also insures that the animals secure about the same feed each day, as otherwise they will eat the more palatable portions of the plants first.

A system of temporary pastures requires accurate knowledge in regard to the date a crop must be sown to be pastured at a particular time, the approximate amount of feed an acre will provide and the length of time during which the crop may be grazed.

Such a system is essentially identical with a soiling system (Par. 36), but it permits the use of some crops not adapted to the latter, such as chufas, peanuts and sweet potatoes.

99. Temporary pasture crop systems for hogs. — Pasture crop systems for feeding hogs continuously have been devised by various investigators. Annuals are best suited to this purpose not only because the period during which they can be used and the feed they will produce may be quite accurately predicted, but because the planting of perennials in small patches is often objectionable. If fields of perennials like clover or alfalfa are available they may well be utilized, however, in some systems. Two systems of temporary pastures are here given as examples, one adapted to the North and the other to the South.

Duggar, at the Alabama Experiment Station, on the basis of extensive experiments suggests the following succession of pasture crops for pigs in that state : —

SYSTEM OF PASTURE CROPS FOR PIGS. ALABAMA

Crops	When Sown	When Pastured
Rape	Fall	January and February
Chufas	Spring	January and February
Rape	Fall	March to April 15
Vetch and oats . . .	Fall	March to April 15
Vetch and oats . . .	Fall	April
Crimson clover . . .	Fall	April
Oats and wheat . . .	Fall	April and May
Rape	Spring	May and June
Turf oats	Spring	June
Sorghum	Spring	July and August
Cowpeas	Spring	July and August
Spanish peanuts . . .	Spring	September to November
Cowpeas	Spring	September to November
Sweet potatoes . . .	Spring	September to November
Sorghum	Spring	September to November
Chufas	Spring	December
Rape	Fall	December

Fisher at the Indiana Experiment Station has arranged the following data, from which a system of temporary pastures for hogs in that state may be selected : —

PASTURE FOR HOGS BY MONTHS. INDIANA

MONTH TO PASTURE	NAME OF CROP	DATE OF SOWING	APPROXIMATE LENGTH OF TIME CROP AFFORDS PASTURE	NO. OF 100-POUND HOGS PER ACRE
April . . .	Rye	August or September	Six weeks	10–15
May	Oats	March 20 to April 10	Six weeks	8–12
	Oats and rape	March 20 to April 10	Four weeks	12–20
	Oats and field peas	March 20 to April 10	Four weeks	12–20
	Rape	April 1–10	Four weeks	12–15
June . . .	Rape and oats	April 10–30	Four weeks	15–20
	Field peas and oats	April 10–30	Four weeks	12–15
	Rape	April 10–30	Four weeks	12–20
July . . .	Rape	April 1–10 and grazed down in May	Four weeks	12–20
	Rape	May 1–20	Four weeks	12–20
	Clover, red or mammoth	March 25 to April 10 without nurse crop	Remainder of season	8–10
	Sorghum	May 10–20	Four weeks	15–20
August . .	Clover, red or mammoth	Spring sown	Remainder of season	8–10
	Rape	April 10–30 and grazed down in June	Four weeks	12–20
	Rape	June 1–15	Four weeks	12–20
	Sorghum	May 20–30	Four weeks	15–20
	Soybeans or cowpeas	May 20 to June 1	Six weeks	12–18
September	Clover, red or mammoth	Spring sown	Remainder of season	8–10
	Soy beans or cowpeas	May 20 to June 15	Six weeks	12–18
	Rape	Second or third growth	Four weeks	12–20
	Rape	June 20 to July 10	Four weeks	12–20
	Pumpkins	May 15 to June 15	Fed in lots	
	Sorghum	May 20 to June 15	Fed in lots	
October . .	Clover, red or mammoth	Spring sown	Remainder of season	8–10
	Rape	Same as September	Four weeks	12–20
	Rye	August 1–30	Remainder of season	8–10
	Soybeans or cowpeas	June 1 to July 15	Four weeks	12–20

100. Bloating or hoven. — Ruminant animals are often subject to bloating when pastured on such crops as alfalfa, red clover or rape. Sainfoin and lespedeza are said never to cause bloating, but most succulent legumes will probably cause the trouble.

Among the prevention measures that have been suggested are the following : —

1. Do not turn the cattle into the pasture when it is wet with dew or rain, or the cattle very hungry.

2. In pasturing rape have an abundance of salt available to the animals.

3. Have a supply of hay or straw or a grass pasture available to the animals. It is said they will instinctively turn to the grass or hay when bloat threatens.

Should bloating occur, several remedies are usually at hand which will afford material relief. A large bit, the diameter of a pitchfork handle, may be tied in the mouth; a piece of rubber tubing may be passed through the mouth to the first stomach; or, as a last resort, the animal may be tapped to allow the escape of gas. For this purpose a trocar, such as is used by veterinary surgeons, is best; but in the absence of this, a small-bladed knife may be used to make the incision about 6 inches in front of and slightly below the left hip bone. A straw or quill may be used to permit the escape of gas. Care should be taken not to allow the straw or quill to work down out of sight into the incision.

CHAPTER VI

THE STATISTICS OF FORAGE CROPS

STATISTICS regarding forage crops are instructive to the agronomist in showing the relative importance and geographical distribution of each crop reported upon. The data from successive censuses also disclose the progress or regression which a crop may have made. Unfortunately only the principal crops are included in the returns. The relative importance of the various forage in different countries varies so greatly that the statistical returns are not directly comparable, as a rule.

101. Classification of crops in statistical returns. — In the Thirteenth United States Census, 1909, the cereal, seed and forage crops are thus classified: cereals include corn, oats, wheat, barley, buckwheat, rye, rice, emmer and spelt, kafir and milo. " Other grains and seeds " include beans, peas, peanuts, flaxseed, grass seeds, flower seeds and vegetable seeds. " Hay and forage " include all crops cut for hay and fodder, excluding the cereals, — except such as are cut for hay,— and also excluding improved pastures.

In considering this classification of crops, it needs to be pointed out that under " cereals " is included a vast amount of produce other than grain utilized as forage. Thus, the herbage of the corn crop, whether preserved as stover, silage or pulled fodder, is used purely as forage, and indeed forms an important percentage of the food of farm animals. It is safe to estimate the value of the herbage of the corn plant at about 50 per cent of the grain, assuming that all the corn is allowed to mature. As a matter of fact, a considerable and increasing amount is preserved as silage. A small part of the corn crop is reported under the item " Coarse Forage."

Of kafir corn and other grain sorghums, probably 75 per cent is harvested entire and thus used as forage.

On the Pacific Coast much wheat and barley is harvested as hay, and throughout the country more or less rye is similarly used, but all this is included under forage as " Grains Cut Green." The straw of small grains, especially that of oats, has considerable value as forage.

In the same way the straw of cowpeas, Canada and garden peas, soybeans and other leguminous seed crops has also a considerable value as forage.

The bearing of these facts is that the relative importance of grain production to forage production is necessarily somewhat inaccurate on account of the classification, the statistics exaggerating the importance of the first, and diminishing that of the latter.

In the Census of Canada, forage crops are included under 8 items; namely, Hay and clover; Alfalfa; Corn and forage; Other forage crops; Mangolds; Sugar Beets; Turnips; Other field roots. The item of " Other forage crops " includes mainly the small grains, either alone or in mixture, cut for hay or for green feed.

102. Forage crops in general, United States, 1909. — In the accompanying table appear the statistics of the Thirteenth United States Census showing the relative importance of forage crops in the different sections of the United States, and in the eleven states which lead in forage production. (Compare Fig. 8.) The data are tabulated to show percentage of total and of improved land occupied by forage crops, and average yield and value to the acre : —

STATISTICS OF FORAGE CROPS, UNITED STATES, 1909

DIVISION	PER CENT OF LAND IN UNITED STATES	PER CENT OF IM- PROVED LAND	AVERAGE YIELD TO THE ACRE 1909	AVERAGE VALUE TO THE ACRE 1909
			Tons	
United States	100.0	15.1	1.35	$11.40
New England . . .	5.3	52.3	1.23	15.57
Middle Atlantic . .	11.8	29.1	1.32	15.31
East North Central .	20.4	16.6	1.38	12.52
West North Central .	37.9	16.7	1.33	7.71
South Atlantic . . .	4.0	5.9	1.02	13.25
East South Central .	3.4	5.7	1.03	11.92
West South Central .	4.5	5.6	1.03	9.09
Mountain	6.9	31.3	1.73	13.38
Pacific	5.8	19.1	1.73	17.69
Iowa	7.0	17.1	1.55	11.76
New York	7.0	34.0	1.40	15.34
Nebraska	6.3	18.5	1.28	7.02
Kansas	5.5	13.2	1.50	8.09
Minnesota	5.5	20.1	1.53	6.77
Missouri	5.0	14.8	1.13	9.33
South Dakota . . .	4.8	21.7	1.06	4.44
Illinois	4.6	11.9	1.30	12.11
Ohio	4.6	17.2	1.37	12.81
Pennsylvania . . .	4.3	24.4	1.19	14.77
Wisconsin	4.3	25.9	1.62	13.27

These figures for hay and forage crops, not including pastures, are also compared with other important crops. The acreage of 72,280,776 acres was 37.8 per cent of that of all cereal crops. It was 73.5 per cent of the acreage devoted to corn, but much larger than that of any other cereal crop. It was 15.1 per cent of all the improved land in the country, but this includes a considerable area of land, especially west of the Mississippi River, on which hay is cut, but which has never been plowed. It will also be noted that over one-third of the hay crop was in the West North Central Division; namely, Minnesota,

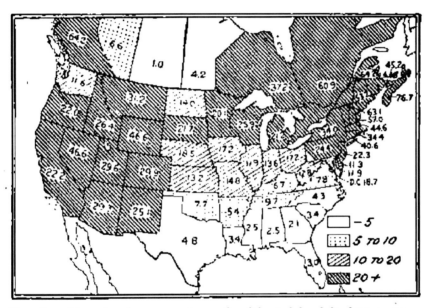

Fig. 8. — Map showing percentage of cultivated land in forage crops, 1909–1910.

Iowa, Missouri, North Dakota, South Dakota, Nebraska and Kansas. Over one-fifth of the crop was in the East North Central Division; namely, Ohio, Indiana, Illinois, Michigan and Wisconsin. These two groups of states produce nearly three-fifths of the hay crop of the country. The Middle Atlantic States — New York, Pennsylvania and New Jersey — produce nearly 12 per cent of the crop. The three groups of states together have 70 per cent of the total United States acreage, and nearly as great a percentage of total production of forage crops.

The states with largest acreage are Iowa and New York, each with over 5,000,000 acres; Nebraska, with over 4,000,000 acres; Kansas, Minnesota, Missouri, South Dakota, Illinois, Ohio, Pennsylvania and Wisconsin, each with over 3,000,000 acres.

103. Hay and forage by classes, United States, 1909. — In the accompanying table is shown the acreage of the different classes of forage crops grown in the United States in 1909, as determined by the Thirteenth Census. The acreage of corn, the principal American crop, and largely used as forage both as roughage and as grain, is added for comparison. Corn roughage is economically comparable to hay made from small grains, but it should be borne in mind that much small grain straw — especially of oats — is also fed as roughage. In the census table several of the categories include more than one crop as regards the plant actually grown. Thus, "Grains Cut Green" include oats, rye, wheat, barley and emmer; "Coarse Forage" covers corn and sorghums and similar plants cut for fodder or silage; "Other tame or cultivated grasses" include all hay grasses and legumes except timothy, red clover, alfalfa and millet.

Timothy and clover. — Perhaps the most striking thing about this table is the preponderating importance of timothy and clover, alone or mixed. The two plants constitute one-half of the total acreage of American forage crops, even if the 17,000,000 acres of wild hay meadows are included. Excluding these wild meadows timothy and clover constitute over three-fourths of the acreage of hay and forage crops. No figures are available for the relative importance of timothy and clover each considered alone, but from various sources of information it is probable that there is about 3 times as much timothy as clover.

Corn. — Notwithstanding the high importance of timothy and clover the fact must not be overlooked that the greatest amount of roughage is produced by corn. In the forms of stover, silage and pulled fodder, the herbage of probably 90 per cent of the corn crop is utilized as feed. On the whole, it is conservative to place the average yield of dry edible fodder from corn at about one ton per acre.

Alfalfa. — The area of this crop approximates five million acres. Due to the fact that this crop can be cut two or more times in a season the average yield is considerably higher than other hay plants. Ninety-five per cent of the acreage is west of the Mississippi.

Grains cut green. — In semi-arid regions and on poor soils in humid regions, small grains are often cut for hay, the total acreage of these harvested in the United States in 1909 being nearly equal to that of alfalfa. In the humid regions oats and rye are most often utilized in this way; in California, and to a less extent in other Pacific States, barley is a common hay crop; in wheat regions it is a frequent practice to get the fields ready for harvesting the grain by cutting the marginal portion for hay. Three-fourths of the grain hay is cut west of the Mississippi.

Coarse forage. — This term includes mainly corn and sorghum cut green for fodder or silage.

Millet. — The different varieties of foxtail millet are much grown in the northern portion of the great plains, over half of the acreage being from this area. Elsewhere, especially in the South, it is sown to obtain a quick crop of hay.

Wild, salt or prairie grasses. — The states in which

TABLE SHOWING AVERAGE PRODUCTION AND RELATIVE IMPORTANCE OF HAY FORAGE CROPS, UNITED STATES, 1909

NAME OF CROP	TOTAL ACREAGE	YIELD TO THE ACRE	TOTAL PRODUCTION	PERCENTAGE OF TOTAL HAY AND FORAGE PRODUCTION
	Acres	Tons	Tons	
Corn	98,382,665	1.	98,382,665	
Oat straw . .	35,159,441	.6	21,095,665	
Wheat straw . .	44,262,592			
Barley straw . .	7,698,706			
Rye straw . . .	2,195,561			
Total hay and forage . . .	72,280,776	1.35	97,453,735	100
Timothy [1] . .	24,457,584	1.22	30,359,698	31.2
Red clover [1] . .	12,274,454	1.29	15,532,602	15.9
Alfalfa	4,704,146	2.52	11,859,881	12.2
Wheat, Rye, Oats, Barley } for hay	4,324,878	1.24	5,367,292	5.5
Other tame grasses	4,218,957	0.99	4,166,772	4.3
Sorghums . . .	2,079,242	1.5	3,118,863	3.2
Millet	1,117,769	1.38	1,546,533	1.6
Cowpea . . .	1,100,000	1	1,100,000	1.1
Redtop [2] . . .	800,000	1	800,000	.8
Kentucky blue-grass	800,000	1	800,000	.8
Alsike [2] . . .	500,000	1	500,000	.5
Bermuda-grass [2]	400,000	1	400,000	.4
Johnson-grass [2] .	400,000	1	400,000	.4
Orchard-grass [2] .	300,000	1	300,000	.3
Crab-grass [2] . .	300,000	1	300,000	.3
Canada peas . .	250,000	1	250,000	.3
Brome	100,000	1	100,000	.1
All others . . .	600,000	1	600,000	.6
Wild grasses . .	17,186,522	1.07	18,383,574	18.9

[1] In the production figures for timothy and for clover, half of the production of timothy and clover mixed has been credited to each plant.

[2] This acreage has been estimated from that of "Other Tame Grasses."

natural or wild hay is most largely harvested are the following: Nebraska, North Dakota, South Dakota, Minnesota and Kansas. It is a surprising fact that the total acreage is over one-half of that of timothy and clover combined, and nearly one-fourth of the total hay and forage acreage.

Other tame or cultivated grasses. — The relatively small importance of all other hay grasses to timothy is striking, their total acreage being less than one-fourth that of timothy. These figures must, however, be considered with due allowance, as some of these grasses are often mixed with timothy, either being sown or appearing spontaneously. The most important of the "other tame grasses" are redtop, orchard-grass, brome, Kentucky blue-grass, Johnson-grass, Bermuda-grass and crab-grass.

Root forage. — Root crops for forage primarily are relatively very unimportant in the United States. They are seldom grown where field corn or sorghum thrive well. For this reason they are utilized mainly in the Mountain and Pacific States. Besides the roots grown for forage a large amount of feed results from the refuse of sugar beets after the sugar is extracted. This is fed fresh, or preserved by drying or by ensiling.

104. Forage statistics for Canada. — The census statistics of forage crops for Canada are compiled under different headings from those used in the United States Census, but in the main they are comparable. The item "Hay and Clover" in the former comprises both the "timothy and clover" and "other cultivated grasses" in the latter. "Other forage crops" includes the same crops as "grains cut green." It will be noted that corn is relatively unimportant in Canada except in Ontario, and that root crops are far more largely grown than in the United States.

ACREAGE OF FORAGE CROPS, CANADA, 1910

	HAY AND CLOVER	ALFALFA	CORN AND FORAGE	OTHER FORAGE CROPS	ROOTS
	Acres	Acres	Acres	Acres	Acres
Ontario	3,216,514	45,625	245,048	26,256	148,493
Quebec	3,224,122	4,046	41,082	19,483	13,964
New Brunswick .	625,911	83	235	2,098	8,611
Nova Scotia . .	542,007	10	561	2,273	9,635
Prince Edward .	215,083	2	191	917	6,537
Manitoba . . .	137,671	539	4,603	73,205	2,099
Alberta . . .	149,973	2,592	1,259	67,304	1,039
Saskatchewan .	37,694	182	675	53,863	2,412
British Columbia	133,217	3,741	355	15,164	2,312
Canada, total .	8,280,192	56,820	294,009	260,563	195,102

CHAPTER VII

TIMOTHY

TIMOTHY is by far the most important hay grass in America. A peculiar interest attaches to this crop because its first cultivation was on this continent, though the plant is of Old World origin. Its American given name has become adopted in all languages.

105. Botany. — Timothy (*Phleum pratense*) belongs to a genus in which botanists recognize 10 species. All of these are confined to the Old World with the exception of Mountain Timothy (*Phleum alpinum*), which also extends to North America, occurring generally through the western mountains, and south as far as the White Mountains of New England. The botanical evidence is strongly against common timothy being native to the New World. It was early introduced, but has never been found in localities where its introduction was improbable. Most northern plants common to the Old and the New World range in North America either from Alaska southward through the western mountains, or southeastward to New England, or else range from Greenland south to New England. It has been thought by some that timothy was native in New England, but as the plant is not native to the northward of New England, nor in Alaska and the Rocky Mountains, it is quite certain that the plant is not endemic to North America.

122

FIG. 9. — Timothy (*Phleum pratense*).
a, glumes; b, floret with glumes removed.

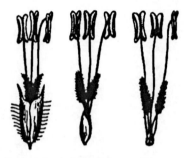

FIG. 10. — Timothy. Florets showing the different parts.

In the Old World timothy is native to most of Europe north to latitude 70 degrees, and eastward through Siberia. It also occurs in the Caucasus region and in Algeria. Through this area occur about 10 different botanical varieties, none of which have ever been cultivated.

106. Agricultural history. — Timothy was first brought into cultivation in the United States. It was first propagated, according to Jared Eliot, by one Herd, who found the grass growing along the Piscataqua River near Portsmouth, New Hampshire. Eliot in 1747 recommends it for Massachusetts under the name Herd-grass. He also cites Ellis to the effect that Herd-grass had even that early been introduced into England from America. The culture of timothy is thus older than that of any other hay grass excepting perennial rye-grass. A

letter to Eliot from Benjamin Franklin under date of July 16, 1747, states that the Herd-grass seed received proved to be " mere timothy." This is the earliest record of the name timothy. This designation is supposed to be derived from Timothy Hansen, who apparently brought the grass from New England into Maryland. Later its culture spread to Virginia, and from there was sent to England about 1760 under the name timothy. In England the grass has been known also as meadow cat's-tail, but the name timothy is now used in nearly all languages. Timothy was the most important hay grass in the United States as early as 1807, and its supremacy has never been seriously threatened.

107. Agricultural importance. — Practically all of the hay grass grown in the northeastern fourth of the United States and in southern Canada is timothy, either alone or in mixtures. An increasing quantity is also being grown in

Fig. 11. — Distribution of timothy, 1909–1910. Figures equal acres.

the irrigated valleys of the northwest and in the mountain states. The total value of the timothy crop, either alone or in mixtures, was, according to the last United States Census, about $300,000,000, which was ⅛ of the value of the corn crop, ¾ of the value of the wheat crop and ⅝ of the value of the cotton crop for the same year.

The total acreage devoted to timothy was as much as that of all other cultivated hay plants combined, including clover and alfalfa. All of the other perennial hay grasses combined occupied but one-fourth the acreage of timothy.

In Europe timothy has never been of the highest importance among grasses, but its use there in recent years seems to be steadily increasing. In other countries it is but little grown.

108. Climatic adaptations. — Timothy is a northern grass, and does not succeed well in the United States south of latitude 36° excepting at higher elevations. It thrives fairly well on the Alaskan coast, but in the interior suffers both from winter cold and summer drought. No definite data regarding the minimum cold that timothy will withstand have been recorded, but it is more cold resistant than most cultivated grasses. At Copper Center, Alaska, a considerable proportion of the timothy plants survived a winter when redtop, tall oat-grass, orchard-grass and velvet-grass were completely destroyed. It has also matured seeds at this place.

It does not well withstand hot, humid summers, and successful fields are rarely found in the area adapted to cotton. Crab-grass and other summer weeds are also destructive competitors. When planted in the cotton belt usually but one cutting of timothy can be obtained, and the plants then disappear. Even this degree of success can be obtained in the Gulf States only in the richest lands. Tracy suggests that the growth stimulated by warm winter weather weakens the bulbs so that the plants are less able to withstand summer heat and drought.

109. Soil adaptation. — Timothy is best adapted to clay or loam soils. It does not possess much drought resistance, but on the other hand thrives best where moisture is abundant.   In moist meadows it is sometimes the practice to sow timothy seed directly without any preparation of the soil, and timothy often makes a splendid stand, largely replacing the native plants.   While timothy is mainly grown in humid regions, it is being more and more grown in irrigated regions, as large yields of readily marketable hay can be obtained, particularly in valleys too cool for the most successful growing of alfalfa.

110. Advantages of timothy. — The importance of timothy in America is due to its rather remarkable combination of qualities, as well as to its splendid adaptation to the same area as red clover.   Its advantages may thus be summarized : —

1. It produces good yields.

2. A stand is usually secured easily.

3. The seed is usually high in purity, germinates well, and the cost per acre is less than that of any other grass.

4. It seldom lodges.

5. It is easily cut and cured.

6. The period during which it may be harvested is longer than that of most grasses.

7. It is the favorite hay for city horses, and the demand and price is therefore greater than that of other hays.

Among the objections that have been urged against timothy are : first, its lateness ; second, the fact that it becomes somewhat woody ; third, its comparatively low nutritive value; and fourth, the small amount of after-math. The last objection affects its value as a pasture plant; the others are not important.

111. Rotations. — Timothy is used in the most common of all rotations in the North; namely, corn, oats, wheat, clover, timothy. The corn may be replaced by potatoes or other cultivated crop, the wheat by rye and the oats sometimes by cowpeas or soybeans, but there is no equally good substitute for the clover and timothy.

In places where timothy is grown for market, or where the land is poor, timothy is often allowed to stand for five years or even more. On such fields the yields may be kept up by top-dressing with barnyard manure or other nitrogenous fertilizers.

Old timothy sod is apt to harbor insects, and therefore it is best to plow in winter, if possible.

112. Seed. — Timothy seed is nearly always very pure, and is never adulterated except with old seed. The small size and characteristic appearance of timothy seed, as well as its low price, make adulteration with other seeds practically impossible. Some of the grains are free.

The purity of good seed should be 99 per cent or more, and the viability 98–99 per cent. Germination ensues in 5–6 days.

The legal weight of the seed is commonly 45 pounds per bushel. It actually varies, however, from 42 to 50 pounds. One pound contains 1,170,500 to 1,320,000 seeds.

The viability of timothy seed is retained better than that of most grasses. Stebler and Volkart state that it loses very little during the first year in viability, about 10 per cent the second year, and 15 to 25 per cent the third year. At the Vienna Seed Testing Station seed 4 years old had lost but 9.4 per cent of its viability. At the

Wisconsin Experiment Station seed retained its viability well for 5 years, and then rapidly deteriorated.

The free grains present in timothy seed show a somewhat lower viability than the grains in the hulls, according to tests at both the Wisconsin and Delaware Experiment Stations.

113. Preparation of seed bed. — At the Utah Experiment Station three methods of preparing the ground for seeding were compared, the plats being one-eighth acre in size : —

" Plat 37 was harrowed twice with a disk harrow, once with a square-tooth harrow, then dragged with a clod crusher, followed by a square-tooth harrow, after which it was sown and again dragged.

" Plat 38 was harrowed once with a disk harrow, again with square-tooth harrow, and the seed was dragged in with a clod crusher.

" Plat 39 was dragged level to receive the seed, passing over the ground but once with the drag or clod crusher, and then the seed was sown and covered by the drag or clod crusher.

*   *   *   *   *   *   *

" Plat 37, it will be observed, was given a large amount of tillage. Plat 38 had a moderate amount of tillage. Plat 39 had none at all. The drag was used on Plats 38 and 39, in order to place the seed in the same relative condition on the surface as the others, that the question of amount of cultivation might have no disturbing factors in the determination of results. Plat 39, as will be seen, was entirely untilled, the dragging was simply for the purpose of leveling the ground before and after covering the seed."

TABLE SHOWING EFFECT OF DIFFERENT METHODS OF SOIL
PREPARATION ON YIELDS OF TIMOTHY.   UTAH EXP. STATION

| PLAT | CROP OF 1892 | | CROP OF 1893 | | TOTAL WEIGHT 1892-3 | TOTAL DRY MATTER |
	Yield an Acre, lbs.	Dry Matter	Yield an Acre, lbs.	Dry Matter		
37	1920	1448.98	1680	1529.81	3600	2978.79
38	2680	Lost	2320	2029.07	5000	———
39	3080	2191.72	2200	2030.16	5280	4221.88

114. Heavy seeds or light seeds. — Heavy seeds and
light seeds separated by means of a brine solution were
compared at the Utah Experiment Station in 1893.   The
first season crop from the heavy seed was larger by 28
per cent, but in the second season the two were alike.

Clark at the New York (Geneva) Experiment Station
separated timothy seed by using salt solutions of different specific gravities from 1 to 1.26.   The percentage
of germination was smallest in the lightest seeds and greatest in the heavy seeds.

Hunt mentions a test at the Cornell Experiment Station
in which three sizes of timothy seed, containing respectively
600,000, 1,200,000 and 2,000,000 seeds to the pound were
grown in similar plots.   The result of a two years' trial
was slightly in favor of the large seeds, both when the same
number and the same weight per acre were planted.

115. Rate of seeding. — The usual rate of seeding
timothy is 12 to 15 pounds to the acre if seeded alone, and
about 9 pounds if red clover is to be added.   Few rate of
seeding experiments have been reported.   Hunt at the
Cornell Experiment Station tested various rates at from
5 to 35 pounds, and concluded that 15 pounds is a desirable
rate.

K

At the Utah Experiment Station seed was sown on poor soil at four different rates; namely, 8, 16, 24 and 32 quarts an acre. The largest hay yield was from the 24-quart seeding the first season and from the 16-quart seeding the second season. The total yield for the two seasons was in favor of the 24-quart seeding, but this was but slightly greater than the 16-quart seeding. In both seasons the 32-quart plot yielded least.

Stebler and Volkart in Switzerland, and Werner in Germany, advise 19 kg. a hectare, which equals 17 pounds an acre.

116. Depth of seeding. — Timothy seed, when sown with a hand seeder or with a grass seeder attachment behind a grain drill, is left on or very near the surface. If the seeder attachment permits the seed to drop in front of the grain drill, the timothy seeds will lie at various depths from the surface to that of the grain. There is reason to believe that timothy seed is ordinarily not covered deeply enough.

Two tests at the Utah Experiment Station in broadcasting as compared with drilling gave contradictory results. In one experiment the drilled plots outyielded the broadcasted by 50 per cent the first year and 32 per cent the second year; in the other, the broadcasted plots gave greater yields by 35 per cent the first year and 53 per cent the second season.

117. Methods of seeding. — Four methods of seeding timothy are in use in America: (1) Seeding in fall with wheat or other grain; (2) Seeding in fall alone on prepared land; (3) Seeding in spring with grain; (4) Seeding in the spring without a nurse crop.

The first method of seeding timothy — namely, with wheat or other grain in the fall — is the most common, probably 60 per cent or more of the timothy being thus sown. In this case a grass-seeding attachment is used on the grain drill, and the seed is allowed to fall either behind or in front of the wheat drill. In the latter case, it is somewhat covered. When thus seeded, timothy makes but little growth the succeeding year and no crop can be harvested. Partly on this account, medium red clover is sown in the wheat early in the spring. As a result a small crop of red clover may sometimes be harvested the same season, or at least some pasturage be secured. The next season the crop is mainly clover, and thereafter practically all timothy. This method of seeding involves a minimum amount of labor, and as a rule gives entirely satisfactory results. In many places it is unsatisfactory because the timothy fields become increasingly foul year after year. The most troublesome weeds are the oxeye daisy (*Chrysanthemum Leucanthemum*) and the white fleabane (*Erigeron ramosus* and *Erigeron annuus*). Both of these weeds ripen all or much of their seed before timothy is cut for hay, and as these seeds live over in the ground for several years and are returned to the land in the manure, timothy fields frequently become badly infested.

The second method — namely, of sowing alone in fall — is best where weeds are troublesome, and in general southward of the principal timothy area. The seed bed should be well prepared after plowing wheat or other grain stubble, and sown to timothy in late summer or early fall. An excellent crop, practically free from weeds, will ordinarily be secured the next season. Southward of the parallel of 36 degrees red clover can quite safely be sown with the timothy, especially if it be seeded rather early. This method should be more generally used. It involves more labor, but produces cleaner and usually larger crops.

The third method — that of sowing in spring with a grain nurse crop — is used quite largely, especially near the northern limits of timothy culture, both in the East and on irrigated lands in the West. Clover may be and usually is seeded with the timothy. As a rule, it is best to sow very early on land that has been plowed the previous fall. A firm seed bed is better than a loose one. With this method practically no timothy is secured the first season.

The fourth method — seeding without a nurse crop in spring — is used on irrigated lands in the Northwest, often with clover or alfalfa, and a fair cutting obtained the same season. It is also used on unirrigated lands in the West, where soil moisture conditions do not permit of fall seeding. In the latter case, the land is sometimes plowed in the fall or winter to conserve soil moisture, and to avoid delay in spring seeding.

Spring seeding, either with or without a nurse crop, is not satisfactory southward, as crab-grass and other summer weeds injure the timothy greatly.

At the Iowa Experiment Station timothy was sown alone March 23 and 30, April 6, 13, 20 and 27 and May 3 and 10. The two May sowings were complete failures, and the April 27 one nearly so. The March 23 sowing gave a very good stand, but the later ones were inferior.

118. Seed bed. — A fine, well-firmed seed bed is probably the most favorable for timothy, as for most grasses. Where fall seeding alone is practiced, a cultivated crop like potatoes or tobacco leaves the land in excellent shape for timothy.

If the ground is loose, rolling is probably advantageous. Rolling the ground after seeding was tested at the Utah Experiment Station, with the result of increasing the yield of hay both where the seed was drilled and where it was broadcasted.

At the same experiment station the effect of different methods of preparing the seed bed was also tested, with the results shown in the following table : —

TABLE SHOWING YIELDS OF TIMOTHY WITH DIFFERENT DEPTHS OF PLOWING. UTAH EXPERIMENT STATION

DEPTH PLOWED	CROP OF 1892		CROP OF 1893		TOTAL 1892-3	
	Hay to the Acre	Dry Matter to the Acre	Hay to the Acre	Dry Matter to the Acre	Hay to the Acre	Dry Matter to the Acre
	Pounds	*Pounds*	*Pounds*	*Pounds*	*Pounds*	*Pounds*
4 inches	2973	2473	2373	2161	5346	4634
10 inches	3227	2748	2507	2345	5734	5093
7 inches	3240	2737	2827	2627	6067	5364
Not plowed, surface har-rowed	4133	3582	4027	——	8160	——

In this series of experiments the yields are in inverse relation to the depth of plowing.

119. Fertilizers for timothy. — Timothy, as ordinarily grown in the corn-oats-wheat-clover-timothy rotation, usually secures only the residues of the fertilizers that are applied to the cereal crops. Where timothy meadows are allowed to stand three years or more, the yield can be maintained by top-dressings of fertilizer, especially barnyard manure. The experiments that have been conducted at a number of experiment stations have uniformly shown markedly increased yields from the use either of barnyard manure or of commercial nitrogenous fertilizers. In most cases, complete fertilizers have also given good results, but the return from phosphorus and potash is rarely so striking as that from nitrogenous fertilizers.

The data in Par. 88 also refer largely to timothy or timothy mixtures.

At Cornell Experiment Station extensive fertilizer trials with timothy have been conducted. The largest yields were obtained by using 20 tons of barnyard manure and very good results by using 10 tons an acre. In all cases, the influence of nitrate of soda was very marked. The most satisfactory commercial fertilizer was found to be 320 pounds nitrate of soda, 320 pounds acid phosphate and 80 pounds muriate of potash an acre. The results indicate that a still smaller proportion of acid phosphate would have been economical.

120. Lime. — On Dunkirk clay loam at the Cornell Experiment Station, applications of lime did not increase the hay yield.

At the Rhode Island Experiment Station top-dressings of lime exercised but little influence, but it was well marked when the lime was harrowed into the soil.

In the rotations at the Pennsylvania Experiment Station burned lime alone actually reduced the yields of grass (timothy and clover), but ground limestone and gypsum each increased the yield slightly.

121. Irrigation. — Timothy is grown with marked success on irrigated lands in the West. An abundance of water is necessary, as timothy is quickly injured by an insufficiency. Extensive experiments on timothy under irrigation have been conducted at the Utah Experiment Station, where it was found better to apply water at frequent intervals. On plots irrigated at intervals of 3, 6, 9, 12, 15 and 18 days, the total amount of water being the same, the total yields of hay to the acre for the three years were respectively 3640, 4380, 4360, 4340, 4080, 3555 and 2100 pounds.

An oversufficiency of water is less injurious than too little. Where the soil was saturated respectively 4, 3½, 2½, 2 and 1½ feet, the total acre yields for three years were respectively 6040, 3900, 7020, 3580 and 4750 pounds of hay.

In another experiment the ground was saturated respectively 31, 27, 33, 12 and 17 inches deep, and the corresponding yields per acre were 3576, 6496, 6096, 1070 and 2260 pounds.

In a different series of experiments the results are thus tabulated : —

Irrigation water applied in inches to the acre	7.50	15	30	60	100
Total yield to the acre in pounds	3982	3844	6054	8406	2214
Yield to inch of irrigation water	531	256	202	140	22

It will be noted that 15 inches of water reduced the yield somewhat, a result also secured with orchard-grass, brome and Italian rye-grass. According to the above figures 30 inches of water on one acre will yield but 6054 pounds of hay; spread over two acres 7688 pounds; and over four acres 11,928 pounds.

Irrigation by means of a network of lateral ditches gave higher yields than by any other method of applying the water.

Irrigating in the day time, 10 A.M., proved better than irrigating in the evening. The average yields for three years were respectively 3033 and 2033 pounds.

Irrigating timothy fields both in the fall and in the spring increased the yield over spring irrigation alone an average of about 25 per cent during four seasons.

122. Time to cut for hay. — The usual time recommended for cutting timothy hay is shortly after the anthers have fallen and not later than when the seed is in the dough stage.

The problem of the best time to cut timothy for hay is a many-sided one, and has been attacked from several standpoints. The stage at which the grass is cut will affect : —

1. The total yield.
2. The palatability.
3. The digestibility.
4. The ease of curing.
5. The convenience of harvesting.
6. The amount of the next season's crop.

The most extensive studies on this problem have been those of Waters and Schweitzer at the Missouri Experiment Station, who conducted their investigations during twelve seasons. In these investigations the timothy was cut at five stages; namely, coming into blossom, full bloom, seed formed, seed in dough and seed ripe. Their findings may be thus summarized : —

The total yield of dry matter is on the average greatest in the hay at the time the seed is just formed. This was the case three seasons out of four, the yield being greatest at full bloom the second season.

The total amount each of protein, ether extract and ash per acre was greatest in the hay cut at full bloom; of nitrogen-free extract when the seed was in the dough stage; of crude fiber when the seed was just formed.

The loss of dry matter and perhaps of other substances as the plants approach maturity is due partly to the storage of material by the bulbs, partly to loss of leaves by drying and breaking off, especially the lower ones, and partly by the solvent action of rain.

The total amount each of digestible protein, nitrogen-free extract, crude fiber and ash is greatest at time of full bloom; of ether extract when the seed is in the dough.

The digestibility of the hay is greatest in the youngest stages and gradually decreases in the later cuttings. This is also true of the protein and the crude fiber, but is less marked in the nitrogen-free extract.

Yearling steers fed only on timothy showed a marked preference to the hays cut at the younger stages, eating the first three cuttings before they would touch the others. Other cattle fed liberally on grain and silage did not show · a decided preference, as was also the case with well-fed sheep.

Timothy cut young is more difficult to cure and more easily damaged by weather.

At the time when timothy is in full bloom, other farm operations, especially the cultivation of corn, are impera- · tive.

Early cutting is thought to weaken the bulbs and to lessen the next year's crop.

Morse at the New Hampshire Experiment Station studied timothy cut every five days from June 4 to July 31. The conclusions were as follows : —

"Timothy grass grows very rapidly until the blossoms appear. Its fastest growth is between the appearance of the head and the beginning of the bloom.

"The amount of grass per acre increases until the time of blossoming. It then decreases. The decrease is due to loss of water.

"Dry substance steadily increases until the plant forms seed.

"The young grass is richest in fat and protein. The mature grass is richest in carbohydrates or fiber and nitrogen-free extract.

"Timothy yields the largest amount of digestible protein when cut at the beginning of bloom.

"The total amount of digestible matter is largest when the grass has passed out of blossom, or gone to seed."

TABLE SHOWING RELATION BETWEEN TIME OF CUTTING AND YIELD IN POUNDS OF TIMOTHY

STAGE WHEN CUT	ILLINOIS[1]	MISSOURI[2] AVE. OF 5 YRS.	CONNECTICUT[3]	PENNSYLVANIA[4]	MAINE[5]
	Water-free	Water-free	Water-free	Water-free	Hay
Well headed	——	——	2749	——	——
Coming into bloom .	——	3411	——	——	——
Full bloom	3287	3964	3301	2586	4225
Anthers half fallen .	3423	——	——	——	——
Out of bloom . . .	——	——	3117	——	——
Seed formed . . .	——	4089	——	——	——
Seed in dough . . .	4012	4038	——	——	——
Late cut	——	——	——	•——	5086
Seed nearly ripe . .	4064	——	3616	3064	——
Seed ripe	——	3747	——	——	——

123. Yields. — The average yield of timothy hay per acre, according to the Thirteenth United States Census, was in tons per acre for the various divisions as follows: New England, 1.12; Middle Atlantic, 1.09; East North Central, 1.26; West North Central, 0.97; Mountain, 1.48; Pacific, 1.62; and for the whole United States, 1.22 tons. In the Canadian Census special data for timothy are not reported.

Different experiment stations have reported yields of timothy in pounds to the acre, as follows: Ohio, 3497;

[1] Illinois Exp. Sta. Bul. 5.
[2] Proc. Soc. Prom. Agr. Sci. 1910, p. 75.
[3] Conn. State Board Agr., 12th An. Rep. 1878-9.
[4] Penn. State College, An. Rep. 1886, p. 273.
[5] Maine Exp. Sta., An. Rep. 1890, p. 65.

Pennsylvania, 3344; Kansas, 5528; Illinois, 4400; Michigan, 3466; Minnesota, 4340; Utah, 2045; North Carolina, 2136; North Dakota, 2470; Cornell, without fertilizers, 2000 to 3600, with fertilizers, up to a maximum of 8940.

Good yields of timothy average about 2 tons to the acre; maximum yields may reach 4½ tons an acre, but such are secured only by heavy fertilizing or on rich irrigated lands in the Northwest.

European yields for the acre are recorded as follows: Vianne in France, 5280 to 13,200 pounds; Sinclair in England, 17,356 to 19,398 pounds; Werner in Germany, 5280 to 6160 pounds; Pinckert in Germany, 4050 pounds; Sprengel in Germany, 3520 to 4400 pounds. The yields of Sinclair are based on very small plots and cannot be realized on a field scale.

124. Pasture. — Timothy alone is not well adapted to permanent pastures, but is a useful element in most mixtures. Most of it will disappear in about three years. For temporary pastures, however, it forms an important element.

The pasturing of timothy meadows in fall and even in spring is a very general practice, both in the East and on irrigated lands in the West. It is very doubtful, however, if the practice is a wise one. The bulbs of timothy are easily injured by the close pasturing of sheep and by the trampling of larger animals.

At the Utah Experiment Station some data were secured to show this effect. On three plots of ⅔ acre each the yields in 1892 were respectively 6633, 6960 and 7333 pounds per acre. The first plot was grazed by 18 head of cattle May 16, 1893; the second was left ungrazed; while the third was grazed by two heifers for two weeks,

November 8–22, 1892. The 1893 yields to the acre were respectively 2933, 5107 and 4800 pounds. Spring grazing thus proved markedly injurious, while light fall grazing was much less so.

125. Pollination. — The pollen of timothy is very light, and with a scarcely perceptible air movement will float 12 feet or more. The grass is normally anemophilous — that is, pollinated by wind — as indicated by the large feathery stigmas and light pollen.

According to Hopkins's observations in West Virginia, timothy flowers begin to bloom 10 to 15 days after the tip of the spike is visible. On each spike the blooming period extends from 7 to 12 days. The flowers open as a rule early in the morning and the stigma is exserted at the time the anthers open, so that self-pollination may easily occur.

No observations are recorded as to whether an individual flower is self-fertile or not. Some seed may be produced, however, by bagging a single head or all the heads of a single plant.

126. Seed-production. — Timothy is one of the most reliable grasses for seed-production. The grass is usually cut with a grain binder and the bundles put in small shocks and allowed to cure for a week or more. Thrashing is done by a grain separator, but special sieves are necessary. The average yield of seed is stated to be about 7 bushels an acre and the maximum 12 bushels.

Some loss from shattering will occur if the seed be allowed to become overripe. Showery weather causes the glumes, by opening and closing, to become looser, so that in thrashing a considerable proportion of the seed becomes freed from the glumes.

The principal seed-producing states in the order of total

yield are Illinois, Iowa, Minnesota, South Dakota, Kansas, Ohio.

In Europe some surplus seed is grown in Germany and in Austria. Werner gives the German yield at 500 to 800 kg. to the hectare. Michalowski at Hohenheim from fall sowings obtained 244 kg. the first year and 554 kg. the second year to the hectare. From a spring sowing the seed yield the second year was 567 kg. the hectare.

The date of harvesting influences the weight of seed obtained. Thus Dorph-Petersen in Denmark harvested from plots at intervals of 3 days, the yields being at the rate respectively of 303, 346, 360 and 414 kg. the hectare.

127. Life history. — If a seedling of timothy is carefully examined, a small bud, the beginning of a corm or bulb, will be found in the axil at the base of each of the leaves. The basal internodes are very short until the one is reached which becomes the primary corm. The smaller axillary corms below develop later and give the false appearance of having arisen from the base of the primary bulb. A single seedling may have during the first year 8 to 18 corms and shoots, each with a more or less well-developed corm, from the base of which roots are produced. Under field conditions all of these shoots do not survive, as crowding and other conditions prevent the weaker ones from securing enough nourishment. Where the plants are isolated, most of the shoots will head at approximately the same height, but if the plants are crowded and the nourishment is insufficient, the weaker shoots head when much smaller than the others. A timothy shoot heads but once, and then dies, including the corm. Before the latter dies, however, a new lateral bulb is usually developed from its base, or if the corm is double from the base of each joint. Normally the shoot develops and heads the season after the bulb is formed, but spring-sown plants may come to bloom the same season.

After a crop of hay has been cut, the stronger basal shoots will under favorable conditions develop and produce heads. Thus, while the plant is a perennial, each shoot behaves much like an annual.

128. Life period. — Few data seem to have been recorded as to the length of life of individual timothy plants, and none as to the maximum length. It is known, however, that many plants endure as long as six years and probably much longer. In meadows it is generally agreed that the yields are best in the second and third years, and thereafter gradually decline.

Stebler in Switzerland planted two areas with a mixture of grass seeds containing 15 per cent timothy, in one case American seed, in the other German. The percentage of timothy plants was determined for each year for the eight years following, with the following results : —

	1904	1905	1906	1907	1908	1909	1910	1911
American	61.7	39.8	15.7	20.0	12.9	5.0	5.0	5.0
German	67.5	51.6	60.2	41.4	37.4	26.7	17.0	12.8

From these results the American strain seems to be less long-lived. This may be due to the fact that in America, timothy is usually allowed to lay but two years, so that short-lived individuals are not eliminated.

129. Depth of root system. — The depth to which timothy roots extend is not great. Ten Eyck at the North Dakota Experiment Station found that they did not reach three feet.

130. Proportion of roots to tops. — Several investigators have secured data on the relative amount of roots in timothy, from which it appears that the roots do not weigh more than half as much as the tops.

At the Storrs, Connecticut, Experiment Station, Woods determined the dry weight of roots in an area 2 feet square for each 6 inches in depth. From these data the weight to the acre for each 6 inches was calculated as follows in pounds: 2170, 274, 58, 14 or a total of 2516 pounds. The dry weight of the tops similarly calculated was 5027 pounds.

At the Utah Experiment Station the dry weight of timothy roots was determined in an area 2 feet square for each inch of depth. On this basis the weight of roots per acre was for each inch of depth as follows, the weights being given in pounds: 541.7; 279.8; 116.9; 103.9; 86.8; 38.4; 24.0; 26.9; 29.9; 24.0; 16.6; 12.0. The total acre weight in the 12 inches was 1303.9 pounds.

At the Arkansas Experiment Station Bennett and Irby determined the weight of roots to tops to be as 83:100. Fifty per cent of the roots were in the top 4 inches, 95 per cent in the top 6 inches and practically none extended deeper than 12 inches.

131. Regional strains. — In Switzerland, Stebler and Volkart report a number of investigations to determine the relative yielding capacity of seeds from different sources. In one small plot test lasting four years the average yield of timothy from Saxony was 25 per cent greater than that from America. The American timothy showed a much greater reduction of yield after the first two years. In both cases the timothy was mixed with the same per cent of red clover.

In another test of 5 years, the average yields of 4

strains in plots of 50 square meters was as follows: Pomerania, 116.6 kg.; Saxony, 112.6 kg.; America, 111.8 kg.; and Mähren (Moravia), 107.4 kg. The differences are not significant.

The trials of the Landwirtschaftsgesellschaft in Germany gave the following yields a hectare in kilograms: Finland I, 4528; Canada, 4500; United States, 4395; Saxony, 4022; Finland II, 3974; Galicia, 3878; East Prussia, 3767; Moravia, 3700.

Definite conclusions can scarcely be drawn from the above limited data.

132. Feeding value. — There are comparatively few feeding experiments reported by which the feeding value of timothy can be compared with other hays.

Experiments at the Mississippi Experiment Station indicate that its feeding value for working mules and for dairy cows is practically identical with that of Bermuda-grass hay.

At the Utah Experiment Station the conclusion was reached that wild hay was more valuable pound for pound in feeding both sheep and cattle than was timothy hay.

Haecker in two series of experiments at the Minnesota Experiment Station finds that prairie hay and timothy have equal feeding value for dairy cows.

At the Illinois Experiment Station alfalfa was compared to timothy in a ration fed to dairy cows. Each of the 16 cows produced considerably more milk when on the alfalfa ration than when on the timothy ration, the increase on the average being 17.7 per cent.

At the same experiment station, timothy and alfalfa were compared for work horses, and the conclusion was reached that with alfalfa less grain is required to prevent them from losing weight than where timothy is fed. In this experiment the saving in grain was 22 per cent in favor of the alfalfa.

At the Indiana Experiment Station red clover hay was found much more efficient than timothy hay in fattening steers when both were fed with grain corn. The advantages that the use of clover hay has over the timothy in fattening steers are that it improves the appetite, keeps the digestive system in good condition, improves the appearance of the coat, causes the steers to make more rapid gains, produces a pound of gain at less expense, and results in a higher finish and a corresponding increase in the value per hundred of the finished steer.

At the same station timothy hay was compared with red clover hay for fattening lambs. As a result of one direct comparison, timothy was found far inferior. When fed with corn alone, the effect of the timothy on the thrift of the lambs was harmful.

Two feeding tests of timothy in comparison with red clover hay for horses have been conducted at the Illinois Experiment Station. From the first test the conclusion was reached that clover hay when fed with a mixed grain ration is more efficient for producing gains than timothy hay. In this test clover hay produced 58 per cent more gain in weight than did timothy.

In the second experiment both hays were compared on work horses. The data indicate that there is but little difference in the value of the two when fed in conjunction with mixed grains consisting of corn, oats, oil meal and bran. The horses fed the clover hay had, however, glossier coats of hair. The laxative effect of the clover was evident, but not to an objectionable degree.

In a feeding experiment with 6 steers at the Maine Experiment Station the animals were fed for 28 days with

L

timothy hay cut when in bloom and for 41 days with timothy hay cut 17 days after bloom. In the first period the steers gained 1.47 pounds per diem and in the second period 1.49 pounds per diem.

133. Injurious insects. — Timothy is not much subject to insect injury, but a few species may at times do considerable damage.

Bill-bug (Sphenophorus zeœ). — The larva of this weevil burrows into the bulbs of timothy and feeds on the interior, thus weakening the culm. In Illinois Forbes found 50 to 75 per cent of the bulbs infested or injured in fields three or four years old, and 10 to 20 per cent in fields two years old. Hopkins expresses the opinion that the bill-bug is one of the prime causes of early failure of timothy meadows in West Virginia, and suggests as a remedy that the stubble be fertilized with stable manure, tobacco dust or lime immediately after hay harvest. As the same insect attacks corn, the timothy sod should, if possible, be plowed in winter to destroy as many of the insects as possible.

Joint-worm (Isosoma sp.). — The larva of this insect infests the stems of timothy, never more than a single larva in a culm. As a result of the injury it causes the head and upper portion of the stem to die prematurely. The dead spikes conspicuously reveal the work of this insect. Where abundant it may reduce the hay yielded 10 to 20 per cent.

134. Diseases. — Timothy is affected by but few fungous diseases that cause damage worthy of notice.

Timothy rust (*Puccinia phlei-pratensis*) occurs in nearly all states east of the Mississippi, and in Minnesota and Iowa. It caused serious injury in timothy breeding plots at Arlington Farm, Virginia, in 1906, where some selections were totally destroyed. It closely resembles wheat rust and attacks both the leaves and culms. The fungus lives over winter on timothy in Virginia. Farther north-ward teleutospores are abundantly produced. The rust has been artificially transferred to oats, rye, tall fescue, orchard-grass and Canada blue-grass, but wheat and barley seem immune.

In fields of timothy the rust seems never to be abundant, and no injury worth while has been reported. On the other hand, wayside isolated plants are often covered with pustules, and apparently more so southward. The cup-fungus (æcidial) stage of this rust is not known. Experiments in inoculating barberry plants, the æcidial host of the wheat rust, have been ineffective.

Another disease which sometimes attacks timothy as well as other grasses is a leaf smut (*Ustilago striæformis*). It causes dark thickened lines on the leaf blades and sheaths, which later burst open and become dusty from the spores. This fungus is rather widespread, and has been reported as damaging timothy in Wisconsin and in Illinois. Severely attacked plants do not form heads.

135. Variability. — Timothy is a very variable grass, as may easily be seen by examining individual plants where they are growing scattered so as to permit the full development of each. Some of the more marked varieties have received names at the hands of botanists. Hays at the Minnesota Experiment Station referred to a number of the commoner variations in 1889, and Hopkins at the West Virginia Experiment Station published more complete studies in 1894.

Clark has made a very full study of the variations observed in 3505 isolated plants in the breeding nursery at Cornell University Experiment Station. Some of the variations observed by him may be thus briefly summarized : —

The leaves vary from 4 to 15 inches in length, and are from .25 to .75 inch broad. They may be flat or concave or loosely twisted; spreading, drooping, or nearly erect. The number to the culm ranges from 3 to 8.

The stems are usually green, rarely reddish or bluish, 18 to 55 inches tall, .05 to .15 inch in diameter, erect to decumbent. The nodes are usually brown, but vary to green.

The heads are normally cylindrical, with a rounded or abruptly pointed tip, but on some plants they have a long tapering apex or a tapering base, or both. They vary in length from 1 to 12 inches; in diameter, from .2 to .4 inch; in color they are usually green, sometimes purple.

The blooming period of the earliest individuals was 18 days earlier than the latest ones in 1907. This difference doubtless fluctuates according to the season, being lengthened by cool weather and shortened by warm weather.

The life period probably varies greatly. Some individuals are apparently annual, and others survived only two years. Most of the plants were still vigorous at the end of nearly six years.

The vigor of individuals varies greatly.

The number of culms per plant ranges from a few up to 280.

The yield of hay to the plant ranges from .01 pound to 1.35 pounds.

The only positive correlation found was that between weight and height.

136. Disease resistance. — The most serious disease that has affected timothy in America is rust. At Arlington

Farm, Virginia, in 1906, this disease completely destroyed some of the selected strains, while others were but slightly affected. None were wholly immune. The relative resistance of these plants was much the same in 1908 and in 1909, but in the latter year the rust was far more abundant. Inoculation experiments in the greenhouse showed that all plants could be inoculated, but that there was great difference in the degree to which the fungus developed in different individuals.

Clark at the Cornell Experiment Station has also recorded the marked variability in the susceptibility of different timothy plants to rust.

137. Breeding. — The first serious attempt made to select the superior individuals from timothy and thus to secure improved strains was by Hopkins, of the West Virginia Experiment Station, in 1893. Among the best of the strains selected by Hopkins were the Stewart, a tall leafy form especially adapted to hay production; the Pasture, the progeny of a plant found surviving in an old, much overgrazed pasture, and conspicuous for the amount of aftermath which it produced; and the Early or Hopkins variety, which matured two weeks earlier than any other. At the West Virginia station, where these varieties were selected, they were found to be distinctly superior to ordinary mixed timothy. These varieties were secured by the United States Department of Agriculture in 1902, and large quantities of seed of these three varieties were grown. The Early remained nearly pure, as it came to maturity before other varieties of timothy were in bloom. The other two varieties, however, became somewhat mixed, but their main characteristics remained evident. These three varieties were tried out on a farm scale in various parts of the United States, but the results were on the whole disappointing, as when taken to new localities these timothies were little, if any, superior to ordinary mixed timothy. In Virginia, they were all found severely subject to timothy rust, a disease which had become prevalent about this time, and which introduced a new factor into timothy breeding. The breeding work inaugurated by Hopkins has been continued by the Department of Agriculture, first in Virginia, and now on a special station in Ohio. In 1903, breeding work was undertaken at the Cornell Experiment Station, and about the same time at the Minnesota Experiment Station. Some of the best of the Cornell selections proved decidedly inferior in comparison with the Hopkins timothies in Virginia, and the reverse of this was the case when they were planted side by side at the Cornell Station. On the whole, the evidence indicates that the bred varieties of timothy will have a comparatively narrow adaptation. The best results are to be expected in breeding timothy for each locality. Beginning in 1905, the breeding of timothy has also been undertaken at Svalöf, Sweden and other places in Europe.

There can be little doubt that the breeding of timothy will be advantageous. Such breeding, however, will necessarily have to be continuous, as timothy, like corn, is almost impossible to keep pure. Similar methods to those used in corn breeding can very well be used in connection with timothy breeding.

138. Methods of breeding. — Webber recommends on the basis of the experience at the Cornell Experiment Station the following plan of conducting timothy breeding, beginning with the selected individual plant. These methods differ but little from those which were employed by Hopkins.

1. The selected plant is propagated vegetatively by digging up and separating the bulbs that are formed in the stooling of the plant. These are taken in early September and a row of sixteen to twenty-four plants grown. These plants, it will be understood, are only transplanted parts of the same individual. From such propagation the character of the individual can be judged better and a more nearly correct idea can be obtained of the yielding capacity of the plant as well as of other characters.

2. Inbred seed is sown carefully in sterilized soil and the seedlings transplanted in rows in field plats as above described, in order to test the transmission of the characters for which the plants were selected.

3. As soon as sufficient seed can be obtained, plats are sown broadcast in the usual way in order to test the yield under ordinary field conditions.

4. As soon as a variety is known or believed to be valuable, isolated plats are planted from inbred seed in order to obtain seed for planting larger areas that will finally give sufficient quantities of seed for distribution.

139. Desirable types of improved timothies. — The main object sought in breeding timothy is to secure varieties that will give increased hay yield. Hopkins also developed an early strain that could be harvested ten days earlier than the ordinary, and which on account of its earliness did not cross much with other strains. He also endeavored to secure a variety that would withstand heavy pasturing, using as the basis a plant that had survived several years in a closely grazed field. Another type was distinguished by the fact that its stems remained green when the seed was ripe, producing presumably a straw with greater feeding value.

Webber at the Cornell Experiment Station has sought

to select early, medium and late varieties, each with the following combination of characters : —

1. Highest yield; 2. tall growth; 3. good stooling capacity; 4. culms numerous and dense; 5. erect, without tendency to lodge; 6. numerous large leaves; 7. culms leafy to near the top; 8. tendency to remain green late; 9. rust resistance in high degree; 10. heads medium sized and bearing abundant good seed.

140. Comparison of vegetative and seed progeny.— When timothy is propagated vegetatively, the progeny are identical, at least in the great majority of cases. When, however, the seed of a single plant is sown, the offspring show considerable diversity. Webber has compared the average yield of selected plants with that of their descendants grown both clonally or vegetatively and from seed. In the latter case some of the plants were grown from open-fertilized and others from self-fertilized seed. The average yield to the plant for all types tested was as follows: original plants, 9.307 ounces; clons or vegetative offspring, 8.769 ounces; open-fertilized seed 6.963 ounces; self-fertilized seed, 5.243 ounces. These data seem to indicate that self-fertilization tends to reduce vigor.

In another series of investigations the yield of clonal individuals was compared to that of seedlings from the same parent. In all cases the seed-propagated plant yielded less than the corresponding clon. A comparison of the average yields, however, shows that as the yield of the clons of an individual was high or low, so was its corresponding progeny produced from inbred seed. The increase in yield, however, from the lowest to the highest was relatively much less in the seed-propagated plants than in the clons.

141. Field trials with improved strains. — At the Cornell Experiment Station 17 improved strains were compared in field plots with commercial timothy. In the first season, 1910, all but three of the selected strains outyielded the check plots grown from commercial seed; the second season, 1911, all of the selected strains outyielded the checks. The data secured were thus summarized : —

	1910	1911
Average yield (17 new sorts)	7451 lb. an acre	7153 lb. an acre
Average yield (commercial seed)	6600 lb. an acre	4091 lb. an acre
Average increase . . .	851 lb. an acre	3062 lb. an acre

CHAPTER VIII

BLUE–GRASSES, MEADOW–GRASSES AND REDTOP

ALL the different species called blue-grass, and most of those called meadow-grass, belong to the genus Poa, for which some early writers used the English equivalent *poe*, now practically obsolete. All of the cultivated poas are much alike agriculturally, being especially useful for pastures.

Redtop and related species of bent-grass (Agrostis) are botanically quite remote from the Poas, but agriculturally very similar. Redtop itself is perhaps equally valuable for pasturage and for hay.

THE BLUE-GRASSES

142. Kentucky blue-grass (*Poa pratensis*). — Kentucky blue-grass is also known as June-grass, or simply as blue-grass. It has been called smooth-stalked meadow-grass to distinguish it from rough-stalked meadow-grass (*Poa trivialis*). In Virginia it was formerly known as greensward. The name of Kentucky is used as a prefix partly because of the famous blue-grass lands of that state, and partly to distinguish it from Canada blue-grass. The narrow-leaved variety of blue-grass was formerly known as " bird grass."

143. Botany. — *Poa pratensis*, in its ordinary cultivated form, is quite certainly not native to North America. Endemic varieties do occur, however, from Alaska south-

154

ward to British Columbia, in Labrador, and probably on the coast of New England. The Alaska and Labrador forms are apparently distinct from any Old World varieties, but have not received distinctive names. A dwarf form on the New England seacoast is apparently identical with var. *costata* Hartm. found on European seacoasts.

European botanists have described many varieties, as the species group is highly variable. Even the cultivated forms occurring in America, which consist wholly or mainly of the typical form and of the narrow-leaved variety *angustifolia*, give by selection a long series of distinguishable strains. There are possibilities in some of these forms of Kentucky blue-grass that may in the future warrant their selection and culture for special purposes.

FIG. 12. — Kentucky blue-grass (*Poa pratensis*). a, spikelet; b, lemma showing attached tuft of hairs.

In the Old World, *Poa pratensis* is native over practically all of Europe, the northern half of Asia and in the mountains of Algeria and Morocco.

144. Adaptations. — Kentucky blue-grass is adapted primarily to temperate regions of relatively high humidity, but in the arid regions succeeds well under irrigation. It is markedly resistant to cold, never freezing out in the most severe winter weather. During summer heat, however, its growth languishes and, even with abundant moisture, shows little vigor during the hot weather of July and August. Its area of usefulness extends farther south than that of timothy, as it survives hot summer weather and makes good pasturage in the fall and spring. It begins growth in the spring earlier than most grasses, and continues to grow as late into the fall as any other grass.

FIG. 13. — A spikelet and florets of Kentucky blue-grass. **a**, spikelet as it appears at maturity; **b**, the same having the florets spread apart, showing jointed rachilla; **c**, back view of a floret, showing the lemma (1); **d**, front view of the floret, showing the edges of the lemma (1), the palet (2) and the rachilla segment (3); **e**, the grain or kernel.

Blue-grass prefers well-drained loams or clay loams, particularly such as are rich in humus. Southward it is especially abundant on limestone soils, where it often grows to the exclusion of other species. The famous blue-grass regions of Kentucky and Virginia are of limestone origin. On poor soils it is never abundant, giving way to other grasses like red-top and Canada blue-grass.

Spillman has pointed out that the distribution of blue-grass in the East closely corresponds with that of the glaciated soils and that southward of this area it is confined almost wholly to limestone soils.

Blue-grass will endure fairly wet soils but not so well

as redtop. It has but little endurance to drought, but even in semi-arid regions, where it is normally burnt brown for two months or more, it promptly recovers with the fall rains.

It is only fairly well adapted to growing in shade, not being nearly equal in this respect to orchard-grass or red fescue.

145. Importance. — Kentucky blue-grass is of relatively small importance in Europe, but in North America it is by far the most important pasture grass and second among grasses in total value only to timothy. In the timothy region, all of the best pastures are wholly or primarily blue-grass, and it is likewise the commonest lawn grass in the same area.

It is difficult to find a satisfactory explanation for the great importance of this grass and of timothy in America. About all that can be said is that these two grasses are much better adapted to the climatic conditions of cold winters and hot, rather dry summers than are any other European grasses used for the same purposes.

Kentucky blue-grass differs from most humid region grasses in that the old dried or half-dried herbage is readily eaten by animals, in this respect resembling some of the grasses native to arid regions. Late fall or winter pasturage may thus be secured by permitting the grass to make considerable growth in the fall.

146. Characteristics. — Kentucky blue-grass grows but slowly at first, and even on lawns where it is planted thickly, a good sod is not formed until the second year. It produces abundant short rootstocks, which finally develop into upright shoots. The blossoms appear earlier than most other grasses, and blue-grass is peculiar in that it blooms but once a year, no matter how favorable the conditions may be after cutting. The plants are very long-lived and under favorable conditions there seems to be no limit to the time endurance of a blue-grass pasture. In the humid region west of the Cascade Mountains in Oregon, Washington and British Columbia, blue-grass is rather troublesome as a weed, especially in berry patches and similar places that cannot be plowed.

The grass is very palatable to all classes of live stock, much more so than any other grass so capable of maintaining itself. It is distinctly exceeded in palatability only by smooth brome-grass.

At the Kansas Experiment Station the roots of blue-grass on an old sod were found to penetrate to a depth of four feet, but there were comparatively few below 18 inches. They are densest in the top six inches.

147. Culture. — Probably 90 per cent of the blue-grass pastures in America have developed spontaneously. On most farms the untillable land is left for pasture, and in the timothy region this is eventually composed mainly of blue-grass with more or less white clover and redtop. On the best blue-grass soils, however, the returns are profitable enough so that large areas of tillable land are kept permanently in pasture.

No definite systems have yet become established for using blue-grass in rotations, primarily because blue-grass pastures improve with age, at least for several years.

Where sown, the seed is best planted in fall. A common method is to sow it with timothy and clover, sowing the seed in fall with the timothy. After two years in clover and timothy for hay, the land is then pastured and the blue-grass finally occupies the land as the timothy disappears. Blue-grass sown in this way adds a little bottom grass to the hay crop of timothy and clover.

The amount of seed to use per acre, if sown alone, is not very definite, due partly to the small extent to which this grass is sown and partly to its very uncertain quality. Werner recommends 20 pounds per acre; Stebler and Schröter 17½ pounds; Spillman 25 to 30 pounds. Hunt says 40 pounds is the usual rate, but that half this amount of good seed would probably suffice. On lawns much greater quantities are desirable, four bushels being the rate commonly advised.

148. Fertilizers. — Blue-grass yields so little, even at its maximum, that but few fertilizer experiments have been conducted on pastures or meadows. Where it is grown on lawns, however, abundant experience shows that blue-grass responds markedly to lime and to nitrogen fertilizers.

At the Massachusetts Experiment Station Kentucky blue-grass top-dressed annually for 5 years with nitrate of soda was found to be much subject to rust and otherwise unsatisfactory. Another plot top-dressed with potash salts and basic slag meal in addition to nitrate of soda produced far heavier and more satisfactory crops.

As shown in the accompanying table, the largest increases were secured by the use of heavy applications of manure, or practically the same by using a complete fertilizer. Nitrate of soda alone had but little effect, and this also true of muriate of potash. Acid phosphate alone gave the best results of any single fertilizing element. The results of the three combined apparently increased the effectiveness of each. Apparently the most far-reaching tests of fertilizers to determine the effect on yield of hay are those of Morrow and Hunt.

TABLE SHOWING THE RESULTS SECURED FROM FERTILIZING
KENTUCKY BLUE-GRASS AT THE ILLINOIS EXPERIMENT
STATION. (MORROW AND HUNT)

PLATE	KIND OF FERTILIZER BOTH SEASONS	QUANTITY OF FERTILIZER USED TO THE ACRE, LB.	YIELD OF FIELD-CURED HAY TO THE ACRE, 1889, LB.	YIELD OF FIELD-CURED HAY TO THE ACRE, 1890, LB.	YIELD OF FIELD-CURED HAY TO THE ACRE, AVERAGE, LB.	INCREASE DUE TO FERTILIZERS, LB.	INCREASE DUE TO FERTILIZERS, PER CENT
1	Horse manure [1]	12 loads	2,340	3,180	2,760	1,165	73
2	None	—	1,220	2,100	1,660	—	—
3	Cattle tankage	500 lb.	1,600	2,400	2,000	405	25
4	Superphosphate	500 lb.	1,880	2,200	2,040	445	27
5	None	—	1,080	2,040	1,560	—	—
6	Horse manure [2]	13 loads	2,160	2,460	2,310	715	45
7	Superphosphate	500 lb.					
	Muriate of potash [3]	200 lb.	2,280	3,060	2,670	1,075	67
	Nitrate of soda	200 lb.					
8	None	—	720	2,000	1,560	—	—
9	Muriate of potash [3]	200 lb.	960	2,320	1,640	45	3
10	Nitrate of soda	200 lb.	1,040	2,340	1,690	95	6
11	Gypsum	500 lb.	780	2,060	1,420	—	—

149. Yields of hay. — Blue-grass is too small to give
large yields of hay and is seldom employed for such purpose, excepting where it comes in naturally.   The hay is
considered to be of good quality, but not equal to timothy.

Yields in pounds to the acre have been reported by experiment stations as follows: Ohio, 2187, 6-year average;
Kansas, 1830, 2-year average; Michigan (Upper Peninsula), 3280; Guelph, Ontario, 3160, 7-year average;
Utah, 1060; Lacombe, Alberta, 1724, 2-year average.

At the Illinois Experiment Station Kentucky blue-grass
gave a yield of 2508 pounds dry matter to the acre when

[1] 24,320 lb. in 1890.   [2] 21,880 lb. in 1890.   [3] Sulfate of potash in 1890.

the seeds were in the milk stage, and 2907 pounds when the seeds were ripe.

In Europe yields ranging from 3500 to 6250 pounds an acre are reported, but most of these are based on very small plots.

Irrigated blue-grass at the Iowa Experiment Station yielded 15,160 pounds green matter, and non-irrigated 10,360, the water contents of the grass being, respectively, 67 and 60 per cent.

150. Seed-production. — Commercial seed of Kentucky blue-grass is gathered mainly in the blue-grass region of Kentucky, especially the counties of Bourbon, Fayette and Clark. In recent years increasing quantities are harvested in northern Missouri and southern Iowa.

The seed is harvested from about the 10th to the 15th of June, as soon as the panicle has become yellow and the grain firm. Where a large acreage is to be cut, however, the harvesting is begun sooner. Some of the seed is gathered by means of hand strippers, but most of it by stripping machines, of which various forms have been devised. The most efficient machines are rotary strippers in which a revolving cylinder studded with rows of nails brushes the heads against a platform and into a receptacle behind.

The stripped heads must be carefully cured in order to secure the best seed. This is commonly done in the open, preferably where the ground has a hard smooth surface. The seed is piled in long, narrow ricks, preferably not over 18 inches high, which must be frequently turned to accelerate curing and to prevent heating. During the first few days each rick should be turned at least three times a day. The viability of the seed is greatly affected by the care used in curing, and lack of

M

care in this process more than anything else injures the quality of the seed. Pieters and Brown found that freshly gathered seed when put in ricks would heat to a temperature of 130 to 140 degrees in less than 16 hours, and that this temperature would entirely destroy the vitality in 16 hours or less.

The seed is mostly cleaned at warehouses with special cleaning machinery. The yield averages about 15 bushels per acre, and 25 bushels is the maximum.

FIG. 14. — Mixture of seeds of Kentucky blue-grass (a) and Canada blue-grass (b). The Kentucky blue-grass seeds are broadest at the center, pointed and have a distinct ridge on each side. Canada blue-grass seed are mostly broadest near one end, blunt and smooth on the sides.

At the Kentucky Experiment Station, seeds were gathered every day or two in June from the time the first ripened. Germination tests gave poorer results for those gathered very early and very late, the best being those harvested between June 14 and June 25.

151. Seed. — Kentucky blue-grass seed is frequently adulterated with the cheaper Canada blue-grass (Fig. 14). This is always an adulteration, as the former matures several weeks before the latter. Pure Kentucky blue-grass is brownish-straw in color, in the bulk considerably darker than Canada blue-grass seed. The percentage of chaff varies greatly, according to the methods of cleaning used, but the best seed has 10 to 20 per cent of chaff.

The purity of commercial seed is commonly 70–80 and rarely 85 per cent. The viability may reach 80–90, but usually is only 65–80 per cent. In some cases very fresh seeds refuse to germinate. The seeds begin to sprout under favorable conditions in 9 or 10 days, but many require a longer time, up to 28 days. Light has no effect on germination, but rapid alternation of temperatures is necessary for the best results.

The legal weight of a bushel is 14 pounds, but the weight varies from 14 to 28 pounds. One pound contains, according to different authorities, 2,400,000 seeds (Stebler); 1,860,000 (Hunter); 2,185,000 (Hunt); 3,888,000 (Lawson).

Among the objectionable weed seeds that may occur in Kentucky blue-grass are buckhorn, yellow dock, and if adulterated with Canada blue-grass, it may contain Canada thistle.

152. Hybrids. — Natural hybrids of *Poa pratensis* with *P. trivialis* and with *P. compressa* have been described in Europe, but both are very rare. Their parentage has not been proven by breeding, but is surmised from structural characters and the association with their supposed parents.

G. W. Oliver of the U. S. Department of Agriculture has successfully hybridized *Poa pratensis* with *P. arachnifera*, Texas blue-grass, using the pistillate plants of the latter. The hybrids show much diversity and produce but little seed due to defective stamens.

153. Canada blue-grass (*Poa compressa*). **Botany.** — Canada blue-grass, also known as Virginia blue-grass, flatstem bluegrass and wire-grass, is native to the Old World, ranging throughout temperate Europe and Asia Minor. It was found near Quebec as early as 1792 by Michaux and in 1823 by Richardson on the upper Saskatchewan. Its wide distribution at so early a date is remarkable, but it is quite certain that the grass is not native.

Typical *Poa compressa* bears 2 to 3 leaves on a culm, a panicle about 2 inches long with the spikelets 5- to 8-flowered. It produces abundant rootstocks, and forms a tough sod. The compressed culms are evenly scattered and are remarkable for remaining green long after the seeds have matured. The whole herbage is pale and glaucous.

154. Seed. — Canada blue-grass seed closely resembles that of Kentucky blue-grass, and as it is cheaper, it has been much used to adulterate the latter. As Canada thistles are often present in fields of Canada blue-grass, the presence of the prickles of the thistles is sometimes used to identify the seed, but neither this nor the paler color of the seed is wholly reliable. The best character to distinguish the two seeds is the less prominent veins of the lemma in the Canada blue-grass (Fig. 14). The seed weighs 14 to 24 pounds to the bushel.

The seed is much cheaper than Kentucky blue-grass seed and much more viable as a rule, the average germination being about 85 per cent. The seed is produced mainly in Ontario and about 650,000 pounds a year were imported into the United States up to 1909.

155. Culture. — In Ontario, where Canada blue-grass is most abundant, this grass is seldom sown as it usually appears spontaneously. It is often plentiful enough in wheat stubble so that good fall pasturage is afforded. Such stands are often left either to be cut for hay or for seed.

The yield of hay is not heavy, usually about 1 ton and never more than 1½ tons, but it bears an excellent reputa-

PLATE I. — PANICLES OF CANADA BLUE-GRASS (LEFT) AND
KENTUCKY BLUE-GRASS (RIGHT).

tion as horse feed, and commands nearly as good a price
as timothy. It is said, however, to have a tendency to
produce colic if fed in large quantities.

There is no particular difficulty in harvesting the seed
of Canada blue-grass, strippers not being required as in
the case of Kentucky blue-grass. The grass is cut when
the heads appear golden, and handled much like hay,
but it should be put into small shocks promptly, as otherwise much seed may be lost by shattering. The seed is
thrashed in an ordinary grain separator, but special screens
are necessary. Canada blue-grass is ripe when wheat is
harvested and some seed is secured when the wheat is
thrashed by using a special screen to separate it from the
chaff and trash. The average yield of seed an acre is
about 200 pounds and the maximum about 500 pounds.

Canada blue-grass is seldom sown pure, but when thus
planted about 15 pounds of seed per acre is required. On
poor rocky or clay soils Canada blue-grass will probably
give as great a return in pasturage as any single grass,
and its planting under such conditions is desirable.

156. Adaptations. — Canada blue-grass is adapted to
quite the same range of climatic conditions as Kentucky
blue-grass, but is more resistant to summer heat and to
drought. It is most abundant in eastern Canada and the
northeastern United States, but it occurs south as far as
South Carolina and central Alabama, and west to the
Pacific Coast.

Unlike Kentucky blue-grass, it is most abundant in
poor soils, whether gravels, thin soil over rock or clay.
This is probably not so much preference as inability to
cope with other grasses on good soils. It is often abundant
on the sides of cuts where the subsoil is exposed, while on
the good surface soil other grasses occur.

It is more drought resistant than Kentucky blue-grass but less well adapted to growing in moist or wet soils. It is primarily a grass of the open and does not succeed well in shade.

157. Importance. — Canada blue-grass is important from its ability to grow on poor soils and produce small crops of hay or good pasturage under conditions where other grasses will scarcely thrive. Under such conditions it is valuable and its good points are being more generally recognized. It has suffered in reputation somewhat, because its seed was used to adulterate Kentucky blue-grass and because it has generally been compared to that grass. Its main usefulness, however, is under conditions which Kentucky blue-grass will not endure.

It is primarily a pasture grass and is grazed upon by all herbivorous animals. It not only will withstand very close grazing but, on account of the stems remaining green, can be used as reserve pasturage late in the season. Cattle raisers who are familiar with Canada blue-grass consider it excellent for fattening.

At the present time Canada blue-grass is most important in Ontario and New York, but it is abundant in Pennsylvania, Virginia, Maryland and West Virginia, and is spreading on the so-called scab lands of the Columbia River Basin. In other countries, Canada blue-grass is of very little importance.

158. Texas blue-grass (*Poa arachnifera*). — Texas blue-grass is a native perennial species in southern Texas and adjacent Oklahoma. In a general way its habits are similar to Kentucky blue-grass, but the plants are larger and coarser. Unlike any other cultivated species of Poa, the plants are unisexual, that is, some are pistillate and some are staminate. The base of each lemma has a tuft of long hairs and so the seed must be gathered by stripping after the manner of Kentucky blue-grass.

Texas blue-grass has been tested at many of the experiment stations, especially in the South and as far north as Maryland. It makes rather more growth than Kentucky blue-grass, and being more bunchy in habit it does not make as satisfactory a lawn. Furthermore, the grass is not aggressive and in time is crowded out by other grasses. This peculiarity as well as the high cost of the seed has prevented any large use of Texas blue-grass, and commercial seed can be found only in small quantities.

Oliver has endeavored to combine the good qualities of Texas blue-grass and Kentucky blue-grass by hybridizing. Hybrids were easily secured by placing pollen of Kentucky blue-grass on the flowers of the female plant of Texas blue-grass. The hybrids were very diverse in appearance, most of them having rootstocks like their parents, but some were entirely without rhizomes. The variability in the leaf was also very marked, some of the forms having much broader leaves than either parent. Unfortunately, none of the numerous hybrids secured showed any better seed habits than those of Texas blue-grass, and most of them were inferior in this respect.

THE MEADOW-GRASSES

159. Fowl meadow-grass (*Poa triflora*). — This grass is also known botanically as *Poa serotina* and *Poa flava* and agriculturally as late meadow-grass and fertile meadow-grass. It is native to both Eurasia and North America, and on this continent ranges from Alaska to California, Colorado, Iowa and Pennsylvania.

Unlike the other cultivated Poas, this species is adapted to wet meadows, but does not grow in standing water.

It is intolerant to high summer heat and, therefore, does not thrive southwards. In the area to which it is adapted it has much the same requirements as redtop and is equally late in blooming.

Fowl meadow-grass was one of the early grasses to receive agricultural attention in America, being considered by Jared Eliot in 1747 as the best grass hay in eastern Massachusetts and decidedly superior to timothy. It first attracted attention on the wet meadows along the Charles River, where it appeared spontaneously and covered extensive low meadows. It was supposed to have been introduced there by water fowl, whence its common name. On suitable land old American reports give the yield as 1 to 3 tons of hay an acre, and state that it can be cut at any time from June till October.

This grass has recently been investigated at the Vermont Experiment Station. It occurs abundantly along Otter Creek on natural meadows which have never been plowed and which yield 1 to 2 tons an acre. These meadows are overflowed each year, a condition adverse to timothy and red clover, which are absent, but some redtop and *Glyceria americana* are mixed with the fowl meadow-grass.

In plot experiments on bottom land, fowl meadow-grass was found slow to start, like Kentucky blue-grass, and the grass was not fully established until the third season. In 1899 a yield of 4400 pounds hay and 136 pounds seed an acre was obtained. Late cuttings when the seed is ripe give a considerably larger yield than if cut when in bloom. The yields of timothy under the same conditions have been about 25 per cent smaller.

On account of the slow growth of fowl meadow-grass, it is advised that it be sown in mixture with other grasses, as follows: timothy, 10 pounds; alsike, 6 pounds; redtop, recleaned, 4 pounds; fowl meadow-grass, 10 pounds. The experimental plots that were sown to redtop and to timothy were nearly pure fowl meadow-grass after 3 years.

It is probable that results comparable to those secured in Vermont could be obtained in any similar lands in the northern tier of states and in Canada.

Commercial seed is grown in Europe and is generally of very poor quality. In the Vermont experiments a yield of 6 bushels an acre, weighing 114 pounds, was secured, and in one instance a small plot yielded at the rate of 7 bushels an acre.

160. Rough-stalked meadow-grass (*Poa trivialis*). — This European grass is very similar to Kentucky blue-grass, but may be distinguished by the roughness of the stalk near the panicle, rough leaves and absence of root-stocks. In Europe it is of more importance than Kentucky blue-grass, but in America has scarcely ever been cultivated and, though sparingly naturalized, has nowhere become abundant.

It is adapted to moist soils and moist climates. In England it was one of the first grasses to be cultivated. In moist mountain regions, it is often the common pasture grass. If cut for hay, a very good yield is often obtained, but the aftermath is very scant.

There is little likelihood that this grass will be found valuable in America, except perhaps in the Pacific Northwest. European authorities advise sowing 26 pounds of seed to the acre.

The commercial seed is harvested mainly in the neighborhood of Hamburg, Germany, and in Denmark. Yields as high as 400 pounds to the acre are reported.

161. Wood meadow-grass (*Poa nemoralis*). — This grass is native both to Eurasia and North America, but immensely variable. In North America, it is native from Alaska to Colorado in the mountains, and southeastward to Minnesota and Pennsylvania. The agricultural seed is, however, gathered almost wholly in Germany, and mainly from wild growing grass in woodlands. Wood meadow-grass is remarkably adapted to growing in shade and, being fine in texture, is much employed for shady lawns. It is, however, far more averse to heat than Kentucky blue-grass and rarely succeeds south of its natural range.

REDTOP

162. Names. — Redtop is so called in most of the United States, but in Pennsylvania and the South is also known as herd's-grass, which same name in the New England States is applied to timothy. In Europe it is commonly called fiorin, and in England is also known as bent-grass. Its scientific name is usually given by seedsmen as *Agrostis alba*, but sometimes *A. vulgaris*, *A. dispar* or *A. capillaris*.

163. Botany. — The botanical relationship of redtop and the numerous closely related forms is a most complex problem. Many botanists consider *Agrostis alba* and *A. vulgaris* a single species, but others hold them distinct. The character most relied upon is the ligule, this being very small in *vulgaris*, but well developed in *alba*. Numerous varieties of each have been described by European botanists. The ordinary cultivated forms of redtop are referable to *A. alba*, which is native to the Old World, occurring over most of Europe and Asia; and in Africa is found in the northern parts and in Abyssinia. It is very doubtful if it is endemic in North America. *Agrostis vulgaris* is, however, certainly native to North America, one form being abundant in the coastal lands of New England and known as " Rhode Island Bent."

Other native American varieties are *aristata* which occurs from Maine to Virginia and differs by having an awn rising from near the base of the lemma; and *maritima* which has long, decumbent, rooting stems, occurring along the coast from Newfoundland to Delaware.

The cultivated varieties are only three; namely, common redtop, which is typical *Agrostis alba* L.; Rhode Island Bent, which is the native American form of *Agrostis vulgaris* Withering; and Creeping Bent of Europe, commonly sold as *Agrostis stolonifera*, but it is not the plant so named by Linnæus.

164. Agricultural history. — Redtop was first brought into prominence by Dr. William Richardson in Ireland in 1807, though apparently this was not its first cultivation, as Vianne states that it was grown in France in 1761. It was early introduced into the United States, but no record before 1807 has been found.

165. Adaptations. — Redtop has probably a wider range of adaptation to climatic and soil conditions than any other cultivated grass. It succeeds well over most of the United States except the drier regions and the extreme South. In resistance to cold it is at least equal to timothy, and it withstands summer heat much better. At Copper Center, Alaska, it matures seed.

It thrives best on moist or wet soils, and will even grow vigorously in the bottom of shallow ponds, which later become dry. When thus growing aquatically, the leaf blades float on the surface and the grass is not readily recognized. Provided moisture is abundant, it does not show marked preference for soil types, but does best in clay loams and loams. Notwithstanding its marked adaptation to wet land, it will withstand considerable drought and on poor uplands, even if somewhat sandy, will thrive better than most other grasses.

It is not well adapted to shade, and is rarely found in such situations.

166. Characteristics. — Redtop, if grown isolated, makes tufts 1 to 3 feet in diameter, usually about 30 inches high, but sometimes 3½ feet. The vigorous rootstocks are shallow and mostly 2 to 6 inches long. These enable redtop to make a dense turf even in pure cultures. If kept closely mown the leaves become much finer, and a very satisfactory lawn results. Wherever the grass is thin, the rootstocks promptly become more vigorous and bear broader leaves.

The grass blooms somewhat later than timothy, so that mixtures of the two cut when timothy is in bloom, rarely show any panicles of redtop.

On account of its characteristics, redtop is perhaps better adapted to pasturing than for hay. It is a common element of all northern pastures, but most abundant where the ground is wet or poor. In pasturing experiments, cattle usually show preference to all other cultivated grasses over redtop.

167. Importance. — Redtop is probably the third or fourth most important perennial grass in America, being exceeded by timothy, Kentucky blue-grass and perhaps Bermuda. It makes up more or less of the pasturage over the whole area to which it is adapted, especially on wet and on non-calcareous soils. As a hay crop it is most important in New England, where it comprises most of the 1,100,999 acres of "other tame or cultivated grasses."

On the poor clayey soils in southern Illinois it succeeds better than any other similar grass.

168. Variability. — Cultivated redtop is very variable and many strikingly different individuals can readily be selected. The leaves may be very narrow or broad, dark bluish green or pale green in color; the panicles large or small, purple or green; the rootstocks very abundant and vigorous, or few, or even wanting. In recent times some attention has been given to the selection of improved strains, but none of these have yet become agriculturally established.

169. Regional strains. — Commercial seed is produced only in the United States and in Germany. Stebler and Volkart report experiments in Switzerland, in which the German strain showed far greater ability than the American to maintain itself. The American strain almost disappeared after 7 years, while the German strain increased markedly and still held its own after 9 years.

170. Culture. — Redtop, like Kentucky blue-grass, is such an aggressive grass that it usually comes in naturally where once established. It is rarely sown alone and usually but a small proportion of seed is included in mixtures. There is little accurate information available as to rates of seeding when sown alone, different writers recommending from 6 to 50 pounds, but not always specifying the quality. Of good " recleaned " seed 10 pounds per acre should be ample, and a correspondingly larger amount if of inferior grades. It may be sown in the same manner as timothy. Stebler and Volkart recommend for Switzerland 14 pounds per acre, germinating 72 per cent.

Redtop is also an exceedingly good grass for lawns if sown thickly and kept closely mowed, under which conditions the leaves are fine and the turf dense.

171. Yield of hay. — The yields of redtop hay on wet lands are usually better than those of any other hay grass. It is, however, much better used in mixture, especially with timothy and alsike. If grown alone the return is as a rule less than that of timothy. American experiment stations have reported yields in pounds to the acre as follows: Ohio, 5634; Kansas, 3399; Illinois, 3600; Virginia (Arlington Farm), 3200; Michigan (Upper Peninsula), 3493; Ontario (Guelph), 5580; North Carolina, 2940.

Vianne in France records hay yields of 6290 pounds to the acre; Sinclair in England of 7600 pounds from the first cutting and 2640 pounds from the second; Nielsen and Lindhard in Denmark secured as the average of 7 plot trials 3000 pounds the first year, 2980 pounds the second year, 2200 pounds the third year.

Fig. 15. — Seeds of redtop representing the "fancy" grade of the trade. **a**, different views of seeds having the white, papery, inner chaff; **b**, two views of a grain, or kernel, with the inner chaff removed; **c**, the same, nearly natural size.

172. Seed-production. — Commercial redtop seed is grown mainly in southern Illinois. The seed was formerly harvested by cutting the crop with a mowing machine, curing thoroughly and then thrashing. In recent years rotary strippers, such as are used for Kentucky blue-grass, have been employed. After the seed is thus stripped, the crop is cut for hay and sometimes is thrashed to secure the seed left by the strippers.

The recleaning of the seed and its separation into grades is done by factories with special cleaning machines.

The annual yield in Illinois has been estimated as 700,000 pounds from 50,000 acres.

173. Seed. — Commercial seed of redtop occurs in three grades: 1. "Fancy," "choice" or "recleaned"; 2. "Unhulled"; and 3. "Chaff" seed. "Recleaned" seed consists of free grains and those covered with the inner silvery chaff. "Unhulled" seed is that which is still inclosed in the outer glumes. "Chaff" is mainly the empty scales and fine rubbish, with but a small percentage of good seed.

Recleaned or fancy seed should have a purity of 95–98 per cent, and a similar percentage of viability. The germination remains good for several years. It is sometimes adulterated

FIG. 16. — Chaff of redtop seed. a, whole spikelets usually devoid of seed in "chaffy" grades; b, separated scales of the same; a and b represent the outer chaff of the seed. (Enlarged.)

with timothy seed. Among the common weed seeds present as impurities are oxeye daisy and buckhorn.

The legal weight to the bushel is 14 pounds, but the actual weight ranges from 12 to 40 pounds. The number of seeds to one pound varies with the quality. Thus, it is given as 4,135,900 by the Illinois Experiment Station; 6,400,000 by the North Carolina Experiment Station; and 7,800,000 by Hunt, quoting from Lawson. Stebler gives the number as 603,000, evidently an error.

CHAPTER IX

ORCHARD-GRASS, TALL OAT-GRASS AND BROME-GRASSES

TIMOTHY is to such preponderating extent the most important hay grass in America that other valuable sorts have been relatively much neglected. The species discussed here have somewhat different adaptations than timothy, and hence are potentially important in regions where timothy does not thrive well. Orchard-grass and tall oat-grass are well adapted to a broad belt south of the area in which timothy succeeds best. Brome-grass is especially valuable in temperate regions of small rainfall.

ORCHARD-GRASS

174. Description. — Orchard-grass, in England commonly called cock's-foot or rough cock's-foot, is a long-lived, perennial grass forming dense circular tufts which may become a foot or more in diameter. It is a typical bunch grass, producing no stolons, and hence never forms a complete sod. The peculiar inflorescence is characteristic and cannot be mistaken for any other cultivated grass.

175. Botany. — Orchard-grass (*Dactylis glomerata*) is native throughout Europe excepting the northernmost portions, much of the northern half of Asia, and in Africa in the mountains of Algeria and in Madeira and the Canaries. Botanists have distinguished a considerable number of varieties. Among the more noteworthy are *hispanica*, which has the branches of the panicle not

stalked but flower-bearing to the base; *maritima*, with
the panicle dark violet; *pendula*, with a looser, somewhat
drooping panicle; *abbreviata*, with a short compact panicle;
and *ciliata*, which
differs from all the
above in having hairy
sheaths and lemmas.

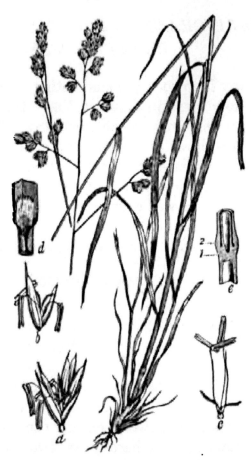

Very closely related
species are *Dactylis
aschersoniana*, which
has creeping root-
stocks and mostly
6-flowered spikelets,
and *Dactylis altaica*.

None of these have
become agricultural
grasses, but variety
pendula was at one
time supplied by Vil-
morin in France.

**176. Agricultural
history.** — Orchard-
grass was cultivated
in Virginia before
1760, in which year
seed was sent to Eng-
land. Its culture in
continental Europe be-
gan about the begin-
ning of the nine-

Fig. 17. — Orchard-grass (*Dactylis
glomerata*). a, spikelet; b, floret; c, stamens and pistil; d, ligule; e, section of
node.

teenth century and became important by 1850. At
the present time it is cultivated in nearly all temperate regions.

177. Climatic adaptations. — While orchard-grass is strictly a temperate grass, it will withstand a greater quantity of heat than timothy, and is also more easily injured by winter cold. In the United States, it is cultivated more abundantly southward than northward. This distribution is due partly to competition with timothy and partly from the fact that fall-sown stands of orchard-grass are uncertain. This uncertainty has been ascribed to late frosts rather than winter cold, but the evidence is not satisfactory. Orchard-grass begins its growth in spring much earlier than most grasses, which is one reason why the late spring frosts are injurious.

At Copper Center, Alaska, it was entirely winter-killed, while a considerable percentage of timothy survived.

At Fort Vermilion, Alberta, orchard-grass planted in spring was completely killed the succeeding winter when the minimum reached was 23° below zero Fahrenheit.

178. Soil preferences. — While orchard-grass will grow in all types of soils, it ordinarily does not succeed well in sands or muck. It is best adapted to clays or clay loams. It is not averse to wet soils, but prefers a moderate amount of moisture. Fair success can be had when the rainfall is rather scanty, as it is somewhat more resistant to drought than is timothy.

179. Adaptation to shade. — Orchard-grass succeeds so well in shady places that this peculiarity has given rise to one of its common names. Its adaptation to shade has been ascribed as due partly to its great leafiness and partly to its early growth before the trees become leafy. However, it succeeds apparently as well in the shade of evergreens as of deciduous trees.

Stebler in Switzerland shaded artificially one portion of a field sown to a mixture of grasses and determined each year the percentage of each grass. The percentage of orchard-grass each year was as follows : —

	1903	1904	1905	1906	1907	1908
Not shaded	0.5	6.6	17.6	21.8	23.3	10.0
Shaded	1.7	21.1	34.4	46.3	40.9	37.8

The percentage increase of the orchard-grass due to the gradual disappearance of the other grasses was more marked in the shaded than in the unshaded area.

180. Variability. — Orchard-grass is exceedingly variable, not less so than timothy. Numerous varieties can easily be selected anywhere from thin fields and from the roadsides. Cross-pollination is the rule so that such individual plants usually give rise to diverse progeny. There can be no question that pure strains much superior to the ordinary mixed progeny can easily be isolated. It is doubtful, however, if the importance of this grass in the United States is sufficient to justify selection and the care necessary to keep strains pure.

181. Advantages and disadvantages. — To illustrate the strong and weak points of orchard-grass it may be compared with timothy. Orchard-grass is better adapted to conditions southward and less so to those northward; it is less well suited to being grown in pure cultures, owing to its bunchy habit; it can be cut for hay much earlier; it becomes woody after full bloom much more rapidly and markedly; the cost of seed per acre is about five times as large; the spring growth is more abundant and much earlier; the aftermath is much greater, often producing a second crop of hay; the plants are more persistent both in meadows and pastures.

In average yield of hay and in feeding value, there probably is but little difference, but the market preference in America is strongly in favor of timothy.

182. Importance. — Orchard-grass is probably fourth or fifth in importance among cultivated perennial hay grasses in America. As a hay grass it should be second or third in importance, as southward it is much better adapted than timothy, and should be more generally employed, especially in mixtures.

At present, orchard-grass is most important in Kentucky, southern Indiana, Iowa, North Carolina, Virginia, West Virginia, Maryland and western Oregon.

The relative importance of orchard-grass is much higher in Europe than in America.

183. Seeding of orchard-grass. — Seed may be sown both in the fall and in very early spring. If sown in the fall, early seedings are preferable as this much lessens the danger of winter-killing. In the seed-growing sections, it is the common practice to sow the grass in February in fall-sown wheat, and it is often sown at the same time on ground which has been in corn during the previous season. It may also be sown with spring oats. Whether sown in fall or in spring, the first year's growth rarely yields a crop of hay, but can be utilized only as pasturage. On this account, as well as the danger of winter-killing, spring seedings are in general to be preferred.

When planting for a seed crop, thin seeding is desirable, and for this purpose one bushel of seed, which weighs about 14 pounds, is commonly used. If planted for hay, double this quantity is very satisfactory as the plants are thicker and the hay less coarse. The seed does not feed well through a drill and so is sown by hand or with a wheelbarrow or other type of seeder. Very shallow covering of the seed apparently gives the best results, and sometimes it is broadcasted with subsequent harrowing.

For Ohio Williams recommends 20 pounds per acre for hay, and 12 to 20 pounds if for seed production.

Werner recommends 35 pounds in Germany, and Stebler the same amount in Switzerland.

184. Life history. — If sown in spring orchard-grass does not come to bloom the first season. Its development is very slow as compared to other grasses. In mixtures it may not bloom till the third season.

Orchard-grass is very long-lived and persists indefinitely when once planted. Individual plants are known to live eight years and they will probably live much longer.

Where orchard-grass seed-production is carried on, fields are usually allowed to lay five to seven years.

185. Harvesting for hay. — Orchard-grass should be cut for hay as soon as it reaches full bloom. If permitted to stand longer, the stems become much more woody. Its period of maturity is usually three weeks to a month earlier than that of timothy. This earlier date of harvesting is advantageous in the case of land badly infested with oxeye daisy and fleabane, as these weeds have not ripened their seed at the time orchard-grass hay is cut, and consequently the use of orchard-grass tends to free the land of these weeds.

After the first crop of hay has been harvested orchard-grass produces a rapid and abundant second growth, which consists largely of leaves, the culms being comparatively few. This second growth is much greater than that of any other hay grass adapted to temperate conditions. The yield of hay from the second crop is usually smaller than the first.

Even when the first crop is cut for seed, the second

growth often makes a fair crop of hay by the end of August or early September.

186. Yields of hay. — While orchard-grass is best suited for sowing in mixture, it will when seeded alone usually yield about as well as timothy.

The yield of dry matter at the Illinois Experiment Station was found to be 2642 pounds an acre when in full bloom and 3232 when the seeds were in the milk.

Yields in pounds per acre have been reported by American experiment stations as follows: Ohio, 2197; Kansas, 2809; Illinois, 2800; Michigan, 2080; Idaho, 5280; Arlington Farm, Virginia, 2880; North Carolina, 1554; Arkansas, 3188.

In Europe yields have been reported as follows: Sinclair in England, 11,685 pounds; Pinckert in Germany, 3520 pounds; Vianne in France, 15,570 pounds.

Orchard-grass was grown continuously on two plots at the Michigan Experiment Station from 1897 to 1905. The yield by acre in pounds on the two plots was as follows: —

YEAR	1897	1898	1899	1900	1901	1902	1903	1904	1905
Yields . . . . {	3000	258	1750	2760	2150	1500	2230	2250	1640
	3000	183	2250	3620	2900	2150	2970	2330	2620

After plowing up the sod in 1906, the plots were cropped to corn in 1906, oats in 1907 and wheat in 1908. Heavier yields were secured on these plots than on plots that had been in fallow continuously or on others which had been planted to regular rotations mostly including clover. The yield of the orchard-grass for the last seven years was quite uniform.

For yields under irrigation see Par. 41.

187. Harvesting orchard-grass for seed. — In the United States most of the seed is grown in the counties of Jefferson, Oldham and Shelby in Kentucky, Clark County, Indiana, Clinton and Highland Counties, Ohio, and in northern Virginia. The average yield an acre, as reported by the better farmers, is ten to twelve bushels. Harvesting usually begins about the middle of June, the crop being ready for cutting as soon as the seeds become straw-colored. This is easily detected by bending the heads in the palm of the hand, and if some of the seeds shatter out, it is ready to cut. The grass is practically always harvested with an ordinary grain binder, care being taken to make small bundles so as to facilitate rapid curing. The bundles are commonly placed three in a shock, which is tied with two bands of straw so as to hold the bundles firmly and prevent the seed from shattering. Depending on the weather, the shocks are left in the field up to four weeks before they are cured thoroughly. Thrashing usually takes place directly from the field. As a rule the grass is cut high so as to avoid low-growing weeds, and also because the undergrowth is thus left for subsequent pasturing or to be cut as hay. The thrashing is done with an ordinary grain thrasher, but using special riddles and but little wind.

188. Weeds. — The most troublesome weeds in orchard-grass fields in the states where the seed is mainly grown are whiteweed (*Erigeron strigosus* and *E. annuus*); sorrel (*Rumex acetosella*); oxeye daisy (*Chrysanthemum Leucanthemum*); milfoil (*Achillœa Millefolium*); and buckhorn (*Plantago lanceolata*).

Some seed growers cut out these weeds with a hoe before the crop of orchard-grass is harvested, but this method is expensive. Spraying with weed-killing chemicals has been used to a small extent, but is not very satisfactory.

A much better method is to use sheep to keep the weeds down. These animals may be turned in the field as soon as the grass begins to grow in spring, and allowed to remain until harvest time, but many growers remove them in early May. As the orchard-grass matures, the sheep eat but little of it, but graze principally on the weeds, especially whiteweed. They do very little damage to the grass when it is dry but should be removed during wet weather. Even when sheep stampede through a field nearly ripe but few culms are broken. This is due to the bunching habit of the orchard-grass which leaves room between the plants for the feet of the sheep, and the stout stems are seldom injured. Cattle are not nearly as satisfactory as sheep, for they trample down too much of the grass.

189. Seed. — Orchard-grass seed is often adulterated with that of meadow fescue and perennial rye-grass, both of which resemble it rather closely, and both of which are much cheaper. Orchard-grass seed, however, may be readily distinguished from these two by the slightly smaller size and the awn-pointed apex of the lemma, which in both of the others is merely acute (Fig. 18).

The best quality of seed reaches a purity of 95–98 per cent and a viability of 98–99 per cent. Germination is complete in 14 days. The seed deteriorates but little the first year, but thereafter more rapidly, so that when four years old it is worthless.

A bushel weighs from 12 to 22 pounds, the usual legal weight being 14 pounds. One pound contains, according to different authorities, 579,500 seeds (Stebler), 426,000 seeds (Hunter), 400,000 to 480,000 seeds (Hunt).

190. Sources of seed. — Commercial seed of orchard-grass is most largely grown in the United States and in New Zealand, but some seed is produced in Europe (southern France, Germany, Hungary, Holland, etc.). New Zealand seed is sometimes imported into the United States in considerable quantity. No American experiments, however, have been reported as to the relative

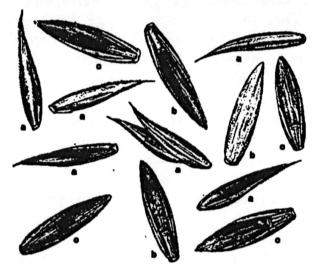

FIG. 18. — Mixture of seeds of orchard-grass (a), meadow fescue grass (b) and English rye-grass (c). The orchard-grass seeds are distinguished from the others by their slender, curved form. The meadow fescue and rye-grass seeds are distinguished by the difference in the section of the seed-cluster axis (rachilla segment) which each bears. (Enlarged.)

yield obtained from seed from different sources. In plots grown side by side in Virginia the New Zealand strain was distinctly shorter and apparently inferior by about 20 per cent.

Under Swiss conditions, Stebler reports that French seed gives the most satisfactory results, but American is scarcely inferior, though a little later; in two out of five trials the American outyielded the French strain. Seed from Switzerland, Holland and Germany gave in each case practically as good results as that from France. The New Zealand strain proved inferior to the French in six trials. It proved to be slower in growth and somewhat less winter hardy.

At three experiment stations in Denmark, tests were conducted for three years to determine the amount of hay produced from seed from different sources; namely, United States, Denmark, Germany, France, Sweden, Australia and New Zealand. The American strain was slightly superior to the European at two of the stations. The Australian and New Zealand strains showed a smaller yield by about 20 per cent.

191. Utilization of stubble and aftermath. — Among orchard-grass seed growers, there is much difference of opinion as to the utilization of the stubble and aftermath, especially as to its effect upon the next year's seed crop. A common practice is to cut the stubble and aftermath in the latter part of August and to utilize it for hay, but some farmers allow it to lie on the field as a mulch. Some farmers cut the stubble as soon as possible after seed harvest, while others believe it is best to leave both the stubble and aftermath uncut.

Pasturing the stubble and aftermath is a very common practice and if done judiciously, especially with sheep, is believed not only not to lessen the next season's crop but even to cause an increase.

192. Mixtures. — Orchard-grass, excepting for seed production, is seldom sown alone as the bunchy nature of the grass does not fully utilize the ground. One of the most satisfactory mixtures is orchard-grass, tall meadow oat-grass and alsike clover, in the following proportions: 10 pounds of orchard-grass, 20 pounds of tall meadow oat-grass, 4 pounds of alsike clover. The tall meadow oat-grass matures with the orchard-grass, and at this time a satisfactory growth of the alsike clover has also been made. On much of the area south of the Potomac and Ohio rivers, this mixture yields much more satisfactory crops than timothy and red clover.

Another mixture commonly used is orchard-grass and red clover, which is very satisfactory wherever red clover succeeds well. In this mixture, orchard-grass is sown at the usual rate and about 10 pounds of red clover used to the acre. This mixture is often used where the orchard-grass is grown mainly for seed, as the clover interferes but little with the harvesting of the seed crop, and adds greatly to the subsequent crop of hay or pasturage.

193. Pasturage value. — Orchard-grass should be a constituent of pastures wherever this grass will grow. Especially is this true on account of its ability to grow in cool weather, as it will furnish the earliest and latest pasturage in the season. Furthermore, it succeeds best under heavy grazing, and produces a continuous succession of young leaves. The most serious objection to it as a pasture grass is that, during unfavorable soil conditions, the plants are apt to be pulled out of the ground by pasturing animals. Where it forms only a portion of the pasture mixture, however, there is but little difficulty from this source.

Cattle graze upon it quite as readily as upon timothy, but prefer Kentucky blue-grass to both.

194. Feed value. — No American feeding experiments with orchard-grass hay have been reported. Judged wholly by its chemical analysis and digestibility, orchard-grass should be considerably more nutritious than timothy hay, and many farmers consider that this is the case both for horses and cows. There is considerable market prejudice against it, however, on account of its relative coarseness.

195. Value as a soil binder. — Orchard-grass is commonly recognized as exceedingly valuable to plant in places where the soil is likely to wash. Thus, planted in rills with rye as a nurse crop, it has proven very effective in preventing further washing. Its effectiveness is apparently more due to the large tussocks that it makes than to any other one character.

Orchard-grass has deeper roots than most grasses. Ten Eyck at the Kansas Experiment Station found that the root system of a large plant extended to a depth of 3½ feet. The root mass was very dense in the top 6 inches, but below 10 inches rapidly became thinner.

At the Arkansas Experiment Station the total weight of the roots was found to be equal to the tops. Fifty per cent of the roots were in the top 12 inches and 90 per cent in the top 30 inches.

196. Improvement by selection. — Orchard-grass is decidedly variable, apparently more so than timothy. The contrasting characters are easily seen when vegetatively propagated rows are grown in a nursery. Marked differences are apparent in height, coarseness, leafiness, color, earliness, number of culms, length of leaves, etc.

In recent years the study of these variations with the object of developing improved strains has received attention both in America and in Europe.

197. Pests. — Orchard-grass is but little troubled by insects or diseases. Occasionally rust is found in small quantity. A very common trouble, however, is the tip burn of the leaves, a characteristic trouble of the grass, which seems not to have been scientifically investigated.

TALL OAT-GRASS

198. Names.—Tall oat-grass (*Arrhenatherum elatius*) is known also as tall meadow oat-grass, tall oat-grass, false oat-grass, French rye-grass and, in the South, evergreen grass. The French name, fromental, has become much used in Germany and Switzerland, and is advocated by Stebler as a convenient and distinctive name for general adoption. Synonyms of the scientific name are *Arrhenatherum avenaceum* and *Avena elatior*.

199. Botany. — Tall oat-grass is native to southern Europe and northern Africa, but ranges eastward into Persia. It is quite variable, eight varieties being considered distinguishable by European botanists.

Fig. 19. — Tall oat-grass (*Arrhenatherum elatius*). **a**, spikelet; **b**, the two florets.

The most noteworthy variety is *tuberosa* which bears a number of bulbs at base like a string of small onions and is therefore called Onion Couch. This is sparingly introduced in the United States. In Europe it occurs mainly on poor pasture lands and not in fields of tall oat-grass. Under some conditions it has been found in Great Britain troublesome as a weed. Some botanists have considered that the bulbs are abnormal and produced by a parasite, but the variety breeds true to seed. Stebler and Volkart report that in small plots it yielded less than half as much hay as tall oat-grass.

Other varieties are *subhirsuta* with sparsely hairy sheaths.; *biaristata* with both florets of each spikelet bearing awns; *flavescens* with the spikelets yellow instead of pale green; and *hermaphrodita* with the spikelets sometimes 3-flowered, and all the florets perfect.

200. Agricultural history. — Tall oat-grass was advocated for culture by Kalm in Sweden in 1747. According to Schreber, however, it was first cultivated by Abbe Miroudet in France, in 1760, but Stebler and Volkart state that it was probably cultivated in southern France before that time and it was commended by Stapfer for cultivation in Switzerland in 1762. It was cultivated in Massachusetts as early as 1807 and in South Carolina in 1824.

201. Adaptations. — Tall oat-grass is adapted to about the same climatic conditions as orchard-grass; that is, it will not endure as much cold as timothy, but will withstand greater summer heat.

It is one of the most drought resistant of all cultivated grasses, being excelled in this respect only by brome-grass and western wheat-grass. Wet soils are distinctly injurious and tall oat-grass will not endure on such land. It does well under irrigation, provided the subsoil be well drained.

It thrives best on loose, deep loams and calcareous soils, but succeeds also on sandy and gravelly soils. Perhaps no other perennial grass will yield as well on very poor land. Nevertheless its yields are greatly increased by the use of fertilizers.

It does not grow well in shade, but rapidly disappears. For this reason, it should never be sown with a nurse crop, as both the thickness and the vigor of the stand is much lessened thereby. For the same reason it is injured in mixtures by any grass which shades the ground too much.

Tall oat-grass is primarily a hay grass. Frequent cuttings reduce the total yield greatly, and under pasturing the return is comparatively small.

In the Southern States tall oat-grass remains green the whole year, whence it has been called evergreen grass. It languishes, however, in midsummer in the moist region near the Gulf of Mexico.

202. Importance. — Tall oat-grass is not an important grass in America. In continental Europe it is considered one of the best grasses and is commonly grown, especially in France. In England it has never been much used. To some extent the grass is cultivated in Australia. In the United States it is mostly employed on poor or gravelly land and near the southern limit of timothy production. In experiments continued over several years at Arlington Farm, Virginia, a mixture of this grass with orchard-grass and alsike clover was found to be far more productive on relatively poor land than any other perennial grass or grass mixture. This mixture has recently been received with much favor in South Carolina, and for much of the area south of the timothy region is probably the best combination of perennial grasses for hay meadows. For this reason the grass seems destined to increase in importance.

203. Characteristics. — Tall oat-grass is a long-lived, deep-rooted perennial. It is strictly a bunch grass, all the new shoots being produced intravaginally and growing perfectly erect. The lowermost joint may, however, be elbowed, due to resistance encountered by the young shoot when developing through the old tuft. The stems grow to a height of about 4 feet, rarely 6 feet. The panicle is pyramidal, loose and pale green, more nearly resembling that of the oat than any other cultivated perennial grass. The spikelets bear two florets, the lower bearing a long, twisted and elbowed awn from its base.

In mixtures where tall oat is not shaded by other grasses, it maintains itself well for five years or even more. The hay is somewhat bitter in taste and on this and other accounts it is better grown in mixtures. At Arlington Farm, Virginia, however, horses ate pure hay of tall oatgrass readily, and most American experiment stations have reported that animals eat it well. Its supposed unpalatability is probably exaggerated and, as in similar cases, it is presumably easy to accustom animals to its taste.

204. Seeding. — Tall oat-grass, whether sown alone or in mixtures, is best sown in the spring in the North, but in the South early fall seeding is preferable. In Tennessee the best time is the latter half of September or else March and April. A well-prepared firm seed bed is most desirable. The seed is rather large and deep seeding is important, about 1 inch in moist soil and 1½ inches when dry.

European authorities recommend for one acre, if sown alone, 80 pounds of seed germinating 50 per cent; that is, about 40 pounds of viable seed.

205. Hay. — Tall oat-grass should be cut for hay promptly when it blooms, as thereafter the stems rapidly become more woody. It cures into hay more readily than most other grasses.

On rich soils it may be cut as many as three or four times in a season, but on poor soils but once or twice. The first cutting is nearly always the largest. The yield the second year is nearly always the heaviest.

European authorities have recorded the following hay yields to the acre: Pinckert, 6340 pounds secured from two cuttings; Sprengel, 8800 pounds. Karmrodt in Germany secured from the same plot in four successive years yields at the rate respectively of 6468, 15,268, 10,384 and 7524 pounds to the acre.

Yields to the acre in pounds have been reported from American experiment stations as follows: North Carolina, 2994; Louisiana, 3400; Kentucky, 8160; North Dakota, 3220; South Dakota, 2083; Ohio, 2247, 6-year average; Kansas, 2453, 4-year average; Illinois, 5480; Arlington Farm, Virginia, 3720; Michigan (Upper Peninsula), 5680; Utah, 2691; Idaho, 5760; Ontario (Guelph), 5520, 7-year average.

In general about 3 pounds of the green grass make 1 pound of hay.

206. Seed-production. — The seed of tall oat-grass is mostly grown in Europe (France, Tyrol, Switzerland, Bohemia) but some is produced in Virginia. Spillman states that at the Washington Experiment Station it shattered very readily within 24 hours after it began to ripen. On the contrary, Stebler says the growing of seed in Europe is very profitable because it yields well, is easily harvested and commands a good price. It is ready to cut for seed when the panicles turn yellowish and the grain can be broken by the finger nail. It is better, however, to cut too early than too late to avoid loss by shattering. If a binder is used in harvesting, early cutting is necessary.

The yield of seed to the acre in Europe is given by Pinckert as 880 pounds; by Walker, as 88 to 132 pounds; by Michalowski as the average of 4 years, 328 pounds; by Jung, 880 pounds, when grown on a large scale; and by Werner as 724 to 880 pounds.

Tall oat-grass is frequently infested with a smut (*Ustilago perennans*) which destroys the attacked seeds.

207. Seed. — The seed of tall oat-grass weighs 10 to 16 pounds per bushel. It loses viability quite rapidly after the first year, and by the fourth year is practically worthless. In common with other grass seeds for which there is small demand in America, seed is quite likely to be old or else mixed with old seeds.

The percentage of impurities in tall oat-grass seed is rather large, on the average 20 per cent, but the other seeds are commonly those of other grasses which occur in fields, such as orchard-grass and meadow fescue, but there is often considerable cockle (*Agrostemma githago*) present. One pound contains about 150,000 (138,000 to 159,000) seeds.

208. Mixtures. — Tall oat-grass should rarely be sown alone unless for the purpose of seed production. Among the reasons for growing it in mixtures are its bunch habit, its relative lack of palatability, the cost of the seed and the fact that it is primarily a top grass. It must not, however, be sown in mixtures containing much Italian rye-grass or other grasses which grow more rapidly and thus injure the tall oat seedlings by shading; nor should it be sown with grasses that mature distinctly earlier or later, as tall oat-grass should be cut when in bloom. It is early and blooms about 10 days sooner than red clover. European authorities recommend that only 10–20 per cent of tall oat-grass should be used in mixtures, but a larger percentage has not been found disadvantageous in America.

The best grasses and clovers for mixing with tall oat-grass are orchard-grass, meadow fescue, alsike and red clover. In the region south of the best area for timothy and red clover the so-called Arlington mixture has been found especially good, the amount indicated to be sown on one acre : —

Orchard-grass . . . . 10 pounds
Tall oat-grass . . . . 20 pounds
Alsike clover . . . . 4 pounds

BROME-GRASS

209. Names and description. — Brome-grass (*Bromus inermis*) is also called smooth brome awnless brome, Hungarian brome, Russian brome and Austrian brome.

It is a long-lived perennial grass, enduring according to Werner 12 to 13 years. Each plant produces many underground rootstocks and thus mats a foot or more in diameter are formed. Single plants under favorable conditions grow to a height of about 4 feet, and each one may possess 100 to 200 culms. The basal leaves are numerous, and the lower half of each culm may bear 5 or 6 leaves.

After two or three years it forms a dense sod and thereafter without special treatment the plants form but few culms. This characteristic makes it better suited for permanent pastures than for hay production.

210. Botany. — *Bromus inermis* is native to much of Europe and extends through Siberia to China. Botanically it is not very variable, though five or six varieties have been deemed worthy of botanical designations. Among these varieties are *pellitus* with lower leaves and sheaths hairy; *divaricatus* with triangular pyramidal panicles and small spikelets; *pauciflorus* with small 3–4-flowered spikelets; and *aristatus* with the lemma short-awned. Very closely related but perhaps distinct is *Bromus Reimanni* with short leaves and small panicles.

211. Agricultural history. — Brome-grass was first culti-vated, according to Schreber, in 1769 as a pasture grass. It is not, however, an important grass in Europe, being grown mainly in Hungary and Russia.

It was introduced into the United States prior to 1884 by the California Experi-ment Station. It

FIG. 20. — Brome-grass (*Bromus inermis*). a, spikelet; b, floret, dorsal view; c, floret, vertical view.

has met with most favor in the region west of the 95th meridian and north of latitude 36°, especially as a grass for unirrigated lands. In North and South Dakota and in the Columbia Basin brome-grass attained con-siderable prominence, but in recent years its cultiva-tion has slowly diminished. More of it has been grown in the Dakotas and in Manitoba than in any other region.

212. Adaptations. — Brome-grass is especially adapted to regions of rather low rainfall and moderate summer temperatures. High summer temperatures and humidity are both adverse. In trial plots the grass has succeeded well enough in the region of timothy and red clover, but has not attained popularity.

It prefers rich loams and clay loams, but has succeeded well in sandy soils. No other cultivated perennial grass has shown a higher degree of drought resistance.

Brome endures winter cold remarkably well and no instances of winter injury have been reported even in North Dakota. At Kenai, Alaska, it succeeds fairly well except in very moist summers.

213. Depth of roots. — Shepperd at the North Dakota Experiment Station found that one-year-old plants had roots 4 feet deep, and two-year-old plants 5½ feet. At the same station brome roots were found to be 5 to 6 feet deep when timothy roots reached only 3½ feet.

Ten Eyck at the Kansas Experiment Station found roots to a depth of 4¼ feet, at which depth solid rock prevented further penetration, but the roots had spread over the rock in a large mass.

214. Method of seeding. — In the regions where it is most grown, brome-grass is nearly always seeded in early spring on a well-prepared seed bed. Fall plowing in some places is preferable as it insures a better supply of moisture. The surface of the seed bed should be well firmed by harrowing, and rolling is also desirable.

Where the rainfall is sufficient the grass is often sown with a nurse crop — wheat, oats, barley or spelt. The grass seed does not feed well through a drill, so it is usually broadcasted after the grain has been drilled, and then covered by harrowing crosswise to the drill rows.

In regions where fall-sown timothy will succeed, brome-grass may be sown in fall either with or without wheat, or the brome-grass may be sown alone in late summer.

At the Nebraska Experiment Station in 1902 brome-grass was sown March 24, April 8 and 21, May 7 and 19, August 7 and 19, September 15, October 1 and 21. All produced good stands except the last seeding which was winter-killed.

215. Rate of seeding brome-grass. — The usual rate of seeding is 1 bushel (14 pounds) to the acre, but under favorable conditions 10 pounds is sufficient. Where only pasture is desired a double quantity of seed is often used, as a dense stand will permit of grazing sooner. At the Wisconsin Experiment Station 32 pounds to the acre gave much better results than 16 or 24 pounds, but in all cases the yield was small. The North Dakota and Nebraska Experiment Stations recommend 20 pounds to the acre.

According to Werner, brome is sown in Europe at the rate of 55 kg. to the hectare; that is, 48 pounds to the acre.

216. Time to cut for hay. — Brome-grass is usually cut for hay just after full bloom at the stage called " the purple." There is a considerable period, however, in which it may be cut with apparently little effect on the hay.

Under favorable conditions of moisture two cuttings can be obtained, the first in June or July, the second in September. The second crop produces but few culms, and the yield is much smaller.

The hay cures less readily than timothy and is more easily injured by unfavorable weather.

At the North Dakota Experiment Station brome-grass cut at three different dates, June 21, June 25 and

July 9, gave respectively 5637, 6456 and 7632 pounds to the acre green substance, or 2290, 2462 and 2802 pounds dry substance. At the first date the grass was in bloom; at the second in the milk stage; and at the third fully mature.

217. Hay. — The yield of hay from brome-grass is usually small the first year, good the second year and best the third year. Thereafter it falls off rapidly unless given special treatment. The average yield of hay is about 1½ tons to the acre, the maximum about 3½ tons. Yields to the acre have been reported from many experiment stations, as follows: Ohio, 2900 pounds in 1905, 5960 pounds in 1910; Wisconsin, 4200 pounds; Michigan (Upper Peninsula), 4295 and 3285 pounds; Nebraska, 4640 pounds in 1900, 2640 in 1903; Kansas, 6016 pounds, average for 4 years; Colorado (San Luis Valley), 3713 pounds; Idaho, 5600 pounds; Wyoming, 4400 pounds; South Dakota, third, fourth and fifth seasons, 3720, 3632 and 7680 pounds respectively; North Dakota, Fargo, 2520 pounds, and Dickinson, 2520 pounds, average for 2 years; Indian Head, Saskatchewan, average of 18 yields in 10 years, 2622 pounds; Brandon, Manitoba, average of 6 yields in 4 years, 4100 pounds.

For yield under irrigation see Par. 41.

218. Fertilizers. — But few fertilizer experiments have been made on brome-grass. Barnyard manure is nearly always helpful, if available. Manured and unmanured plots yielded respectively 2012 and 1242 pounds per acre at Dickinson, N.D., and 5500 and 3920 pounds per acre at Fargo, N.D.

At the Nebraska Experiment Station a small plot fertilized at the rate of about 6 tons of rotted horse manure and 320 pounds nitrate of soda in spring yielded the following year at the rate of 5666 pounds to the acre against 2166 for a check plot.

At the Central Experimental Farm, Ottawa, Canada, 400 pounds superphosphate to the acre gave a greatly increased yield.

219. Treatment of meadows. — In the Dakotas and adjacent Canada, brome-grass fields as a rule yield the first season nothing but a small amount of pasturage; the second year, a good crop of hay; the third year, a maximum crop; the fourth year, a decidedly diminished yield; and thereafter, but little unless special treatment is given.

In the Columbia Basin a good amount of pasture is secured the first year, the second year the grass yields but moderately if cut for hay, but bears a heavy crop of seed. The third year the hay crop is at a maximum.

Brome-grass, after the third or fourth year, falls off in yield rapidly on account of what is called a "sod-bound" condition, apparently due in part to the spreading of the grass, and in part to the increasing compactness of the soil. Loosening the soil thoroughly will renew the vigor of the grass. On loose or sandy soil harrowing with disk or spike-tooth harrow is fairly effective. On heavier soils plowing is necessary, the time depending largely on the soil moisture conditions. But little of the grass is killed by plowing. Several methods have been used: —

1. Plowing about 2 inches deep in spring, a method advocated by the Saskatchewan Experiment Farm.

2. Plowing after the hay crop is harvested, advocated by the Brandon, Manitoba, Experiment Farm.

3. Plowing in spring and seeding to oats or other grain, to which some brome seed may be added. In this way a crop of grain is secured and a full grass crop the next year.

4. Breaking the sod in fall, and sowing oats or other small grain in spring. The next season a full crop of grass is obtained.

220. Seed-production. — The seed of brome-grass is mainly grown in North and South Dakota, and in Manitoba and Saskatchewan. It is cut at the stage called "brown" when the seed is fully formed and nearly ripe. It is usually harvested with a binder, more rarely with a header and occasionally with a mowing machine. When a binder is used, the grass is cut as high as possible and the bundles then shocked for curing. The tall stubble is then cut for hay and yields about one ton per acre. Harvesting the seed with a header leaves a larger amount of the grass for hay.

The seed is thrashed with an ordinary thrashing machine, using special riddles, and with the wind shut off to prevent the seed from blowing over. The seed usually contains fragments of straw which cannot all be separated even with a fanning mill.

Seed yields average from about 250 to 350 pounds to the acre. At the Saskatchewan Experimental Farm as high as 600 pounds to the acre were secured. At the Iowa Experiment Station 300 pounds were obtained. At North Platte, Nebraska, three plots yielded respectively 157, 200 and 700 pounds to the acre, the first plot being on land previously in alfalfa.

221. Seed. — Although brome-grass seed is easily distinguished, it is sometimes adulterated with meadow fescue, perennial rye-grass and cheat. European seed sometimes contains quack-grass as an impurity, and the seeds of this are very similar to western wheat-grass, which may occur in American seed.

The best commercial brome-grass seed attains a purity

of 98–99 per cent, and a viability of 90–95 per cent. Germination tests should continue 14 days.

The seed weighs 12 to 20 pounds to the bushel. One pound contains 137,000 seeds, according to Stebler.

222. Pasture value. — Brome-grass is better adapted for pasture purposes than for hay. Under semi-arid conditions in the Northwest, brome-grass is without question the best pasture grass for cultivated lands yet discovered. Its ability to withstand drought is as great as that of alfalfa. Other characters that emphasize its pasture value, especially on sandy lands, are its sod producing habit, which enables it to withstand trampling and prevents uprooting.

Comparative tests have shown that it is one of the most palatable of all grasses, cattle grazing upon it in preference even to blue-grass. It begins to grow very early in the spring and continues growth into late fall. After frost the leaves become purplish, but the grass does not seem to lose in palatability.

At the North Dakota Experiment Station brome-grass cut five times during the season yielded 5538 pounds of green grass against 4682 pounds for timothy.

223. Mixtures. — Several mixtures with brome-grass have been employed and are especially satisfactory in that they tend to delay the sod-bound condition. Timothy has been most used in mixtures, but alfalfa, red clover, orchard-grass, slender wheat-grass and meadow fescue have also been found desirable. At the Indian Head, Saskatchewan, Experimental Farm, a mixture of brome-grass and slender wheat-grass has proven particularly desirable.

224. Variability. — Brome-grass, like most other grasses, shows a wide range of variability in desirable characteristics.   Numerous strains have been selected by Leckenby, by Evans and by Dillman of the U. S. Department of Agriculture, by Keyser of the Colorado Experiment Station and others.   As yet no pure strains have become established.

The progeny of some individuals is quite uniform; in others, very diverse.   Keyser has selected 121 distinct strains, and has recently published illustrations and notes on the most striking.   The individual plants vary in vigor, height, number of culms, amount of stooling, coarseness of stems, color of leaves and panicles, length and breadth of leaves and earliness.   For pasture purposes the most desirable type is apparently one that stools vigorously and produces an abundance of leaves.   For hay purposes, one that is relatively bunchy with tall, leafy culms is probably best.

CHAPTER X

OTHER GRASSES OF SECONDARY IMPOR-TANCE

THE grasses discussed in this chapter are all important in limited areas in America. Most of them thrive well over wide regions in which they are little or not at all used. With the increasing value and importance of grass lands in general agriculture, their greater utilization in the future scarcely admits of doubt.

MEADOW FESCUE (*Festuca elatior*)

225. Botany and history. — Meadow fescue occurs naturally over all of Europe and in much of temperate Asia. The species is not very variable, but eight or more varieties based on slight characters have been described and named by botanists. From a botanical point of view *Festuca pratensis* Hudson is considered identical with *F. elatior* Linnæus, but seedsmen use these names as the equivalents, respectively, of two cultural varieties; namely, meadow fescue or English blue-grass, and tall fescue. The former has also been known as Randall grass in the South, but this name has sometimes been applied to tall oat-grass, perhaps erroneously.

Meadow fescue was first recommended for cultivation by Kalm in Sweden in 1747.

204

226. Characteristics. — Meadow fescue is a tufted, deep-rooted, long-lived perennial. It produces an abundance of dark green leaves on sterile shoots, and comparatively few culms or fertile shoots. The sterile shoots are about 4 times as numerous as the fertile ones. The culms are not very leafy, and grow commonly to a height of 18 to 24 inches or rarely 3 feet. Although the grass possesses no rootstocks it is not bunchy, but makes a fairly good sod. If cut either for hay or for seed, it produces a good amount of aftermath. If cut early, the second crop will produce culms, but otherwise mostly leaves. It withstands pasturing very well.

Fig. 21. — Meadow fescue (*Festuca elatior*). a, spikelet.

Old fields of meadow fescue are plowed without difficulty, and the grass is as readily destroyed as timothy.

227. Adaptations. — Meadow fescue is adapted to

practically the same area as timothy. It prefers rich, moist or even wet soils, but does not succeed well in sandy land. In shady places it thrives quite as well as orchard-grass. It is better adapted for pastures than for meadows, but may be used for both purposes. The grass was early introduced in the United States and occurs spontaneously over the whole region to which it is adapted, but it seems never to be abundant under natural conditions. The grass is probably just as hardy as timothy and has succeeded as far north as Kenai, Alaska.

228. Importance. — Meadow fescue is a grass of small importance in American agriculture, except in eastern Kansas, where much seed is grown principally for export to Europe. This industry began in 1877 and has developed greatly since 1885. In 1903 the yield of seed was estimated at about 400,000 pounds. Both the yield and the prices fluctuate greatly, which has led to a larger utilization of the grass crop for hay and pasture.

In Europe the grass is much employed both in meadow and in pasture mixtures.

229. Seeding. — Meadow fescue should be sown on a well-prepared and thoroughly firmed seed bed. It may be seeded either in fall or in spring, but early fall is the usual time. Nurse crops are seldom used, as if fall sown a full crop ensues the first year. The usual rate of seeding is 10 to 15 pounds to the acre where a seed crop is desired. Heavier seedings are better for hay or for pasture, but probably reduce the seed crop. Red clover is sometimes mixed to improve the subsequent crop of hay or pasture.

In Europe the rate of seeding when sown alone is given at 40 pounds per acre by most authorities, but the grass is usually sown in mixtures.

230. Hay. — Meadow fescue should be cut for hay just as it comes into bloom, if the best quality is desired. The hay is somewhat stemmy and rather laxative. No American feeding experiments are reported, but the hay is as palatable as timothy, and stockmen consider it more fattening for cattle. It is probably too laxative to use exclusively as horse feed.

In favorable moist seasons a crop of hay can be cut after one of seed is harvested, but this second crop is mainly leaves and but few culms.

Meadows fertilized with barnyard manure remain productive a long time, in some instances as high as 17 years. It is considered better practice, however, to allow the fields to lie but 5 or 6 years.

The average yield of hay in Kansas is given at 1 to 1.5 tons to the acre, but on fields fertilized with barnyard manure, these yields may be doubled.

Acre yields have been reported from various experiment stations as follows: Ohio, 2100 pounds, average of 6 years; Kansas, 2155 pounds, average of 4 years; Illinois, 3775 pounds; Michigan (Upper Peninsula), 6070 pounds; Utah, 2200 pounds; Idaho, 5280 pounds; Arlington Farm, Virginia, 3080 pounds; Nebraska, 2400 to 3450 pounds.

At the Illinois Experiment Station the yield of dry substance was found to be 1424 pounds to the acre when in full bloom, and 1954 pounds when the blooming was completed.

European authorities give the yield of hay as ranging from 3500 pounds to 10,000 pounds to the acre.

231. Seed-production. — Meadow fescue should be cut for seed as soon as the fields assume a characteristic yellowish-brown color and the heads begin to droop from the weight of grain.   This is early in July in Kansas.   The grass is commonly cut with a binder and cured in small shocks.   Thrashing is done with an ordinary grain thrasher, but preferably using a special screen.

Where a seed crop is the object, it is probably best not to pasture in spring.   The opinions, as well as the practices, of seed growers, however, differ on this point.   A moderate amount of fall pasturing is probably not injurious to the next seed crop.

The average yield of seed is 8 to 12 bushels, and maximum yields about 25 bushels to the acre.   First-class seed weighs 25 pounds to the bushel.

The commonest weeds that occur with meadow fescue in Kansas are flea bane (*Erigeron ramosus*), cheat (*Bromus secalinus*) and Japanese cheat (*Bromus japonicus*).   The last two are particularly objectionable because of the difficulty of separating their seeds from the fescue seeds.

Some seed is grown in Europe.   Werner states that the yields in Germany range from 350 to 700 pounds to the acre.

232. Seed. — Meadow fescue seed often contains a small percentage of cheat as an impurity, usually less than 5 per cent, but sometimes much more.   Perennial rye-grass has in some cases been used as an adulterant, but this may be distinguished by the joints of the rachilla being flattened, slightly wedge shaped and not expanded at the apex.

The best commercial seed attains a purity of 99 per cent and a viability of 95–98 per cent.   It loses about 5 per cent viability the first year, but thereafter falls off more rapidly, three-year-old seed being nearly valueless.

The weight of a bushel ranges from 15 to 30 pounds. One pound contains about 250,000 seeds.

233. Pasture value. — Meadow fescue is better adapted for pasturing than for hay. It begins its growth early in the spring, and continues late in the fall. It is quite as palatable as Kentucky blue-grass, and stockmen in Kansas and Nebraska consider it especially valuable for fattening cattle.

Meadow fescue is well adapted to growing in mixture with other grasses, especially in moist lands. It should probably be included in such mixtures throughout the timothy region. When grown alone, it endures in Kansas and Nebraska for 6 to 8 years, or, if manured and well cared for, 12 to 15 years. In mixtures it usually maintains itself for about five years, but is at its best the second and third years.

234. Pests. — The only serious enemy that has attacked meadow fescue in America is a rust (*Puccinia lolii*). This fungus greatly injures the leaves of the aftermath, practically ruining the fall pastures. It also weakens the plants so that but few culms are produced the following season.

Tall fescue, when growing adjacent to infected meadow fescue, remains almost wholly free from the fungus, but is not entirely immune.

Strebel states that in Germany meadow fescue from American seed is far more subject to rust than that from German seed.

235. Hybrids. — *Festuca elatior* is a remarkable grass because of its ability to make hybrids. Natural hybrids with *Festuca arundinacea*, *F. gigantea*, *Lolium perenne* and *L. multiflorum* have been described. None of these has been utilized agriculturally.

P

OTHER FESCUES

236. Tall fescue. — Tall fescue differs from meadow fescue, mainly in being 6 to 12 inches taller, in its somewhat looser panicles and in its resistance to rust. The seeds of the two are quite indistinguishable, but those of tall fescue command a much higher price. From limited experiments in Kansas and in Washington, tall fescue appears to yield only half as much seed as meadow fescue. The culms are comparatively few and the seeds ripen unevenly. Owing to its rust resistance, it may replace meadow fescue, especially as it yields larger crops of hay and the seed commands a higher price.

At the Ohio Experiment Station tall fescue produced in four years on one-twentieth acre plots an average yield of 4870 pounds of hay per acre.

237. Reed fescue (*Festuca arundinacea*). — Reed fescue is native to Europe, North Africa and western Siberia. It is more variable than its close relative, *F. elatior*, about twelve varieties being botanically distinguished in Europe.

By some botanists it is considered a variety of meadow fescue. It is, however, a larger and coarser plant in every way. It is perhaps most easily distinguished from tall fescue by the upper part of the culm, the lower sheaths and upper surface of the stiffer leaves being very scabrous.

The seed is indistinguishable from tall fescue and it is sometimes sold for that by unscrupulous dealers.

Reed fescue has from time to time been extravagantly praised, but has nowhere attained any definite agricultural status.

It produces large yields of hay, which is said to be readily eaten by horses and cows. Sheep, however, refuse it, both as pasturage and as hay. So far as growth and seed production are concerned, it is far superior to both meadow fescue and tall fescue, but its lack of palatability has kept it from being much used.

PERENNIAL OR ENGLISH RYE-GRASS (*Lolium perenne*)

238. Name. — The name " rye-grass " or " ray-grass," as applied to species of *Lolium*, did not originate from any fancied resemblance to rye. The name is probably derived from the French appellation for darnel (*Lolium temulentum*), "fausse ivraye" or "ivrai." From this the English designation was easily derived by abridgment into ray or rai = rye. In distinction to Italian rye-grass, it is known either as perennial or English rye-grass.

239. Agricultural history. — Perennial rye-grass was the first of all perennial grasses to be grown in pure cultures for forage. According to Sutton it was first mentioned in agricultural literature in England in 1611. Werner states that it was first cultivated by Eustace, who lived in Oxford about 1681.

Sinclair, refers to a mention of its cultivation in Worlidge's " Husbandry," published in 1669, but it is not clear that Worlidge really referred to perennial rye-grass.

240. Botany. — Perennial rye-grass occurs naturally in all of temperate Asia and in North Africa. Botanists have distinguished and named about 10 varieties. Hybrids are known with *Festuca elatior*, *Festuca gigantea* and *Lolium multiflorum*.

241. Characteristics. — This rye-grass is a short-lived, rapid-growing perennial, living only two years on poor lands, but persisting much longer under favorable conditions, especially in lawns and pastures. If grown in hay mixtures, it is apt to disappear after the first year, as it does not withstand shading by taller grasses. It closely resembles Italian rye-grass, but can nearly always be distinguished by the awnless lemmas. The young leaves are folded and not convolute, as in Italian rye-grass.

242. Adaptations. — This grass is primarily adapted to moist regions with mild winter climate. It continues to grow at low temperatures and partly on this account does not well withstand severe winter cold. In winter hardiness it is about equal to orchard-grass. It thrives best on rich, moist, well-drained soils, and does not do well on sandy soils, nor will it endure standing water near the surface.

243. Importance. — In America, perennial rye-grass is of small importance, being seldom employed except as an admixture in lawn grasses. It succeeds well enough wherever red clover thrives, but has not won for itself a place in American agriculture.

In Europe it is the principal pasture grass, being much employed on rich bottom or moor lands, usually in mixture with white clover, but it is also used as an element in practically all pasture land mixtures. In Europe it holds much the position which Kentucky blue-grass does in America. As a hay grass it is much inferior in yield to Italian rye and other grasses. It is also much cultivated in New Zealand.

244. Agricultural varieties. — Besides being the oldest cultivated meadow-grass, perennial rye-grass was also the first in which cultural varieties were developed. Apparently this grass is little subject to cross-pollination and hence varieties are not difficult to maintain. Sinclair in 1825 mentions six different named varieties in England, and intimates that others were known to him.

At the present time English seedsmen advertise several varieties of this grass, but in some instances these "varieties" are merely seeds of different weights or sizes separated by machinery.

245. Culture. — Perennial rye-grass may be sown either in the fall or in the spring, the former being preferable, as but little return can be obtained the first season if spring sown. The young plants grow more rapidly than most perennial grasses, so that some winter and early spring pasturage is afforded, in regions of mild winters. If used for pasturage the European practice is to pasture heavily enough to keep the culms from developing, as animals will not eat these. If grown for hay, one good cutting and a second smaller one may be secured. In common with most grasses, it should be cut when in full bloom.

In pure cultures perennial rye-grass lasts three or four years when cut as hay, and somewhat longer if kept closely pastured. In mixed hay meadows it soon disappears.

When sown alone, 25 to 35 pounds to the acre is used.

246. Hay yields. — The hay yield of perennial rye-grass is not as large as most hay grasses. In Europe Werner gives the average yield to the acre as 3800 pounds, but as high as 7400 pounds has been recorded. Karmrodt in four successive years on the same plot secured yields to the hectare of 6791, 10,432, 9407 and 6653 kilograms, the yield being decidedly best in the second and third years.

American experiment station yields to the acre in pounds are reported as follows : North Carolina, 5229; Kentucky, 4640; Ohio, 1822, 6-year average; Kansas, 1050, 2-year average; Arlington Farm, Virginia, 2800; Utah, 1410.

and 1560; Idaho, 4000; Ontario (Guelph), 2500, 7-year average.

247. Seed-production. — The seed habits of the grass are excellent and under very favorable conditions two crops may be harvested in the same season. More usually the first is cut for hay and the second for seed. The grass should be cut before the seed is fully ripe; otherwise, there is some loss by shattering. Practically no seed is grown in America, the commercial supplies coming from Europe and New Zealand.

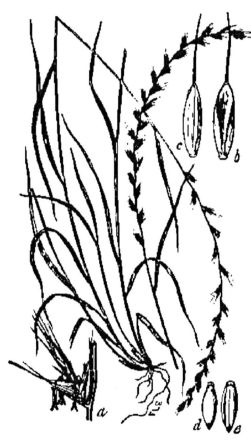

248. Seed. — Seed of perennial rye-grass is grown mainly in Scotland and Ireland. None is grown in America. On account of shattering, the crop is cut before the seeds are fully ripe. Care is necessary in curing, as, if the hay becomes heated in drying, the germination of the seed is injured. The yield per acre varies from 250 to 500 pounds per acre and maximums of 1050 pounds are reported.

FIG. 22. — Italian rye-grass (*Lolium multiflorum*). a, spikelet; b, c, lemma; d, e, seed.

The seed is recleaned and graded according to weight and size. The small seeds are sold as short-seeded rye-grass, and sometimes as Pacey's rye-grass.

ITALIAN RYE-GRASS

249. Characteristics. — Italian rye-grass (*Lolium multiflorum*) is readily distinguished from perennial rye-grass by the lemma being awned, except in one variety, but in all forms the young leaves are convolute, not folded as in perennial rye-grass. Agriculturally it is distinguished by its short life, — seldom over two years, unless heavily manured, — its very rapid growth and prompt recovery after cutting.

250. Botany. — Italian rye-grass is native in the region about the Mediterranean; namely, southern Europe, northern Africa and Asia Minor. Varieties have been distinguished by the awns; namely, *longiaristatum*, the ordinary long-awned form; *submuticum*, with the occasional awns short; and *muticum*, which is awnless.

On the length of life are differentiated *Gaudini*, the annual forms, and *perennans*, which lives 3–4 years. Stebler and Volkart state that the former includes a summer annual form, to which belongs Argentine rye-grass; a winter annual form, which includes Rieffel's rye-grass, cultivated in Brittany; and Bailly's rye-grass, which differs only in being awnless. The forms which endure more than one year are Westernwolth rye-grass, which blooms the first season if spring sown, and ordinary Italian rye-grass, which does not bloom the first season.

251. Agricultural history. — Italian rye-grass seems to have been first cultivated in northern Italy. It was known in Switzerland in 1820 and in France in 1818. It was introduced into England in 1831. In France and

England especially, it is largely cultivated and furnishes the largest proportion of the market hay. Elsewhere in Europe it has not become of much importance.

252. Adaptations. — This rye-grass is primarily adapted to moist regions with mild winter temperatures. It succeeds well in most of western and southern Europe, Argentina and New Zealand. In North America the best results have been secured in the Atlantic States, practically in the same area as that adapted to crimson clover, and on the Pacific Coast. When seeded in fall it is not injured by a temperature of $-10°$ Fahrenheit and probably will withstand more severe cold.

It prefers loam or sandy loam soils, but does fairly well on clay loams. It does not endure standing water, but on well-drained land is well adapted to irrigation farming.

253. Culture. — Italian rye-grass is mostly sown alone at the rate of 35–40 pounds to the acre. It may be sown either in fall or in spring, with or without a nurse crop. In the south Atlantic States and on the Pacific Coast, fall seeding gives the most satisfactory results. The grass is not well adapted to sowing in permanent meadows, as it disappears after the second year, and sometimes after the first. Furthermore, the rye-grass by its rapid early growth injures the other grasses so that in some experiments it has actually reduced the yield.

In Europe it is sometimes mixed with crimson clover, which requires much the same conditions, and the two are ready to cut for hay at the same time. A test of this mixture at the Delaware Experiment Station gave a good yield, and enough of the seed of the Italian rye-grass shattered to produce a volunteer crop.

254. Irrigation. — Italian rye-grass succeeds well under irrigation, and this method of culture has long been pursued in northern Italy.

At the Utah Experiment Station the following results were secured with irrigation : —

Irrigation water applied, inches	7.50	15.00	45.00	102.00
Total yield of Italian rye-grass, pounds	2357	2218	3201	2357
Yield to the inch of irrigation water	314	148	71	2

255. Hay yields. — Italian rye-grass is remarkable for the number of cuttings that can be made in a season and the large total yield under the most favorable conditions. No other temperate grass grows so rapidly or recovers so promptly after cutting. Ordinarily but two cuttings can be obtained in a season, the second smaller than the first. With abundant moisture and fertilizer, however, the grass has yielded 5 cuttings at Christiana, Norway; 5 or 6 in Germany; and as many as 7 to 9 in England and Switzerland, in a single season. It is possible that these results might be duplicated west of the Cascade Mountains in Oregon, Washington and British Columbia; but in the East, Italian rye-grass languishes under midsummer heat. Werner thinks that the very rapid growth of Italian rye-grass when irrigated with liquid manure is partly due to the fact that it produces numerous fine roots from the lower nodes. The growth is so rapid that a growth of 30 inches has been recorded in three weeks.

Some of the yields recorded for Italian rye-grass in Europe border on the marvelous. In England on land watered with liquid manure, annual yields of 60 to 120 tons of grass, or 12 to 20 tons of hay, to the acre are said to have been secured. Werner records yields of 52,040 pounds of grass, or 10,560 pounds of hay to the acre near Milan, Italy, in 6 cuttings during a season. Karmrodt in four successive years secured on the same piece of ground hay yields respectively of 8077, 8100, 7058 and 7196 pounds to the acre.

Yields reported by American experiment stations are very moderate, being in pounds to the acre: Kentucky, 4480; Missouri, 6800; Ohio, 5120, 6-year average; Kansas, 2341, 2-year average; Virginia (Arlington Farm), 3200; North Carolina, 5557 and 5500. At the Western Washington Experiment Station 3 cuttings were secured in one season. The Westernwolth variety gave a yield of 3432 pounds an acre in Prince Edward Island.

256. Seed-production. — The seeding habits of Italian rye-grass are essentially the same as those of perennial rye-grass, and the seed is just as easily harvested. It shatters, however, somewhat more readily and so needs to be cut promptly when the seeds are in the late dough stage. Commercial seed is grown in Europe, Argentina and New Zealand. The average yield in Europe is given at about 500 pounds an acre, the maximum at double the quantity.

Seed from various sources gave very much the same hay yields according to experiments in Switzerland.

257. Seed. — The seed of Italian rye-grass is usually quite free from weed seeds, and of good viability. At the Zurich, Switzerland, Seed Control Station, the average purity of 7000 samples has been 95.4 per cent and the average germination 82 per cent. Very good seed will reach 98 per cent purity and 95 per cent germination. Two-year-old seed loses about 25 per cent in viability, and three-year-old seed is nearly worthless. Owing to the cheapness of the seed it is rarely adulterated.

Ordinarily it is easily told from perennial rye-grass by the awns. If these are absent, the two may be distinguished by the palea, this being far more abundantly toothed on the margin and more deeply notched in Italian rye-grass.

The seed weighs 12 to 24 pounds to the bushel, and the quality varies accordingly. One pound contains 270,000 to 285,000 seeds.

SLENDER WHEAT-GRASS (*Agropyron tenerum*)

258. Slender wheat-grass, known in Canada as western rye-grass or McIvor's rye-grass, is the only example of a native North American grass that has proven valuable under cultivation. It is widespread, but variable, occurring abundantly from British Columbia to Manitoba, southward to Arizona and Oklahoma and sparingly eastward to Pennsylvania and Newfoundland. It is strictly a bunch grass with numerous slender erect stems, 2 to 4 feet high and narrow, flat, rather stiff leaves. The spikelets are crowded, scattered in a spike 4 to 6 inches long. Its root system was found at the North Dakota Experiment Station to be quite as deep as that of brome-grass, but with fewer roots.

Slender wheat-grass was first brought into cultivation about 1895. It is now grown to a considerable extent in Manitoba, Alberta, Saskatchewan and the Dakotas, and has given good results in Ontario and Washington.

Slender wheat-grass is usually seeded in spring. A firm, well-prepared seed bed is desirable. The seed may be sown broadcast and then harrowed, but is better sown with a drill. Good stands have been secured with 10 to 15 pounds per acre in Saskatchewan, the heavier seeding being best. Elsewhere as high as 30 pounds an acre have been used without the stand being too thick.

The grass is somewhat subject to a rust (*Puccinia rubigo-vera*), but otherwise is free from diseases.

At Indian Head (Saskatchewan) Experimental Farm, yields of hay in large plots have been reported since 1901. The yields have varied from 2000 to 9000 pounds an acre, the average of 14 fields during 9 years being 4800 pounds. The best yields were nearly always secured the second season after seeding, unless the field was renovated by manuring.

At Brandon, Manitoba, the average yields for 7 years have been 4694 pounds an acre.

A plot of one-fourth acre at the South Dakota Experiment Station was not cut during the first two years. The hay yields during the three following years were respectively 980, 908 and 1920 pounds an acre.

Fig. 23. — Slender wheat-grass (*Agropyron tenerum*). **a**, glumes; **b**, spikelet with glumes removed.

At Guelph, Ontario, it has yielded the most heavily

of 15 grasses during trials of 7 years, the average yield for the period being on small plots at the rate of 8720 pounds an acre. In other trials where the plots were cut 6 times each season during 4 years, slender wheat-grass was exceeded only by tall oat-grass and orchard-grass.

Acre yields have been reported from other experiment stations as follows: Minnesota, 4700 pounds; Michigan (Upper Peninsula), 5440 pounds; North Dakota (Dickinson), 2950 pounds, 2-year average; Wyoming, 2065 pounds; South Dakota " nearly as large yields as brome-grass."

Slender wheat-grass has also given good results in mixtures, especially with brome-grass; with red clover; with red clover and timothy; and with alfalfa.

At Brandon, Manitoba, in a feeding experiment comparing slender wheat-grass with brome-grass, 4 steers fed brome-grass gained 675 pounds and 4 fed slender wheat-grass gained 660 pounds. At Indian Head, Saskatchewan, in a similar trial 5 steers gained 910 pounds on brome and 5 others 830 pounds on slender wheat during the same period.

WESTERN WHEAT-GRASS (*Agropyron occidentale*)

259. Western wheat-grass is also known as blue-stem, blue-joint and Colorado blue-stem in various parts of the West. It is native over practically the whole region west of the 98th meridian from Saskatchewan to Mexico. In a general way it resembles slender wheat-grass, but the whole herbage is glaucous and the grass spreads by numerous creeping rootstocks.

Western wheat-grass is quite resistant both to drought and to alkali, but it is seldom abundant except where the ground is naturally or artificially irrigated. Under such conditions excellent crops of hay are cut and where the grass is well known it has long borne a reputation for horse feed equal to that of timothy.   In Texas the bottoms of shallow desiccated ponds are often covered with a pure growth of this grass.   In parts of Montana it is only necessary to irrigate the land in order to secure a good stand of western wheat-grass.   After several mowings the grass seems to become sod bound, so that rejuvenation by disking is necessary.

Attempts to domesticate this grass have thus far not resulted satisfactorily, mainly because the seed is poor in quality even when gathered with the utmost care.   While this grass possesses creeping rootstocks, it has never been reported troublesome as a weed.   Its excellent qualities make it worthy of further efforts at domestication.

CHAPTER XI

PERENNIAL GRASSES OF MINOR IMPOR-TANCE

It has already been pointed out that a number of grasses agriculturally utilized in Europe are scarcely at all used in America. From the fact that commercial seed is abundant, and from their European reputations, their exact status as regards America is important to the student. Some of them are not at all well adapted to American conditions, while others are useful only in very restricted areas, or on peculiar soils.

SHEEP'S FESCUE AND CLOSELY RELATED SPECIES

260. Sheep's fescue and its close relatives form in all probability the most puzzling group of forms of all the grasses. About 70 varieties have been described from Europe alone, and these are variously regarded as forms of one species or of several. All are densely tufted perennials with numerous fine, stiff leaves, and slender erect culms usually 12 to 18 inches high, but under very favorable conditions taller. The following four varieties are used in agriculture : —

Sheep's fescue (*Festuca ovina*) with folded leaves not broader than thick, .3 to .6 millimeter wide.

Hard fescue (*Festuca ovina duriuscula* or *Festuca duriuscula*) differing from the preceding mainly in having the leaves broader than thick, .7 to 1 millimeter wide.

Various-leaved fescue (*Festuca ovina heterophylla* or *F. heterophylla*) is sometimes considered a variety of *Festuca rubra*. Some of the shoots are extravaginal. The radical leaf blades are long, soft and folded, while the culm leaves are flat and expanded, whence its name.

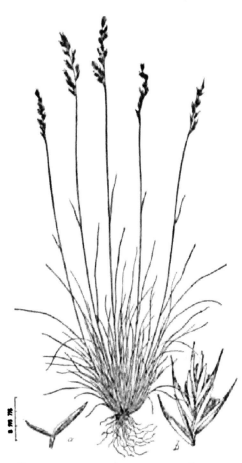

Fig. 24. — Sheep's fescue (*Festuca ovina*). a, glumes; b, spikelet with glumes removed.

Fine-leaved fescue (*Festuca ovina tenuifolia* or *F. tenuifolia* of the seedsmen; *Festuca ovina capillata*) has very fine leaves and awnless lemmas.

The forms of *Festuca ovina* native to North America are much fewer than in Europe. Typical *Festuca ovina* occurs rather sparingly as a native in the Rocky Mountains from Alberta to New Mexico, in the Black Hills and about the Great Lakes. *Festuca ovina ingrata*, the "Blue bunchgrass" of the stockmen, is an important range plant from British Columbia and Alberta to Colorado and Utah, especially in the Co-

lumbia Basin. Farther south it is replaced by the larger
Arizona fescue (*Festuca ovina arizonica*) which extends
into Mexico. The few other native American forms are
of no economic importance.

261. Importance and culture. — None of these fescues
has as yet attained any considerable importance under
cultivation in America. Fine-leaved fescue is used
sparingly in lawn grass mixtures. Various-leaved fescue
has apparently been tested only in grass gardens. Hard
fescue also seems to have been grown only in trial grounds,
as most of the commercial seed is the indistinguishable
sheep's fescue. Sheep's fescue has become widely introduced, and on poor stony or sandy land is a valuable
pasture plant for sheep and deserves more attention for
such purpose than it has yet received in America.

Sheep's fescue should be sown only for pasturage and
only on land that will not produce better grasses, such
as stony or gravelly hills, and poor sandy soils. It is
too small to make it worth while to sow for hay on good
land, even in mixture with other grasses. It possesses
abundant deep, strong roots, and is never injured by uprooting, nor does it suffer under trampling and close
grazing. Sheep eat it quite readily, but cattle avoid
it if other grasses are present. The animals should have
access to the pastures early in the spring, as the grass is
more palatable if kept closely grazed. European authorities state that the grass yields most during the second
and third years, and should be plowed under after four
or five years, where possible.

Sheep's fescue is a northern grass, and not well adapted
to conditions south of about latitude 40 degrees, except
in the mountains. Northward its limit is that of any
possible agriculture. On very poor land it will thrive

Q

where no other cultivated grass will grow, but on somewhat better pasture land should be grown in mixtures with redtop, Kentucky blue-grass, Canada blue-grass and white clover. In pure cultures, European writers recommend sowing 28 pounds an acre.

262. Seed. — Seed of all these fescues is grown in Europe. That of sheep's fescue is easily gathered and is low in price.

A bushel weighs ordinarily 10 to 15 pounds, but the best quality reaches 30 pounds. One pound contains 680,000 seeds, according to Stebler. The purity should be 90 per cent and the viability at least 50 per cent.

RED FESCUE

263. Red fescue (*Festuca rubra*) is best distinguished from *Festuca ovina* by having creeping extravaginal shoots or rootstocks. *Festuca heterophylla* with some extravaginal non-creeping shoots is intermediate between the species. Red fescue occurs naturally in Europe, Asia and North America. · It is very variable and numerous varieties have been described. In North America it ranges from Greenland southward near the seacoast to Virginia, and from Alaska to California and New Mexico. One form occurs rarely in Tennessee and North Carolina.

It has never been used under cultivation in North America, except as a lawn plant, for which it is well adapted in the Northern States and Canada, especially on sandy soil near the seacoast. In some of its forms it is probably the most beautiful of all lawn grasses.

Red fescue is a long-lived perennial. In Europe it is somewhat used as a pasture plant, especially on moist, sandy soils. Under favorable conditions it makes a dense growth and may reach a height of two feet or more. In such dense growths the lower leaves turn brown readily. Hay yields of 1½ and 2 tons to the acre are recorded, but this is exceptional. It should not be planted where better hay grasses can be grown.

At present the commercial seed supply of red fescue comes from Europe. It is often mixed with or adulterated with other fescues, where seeds can scarcely be distinguished. In recent years a variety known as Chewing's fescue has been exported from New Zealand. It is identical with the European, at least for all practical purposes. The variety sold as *Festuca dumetorum* is apparently *Festuca rubra grandiflora*, which is somewhat larger than the typical form.

MEADOW FOXTAIL (*Alopecurus pratensis*)

264. Meadow foxtail is native to the temperate portions of Europe and Asia. It is quite variable, 6 or 8 varieties having been botanically named, but none of these have come into agricultural use.

The culture of meadow foxtail dates from about the middle of the eighteenth century, when it was recommended by Kalm in Sweden and especially by Schreber in Germany.

265. Characteristics. — Meadow foxtail is a long-lived perennial grass producing loose tufts with numerous basal leaves. The rootstocks are comparatively few and but 2 to 4 inches long as a rule. The culms grow usually to a height of 3 feet, but rarely reach 6 feet. Under very favorable conditions three cuttings may be secured in one season, but usually only two cuttings.

It begins its growth very early in spring, more so even than sweet vernal-grass. The grass should be cut for hay when in full bloom, but it is said to retain its feeding value for a considerable time thereafter.

266. Adaptations.—Meadow foxtail is adapted primarily to moist cool regions. Its culture is prominent in northern Europe, but elsewhere it is but little grown. It has no particular soil preference so long as the water supply is abundant. This peculiarity makes it well suited to growing under irrigation, but it will not withstand drought. Though primarily adapted to open meadows it endures shade fairly well. Better than any other grass, it withstands cold weather in early spring after its growth has begun, and it is perhaps the most winter hardy of any cultivated perennial grass.

267. Culture. — Meadow foxtail is but very little grown in North America, most of the data concerning it being those obtained at experiment stations.

In northern Europe it is a favorite hay grass, especially for wet meadows. European authorities recommend the sowing at the rate of 22 pounds an acre. It is seldom sown alone, however, but usually in mixtures with such grasses as meadow fescue, timothy and orchard-grass. In recent years its improvement by breeding has been undertaken at Svalöf, Sweden.

Sinclair in England reports a yield of 8844 pounds an acre; Vianne in France, 8932 pounds.

Few yields have been reported by American experiment stations. At the Michigan (Upper Peninsula) Station it gave a yield of 2906 pounds of hay to the acre; at the Utah Experiment Station, 1500 pounds; and the 7-year average at Guelph, Ontario, was 3100 pounds an acre.

268. Seed.—Seed of meadow foxtail is grown in Finland, Sweden, Denmark and Holland, but most of the commercial supply is from the first-named country. A small amount is also exported from New Zealand. The average yield in Europe is said to be about 170 pounds to the acre.

The results of tests at the Zurich Seed Control Station indicate an average purity of 75 per cent and viability of 69 per cent. A bushel weighs 6 to 14 pounds. One pound contains 907,000 seeds (Stebler); 490,000 (Hunter); 1,216,000 (Hunt).

SWEET VERNAL-GRASS (*Anthoxanthum odoratum*)

269. Botany. — Sweet vernal-grass is native to temperate Europe and Asia and Northwest Africa. It is wholly an introduced plant in North America, except perhaps in South Greenland.

Sweet vernal-grass receives its name from the fact that the whole plant contains cumarin, giving it a vanilla-like odor but also a bitter taste. This is present even in the very young seedlings, which may thus be recognized. On account of its agreeable odor, sweet vernal-grass has long been recommended as a desirable addition in mixed grass meadows. It is not clear, however, that the grass with its pleasant odor really makes the hay more palatable to animals.

The grass is a long-lived perennial, growing in small, dense tufts, the culms reaching a height of 18 to 20 inches as a rule. It is one of the earliest grasses to appear in spring, but is not much liked by cattle as a pasture grass. It is quite resistant to both cold and drought. The best growth is made on fertile soil, but sweet vernal-grass will thrive on almost any type of soil if not too wet. Near Washington, D.C., old neglected pastures on hard clay soils are sometimes covered with nearly pure growths of this grass.

270. Culture. — Sweet vernal-grass has never been utilized in America except as it may be a spontaneous element in pastures and meadows. Its small growth, however, does not commend it. In Europe it is used in small quantities in mixtures with other grasses because of the sweet odor it imparts to hay. It is never sown alone except in experimental work. Vianne in France records hay yields of 1760 to 2640 pounds an acre, but this must be far above what can ordinarily be expected. The seed is gathered mainly in Germany. At the Zurich Seed Control Station, the average purity of numerous samples was found to be about 92 per cent and the average viability 52 per cent. If sown pure, about 20 pounds of such seed are needed to the acre.

REED CANARY-GRASS (*Phalaris arundinacea*)

271. Botany and agricultural history. — Reed canary-grass is native to the temperate portions of Europe, Asia and North America. It grows naturally in wet soils, especially river bottoms and lake shores, where it is subject to periods of inundation. No botanical varieties have been named except the variegated " ribbon grass " of the gardens (*P. arundinacea picta*). The grass is, however, decidedly variable, about ten strains having been grown for several years at Arlington Farm, Virginia. The strains differ in size, coarseness, earliness, breadth of leaves and other characters, but all shatter their seeds readily.

It was first cultivated in England before 1824 and in Germany about 1850. It has never been much used in America, but is cut for hay where it occurs naturally.

272. Characteristics. — Reed canary-grass is a long-lived, rather coarse perennial grass. It produces numerous short extravaginal stolons, which at the tip develop into upright culms. Each plant finally forms a rather dense tussock, one to two feet in diameter. The culms are perfectly erect, usually about four to six feet high but often taller, and so stout that they never lodge.

Reed-canary is adapted mostly to cool climates, but the ribbon grass form, at least, succeeds well in the Southern States. It is never injured by severe winter weather. Though naturally a wet land grass, it succeeds well in ordinary cultivated land, especially in clays and clay loams. It also succeeds well in sand if there be an adequate moisture supply, but is said not to thrive in peaty soils. Owing to its moisture-loving proclivities, it is well adapted to irrigation.

Growth begins early in spring and continues late into the fall. Seed is produced in abundance, but shatters easily. This, perhaps more than anything else, has militated against its general use.

273. Culture. — Reed canary-grass is sparingly cultivated in Europe. If cut before bloom, three cuttings may be secured, but only two if allowed to bloom. At Arlington Farm, Virginia, the second crop of plants in rows is about two-thirds as large as the first. The hay is palatable if cut young, and yields of 12,000 to 17,000 pounds an acre are recorded in Europe. These yields, however, are based on very small plots.

Seed is gathered by cutting off the panicles before they are ripe, and the yield is stated to be about 180 pounds an acre. It weighs 44 to 48 pounds to the bushel.

It is best adapted to pure cultures, as its habits do not coincide with other grasses. Commercial seed germinates as a rule but 60 per cent, and 20 to 25 pounds to the acre should be sown.

This grass would be worthy of serious attention if its seeding habits could be improved. It is possible that a strain may be found or developed which will not seriously shatter its seed.

VELVET-GRASS (*Holcus lanatus*)

274. Velvet-grass is also known in England as York-shire Fog, and meadow soft-grass. On the North Pacific Coast, where it is extraordinarily abundant, it has acquired the name " mesquite."

It is native to temperate Europe, and Asia, and extends southward into Algeria and the Canary Islands. It is adapted primarily to moist, cool climates, and under such conditions is not particular as to soil. In hardiness it is much like orchard-grass, but is more injured by late spring frosts. It does not endure shade.

Velvet-grass forms thick, rather high tussocks, which make mowing somewhat difficult. The culms are usually about 30 inches high. The whole plant is very hairy and probably on this account is not readily eaten by animals either as hay or pasturage. It possesses very little substance, the hay being probably the most bulky of all grasses. Under favorable climatic conditions two cuttings of hay may be obtained. European authorities state that the hay yield is best in the third year. Sinclair in England records a yield of 6160 pounds an acre, and Vianne in France, 6950 pounds.

In America the grass is utilized to a slight extent in western Virginia, and to a great extent on the North Pacific Coast. In all the region west of the Cascade Mountains — in Oregon, Washington and British Columbia — it is very aggressive, and in the very moist region near the ocean occupies the land practically to the exclusion of other grasses. Under such circumstances its use is a matter of necessity rather than choice, but the returns are not unsatisfactory. The grass is best cut when in full bloom, at which time the rays of the panicle are spreading, but after blooming they become erect.

Velvet-grass should perhaps never be intentionally sown, and at any rate merely as an admixture with other grasses.

Commercial seed is produced mainly in Denmark, and this averages about 63 per cent in purity and 84 per cent in germination. New Zealand seed is somewhat better. The yield in Germany is given by Werner as about 90 pounds to the acre, and as the price is very low, the financial return is small. European writers recommend 20 pounds of seed per acre, if sown pure.

It is sometimes desirable to eradicate velvet-grass so as to plant the land to more valuable grasses. To do this the grass must be cut before the seed is ripe, generally June 10 to 20. About July 1 give the field a thorough but shallow disking. Repeat the shallow disking every week until August 1, and then treat with a spring-tooth harrow and disk again. The shallow cultivation during the driest weather will kill the roots and leave the ground with a very fine mulch on top and plenty of moisture in the subsoil. The land may then be reseeded to clover or planted to any other crop desired.

ERECT BROME (*Bromus erectus*)

275. Erect brome, upright brome or **meadow brome** is a perennial species that has long been cultivated in southern France and in recent years in other countries. The grass is native to much of temperate Europe and Asia and Algeria. It is especially adapted to dry calcareous soils that are too shallow for sainfoin, and on such soils is said to give better results than any other grass, either for pasture or for hay. It bears the same relation to poor, dry, chalky soils that sheep's fescue does to poor sandy soils. On good land it has no place, as other grasses produce larger and better crops.

Both the hay and the pasturage are of mediocre quality, but the fields last many years on suitable calcareous soils. The yield is best the second year and the plants bloom but once each season. It is rarely sown alone, but usually mixed with sainfoin if the land is good enough.

The seed weighs about 15 pounds to the bushel, and 50 pounds to the acre is sown. It is often adulterated with the screenings of tall oat-grass.

Erect brome has been but little tried in America. At the Kansas Experiment Station yields of 1844 and 1720 pounds per acre were obtained in 1904 and 1905 respectively. At the Michigan Upper Peninsula Substation a small plot yielded at the rate of 3706 pounds an acre.

YELLOW OAT-GRASS (*Trisetum flavescens*)

276. Yellow oat-grass, also known as golden oat-grass, is native over much of temperate Europe and Asia and in North Africa, and several botanical varieties are described. It is of only secondary importance in European agriculture, but is practically unknown in America. It is a loosely tufted, long-lived perennial. It is used almost wholly as an admixture with other grasses. It was apparently first brought into cultivation in England before 1785. The seed, which is mainly grown in the south of France and in Tyrol, is scarce and expensive, and this has probably prevented the greater use of the grass.

Yellow oat-grass is decidedly drought resistant and adapted only to well-drained soil. It is said to prefer calcareous soils rich in humus. It is seldom grown in pure cultures except for purposes of seed-production. Vianne records a yield of 5020 pounds hay an acre in France, and Sinclair in England records that he obtained 2859 pounds hay cut in bloom, and 4900 pounds cut when the seed was ripe.

The aftermath is only moderate. When sown alone, about 30 pounds of ordinary quality of seed is needed to the acre.

The seed weighs 5 to 14 pounds a bushel, depending on quality. The average purity is about 70 per cent and the viability 63 per cent, but the best heavy seed is guaranteed by some seedsmen to germinate 70, or even 80 per cent. One pound of seed contains 1,400,000 seeds according to Hunter, and 2,045,000 according to Stebler. Yellow oat-grass is sometimes used for lawns and, if kept closely cut, makes a good fine turf, but rather pale in color.

Fig. 25. — Crested dogstail (*Cynosurus cristatus*). a, b, fertile spikelets; c, sterile spikelet.

CRESTED DOGSTAIL
(*Cynosurus cristatus*)

277. Crested dogstail is a highly appreciated grass in Europe as an admixture both for pastures and for meadows. It makes up a portion of the grass upon the best pastures of England, Holland and Switzerland. It is considered very nutritious, but the yield is only moderate. It is adapted primarily to cool, moist regions.

Crested dogstail is another example of a European grass that fails to thrive under American conditions, probably on account of summer heat. It has often been planted, but has become only very sparingly introduced and has nowhere shown any ability to increase and spread.

It may prove of some value on the North Pacific Coast, but elsewhere it has shown no promise.

CHAPTER XII

SOUTHERN GRASSES

THE climate of the cotton region is not closely paralleled by that of any portion of Europe, and European grasses are therefore ill adapted to the conditions in the South. Most of the grasses useful in the Southern States have originated in countries having humid subtropical climates. Several of the most valuable have poor seeding habits, but are easily propagated vegetatively.

BERMUDA-GRASS (*Cynodon dactylon*)

278. Botany. — Bermuda-grass is native to India and perhaps other parts of the Old World in tropical and sub-tropical localities. In India it is a most valued pasture grass and called *doob* or *hariali*. In Virginia, where its growth is not sufficient to make it valuable, but only troublesome, it is generally known as wire-grass. It is also known locally as dogs'-tooth grass, Bahama-grass and Scotch-grass.

Several varieties have been named by botanists, some as distinct species. The interrelation of the numerous forms is not, however, clear.

279. Characteristics. — Bermuda-grass is a long-lived perennial with numerous branched leafy stems 4 to 6 inches high, or under very favorable conditions 12 to 18

237

inches high. Where the aërial stems are supported by shrubs, they may reach a height of 3 feet. The leaves are flat and spreading, and differentiated from all similar grasses by the ligule which consists of a circle of white hairs. The flowers are in slender, spreading spikes one-half to one inch long, arranged in umbels of 4 to 6.

In the ordinary form of Bermuda-grass, numerous stout rootstocks as large as a lead pencil are produced, and by the growth of these a single plant may cover an area of several square yards. In very hard soil the rootstocks become stout runners 1 to 3 feet long, with much longer nodes and shorter leaves than the aërial

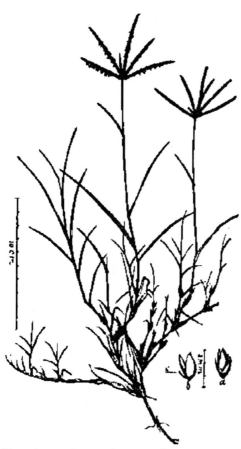

Fig. 26. — Bermuda-grass (*Cynodon dactylon*). a, spikelet; b, floret.

stems. St. Lucie-grass and other forms have no underground rootstocks, but are much less hardy.

280. Agricultural history. — The date of the introduction of Bermuda-grass into the United States is not definitely ascertained. Spillman gives a circumstantial account of its introduction in 1812 at Greensboro, Georgia.

However, a definite and unmistakable account of Bermuda-grass in the United States is given by Mease, "Geological Account of the United States," p. 227, published in 1807.

281. Adaptations. — Bermuda-grass occurs in the United States generally from Pennsylvania west to central Kansas and south to the Gulf of Mexico; also in Arizona, New Mexico and California.

It extends somewhat farther northward, being found in Massachusetts and Washington, but its continued existence in the Northern States is precarious. Much of it survived the cold of January, 1912, in the District of Columbia, when the temperature fell to $-18°$ F. The spread and growth of the grass about Washington, D.C., in the past ten years seem to be more vigorous than formerly, which may be due to gradual acclimatization. That Bermuda-grass does become more hardy seems to be demonstrated by investigations at the Oklahoma Experiment Station, where the local established strain was able to withstand $-18°$ F. while plots grown from Australian seed usually become winter-killed.

In general, however, Bermuda-grass is best adapted in the United States to the same general area as cotton, and in this region is relatively as important as is Kentucky blue-grass in the North. It has also become abundant in California and Arizona, but in these states it is looked upon as a pest because of the difficulty it causes in alfalfa as a weed, whence it is sometimes called "devil-grass."

Bermuda will grow in all types of soil, but makes its best growth on rich, moist bottom lands, but the soil must be well drained. It has marked ability to withstand close grazing or close clipping, and on this account is much used as a lawn grass. The slightest touch of frost, however, causes the leaves to turn brown.

On account of its ability to grow on any type of soil, and its creeping character, Bermuda is an excellent soil binder on sandy soil, on eroding slopes of clay and in gullies. It is very abundant and useful for this purpose on the levees of the Mississippi River.

Bermuda is not well adapted to shade and perhaps for this reason tends to disappear in fields where it is densely shaded by other crops.

282. Variability. — Bermuda is a very variable grass, and many forms have been considered distinct species by botanists. Even the common form introduced into the United States is very diverse, and Moorhouse at the Oklahoma Experiment Station has secured numerous differing forms by selection. Some of the forms are very distinct and may become important. One of these recently introduced from Brazil produces superficial runners 15 feet or more long in a single season.

In Florida occurs a form known as St. Lucie-grass, which differs from ordinary Bermuda in never having underground rootstocks.

As Bermuda is easily propagated by cuttings, any selected form is easily maintained.

283. Importance. — Bermuda-grass is the most important perennial grass in the Southern States, filling much the same position in respect to pasturage as Kentucky blue-grass in the North. Bermuda is also a hay grass and large quantities are thus harvested, especially in rich or alluvial soils. Its area of marked value is mainly south of latitude 36° — that is, the north line of Tennessee — west to central Oklahoma. In this area it is even more aggressive than Kentucky blue-grass in the North, and, like the latter grass, is seldom sown. The fact that both of these grasses volunteer so readily is probably the reason why so few definite experiments have been conducted with either.

284. Culture. — Bermuda-grass is planted either by sowing the seed or by planting " roots." The seed is very fine and rather expensive; therefore the seed bed should be well prepared and firm. The seed is best sown in spring, using about 5 pounds to the acre. To scatter it evenly, it is advisable to mix with meal or soil so as to make a larger bulk. After sowing the ground should be rolled or lightly harrowed.

The more common method is to cut or tear the sod into small pieces and then drop them in furrows on plowed ground or merely press them in with the foot. The pieces should be scattered about 2 or 3 feet apart each way. Planting in this way is best done when the weather is likely to be moist, at any time from spring till midsummer. Under such conditions the pieces of sod are very sure to grow.

To save the loss of the land while the Bermuda is starting, it may be planted in the rows of any intertilled crop after the last cultivation.

Bermuda-grass meadows or pastures tend to become sod bound and fall off in yield. When this is the case, the field should be disked or plowed and harrowed, after which the growth will be much more vigorous.

Where conditions are not such that Bermuda will grow in spite of bad treatment, care is necessary to insure a good stand. At the Oklahoma Experiment Station pieces of sod were planted in well-prepared land in 4 ways: 1. By placing in furrows three feet apart and covering each root; 2. By scattering pieces of sod evenly and then working them into the soil with a smoothing harrow; 3. Seeding

R

followed by light harrowing; 4. Treated the same as in 2, and then planted to kafir corn which was cultivated in the usual way. A good stand was secured by the first method, a partial stand by the second, but the other two were failures.

285. Yields of hay. — But few reliable yields of Bermuda-grass hay have been recorded, but statements have been published to the effect that 3 to 4 tons an acre are secured at times. Probably the average yield does not exceed 1 ton an acre.

At the Oklahoma Experiment Station a field of 2½ acres planted in June, 1905, yielded 2584 pounds hay an acre at the end of September, and in 1906 three cuttings gave a yield of 10,160 pounds an acre. Another plot yielded during three years to the acre respectively, 5850, 1635 and 1667 pounds of hay.

Newman states that a field on bottom land in Georgia yielded in three cuttings 13,000 pounds of cured hay to the acre.

286. Rootstocks. — According to Duggar, the stout rootstocks when plowed up are readily eaten by hogs. In the tropics where Bermuda-grass is sold green in bundles for horse feed, the rootstocks are often pulled up when the top growth is scanty. The same use of the rootstocks is made in Naples, Italy, where they are fed to cab horses.

287. Pasture value. — Bermuda alone or in mixtures makes excellent pasturage, but it is best when closely grazed. The stems become rather tough and wiry with age, and where there are not enough animals to keep it closely grazed they feed only in spots.

Bermuda is so aggressive that few other plants will grow with it during summer. Lespedeza will hold its own in spots and the combination of the two is excellent.

Bermuda does not grow in winter, but if bur clover be sown it will make good winter pasturage and reseed itself from year to year. Hairy vetch is also useful for the same reason, but does not reseed itself so well. Another excellent plan is to seed Bermuda pastures in the fall to Italian rye-grass, which grows rapidly and furnishes pasturage until the following summer. This grass is also often sown in Bermuda lawns to make a green lawn in the winter. White clover is also an excellent plant to grow with Bermuda for pasturage.

Good Bermuda pastures will carry one cow to the acre during the summer and the best Bermuda and lespedeza mixed pastures will support two cattle to the acre during the summer.

288. Feeding value. — The only feeding experiments reported are by the Mississippi Experiment Station. In one experiment Bermuda was compared with timothy as a hay feed for work mules, and the conclusion reached that they were of equal value.

In experiments with dairy cows during three years the results indicate that Bermuda hay has practically the same value as timothy hay for the production of milk and butter.

289. Seed-production. — Commercial seed of Bermuda-grass has heretofore been obtained wholly from Australia, but recently it has been gathered in Arizona and southern California. The culms are often only four or five inches high, but the seed is held firmly long after it becomes ripe. No data concerning the yields of seed seem to have been recorded.

In humid regions Bermuda sets seed sparingly or only in periods of unusually dry weather. Seed has been found in Louisiana, Florida and North Carolina, while at Washington, D.C., it is quite freely formed.

The viability of Australian seed ranges from 56 to 84 per cent. According to Hunt, one pound contains 1,800,000 seeds.

JOHNSON-GRASS (*Andropogon halepensis*)

290. Botany. — Johnson-grass is native to South Asia and about the borders of the Mediterranean in Africa and southernmost Europe. The specific name comes from the city Aleppo, whence it first became known to European botanists.

Two varieties occur in Europe; namely, the ordinary form with awned spikelets, and the awnless variety *submuticus*. Both of these also occur in the United States. In India there is another variety distinguished by having a loose drooping panicle.

Andropogon halepensis is distinguished from all forms of *Andropogon sorghum* by possessing underground rootstocks and thus being truly perennial.

291. Agricultural history. — Johnson-grass was introduced into South Carolina from Turkey about 1830. It derives its common name from Col. William Johnson, who grew it extensively near Selma, Alabama, beginning about 1840. In South Carolina it is still known as Means grass. Governor Means of that state had sent a planter to Turkey to instruct the Turks in cotton culture, and this planter on his return brought back many seeds, including Johnson-grass.

Numerous other local names have been attached to Johnson-grass, among them Aleppo-grass, false guinea-grass, evergreen millet, racehorse-grass, etc.

In its wide spread since 1840, Johnson-grass has usually been considered more as a weed than a cultivated plant, but as late as 1884 and 1885 it was distributed by the California Experiment Station as a desirable new forage plant.

292. Adaptation and utilization. — Johnson-grass is adapted to the whole region in which cotton culture is carried on, and also New Mexico, Arizona and California. It grows well during the summer north of latitude 37°, but in cold winters is usually destroyed. In favorable years it lives over winter in Iowa and the District of Columbia. It grows in all types of soil, but prefers rich land and an abundant supply of moisture.

This plant can scarcely be called a cultivated grass, as when once planted it is difficult to eradicate, and therefore it is rarely sown intentionally. Indeed in regions where it does not occur, great care is taken to keep it out. Where, however, it is established, it is abundantly utilized both for hay and for pasture. On good soil two crops and sometimes three may be cut in one season. Johnson-grass quickly becomes "sod bound," and unless plowed up every year, or at least every two years, the yield becomes very small. Just why the grass becomes "sod bound" is not clear, but perhaps it is connected with the great development of rootstocks.

Where Johnson-grass is very abundant, a common plan is to plow in fall and plant to oats or oats and vetch. After this crop is removed, two good crops of Johnson-grass hay are usually obtained the same season.

North of the south line of Virginia and Kentucky there is no good reason why Johnson-grass should not be utilized as an annual crop. Sown in the spring, it produces a large crop of hay and nearly always is killed in the winter. At Arlington Farm, Virginia, it has several times been planted in mixtures with cowpeas, for which purpose it is well adapted. It is rare that any of the grass survives the winter.

Johnson-grass probably produces more of the hay grown

in the South than any other perennial grass, unless it be
Bermuda-grass. In sections where Johnson-grass has
become very abundant, more attention is now being given
to its profitable utilization rather than to undertake the
expense of eradicating it.

On rich black soils three cuttings are sometimes secured
in one season, the total yield reaching a maximum of
about 6 tons. Probably about 1½ tons is an average cutting, and 2 the usual number saved. At the Mississippi
Experiment Station the yield to the acre on unfertilized
plots was 3.75 and 4.83 tons, an average of 4.29 tons in
two cuttings. The use of 187 pounds cottonseed meal an
acre increased the yield of hay to 5.54 tons, and 460 pounds
to 5.82 tons; 94 pounds of nitrate soda an acre increased
the yield to 5.54 tons, and 189 pounds to 5.92 tons. Mixed
with cowpeas two cuttings were obtained, aggregating 3.85
tons to the acre. At the North Carolina Experiment Station a thin stand yielded 5139 pounds of hay to the acre.

The rootstocks of Johnson-grass are also readily eaten
by farm animals, especially hogs. In Texas fields are
sometimes plowed up in winter to furnish feed in this
manner.

293. Poisonous qualities. — Under some conditions
Johnson-grass may cause the death of cattle in the same
manner as do the sorghums; namely, by the formation of
hydrocyanic acid. Cases of this kind were reported from
Miles City, Montana, in 1885, and from California in 1905.
It has also been reported by Duthie that Johnson-grass in
India often causes the death of cattle, especially in dry
seasons when the grass is stunted. No case of this kind
has ever been reported from the Southern States where
Johnson-grass is most abundant.

294. Seed. — Seed of Johnson-grass is mainly grown in

Texas, but to some extent in Mississippi, Louisiana and Alabama. The demand for it is not large. The grass is commonly cut with a binder, cured in the shock and thrashed with a grain separator. The yields are said to be 8 or 10 bushels per acre, but a crop of hay can be harvested after the seed crop. The commercial seed is often low in viability, seldom testing as high as 70 per cent.

JAPANESE SUGAR-CANE (*Saccharum officinarum*)

295. History and characteristics. — The Japanese or Zwinga sugar-cane was introduced in the United States Department of Agriculture, in 1878, from Japan. At first it was used mainly for sirup, but in recent years it has been employed largely as forage.

Japanese sugar-cane differs from the varieties grown for sugar in having more numerous, more slender stems; firmly attached leaf sheaths which make it difficult to strip the canes; narrower, smoother leaves than the varieties grown primarily for sugar; and especially in its long period of productivity, new canes growing from the old roots for 12 years or more, apparently without any tendency for the yield to lessen on account of age of the plants. According to Scott, a new system of roots is developed each season.

296. Adaptations. — Japanese sugar-cane in the United States is adapted only to the region south of latitude 33°, except in California, where it has succeeded fairly well in the Sacramento Valley. A temperature of about 15° F. is about the minimum the roots will withstand. It is apparently more resistant to cold than any other variety.

Sugar-cane will grow in any type of soil if fairly well drained, but large yields are secured only on fertile soils.

297. Planting. — Japanese sugar-cane, like other varieties, has never been known to bloom in the United States. It is propagated by laying the mature canes in shallow furrows 6 to 8 inches deep and then covering. To insure a full stand it is best to lay two canes side by side for the whole length of the furrow, breaking joints in laying, as the basal nodes are most sure to sprout. The canes may be cut into pieces of 3 or 4 joints, and this is necessary if the canes are crooked. In the tropics the tops of the canes are often used for immediate planting.

The rows are usually planted about 8 feet apart, as the individual plants stool greatly with age, and narrower rows do not leave room to cultivate.

The canes are sometimes planted in November, which is satisfactory in central and south Florida, but farther north spring planting is advisable, as otherwise there is danger of winter-killing.

298. Culture. — Japanese cane is cultivated much like corn. Deep cultivation is desirable in early spring as soon as growth begins. Later cultivations should be shallower.

The use of fertilizers increases the yield greatly, and the yield promptly falls off if fertilizers are not used, at least on ordinary Florida soils. The experiments thus far reported do not show clearly what fertilizers are best to use.

299. Utilization. — Japanese cane may be utilized as dry fodder, silage or pasture. The crop should be allowed to become as mature as possible without danger of frost injury. If cut early, the plants are much weakened or even killed. '

The experience of the Florida Experiment Station is that the silage keeps well and is relished by all live-stock.

Under Florida conditions Japanese cane silage is about one-third cheaper than corn or sorghum silage on account of the larger yields.

The dried fodder also makes excellent feed, but on account of the hard stems is best shredded. When stored in a barn it keeps well for six months or more, but there is considerable loss if left in the field in shocks.

The cheapest way to utilize the crop is by pasturing to cattle and hogs, which may be done from November till March. The animals eat the leaves and tops first, but finally leave nothing but the hardest stubble.

At the Louisiana Experiment Station the experience has been less favorable, the hard canes making the mouths of cattle sore, and even when preserved as silage being but little better.

300. Yields. — There are no definite figures as to the yield of Japanese sugar-cane, but in the region to which it is adapted, it far outyields any similar plant. Good yields probably amount to about 30 tons green matter an acre, and maximum yields to double this or even more.

301. Seed cane. — Canes for propagation should be fully mature if possible, but in any event should be harvested before frost. To preserve them for spring planting, they must be protected from frost in a well-drained place. The usual method is to dig a trench where the ground is well drained and to cover the stripped and topped canes with enough soil or trash to protect them from freezing. It is considered safer to bank the canes in several small trenches rather than in one large one. Sometimes the canes are simply piled on the surface and then covered with soil, manure or straw.

To plant an acre in rows 8 feet wide requires about 3000 whole canes.

OTHER SOUTHERN GRASSES

302. Carpet-grass (*Axonopus compressus*). — Carpet-grass or Louisiana-grass, called by the Creoles in Louisiana " petit gazon," is now widespread in the tropics and subtropics of both hemispheres, but it is probably native to America. It was first described from Jamaica in 1788, next from Porto Rico in 1804. It may be native to Florida.

Carpet-grass is a perennial with creeping rootstocks and numerous short, rather broad, flat leaves. The slender culms rarely reach a height of two feet. This grass has been known in the Southern States for many years and is now widespread from about latitude 32° to the Gulf of Mexico and west to central Texas. It thrives best in sandy land, especially where moist, and in such situations makes a fine dense sward.

On sandy lands in Florida and near the Gulf Coast carpet-grass is very aggressive, and wherever the land is closely pastured, it is the principal grass. It stands trampling and heavy pasturing without injury and seems to thrive best under such conditions.

Carpet-grass can scarcely be considered a cultivated grass, and commercial seed is seldom obtainable. This grass now occurs in nearly all the area to which it is adapted so that it is rarely necessary to plant it especially. Where this is desirable, however, carpet-grass may be planted by scattering small pieces of sod, as in the case of Bermuda-grass. Or better, the grass may be permitted to seed, mowed when mature and the straw with the attached seed scattered over the field where it is desired.

Carpet-grass requires both abundant heat and moisture for its best development, and under such conditions may be pastured from May until November. During the cool weather of winter it makes practically no growth.

PASPALUM

303. Paspalum (*Paspalum dilatatum*) is a native of Argentina and perhaps also of the Gulf States. At any rate it occurs apparently native from North Carolina to Florida and west to Texas. The probabilities are, however, that it was introduced into the Southern States where it has been known at least 50 years. It is readily distinguished from related native species by having the glumes and sterile lemma ciliate with long hairs.

This grass is known also under the names of large water-grass, golden crown-grass and hairy-flowered paspalum. It is a smooth perennial, with a deep, strong root system, and grows in clumps or bunches 2 to 4 feet high. The leaves are numerous near the ground, but few on the stems. The stems are weak and spreading, seldom erect unless supported by other grasses. Its habit makes it much better adapted to pastures than for meadows, but where abundant it is cut for hay.

Paspalum can scarcely be called a cultivated grass in the United States, as it is seldom sown, but is welcomed in pastures where it appears spontaneously. Some farmers collect seed and scatter in pastures to induce its spread. The best seeds are produced late in the season. As a pasture grass it is desirable from the abundance of leaves it produces, and the fact that it remains green and grows in all but the very coldest part of the year. It is quite tussocky in habit, however, and so is best in mixtures.

In New South Wales, paspalum has proven valuable as a hay and pasture grass and has there been greatly praised by agriculturists. It is said to remain green when all other grasses are dried up, and several successive cuttings, aggregating 13 tons (green feed) an acre, were obtained at the Wollongar Experiment Station the season following the seeding. In the Tweed district paspalum pasture is said to support one dairy cow to the acre the year round.

In the United States paspalum is adapted to practically the same area as the cotton plant, excepting that it does not spread west of the humid eastern portion of Texas. While it occurs on all types of soil it is most abundant on rich black soils and bottom lands.

FIG. 27. — *Paspalum dilatatum.* a, showing arrangement of spikelets; b, a single spikelet; c and d, floret.

Paspalum has given fair results under irrigation in the San Joaquin Valley, California, but does not yield heavily enough to warrant cultivation.

It produces seed freely, but it ripens unevenly and shatters easily. In the Southern States the flowers are nearly always affected by a black fungus and apparently only a small percentage of the seed is good. Commercial seed comes wholly from Australia, but it rarely germinates over 50 per cent and is high priced.

PARA-GRASS

304. Para-grass (*Panicum barbinode*). — Para-grass is probably native to South America and first became known to botanists from Brazil. It is a coarse growing species, differing from most other grasses by producing stout runners as thick as a lead pencil which reach a length of 15 to 40 feet. These runners take root at the nodes and thus give rise to independent plants. Where there is shrubbery to support them they may reach a height of 15 feet. The leaves are rather short, rarely longer than one foot and about one-half inch wide. The sheaths are quite pubescent as are the nodes also. When growing thickly para-grass will under favorable conditions make a dense mass of herbage 3 or 4 feet high.

Para-grass is a tropical species and adapted to wet or moist land. In Brazil, Ceylon and elsewhere it is much grown and fed green to animals. It is sometimes difficult to eradicate in the tropics and is especially troublesome in sugar-cane fields. In the United States it is adapted only to Florida and the Gulf Coast to southern Texas. In Arizona and California it has been tried under irrigation, but has not done very well, apparently requiring a humid climate. Para-grass has survived the winter at Charleston, S.C., and can probably be grown wherever the winter temperature does not fall below 18° F. It often grows along stream banks where it is covered with water for a month or more at a time, conditions which do not harm it in the least. On the margins of ponds it is frequently seen growing in shallow water.

On account of its coarseness and rapid growth, para-grass makes an enormous yield. In Florida it is often cut three and four times during a season, and yields as high as 4 tons may be harvested in a single cutting. There is no particular time to cut para-grass, but it is usually done when the grass is 2 to 3 feet high. The hay is coarse but readily eaten by both horses and cattle.

To secure the best yields, it is desirable to plow the field each spring, which stimulates the growth of the grass. Some planters sow the plowed land to cowpeas and then get a mixed crop of cowpeas and grass at the first cutting.

Para-grass is coming into larger use in southern Texas and some extensive fields are now grown under irrigation. Where the climate is warm and moist no other grass produces equally large yields on wet lands.

This grass is easily propagated by cuttings of the long prostrate runners. These are cut into lengths of 2 or 3 joints, and then merely pushed into the ground at intervals of 5 to 10 feet or even more. This may be done on specially prepared land or in between the rows of cultivated crops. During the first season para-grass usually produces only prostrate runners unless the cuttings are planted thickly. After the ground has become well covered with the runners, upright branches are produced, and when growing thickly all the shoots become ascending.

The seed of para-grass is not very satisfactory, and, as it shatters very readily, is seldom gathered. It is produced most abundantly during dry weather when the growth becomes reduced.

305. Guinea-grass (*Panicum maximum*). — Guinea-grass is native to Africa and has been considered native in Brazil, but first became known to botanists from the West

Indies. It was known in Jamaica before 1756 as guinea-grass; in Guadeloupe before 1786; in Dominica before 1791, and in Cuba in 1804. According to Trimen it was introduced into Jamaica in 1774 from west tropical Africa by John Ellis as food for some birds he had imported. From Jamaica it was introduced into India in 1808. It is now quite generally grown in the tropics and cut green as feed for horses and cattle. In Cuba large areas are now covered with a spontaneous growth of the grass. It was introduced into the United States as early as 1813 when it was grown at Natchez, Mississippi. It is well adapted only to Florida and a narrow strip along the Gulf Coast to southern Texas. In Arizona and California it does fairly well under irrigation, but has not come into agricultural use in these states.

Guinea-grass is a long-lived perennial, with short creeping rootstocks, single plants often making tufts 4 feet in diameter. The culms are about as large as a lead pencil and in the ordinary form strictly erect, reaching a height of 6 to 10 feet. The leaves are 1 to 3 feet long, flat and about one-fourth to one and one-half inches wide. The panicles are erect, pyramidal, loose and open, a foot or more long. The spikelets shed promptly as they mature.

Guinea-grass from different sources shows considerable variation. One form from South Africa is smaller, 4 to 6 feet tall, and the culms are decumbent at the base, and rooting at the nodes. Another, too late even to bloom at the Florida Experiment Station, has leaves as broad as those of corn.

In the tropics guinea-grass is used wholly for soiling, and on uplands no other grass will yield as well. In Florida and along the Gulf Coast, it may be cut from 4 to 6 times, if cut when it is two feet high or less. It should not be allowed to bloom, as the stems are rather hard and woody.

Guinea-grass is not well adapted for hay on account of its bunch habit, but this is much less pronounced when it is grown thickly. The seeds shatter promptly as they mature, but can be secured by cutting off the panicles before they are fully mature and curing in the shade.

This grass may be propagated by root divisions, or seedlings may be grown and then transplanted. The best results are secured when the grass is planted in rows 5 or 6 feet wide and 3 feet apart in the row, so that it can be cultivated. Thus planted it will yield an enormous amount of green matter, probably more than any other similar grass. Guinea-grass is killed when the temperature reaches about 18° F.

306. Rescue-grass (*Bromus unioloides*), also known as Schrader's brome-grass, Arctic-grass, Australian brome and Australian oats, is native to Argentina, but was early introduced in the Southern States, where it now appears spontaneously in many places. The first definite record of its introduction is 1853, in which year it was advertised and highly praised by B. V. Iverson of Columbus, Georgia, who apparently first used the name rescue-grass.

Rescue-grass is a short-lived perennial, but under cultivation behaves practically as an annual. It commonly grows to a height of 2½ or 4 feet, the culms terminated by a large, open, somewhat drooping panicle.

It is naturally adapted to humid regions of mild winters, springing up in the fall, growing through the winter and maturing in early summer. It does not make much growth on poor land, but on rich soils is probably the best grass for temporary winter pastures in the South. On such soils it also grows large enough to cut for hay, and under favorable conditions two cuttings may be obtained.

In the North rescue-grass survives the winter at Arlington Farm, Virginia, and in the grass garden survives 4 or 5 years, but it cannot compete with the better northern grasses in yield.

In Australia rescue-grass has become quite important and practically all of the commercial seed is grown there. The seeding habits are excellent and the seed moderate in price.

Rescue-grass is probably deserving of more attention in the South than it has received, especially for winter pasturage on good land. It should be sown in early fall, and may often be

Fig. 28. — Rescue-grass (*Bromus unioloides*). **a**, glumes; **b**, lemma; **c**, palea.

pastured by December but usually not till February. The seeding rate generally recommended is 30 to 40 pounds per acre. It is always a desirable constituent of mixed pastures with such winter-growing plants as bur clover, vetches, orchard-grass and Italian rye-grass.

s

307. Crab-grass (*Digitaria sanguinalis*) is a native of the Old World, early introduced into the United States as a weed. The older agricultural writers mostly speak of it as " crop-grass," of which the more modern term seems to be a corruption. It is an annual weedy grass that appears with the advent of hot weather and is promptly killed by the first frost in fall. It makes an abundant growth in cultivated ground from which winter crops have been harvested, or even after early summer crops, such as oats and potatoes. Perhaps more crab-grass is cut for hay in the South than any other one grass. The hay is considered fair in quality if cut about the time the first heads mature.

Crab-grass is always a spontaneous crop and is never sown, nor is the seed handled commercially. In lawns it becomes a destructive weed, as it makes dense mats which smother out other grasses.

308. Natal-grass (*Tricholœna rosea*) is an annual, native of Natal, South Africa, now grown commonly in India, Australia, the Hawaiian Islands and other warm regions. Sometimes it is called Australian redtop or Hawaiian redtop, but it has no relation to true redtop. It is a summer annual and in America is adapted only to Florida and the Gulf Coast region. The dark rose-colored, loose panicles are very attractive. It is similar to common crab-grass in its habit of growth, but is larger, more leafy and bears moderate frosts with less injury. The best growth is made on rather sandy soils, and in Florida after the ground is once seeded it makes an abundant volunteer growth after Irish potatoes, melons, oats and other early crops have been gathered. It was introduced into Florida about twenty years ago and is now very abundant in scattered areas through that state. For fall and winter grazing it is excellent and the hay is of good quality, especially when mixed with cowpeas. It begins its growth so early in the season that it is usually killed by any summer cultivation which may be given the field, so that it is rarely seen in cotton or corn fields. The glumes are very hairy and light, so the seed must be gathered by stripping. Seed may be sown broadcast at any time from November to April and needs no special attention.

Natal-grass is valuable wherever it will continue to volunteer from year to year, but its seed habits and small yield do not commend it for growing in rotations. Some commercial seed is grown in Australia.

Seeds from different sources show that the plant is quite variable, and some forms are decidedly more valuable than others. A related species, *T. teneriffæ*, is perennial and may prove valuable for permanent pastures in Florida.

CHAPTER XIII

SORGHUMS

SORGHUM (*Andropogon sorghum*)

THE numerous varieties of sorghum are cultivated in the Old World for three distinct purposes; namely, grain, sirup and brooms, and but incidentally for forage. In the United States the utilization of the crop for forage far exceeds its other uses at present, though the culture of broom-corn is important, and the harvesting of the crop as grain is increasing. Sorghum is potentially of enormous importance in America because of its adaptation to regions too dry for Indian corn.

309. Botany. — The botanical origin of the cultivated sorghums is a complex problem. Hackel on the basis of extensive studies reached the conclusion that all the cultivated forms as well as the different forms of Johnson-grass represent but one botanical species. However, the wild forms easily separate into two groups; namely, the perennials with rootstocks like Johnson-grass and its 3 or 4 varieties; and the annuals which lack rootstocks, like Sudan-grass, Tunis-grass and others. As the latter cross spontaneously and abundantly with the cultivated sorghums while the former can be crossed only with difficulty, it seems more logical to admit two species, Johnson-grass and its varieties (*Andropogon halepensis*) and the annual sorghums (*Andropogon sorghum*) including Sudan-grass.

The wild annuals so far as known are confined to Africa, but one occurs perhaps introduced in Tahiti and Samoa. From this fact the cultivated sorghums probably originated in Africa, a conclusion also supported by the fact that the diversity of the African varieties both wild and cultivated is far greater than that of all other regions. Tunis-grass may be considered very near the wild original form and Sudan-grass a variety somewhat improved by cultivation. There are several other wild forms in different parts of Africa concerning which but little is known.

310. Agricultural history. — The culture of the sorghums is doubtless very ancient, far antedating history. The first definite records are illustrations on ancient Egyptian ruins dating from about 2200 B.C. of what is, with scarcely a doubt, some variety of sorghum. Bretscheider finds evidence in Chinese writings that sorghums were cultivated in China as early as the third century of the Christian Era. Old Sanskrit writings, dating back 1900 years, mention what is quite surely a grain sorghum grown in India at that time. In ancient Greek writings there are no clear references to sorghum, but the plant was known to Pliny, who states that it was introduced into Italy from India about 60 A.D.

More potent than the brief records of ancient history is the mute testimony that the plant itself affords by its early wide distribution and the astonishing diversity of its cultivated forms. Its culture probably extended throughout Africa in prehistoric times and early spread to the southern half of Asia as far northeast as Manchuria. In the latter country an entirely distinct group of forms has been developed, the kowliangs; and the East Indian forms also are very different from those of Africa.

In America, the first sorghum to be introduced was

doubtless the Guinea corn, brought from Africa to the West Indies before 1707, at which date it was much cultivated in Jamaica. In the United States broom-corn sorghums were grown in colonial times, but the first definite record of a sweet sorghum was that introduced in 1853 from France, the variety then called Chinese sorghum and much like that now called Amber. In 1857 it was widely distributed by the United States Patent Office.

Since 1857 numerous varieties have been introduced into the United States, mainly by the Department of Agriculture, from all parts of the world where the crop is grown, as with the agricultural development of the semi-arid region the sorghums have become increasingly important.

311. Adaptations. — Sorghums are adapted to regions having a warm summer climate. The earliest known varieties will mature with three months of warm weather, but some of the tropical African varieties barely come into bloom in Florida in 7 months. In regions of long, cool summers like northern Europe, sorghums are of but little value.

No degree of summer heat seems too intense for the sorghums, but they are injured both in spring and in fall by light frosts.

Sorghum has no marked preference for soil except that it be well drained. On account of its deep roots a permeable subsoil is desirable.

In general the climatic and soil adaptations of sorghums are nearly identical with those of corn. Sorghum, however, suffers less than corn from intense heat, lack of humidity or insufficient soil moisture, often remaining fresh and green when corn is completely destroyed, or remaining semi-dormant during short periods of extreme drought and again growing with the advent of favorable weather. On these accounts it is especially well adapted to agriculture in semi-arid regions.

312. Root system. — In Ten Eyck's studies at the Kansas Experiment Station, the roots of kafir and of Folger sorgo were found to extend to a depth of 3½ feet, but at that depth were less abundant than those of corn. Both varieties, especially the kafir corn, produced an enormous amount of roots in the upper 18 inches. The sorghums therefore have a root system especially well adapted to use shallow moisture promptly.

In Russian investigations the roots of two varieties of sorghum penetrated respectively 106 and 110 centimeters, while corn roots went to a depth of 113 centimeters and spread laterally to a greater extent than the sorghum.

The drought resistance of sorghums would therefore seem not to be especially associated with the development of the root system.

313. Agricultural groups. — No other cultivated crop exhibits as great a diversity as does sorghum. Varieties have been developed for three distinct purposes; namely, grain, sugar and broom-straw. All three of the groups also produce forage as a by-product. A satisfactory classification of the very numerous forms of tropical Africa is not at present possible, but very many of them have been named by botanists. So far as the forms cultivated in America are concerned, the classification into groups as proposed by Ball is here adopted, adding another group, however, to include Sudan-grass and Tunis-grass.

* Stems slender, rarely exceeding 6 mm. in diameter; leaves relatively narrow, 12 to 30 mm. broad; panicles loose; spikelets

lanceolate, 2 to 3 mm. broad, readily shattering (Tunis-grass) or persisting (Sudan-grass).   I *Grass sorghums.*

** Stems stout, usually 18 to 30 mm. in diameter; leaves broader, 45 to 75 mm. broad; panicles various.

I. Pith juicy.

    A. Juice abundant and very sweet.

        1. Internodes elongated; sheaths scarcely overlapping; leaves 12–15 (except in Amber varieties); spikelets elliptic-oval to obovate, 2.5–3.5 mm. wide; grains reddish brown.   II *Sorgo.*

    B. Juice scanty, slightly sweet to subacid.

        1. Internodes short; sheaths strongly overlapping; leaves 12–15; peduncles erect; panicles cylindrical; spikelets obovate, 3–4 mm. wide; lemmas awnless.   III *Kafir.*

        2. Internodes medium; sheaths scarcely overlapping; leaves 8–11; peduncles mostly inclined, often recurved; panicles ovate; spikelets broadly ovate, 4.5–6 mm. wide; lemmas awned.

                VIII *Milo.*

II. Pith dry.

    A. Panicle lax, 2.5–7 dm. long; peduncles erect; spikelets elliptic-oval or obovate, 2.5–3.5 mm. wide; lemmas awned.

        1. Panicle 4–7 dm. long; rhachis less than one-fifth as long as the panicle.
        a. Panicle umbelliform, the branches greatly elongated, the tips drooping; grains reddish, included.   IV *Broom-corn.*
        2. Panicle 2.5–4 dm. long; rhachis more than two-thirds as long as the panicle.
        a. Panicle conical, the branches strongly drooping; glumes at maturity spreading and involute; grains white or somewhat buff.   V *Shallu.*

   b. Panicle oval or obovate, the branches spreading; glumes at maturity appressed, not involute; grains white, brown or reddish.

                    VI *Kowliang.*

B. Panicle compact, 1–2.5 dm. long; peduncles erect or recurved; rhachis more than two-thirds as long as the panicle.

  1. Spikelets elliptic-oval or obovate, 2.5–3.5 mm. wide; lemmas awned.   VI *Kowliang.*

  2. Spikelets broadly obovate, 4.5–6 mm. wide.

    a. Glumes gray or greenish, not wrinkled; densely pubescent; lemmas awned or awnless; grains strongly flattened.   VII *Durra.*

    b. Glumes deep brown or black, transversely wrinkled; thinly pubescent; lemmas awned; grains slightly flattened.   VIII *Milo.*

Of the above eight groups, Durra, Milo, Shallu, Kowliang and Kafir were primarily developed as grain crops, though the last also contains sugar; Sorgo was developed for its sugar; Broom-corn for its stiff fascicled straws; and the grass sorghums are useful primarily for fodder. The waste herbage of each group is, however, used as fodder wherever cultivated. In America probably three-fourths of the total herbage produced by all the sorghums is consumed as coarse forage. Indeed, the only portions not thus harvested are the brooms of broom-corn; the stalks from which sirup is extracted; and the increasing proportion of milo, kafir and durra which is headed for grain, at the present time not over one-half the acreage.

Sorghums are sometimes classified into *saccharine* and *non-saccharine,* depending on whether they contain sugar in the stalks. The discussion of *forage* sorghums is here limited to the varieties and methods used where the whole plant is usually harvested and thus utilized.

314. Importance. — The relative importance of the sorghum as forage in America is difficult to estimate, mainly on account of the four purposes — grain, forage, sirup and brooms — for which the crop is grown. The importance of the crop for much of the semi-arid region, especially the unirrigated lands between longitude 98° W. and the Rocky Mountains, is so great that over much of the region it forms the basis of possible agriculture. In more humid areas it comes into competition with corn. Other competitive crops like teosinte and penicillaria have practically been driven from American agriculture by sorghum, but in Florida and the Gulf Coast region Japanese sugar-cane will give larger forage returns than sorghum, but the latter is grown on account of its usefulness in rotations.

The statistics of sorghums, at least the sweet sorghums, are not very satisfactory. According to the Thirteenth United States Census the total acreage of sorghum was as follows : —

Sorghum for sirup	444,089 acres
Broom-corn	326,102 acres
Kafir and milo	1,635,153 acres
	2,405,344 acres

Some of the sorghum is also reported under the heading " Coarse forage," but it is impossible to estimate how much.

According to the Kansas State Board of Agriculture, there was grown in that state in 1910 acreage as follows: sorgo, 512,621 ; milo, 100,700 ; kafir, 636,201. Of the sorgo the product of only 12,879 acres was pressed for sirup.

315. Culture. — Sorghum is grown for forage either in

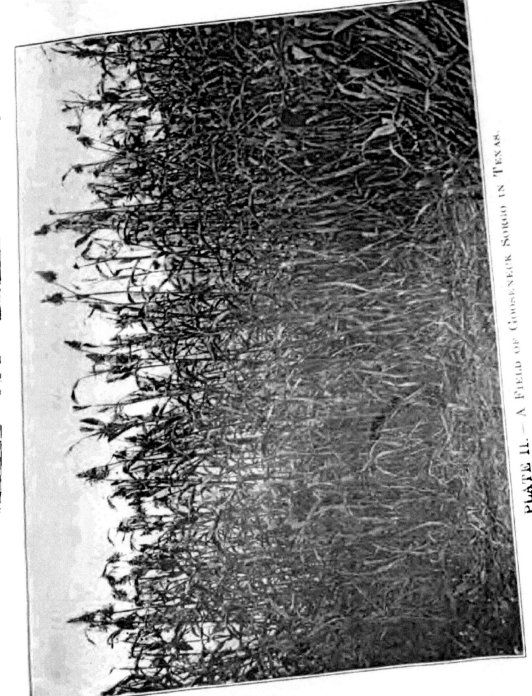

PLATE II. — A FIELD OF GOOSENECK SORGO IN TEXAS.

rows sufficiently wide to cultivate with horses, or less commonly, broadcasted or drilled thickly for hay. Sometimes it is planted in a mixture with cowpeas, soybeans or other legumes.

Good preparation of the seed bed is desirable, especially to secure a firm seed bed and freedom from weeds. Sorghum seedlings grow slowly at first, the more so if the weather be cool, and so are likely to be injured by weeds or even destroyed in broadcasted sowings.

When planted in rows sorghum is cultivated often enough to keep down weeds. In the semi-arid region frequent cultivations are believed to conserve the soil moisture.

Whether broadcasted or sown in rows, sorghum can be harrowed until about 6 inches high with practically no injury to the young plants. Rows 24 to 30 inches wide may be cultivated with a weeder till 2 feet high.

316. Time of sowing. — Sorghum should not be sown until the soil is thoroughly warm in the spring, and usually a little later than corn. Early sowings often given imperfect stands. Later seedings can be made at any time in the summer provided there is likely to be sufficient moisture and time enough to mature before frost.

317. Seeding in rows. — Sorghums may be sown in cultivated rows in widths varying from 18 inches to 44 inches. Cultivation with horses is difficult, however, if the rows are narrower than 28 inches, and 42 or 44 inches is the usual distance used. The thickness of the seeding in the rows may also be varied. Thick seeding will produce finer stems and a larger proportion of leaves, and this is therefore desirable where moisture is ample. In dry regions, however, where the moisture supply may be very scanty, thin seedings are most satisfactory in the long run, even if the yield be somewhat reduced, and the plants coarser.

If the rows be 3 feet wide and the plants 1 inch apart in the rows, an acre will contain 174,240 plants. Six pounds of seed of a sweet sorghum would, therefore, be sufficient if they all grow. Four to 6 pounds of seed to the acre is, however, commonly used in the drier regions, and in humid regions up to 8 to 10 pounds.

In the semi-arid regions sorghums are usually planted in furrows made with a lister, as this is believed to make the plant more firmly rooted, especially as the later cultivations throw the soil about the base of the stems. At Chillicothe, Texas, however, flat planting gave better yields in average seasons.

318. Seeding broadcast. — Where sorghum is sown broadcast an average of about 40 pounds to the acre is best. Such seedings are usually confined to the sweet sorghums the seeds of which do not differ greatly in size in the different varieties. This amount of seed if drilled will sow 1 seed each inch in 7 inch drill rows. In drier regions somewhat less seed is more desirable, but in the humid regions 1 to 2 bushels is the usual rate of seeding.

At the Iowa Experiment Station but slight differences in yield were obtained when sown at the rates of 40, 80 and 100 pounds an acre, excepting that in the thicker seedings the stalks were not as coarse.

319. Number of cuttings. — As a rule sorghum is cut but once for fodder. This is all that is possible in the Northern States or in the semi-arid regions on unirrigated land. In the South, however, where the rainfall is ample or where irrigation is available, two or three cuttings may be secured in a season, new shoots developing from the stubble. To secure a better second crop the rows or broadcasted stubble are sometimes cultivated after the first cutting is removed.

320. Yields of forage. — The yields of forage from the sorghums vary greatly and, as is the case with similar coarse plants, are not often weighed. Maximum yields probably reach 40 tons of green and about 10 of dry forage. Very large yields can be obtained by growing very coarse varieties, but smaller yields of less coarse fodder are more desirable. In general, 3 tons an acre may be considered a good yield and 6 tons a large yield.

321. Seed. — The seeds of the sorghums differ greatly according to variety in size, shape, color and hardness. The weight to the bushel will vary from 54 pounds to 62 pounds per bushel, depending upon the freedom from hulls and the variety. The legal weight to the bushel is 30 pounds in Iowa and Nebraska; 42 pounds in Missouri and Mississippi; 50 pounds in Arkansas and Tennessee; 56 pounds in Kansas; 57 pounds in Minnesota.

According to the last census (1909) there was produced 833,707 bushels of seed on 72,497 acres. Of this Kansas produced 565,522 bushels on 53,706 acres. Other important seed-producing states are Nebraska, Texas and Oklahoma.

The number of seeds in one pound of different varieties is as follows: Sumac, 35,000; Orange, 23,500; Amber, 23,000.

322. Agricultural varieties. — The agricultural varieties of the sorghums important for forage include all the sorgos or sweet sorghums, the kafirs, milo and feterita, as well as Sudan-grass. The broom-corns, the kowliangs, shallu and many of the Indian and African-grown varieties have dry, pithy stems and are therefore much less valuable for forage.

The principal sorgos are Amber, Orange, Sumac, Gooseneck, Honey and Planter; there are four important varieties of kafir, two of milo and one durra (feterita) commonly grown for forage.

Amber. — Amber was the first sorgo introduced into America. It is said to have been developed in Indiana from the Chinese sorgo brought to France in 1851 from Tsungming Island, China. Amber sorgo has open, usually pyramidal panicles with the lower branches drooping; glumes black, slightly hairy, shiny, nearly inclosing the elliptical reddish-yellow grains. It will mature in Ontario and Minnesota.

Red Amber. — This variety was introduced in 1903 from Australia, where it is called Early Orange. It differs from amber in the glumes being dark red or reddish-brown. It is not early enough to use north of Kansas and Maryland.

Orange. — Orange sorgo was one of the forms introduced from Natal in 1857. It has moderately compact heads, 5 to 8 inches long, oblong, cylindric or spreading at the top; glumes reddish to black, two-thirds as long as the reddish yellow grains, which become paler when fully ripe. Usually it is two weeks later than Amber and about one week earlier than Sumac.

Planter. — This variety is much grown in Australia under the name Planter's Friend and in America has been called Sourless from the idea that the juice in the stems would not ferment as quickly as that of other varieties. Its origin and early history are obscure, but forms much like it came from South Africa. It much resembles Orange, but is less sweet and juicy. The heads vary in compactness and may be spreading above; glumes pale brown, very acute, half inclosing the straw-colored grains.

Planter is not considered a desirable variety under American conditions.

Sumac. — Sumac sorgo, also known as Redtop or Redhead, was introduced from Natal in 1857. Sumac varies but little and may be easily distinguished by its erect, cylindrical, quite dense heads 6 to 9 inches long, sometimes loose at the top; glumes dark red or black, hairy, much shorter than the seeds; grains very small, obovate, brownish red. Sumac is too late to mature north of a line from northern Virginia to southern Kansas.

Honey. — Honey has also been called Japanese seeded cane. It was found growing in Texas in 1904, but its earlier history is uncertain. Stems tall, very juicy, sweeter than any other variety known; leaves 14 to 16; panicles erect, pyramidal, very loose and open, 9 to 11 inches long, the slender branches more or less drooping; glumes reddish, nearly smooth and about equal in length to the dark red-brown grains; late, maturing with Sumac.

This variety is probably the best of all in its ability to remain erect until maturity.

Gooseneck. — This is also known as " Texas Seeded Ribbon Cane." It has been known since 1876 and is perhaps one of the varieties from Natal. Stems very tall and stout, 12 to 14 feet high, very sweet and juicy; heads ovoid, rather dense, 5 to 9 inches long, 3 to 5 inches broad, all recurved or at least inclined at maturity; glumes hairy, black, the lower one awned; grains obovate, reddish yellow, inclosed by the glumes; later than Sumac by about one week.

Gooseneck is better for sirup than for forage. It does not lodge much in spite of its great height.

Kafir or Kafir corn. — Kafirs are all originally from southeast Africa, whence they were introduced in 1876, but were not much grown until ten years afterwards. They differ from other grain sorghums in having the stems quite sweet, being intermediate in this respect between the sweet sorghums and the pithy-stemmed sorghums. They are characterized by stout, short-jointed stems, numerous (12–18) broad, rather stiff leaves, and especially by the dense, erect, cylindrical or oblong heads. The grains are oval, half covered by the short glumes.

The most important variety is Blackhull kafir with heads 10 to 14 inches long, and nearly white grains with black glumes. Less important is Red kafir with longer, more slender heads, 12 to 18 inches long and dark red grains with yellowish to dark gray glumes. Pink kafir recently introduced from South Africa, with pink grains, is otherwise intermediate between the Blackhull and the Red varieties. White kafir with white glumes and grains is the earliest variety of kafir, but its heads often remain inclosed in the upper sheath.

Feterita. — Feterita or Sudan durra is an erect-headed durra introduced in 1906. It is much cultivated in Sudan in the region about Khartum. Feterita has rather slender stems, 5 to 7 feet high, slightly juicy and sweet and inclined to produce branches; heads erect, cylindrical, dense but not so compact as milo; grains bluish white, subglobose, much larger than those of milo or kafir; glumes black, shiny, densely hirsute on margins only half inclosing the seeds; early, maturing about one week before milo.

Milo. — Milo is also called milo maize and in northern Texas is often known simply as maize. It was first grown in South Carolina or Georgia between 1880 and 1885. With scarcely a doubt it came from Africa, but nothing exactly like it has since been obtained from that continent, but the yellow durra or *durra safra* of Egypt is more nearly like milo than any other known variety.

Milo is characterized by having stout, rather pithy stems; dense ovate heads, nearly always recurved; glumes dark colored; florets awned; grains pale yellow. A white-seeded form has also been developed near Chillicothe, Texas. Milo seems to be entirely immune from kernel smut and head smut.

323. Seed-production. — The seeding habits of the sorghums are excellent and the yield an acre large. The grain varieties, kafir, milo and feterita, commonly yield 25 bushels an acre and maximums of 75 bushels are reported for kafir, 46 bushels for milo and 80 bushels for feterita. The average yield an acre according to the United States Census was 19.4 bushels in 1899 and 19.8 bushels in 1909. The commercial seed of these grain sorghums is usually excellent both in purity and germination.

The seed yield of sorgos is much less definitely known. The census of 1909 shows a total production of 833,707 bushels on 72,497 acres or 11.6 bushels an acre. Over 70 per cent of this was produced in Kansas, the other important states being Nebraska, Texas and Oklahoma. Of the total amount probably over one-half was Amber sorgo. Good yields range from 20 to 40 bushels an acre.

The commercial seed of the sorgos often leaves much to be desired, as there is usually a mixture of varieties and seldom a pure strain. There is, however, no greater difficulty in growing pure seed than in the case of the grain sorghums.

The seeds of most sorghums retain their viability well for several years, but no detailed studies have been recorded.

T

324. Utilization. — Sorghums for forage may be utilized as soilage, hay, fodder or silage, and with due precautions, may be pastured. The crop should be harvested before frost, if possible, but light frosts do but little damage. If the crop becomes injured by frost, the harvesting should be completed as rapidly as possible.

325. Soilage. — Sorghum is an excellent crop to feed green, and is probably thus used to a greater extent than any other forage crop in America. For this purpose it may be cut at any time after it is 2 or 3 feet high. It is not desirable to cut, however, until it heads, as both the yield and the quality are better at that time. The second growth is more rapid if it be cut before heading than afterwards, but the total yield is probably reduced if cut either before heading or after the dough stage of the seeds is reached.

In growing sorghum for soilage, sowings may be made at intervals of about 15 days, as this is about the length of time that a sowing will afford desirable green feed. Or early and late varieties may be used. The average yield of green forage an acre may conservatively be placed at 15 tons.

326. Fodder. — Sorghum in cultivated rows is harvested much the same as corn, being cut either with a row binder or with a corn knife. The crop is commonly cut for this purpose when the seed is in the early dough stage.

The thick, juicy stems cure with difficulty. It is best, therefore, to begin the curing by having the stalks in small shocks, and to combine these into larger ones as the curing progresses. The large shocks are put under cover when dry enough, or they may be left in the field until used. If left in the field, they should be capped or at least tied closely at the top so as to shed rain water.

When only small areas are harvested, the curing may be done with the aid of a pyramid.

Sweet sorghum fodder, if left in the field, is likely to become sour after about three months, due to the fermentation of the sugar by yeasts. This difficulty is greatest with the saccharine sorghums in humid climates, and probably in nearly direct proportion to their sugar content.

327. Hay. — Where sorghum is sown broadcasted or in close drills, it is usually cut for hay when the seeds are in the early dough stage. In dry regions it may be cut with a binder and allowed to cure in the bundles. In more humid localities, methods must be used to insure as rapid curing as possible, as the rather thick, juicy stems dry out but slowly.

328. Silage. — Sorghum has long been used as silage and the results are nearly as satisfactory as corn. Even in the semi-arid regions the use of the silo has become common in recent years, and an increasing proportion of the sorghum crop, both saccharine and grain varieties, is thus preserved. With the grain sorghums an incidental advantage is secured by the softening of the seeds during silage fermentation, so that practically none are voided by the animal undigested.

For preserving as silage, sorghums should be allowed to become fully mature. In palatability and feeding value sorghum silage has proven to be nearly as good as corn silage.

329. Sorghum and legume mixtures. — A mixture composed of sorghum and cowpeas for hay has long been used. The advantages of the mixture are that the sorghum supports the cowpeas and in curing keeps the leaves from becoming matted. The yield is probably somewhat decreased, but the mixed hay is better than sorghum alone. Amber sorgo is generally used in such mixtures, but in Texas, Sumac is preferable because it is later. Any of the medium late cowpeas may. be employed, such as Whippoorwill, Brabham and Unknown.

Where moisture is ample, the seeding may consist of ½ to ¾ bushel per acre of sorghum and 1 bushel of cowpeas.

When planted in rows under dry-land conditions, the rate of planting needs to be regulated in accordance with the probable amount of moisture. Theoretically there should be one plant of cowpea to two of sorghum. At Chillicothe, Texas, 6 pounds of Whippoorwill cowpeas to 1 pound of Amber sorghum proved very satisfactory.

Other legumes that may be used in place of cowpeas are soybean, bonavist beans and kulthi beans.

330. Pasture value. — Sorghum may be used as pasturage, but on account of the danger of poisoning has never been much employed for this purpose alone.

It is a common practice, however, to turn live stock into a field of sorghum from which the heads have been removed for seed, and when thus utilized there have been no reports of deaths resulting.

The principal danger from sorghum seems to be when the young second growth from the stubble is pastured.

331. Poisoning. — That green sorghums are poisonous under certain circumstances has long been known. The cause is now generally admitted to be due to prussic acid, which under some conditions is formed in the leaves both of young and old plants, but has not been found in the roots or seeds. The conditions under which prussic acid is formed is not clearly understood, but it seems more likely to occur when for any reason the growth of the plant has been checked. As the same phenomenon occurs in

Lima beans, Hyacinth beans, Guinea-grass and other plants, it is quite certainly not due to a parasite. Poisoning has been most frequently reported when cattle were pastured on second-growth sorghum, and on account of the danger this is rarely advisable. A few cases of poisoning by Johnson-grass are also recorded.

332. Diseases. — Three diseases cause more or less damage to the sorghums; namely, kernel smut (*Sphacelotheca sorghi*); head smut (*Sphacelotheca reiliana*); and Red spot or Sorghum blight (*Bacillus sorghi*).

Kernel smut affects only the individual grains, and all or nearly all the seeds in a head are destroyed, but the appearance of the head is but slightly changed. Kernel smut may be controlled by treating the seed with formalin or with hot water.

Head smut destroys the entire head, which, as it emerges from the sheath, is practically a mass of smut spores covered with a whitish membrane. No satisfactory treatment for this smut has yet been found.

Red spot or blight causes characteristic red spots to appear on the leaves and stems. When abundant the leaves die prematurely. All varieties of sorghum and Johnson-grass are subject to the disease, but by selection strains that show a high degree of resistance may be secured.

333. Insect pests. — Only a few insects cause serious damage to sorghums. The most important are the sorghum midge, the chinch-bug, the corn-worm and the fall army-worm.

Sorghum midge (Diplosis sorghicola). — It has long been known that the sorghums seldom produced good seed crops in southern Texas. The cause of this is the sorghum midge, as first demonstrated by C. R. Ball in 1907. This little fly lays its eggs in the flower when in bloom and the young larva feeds on the juices of the developing ovary, preventing the formation of the seed. If a head of sorghum be bagged before it blooms so as to exclude the insect all of the seeds may develop. The insect also lives in *Setaria glauca, Tridens flava (Sieglingia seslerioides)* and probably other grasses. Its occurrence is probably general in the Southern States over about the same area as cotton.

Corn-worm (Heliothis armiger).—The larva of the corn-worm is often found in the heads of sorghum, but mostly in those which are rather dense.

Chinch-bug (Blissus leucopterus). — Chinch-bugs, when abundant, do serious damage to young sorghum plants.

Fall army-worm (Laphygma frugiperda). — The fall army-worm, when abundant, may do serious damage to sorghums. The larvæ usually feed in the young leaves while still coiled, perforating them so that they may break off after they have expanded. Sometimes the larvæ tunnel into the young stem below the developing head, which may later break where weakened.

Sorghum aphis (Sipha flava). — This plant louse is sometimes abundant, but rarely does much damage.

334. Sorghum improvement. — The improvement of sorghums by breeding presents no particular difficulties, but care is necessary to keep any strain pure. Sorghum, like corn, is wind pollinated, and different varieties grown close together cross freely. Uncontaminated seed can easily be obtained by bagging the heads before the stigmas are exposed. After the seeds have set, the bags should be opened to prevent molding. Natural crosses may be found in almost any field of sorghum. Heterozygote plants are often prominent from the fact that they grow much taller than the other plants. Artificial crosses are not particularly difficult to make, but the blossoms must be emasculated before the anthers open.

Selections can easily be compared by the head-to-row method; that is, planting each row from a single head, preferably in duplicate so as to permit of careful comparisons.

Among the sweet sorghums, selections should be for leafiness, disease resistance, sweetness, juiciness and erectness, as well as yield. Yield, indeed, is a secondary matter, as otherwise the tallest and coarsest varieties would be preferred.

Among grain-producing sorghums the yield of seed is the paramount consideration, but in dual-purpose sorghums, like milo, kafir and feterita, the other points should be considered.

When a desirable strain is determined upon, the heads in the row test should be bagged, and from the seed thus secured, a field isolated from other varieties should be planted. As soon as a stock of seed is secured, the variety may be kept practically pure by saving the seed only from the central portions of a field and by promptly removing any rogues that may appear.

SUDAN-GRASS (*Andropogon sorghum* var.)

335. Description. — Sudan-grass is probably native to Egypt, where it is cultivated under the name "garawi," but it may have originated farther south in Africa. It was first introduced into the United States in 1909. There are strong reasons for believing this plant to be the wild original form of the cultivated sorghums, with which it spontaneously crosses wherever the two are planted near each other.

It is a tall annual grass, growing under favorable

conditions to a height of 6 to 10 feet, but when broad-casted thickly it grows only 4 to 5 feet high. The stems are fine, the largest stalks seldom larger than a lead pencil. Where the plants are scattered they stool abundantly, as many as 20 to 100 stalks coming from a single root. In general appearance Sudan-grass is very much like Johnson-grass, but the two are entirely distinct, for Sudan-grass lacks rootstocks and, therefore, never becomes troublesome as a weed. The stems are leafy, perfectly erect and seldom lodging. The sugar content is small, but enough to give a decided sweetish taste. The panicle is loose and open, pyramidal in form and 6 to 18 inches long.

336. Adaptations. — Sudan-grass is adapted to the same general conditions as the sorghums, but it ripens earlier than any sorghum, and will probably mature as far north as latitude 49°. It has been grown with marked success in the semi-arid region from South Dakota to Texas, where it is quite as drought resistant as any other sorghum. It grows equally well through the humid regions and has given splendid results from Maryland to Louisiana. Along the Gulf Coast and in Florida, however, it has not succeeded very well, probably on account of the great humidity. Under irrigation it seems destined to become important, judged from the results secured in Colorado, Arizona and California.

337. Culture. — Sudan-grass may be sown broadcast, drilled or in cultivated rows. Where there is sufficient moisture, broadcasting or drilling is preferable; otherwise the grass is likely to be coarse. In seeding this way three pecks of seed to the acre should be used.

Under conditions of light rainfall Sudan-grass is probably best sown in cultivated rows, though excellent

PLATE III. — SUDAN-GRASS AND NATURAL HYBRIDS.

[The three rows on the left resemble Amber sorghum in general habit of growth, while those on the right are typical Sudan-grass.]

results have been secured in dry regions from broad-casting. In rows 36 inches wide, 3 pounds of seed to the acre are sufficient, even with rather thick seeding, which is recommended when grown for hay. For seed-production much thinner seeding has given excellent results.

It is sometimes practicable in humid regions to sow in 18-inch rows and cultivate. This is especially desirable where the land is very weedy. The grass grown under such conditions does not become too coarse, and further-more, the dense shade kills out the weeds. Five pounds of seed to the acre should be used when thus sown. For drilling or broadcasting 15 to 25 pounds of seed per acre, depending on rainfall, should be used. The seed should not be sown until the ground is warm, that is, about the time for planting corn. Some experiments indicate that Sudan-grass may be seeded considerably earlier, but further experiments are needed before this can be stated definitely. The young plants will withstand slight frosts without injury.

338. Utilization. — Sudan-grass may be compared to the millets in that it makes a large crop of hay in a short season of warm weather. It is preferable to the millets, however, in that the hay is much superior and can be fed to all kinds of live stock without injury to them. While it is closely related to the cultivated sorghums, it has much finer stems, enabling it to be cured into hay readily and thus filling a somewhat different function on the farm.

It is probable that the same precautions will need to be taken in pasturing Sudan-grass aftermath as with the sorghums.

339. Hay. — Sudan-grass may be cut only once in a season at the northern limit of its growth, but southward may be cut two, three or even four times, depending on the length of the season and moisture conditions, and the time of cutting. Sudan-grass is probably best cut when in full bloom, and early cutting is advisable where two or more cuttings are expected. There is little if any deterioration, however, if the grass be allowed to stand longer, as the later culms of the same stool continue to appear over a considerable period.

The grass can be cut with a mower, but more conveniently with a binder, especially in dry regions, as the hay cures very readily in bundles.

At Chillicothe, Texas, 4 cuttings were obtained in 1912 from a broadcasted tenth-acre plot, the yield being at the rate of 8800 pounds of hay per acre. At Arlington Farm, Virginia, single cuttings yielded at the rate of 2.8 tons and 3.5 tons per acre.

340. Hay mixtures. — Sudan-grass is well adapted for growing in mixtures with cowpeas and soybeans or both, as they mature well together and the stems of the Sudan-grass prevent the leaves of the legumes from matting together in curing. At Arlington Farm, Virginia, a plat of Sudan-grass and Black cowpeas yielded at the rate of 4.6 tons an acre, about one-fourth being cowpeas, while Johnson-grass and Black cowpeas yielded but 2.8 tons.

A similar mixture of Sudan-grass and Arlington soybeans, a twining variety, yielded at the rate of 4.4 tons per acre, about one-fourth of the material being the legume.

In these trials, Sudan-grass was seeded at the rate of 20 pounds, and the cowpeas and soybeans 30 pounds an acre.

341. Chemical analysis. — As far as chemical analyses can determine, Sudan-grass does not vary greatly in composition from before heading until the seed is ripe. As

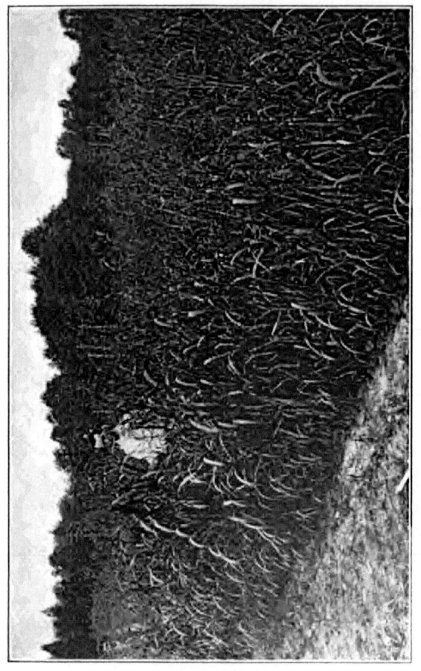

PLATE IV. — A FIELD OF SUDAN-GRASS IN VIRGINIA.

the leaves dry more or less after full bloom, it is probably best cut at that time. In the following analyses, perhaps the most important point shown is the close comparison of the mature plant with that cut in bloom : —

| SUBSTANCE | CUT AUG. 7 | | | | CUT SEPT. 1, BEFORE HEADING | CUT OCT. 1, SEED WAS FULLY MATURE |
	Before Heading	Heads just Appearing	Just beginning to Bloom	In Full Bloom		
	Per cent	Per cent	Per cent	Per cent	Per cent	Per cent
Moisture . .	4.13	3.54	3.46	3.51	4.82	4.38
Ash	6.61	5.55	5.02	5.64	7.12	5.59
Ether extract	1.72	1.39	1.23	1.27	1.49	1.48
Protein . .	7.75	6.06	5.16	4.66	5.63	4.19
Crude fiber .	30.68	31.94	33.23	35.62	34.30	34.44
Pentosans .	21.82	24.01	24.70	24.51	23.38	26.70
Undetermined	27.29	27.51	27.20	24.79	23.26	26.70

342. **Seed-production.** — Sudan-grass yields excellent crops of seed, especially if planted in cultivated rows. At Arlington Farm, Virginia, a yield of 12.8 bushels an acre was obtained when planted in 18-inch rows, while but 3.7 bushels were secured from broadcasted plats. At Chillicothe, Texas, under farm conditions a yield of 356 pounds an acre was secured from 36-inch rows, and on another farm 642 pounds from 42-inch rows. At the South Dakota Experiment Station small plots have yielded at the rate of 1000 to 1500 pounds an acre. The seed weighs 32 to 44 pounds a bushel.

Seed for commercial purposes should be grown on land not infested with Johnson-grass, as the seeds of the two are distinguishable only with difficulty. Where Johnson-grass is abundant, Sudan-grass for seed should be grown only in cultivated rows, taking great care to hoe out any Johnson-grass that may appear in the field.

Sudan-grass crosses very readily with all of the cultivated varieties of sorghum, so that when it is grown near any such variety, more or less numerous hybrid plants will appear in the progeny. These hybrids do no harm in the fields intended for hay, but where a crop is to be harvested for seed the hybrid plants should be rogued out. This should be done preferably as soon as the hybrids appear in bloom, so as to prevent further crossing in the field, but in any event it should be done before the Sudan-grass seed is harvested.

CHAPTER XIV

MILLETS AND OTHER ANNUAL GRASSES

THE millets furnish another example of a crop utilized in the Old World for human food, but in America grown only for forage. They are important mainly as short-season summer catch-crops, but their culture is diminishing steadily. As hay producers they are far less important than the small cereals, namely, oats, barley, wheat and rye.

The term millet has been used agriculturally with a wide meaning, having been applied to about 10 species of grasses belonging to the genera *Setaria* or *Chætochloa*, *Panicum*, *Echinochloa*, *Pennisetum* and sometimes others, including *Paspalum*. The sorghums, too, have frequently been called " giant millets." All the " millets " are rapid-growing summer annuals.

343. The principal millets are the following : —

Foxtail millet (*Setaria italica*), including the varieties known as Common, German, Italian, Hungarian, Siberian and many others. In Europe and America they are used wholly as forage, but in other countries have been grown for human food.

Broom-corn millet, Hog Millet or Proso (*Panicum miliaceum*), cultivated in Russia and other countries as human food and now grown to a considerable extent in America, mainly as a cereal crop, though sometimes cut for hay. This is the "Common millet" of Europe, the *Milium* of the Romans from which the name millet is derived.

Japanese barnyard millet (Echinochloa frumentacea). — This is also known as Sanwa millet and Billion-dollar grass. In America it is grown purely as a forage crop, but in Japan and India the grain is used as a cheap human food. The very closely related *Echinochloa crus-galli* is the common Barnyard millet.

Ragi or finger millet (Eleusine coracana) is much grown in India as a cereal, but has never attained favor in America.

Pearl or cat-tail millet (Pennisetum glaucum) is as tall and coarse as the sorghums and is extensively grown in India and Africa as human food. In the United States it is sparingly grown as forage and often called Penicillaria.

The fruit of the true millets, Panicum, Setaria and Echinochloa, differs from that of nearly all other grasses in having the grain inclosed in a firm box composed of the firmly interlocked lemma and palea. This peculiar fruit deserves a distinct name and for it the name *caryocist* — from the Greek words meaning grain and box — seems appropriate.

344. Foxtail millet (*Setaria italica*). — There is general agreement among botanists that the cultivated foxtail millets have been derived from the green foxtail (*Setaria viridis*), now a cosmopolitan weedy grass, especially in the tropics and warmer portion of the temperate zone. Green foxtail is native in temperate Eurasia and botanists have distinguished about 8 varieties, largely based on the relative length of the awns.

345. Agricultural history. — Foxtail millet is a plant of very ancient cultivation. It is probably a native to southern Asia and with little doubt its cultivation began in that region. According to Bretschneider it was mentioned in connection with religious ceremonies in Chinese records about 2700 B.C. Its cultivation is also very ancient in India and it had early spread west to Switzerland as its seeds there occur in the remains of the lake dwellers of the stone age.

346. Adaptations. — The foxtail millets are very rapid-growing, erect annuals, which delight in great summer heat. In general they require the same climatic conditions as sorghum, but as they mature in a shorter time, are adapted to regions where sorghums will not develop sufficiently. They are quite as drought resistant as the sorghums and are im-

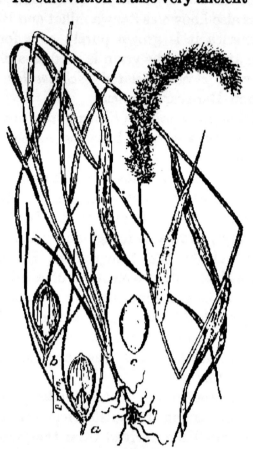

Fig. 29. — Foxtail millet (*Setaria italica*). a and b, dorsal and ventral views of a spikelet; c, lemma.

portant in much the same areas, but as the sorghum will produce greater yields of better forage the foxtail millets are now used mainly as catch-crops when the time is too short for other crops to mature.

Millet bears the reputation of being " hard on the land " — that is, reducing the yield of subsequent crops — but this is probably no more the case than with any similar crop that produces equal yields.

347. Importance. — The foxtail millets are still important as cereals for human food in China, India and other Asiatic countries. In mountainous regions of North Asia they are cultivated by many wild or half savage tribes.

In Europe the variety known as Hungarian millet or Mohar is extensively cultivated for forage on sandy lands in Austria, Italy and the Balkan region.

In America the foxtail millets are grown wholly for forage, their culture being most important in the semi-arid regions, but by no means insignificant in humid areas.

The area planted in the United States in 1909 was 1,117,769 acres, yielding 1,546,533 tons, an average of 1.33 tons an acre. The acreage decreased about one-third between 1899 and 1909. The states where millet is most important are Kansas, Missouri, Nebraska, Texas and North Dakota. Some, however, is grown in every state of the Union.

348. The agricultural varieties of foxtail millet are very numerous and many of them have been given two or more names, which unfortunately have become variously used by different seedsmen. The problem of determining the original or proper application of each name is very involved, and it is very doubtful if this can now be done satisfactorily. The most prominent commercial varieties now used in the United States and Canada are the following : —

Common. — This is the best known and perhaps the

most widely grown variety. It is fine-stemmed and leafy, with a small cylindrical head, compact except near the base, and numerous yellow fruits. It has a short season of growth and produces a fair yield of good quality hay. The California and the Gold Mine are heavy-yielding strains of common millet.

Other names that belong here, in the main at least, are Small millet, Dakota millet, Early Harvest millet, Missouri millet and American millet. This variety has long been cultivated in the United States, but its early history is obscure.

German. — This variety is coarser than the common, with broad leaves and a distinctly lobed, much larger and somewhat looser head. The individual fruits are yellow like the common, but smaller and less flattened. The season of growth is fully two weeks longer, and the hay yield is larger but not quite so good in quality.

The Golden Wonder is a selected type of the German in which the head is distinctly lobed but more compact, longer and more slender. It makes good yields of both forage and seed.

Other names that have been applied to German millet are Southern millet, Mammoth millet, Golden millet and Bengal-grass. German millet was introduced into the United States before 1870, at which time it was well known in Tennessee. It has always been the most important millet in the South. Owing to its coarser habit it yields more per acre than other varieties. It is, however, not so resistant to severe drought. The original source of German millet is doubtful, probably India, but its introduction into Tennessee was from France.

The Golden Wonder variety is said by Crozier to have originated in Michigan in 1884, and its introducers

U

claim it is a cross between German and Hungarian millets.

Hungarian. — This variety possesses a small, compact head with seeds much the same shape as those of common millet. The color of the fruits is mixed, some being yellow, others black or very dark purple, both colors being found in one head. The season of maturity is intermediate between the common and German, but the yield is practically the same as the common, except under dry climatic conditions, when it is apt to be less. It is better suited to the humid than to semi-arid conditions, but is sometimes objectionable on account of its tendency to volunteer.

Hungarian millet is commonly called Hungarian-grass. It is the German millet of Europe, but not that so-called in America. It was introduced into the United States as early as 1830 and probably much earlier, but did not become prominent until after the seed had been distributed by the Patent Office in 1854.

Siberian. — This variety was introduced from Russia about 1896. It is very similar to common millet, except that it has orange-colored fruits. The season of growth is a few days longer than the common and the yield slightly larger, especially in the semi-arid districts.

Another strain of it, called the Kursk, was introduced by the U. S. Department of Agriculture in 1899 from Kursk Province, Russia, and has since been improved by selection. This is the best millet for the semi-arid regions from Kansas and Colorado northwards.

Still other varieties of foxtail millets occur in Japan, Korea and Manchuria, but none of these have attained a place in American agriculture.

349. Culture. — Foxtail millets are mostly sown broadcast or drilled on specially prepared ground, but in the semi-arid regions row culture is sometimes used, especially with the larger varieties like German millet. A well-prepared, firm seed bed is best, but sometimes millets are sown, with very little soil preparation, as on disked corn stubble.

The seed should not be sown until the ground is warm, not earlier as a rule than two or three weeks after the usual time for planting corn. From this time on, millet may be sown at any time in summer if there is sufficient moisture and time enough before frost to mature. The least touch of frost is fatal to millet. Under the most favorable circumstances a crop of millet may be cut in 40 to 50 days after seeding. Towards the end of the season from 60 to 90 days must be allowed.

350. Seeding. — The rate of seeding recommended by different authorities ranges from 2 to 4 pecks to the acre. Crozier on the basis of trials at the Michigan Experiment Station concludes that 2 pecks is the best for Hungarian and common millets on ordinary soils.

For seed-production, however, thin seedings are best and 1 peck to the acre is usually recommended. Under semi-arid conditions millets for seed-production are sometimes grown in cultivated rows.

At the Ontario Agricultural College three millets were sown at six different dates for five years. Japanese broom-corn millet yielded best when sown June 1; Japanese barnyard millet, when sown June 16; and Hungarian millet when sown July 1.

351. Hay. — Millet should be cut for hay just after blooming, but for cattle and sheep it may be left until the seed are in the late milk stage of development.

The quality of hay produced is rather inferior, especially if allowed to become too ripe before it is cut. No danger is experienced in feeding it to either cattle or sheep, but instances of unfavorable results when fed to horses are numerous. Hay intended for feeding horses should be cut before the seed has formed; such hay is more palatable and is not as dangerous.

352. Feeding value. — Armsby, on the basis of calorimetric experiments, finds that Hungarian millet hay is superior to red clover, alfalfa, cowpea or timothy hay for beef production by cattle. This finding gives a much higher value to Hungarian hay than has heretofore been supposed.

At the Connecticut (Storrs) Experiment Station, however, Hungarian millet proved inferior to red clover when fed to dairy cows : —

" In these experiments when clover was fed, the amounts of milk and butter were considerably increased and the percentages of fat were higher than during the test with Hungarian-grass just before and after those with clover. The average product from four cows during the first series of clover tests (August 10, 14 and 18) of 1891 was 281 pounds of milk and 15.6 pounds of butter, and the average percentage of fat was 5.3 per cent; while for the test with Hungarian-grass (August 3 and 27) the average quantity of milk was 249 pounds, and of butter 12.9 pounds, and the average percentage of fat 5 per cent."

353. Silage from foxtail millet. — Millet has sometimes been tried as silage, but is not well adapted for this purpose. At the Michigan Experiment Station millet preserved in the silo was dry and fluffy when removed and much like hay. It had a pleasant odor, however, and was readily eaten by cows.

At the Vermont Experiment Station two cows fed with

Hungarian millet silage after hay showed a slight improvement in milk production. One cow that had been fed on corn silage lost in quantity and quality of milk when changed to Hungarian millet silage, which she ate greedily.

354. Injurious effects. — Foxtail millet has long been regarded as an unsatisfactory feed for horses unless fed sparingly. The experiment at the North Dakota Experiment Station in which horses were fed millet hay for a long period led to the conclusion " that millet when used alone as a coarse· food is injurious to horses, — first in producing an increased action in the kidneys; second, in causing lameness and swelling of the joints; third, in producing infusion of the blood into the joints; fourth, in destroying the texture of the bones, rendering it softer and less tenacious, so that traction causes the ligaments and muscles to be torn loose."

Millet is both laxative and diuretic in its action, but except in horses never seems to produce injurious effects. It is probable, however, that it is always better to feed in connection with other roughage instead of alone.

355. Seed-production. — Millet produces abundant seed and is usually harvested with a binder, cured in shocks and thrashed with a grain separator. It is commonly cut when the seeds are nearly mature, as later cutting results in some loss from shattering.

In a comparative test of 5 years at the Ontario Agricultural College, Siberian millet averaged 47.5 bushels an acre; Hungarian, 45.2 bushels; German, 38.8 bushels; Golden Wonder, 18.5 bushels.

356. Seed. — The seeds of different varieties of millet vary considerably in size and in weight per bushel. In most states the legal weight of common and German millets is 50 pounds, and of Hungarian-grass 48 pounds per bushel. The actual weight, however, varies from 40 to 55 pounds. One pound contains from 175,000 to 250,000 seeds.

357. Diseases and insects. — The only important disease of foxtail millet is smut (*Ustilago crameri*) which replaces the grain with a mass of black spores. The disease is transmitted by smut spores on the seed, and can be prevented by treating the seed with hot water in the same manner as the bunt of wheat.

The chinch-bug is very injurious to millets of which it seems especially fond. On this account millet is sometimes sown around or in strips through a field of wheat to attract the bugs. The insects and their eggs may then be destroyed by plowing under the millet.

358. Japanese barnyard millet (*Echinochloa frumentacea*). — This millet is known as sanwa millet in India and in America has been called billion-dollar grass. It is cultivated in Japan, India and other oriental countries for human food. It has probably originated from the common barnyard millet (*E. crus-galli*), now a cosmopolitan weed in the tropics and in warm temperate regions. The cultivated plant differs mainly in its more nearly erect habit, more turgid seeds and in always being awnless.

Japanese millet is a coarser plant than any foxtail millet, and on account of its thick stems does not cure readily into hay. It has been recommended for silage, but on the whole is probably best used for soiling. Reports differ as to its palatability, probably due to the fact that it is palatable when young and before heading, but much

less so as it approaches maturity. It is not known ever
to cause any ill effects either on horses or on other
animals.

The yields are large when there is ample moisture.
At the Massachusetts Experiment Station it has produced
as high as 6 tons of hay per acre and seed yields of 67
bushels per acre.

359. Broom-corn millet (*Panicum miliaceum*) is of
prehistoric cultivation in Europe as indicated by seeds
found in Switzerland and Italy with human remains of the
stone age. It was probably even more ancient in central
Asia, in which region it appears to be native.

The cultivated plant is sometimes divided into three
botanical varieties: *effusum* with loose panicles; *con-
tractum* with the panicles denser above; and *compactum*
with dense panicles.

The numerous agricultural varieties are distinguished
primarily by the panicles, secondarily by the color of the
glumes which may be red, black or white.

Broom-corn millet is cultivated largely in Europe,
especially in Russia and throughout temperate Asia.
It is invariably grown as a cereal crop, but to some
extent is used as forage. In America it has been grown
most in the Dakotas and Manitoba, though it is well
adapted to a large portion of the West, and fairly well to
the East.

From a forage standpoint, broom-corn millet is not as
desirable as the foxtail millets, the yield being less as a
rule and the stems more woody and less leafy. For seed-
production they are, however, at least as good as the foxtail millets.

The culture of broom-corn millet is essentially the same
as that of foxtail millet.

360. Comparative Hay Yields in Pounds to the Acre of Different Millets at Several Experiment Stations

Variety	Michigan Experiment Station	Ontario Agricultural College	Virginia Experiment Station	Minnesota Experiment Station	Tennessee Experiment Station	New Hampshire Experiment Station
	Hay	*Hay*	*Hay*	*Hay*	*Hay*	*Green*
German from Dakota .	4000					
Common from Dakota	4840					
German from Tennessee	3800					
German from south .	2136					
German	5248	5600	7700	2611		
Common	2952	5600		3360		14520
Hungarian	2240	6600	4840	4820	3500	
Hungarian	2328					
Japanese foxtail . . .	3440					
Japanese broom - corn (*P. miliaceum*) . .	4232	8600	5600			
Hog (*P. miliaceum*) .	2632		3320	3000	1150	21054
Golden Wonder . . .		7000			5000	17908
Siberian foxtail . . .		6400	3420			10406
Japanese barnyard . .		6200			5250	32912

361. Shama millet (*Echinochloa colona*) is a native of India where it is more or less cultivated for human food, but it is now generally spread through the tropics and in the warmer parts of the temperate zone. It is not uncommon in the southern portion of the United States, especially the southwest and in Mexico. It has a general resemblance to barnyard millets, but is much smaller in every way. The panicle is narrow and open and the spikelets unawned. The grass has been tested at many experiment stations on small plots, but has not been found valuable enough in comparison with other millets.

362. Ragi, finger millet or coracan (*Eleusine coracana*) is much cultivated in India and to some extent in Africa as a cereal. It produces large crops of rather poor grain which is therefore very cheap. The cultivated plant is supposed to be a deriva-tive of the wild *Eleusine indica*, native to India. It is markedly charac-terized by having 5 to 7 elongate one-sided spikes arranged in an umbel.

Ragi has much the same adaptations as foxtail millet, but is coarser and more leafy. The varieties are nu-merous. In small tests it has succeeded well throughout the South-ern States, but has never come into use as a forage crop in America.

363. Texas millet (*Panicum texanum*).— This annual grass is native to Texas and adjacent Mexico. It occurs mainly on the

FIG. 30. — Texas millet (*Panicum texanum*). a and b, dorsal and ventral views of a spikelet; c, lemma.

bottom lands along streams, and from its occurrence along the Colorado River, Texas, is most commonly known as

Colorado-grass. It has shown a marked tendency to volunteer in cultivated fields after the manner of crab-grass, not only in Texas, but also in Alabama and other Southern States where it has been introduced.

The hay of Texas millet bears an excellent reputation, and as it is practically always a volunteer crop, it is highly esteemed. The seed habits are good, and more or less seed is handled by Texas seedsmen. As a crop to be planted, however, it cannot compete with the foxtail millets, as it does not yield so heavily. In the southern half of the Gulf States it is probably worth while to establish it generally so that it will make a portion, at least, of the volunteer grasses that hold their own in cultivated land. It rarely does well, however, except on loams and clays, so there is little use to plant it on sandy lands.

CEREALS FOR HAY

364. All of the common small grains, namely, wheat, spelt, emmer, rye, oats and barley, may be and are utilized more or less for hay production, either alone or grown in mixtures with such legumes as crimson clover, vetches and field peas. The production of hay from such crops is most important in regions where the rainfall is comparatively light. Thus wheat is very commonly cut for hay in the Columbia Basin region of Washington, Oregon and Idaho; barley in the same region, but more so in California. Rye and oats are more or less utilized for this purpose in all regions where these cereals are grown. According to the Thirteenth United States Census, the total area of small grains thus cut for hay aggregates 4,324,878 acres, with an average yield of 1.24 tons an acre. This total acreage is slightly greater than that of alfalfa and nearly four times as large as that of the millets. Such cereal hays are mostly utilized for feeding to cows, but with care may be satisfactorily fed to horses. Rye is somewhat objectionable on account of awns on the heads, and the same thing applies to awned varieties of wheat and barley.

The straw of all of these cereals is also utilized as feed, that of oats being considered far more valuable than any of the other small grains.

The same use of small grains for hay is made in Australia and New Zealand. In Australia over half of the total hay crop is made from wheat and nearly half of it from oats. In New Zealand over half of the hay crop is produced by oats.

Where cereals are thus cut for hay, it is the usual practice to cut them in the late milk or early dough stage. In the western United States, where wheat is largely harvested by headers or by harvesters, it is a very common practice to open up the field; that is, cut one or more swaths clear around the field and one or more across the field so as to make a passage for the grain harvesting machinery. The grain cut in opening up the field is commonly used for hay.

OTHER ANNUAL GRASSES

365. Chess or cheat (*Bromus secalinus*). — Cheat is an annual grass native to the Old World and frequently occurring as a weed in wheat fields. The adaptations of the two plants are very similar and formerly the idea was held that cheat is a degenerate or changed form of wheat, whence its name.

Cheat is sometimes grown as an annual crop for hay, planting it in the fall like winter wheat. Formerly it was quite largely grown in western Oregon. In recent years it has been cultivated in northern Georgia under the name of Arctic-grass.

Cheat is easily grown and produces good crops of hay. In Georgia, liverymen consider it equal to timothy, especially if it be cut when the seeds are in the dough stage. For hay purposes it probably has no advantage over the ordinary small grains.

366. Canary-grass (*Phalaris canariensis*) is, with little doubt, native to the countries about the western end of the Mediterranean, though there is doubt about its nativity on the Canary Islands, whence its name is derived. It was introduced into the Netherlands from Spain about the middle of the sixteenth century, which seems to be the first definite mention of the grass. At the

FIG. 31.— Canary grass (*Phalaris canariensis*).

present time it is cultivated mainly in Turkey and adjacent countries for the seed, which is used to some extent as human food, but largely as feed for cage birds.

Canary-grass is an annual species, growing to a height of 3 to 4½ feet, several culms usually stooling from the same root. It is conspicuously characterized by its dense oblong head-like panicle, the white glumes having green nerves.

Canary-grass has succeeded very well in California planted in fall, and in Saskatchewan sown in spring. It will probably succeed wherever barley can be grown, but the demand for the seed is limited. As a hay crop it has no apparent advantage over wheat, oats or barley. Its mode of culture is identical with that of the small grains. At Indian Head, Saskatchewan, yields of 29 bushels of seed and 3960 pounds of straw per acre have been secured, and in California 23,952 pounds of seed were grown on 40 acres in 1905.

367. Penicillaria (*Pennisetum glaucum*). — Penicillaria, Pencilaria or Cat-tail millet is most commonly known as Pearl millet, and there are several synonyms of its scientific name. It is probably native to Africa, where it is largely cultivated by the natives, but it is most cultivated in India. It was early brought to the West Indies from Africa. It is a tall, erect annual, usually growing 5 to 8 feet high, but in Florida attaining a height of 16 feet on rich soil. The stems are not quite as stout as sorghum, but have shorter nodes, more woody cortex and rather dry pith without sugar content. The head is cylindrical, very dense, 4 to 14 inches long and bearing numerous round white exposed grains.

There are several varieties, eight or more having been introduced by the United States Department of Agriculture. The common variety seems to be that grown extensively in India, where it is known as *bajri*. In one variety from South Africa, the heads are much shorter and nearly as thick as long.

Penicillaria is adapted to practically the same conditions as the sorghums. The common American variety will mature seed as far north as Maryland and Nebraska, but doubtless earlier-maturing sorts could be developed.

It was formerly grown to a greater degree than at present, both in the South and in the semi-arid regions, but it has given way in competition with the sorghums. As a forage it is not so desirable on account of the harder pithy stems. As a cereal it has never had any standing in America, as the yield in grain is meager and of poor quality, and furthermore is subjected to much loss by birds.

As a soilage crop, penicillaria will in the South yield very heavily and perhaps is exceeded by no other grass.

For this purpose it is a very useful forage plant. It should be cut preferably when 3 or 4 feet high before the stems become hard and pithy. In the southernmost states it can be cut three or four times in a season and on very rich soil as many as six cuttings may be obtained.

Penicillaria has been recommended for silage, but for this purpose is not as desirable as corn or sorghum.

The culture of penicillaria is practically like that of corn or sorghum. It is most commonly planted in rows 3 feet wide and 3 to 6 inches apart in the rows, under which conditions it stools abundantly. For thus planting, about 4 pounds of seed per acre are needed. It may also be planted thickly, either drilled or broadcasted, under which conditions it does not stool so much nor grow so large. Thus sown it may be cut and cured as hay, but on account of its thick stems is not easily dried. For this purpose about 30 pounds of seed should be sown to the acre. Sowing should take place about the same time as corn, as the plant does not withstand frost either in spring or fall.

On good soils penicillaria will yield as large or larger crops of forage than sorghums, but on poorer soils not so much. Yields to the acre of green fodder have been recorded by experiment stations as follows: South Carolina, 6 cuttings, 94,424 pounds; Georgia, 52,416 pounds in 3 cuttings; Alabama, 13,800 pounds; Louisiana, 16,000 pounds; Kentucky, 80,320 in 2 cuttings; Delaware, 9964 pounds; New Mexico, 56,600 pounds; Arkansas, 9600 pounds; California, 63,000 pounds; New Jersey, 24,000 pounds.

Dry fodder yields to the acre are reported as follows: North Carolina, 6806 pounds; Kentucky, 32,800 pounds; Georgia, 19,474 pounds; Alabama, 2900 pounds; Arkansas, 9600 pounds; Washington, D.C., 15,440 pounds.

Notwithstanding large yields, penicillaria has not become popular, as have other coarse forage grasses, especially sorghum and Japanese sugar-cane.

At the Kansas Experiment Station, penicillaria stover was compared with kafir corn stover in feeding cattle. In a 22-day test the cattle ate only half as much of the former as of the latter. Those eating the penicillaria stover lost an average of 30 pounds each, while those fed on kafir corn gained an average of 6.9 pounds each.

American seed is at present grown mainly in Georgia, where the yield is said to average 500 pounds to the acre. Where English sparrows are abundant, it is useless to try to get a seed crop.

368. Teosinte (*Euchlœna mexicana*) is a coarse annual grass, growing 8 to 12 feet high, and commonly producing many stems from the same root. It is a native of tropical America, probably Mexico, and is closely related to corn, with which it forms hybrids.

Teosinte requires a rich soil and a long season of moist hot weather for its best development. It never has matured north of central Mississippi, but as a fodder crop is occasionally grown as far north as Maryland. The first frosts of autumn promptly turn the leaves brown.

In recent years its culture in the United States has dwindled. On soils of moderate fertility it does not yield as well as the sorghums and on rich soils not so heavily as Japanese sugar-cane. The rather high cost of the seed has perhaps also been a factor in reducing the culture of teosinte.

Teosinte may be used in the same way as sorghum; namely, as fodder, green feed or silage. If cut green for silage two cuttings each 4 or 5 feet high can be secured in a season. The stems contain a small amount of sugar and the herbage is readily eaten by animals.

On account of its abundant tillering, teosinte is best planted in hills 4 to 5 feet apart each way, which requires about 3 pounds of seed per acre; or it may be planted in rows 4 to 5 feet wide.

Yields to the acre have been reported by various experiment stations as follows: Louisiana (Audubon Park), 50 tons green weight; Georgia, 38,000 pounds green weight; Mississippi, 44,000 pounds green weight; North Carolina, 4021 pounds dry fodder against 4576 pounds for Orange sorghum; South Carolina (Charleston), 43,923 pounds green weight in 6 cuttings; New Jersey, 9 tons, as compared to 12.4 tons for milo.

CHAPTER XV

ALFALFA

ALFALFA is at the present time the third most important forage crop in America, being exceeded only by timothy and red clover. Under irrigation in semiarid regions no other perennial forage crop is known which will yield so bounteously. The future agricultural development of western America will to a large degree be associated with the culture of this plant. Further, it may be safely prophesied that alfalfa will become of increasing importance in the east, as the peculiar requirements for its successful culture become better known.

369. Agricultural history. — Alfalfa was cultivated by the Greeks and Romans. According to Pliny, it was introduced into Greece from Media at the time of the Persian wars with King Darius; that is, about 470 B.C. Pliny's statement agrees with the earlier account of Strabo. Perhaps both are based on the authority of Greek writers on agriculture whose works are referred to by Pliny, but which have been lost. Most writers have accepted the statement of Pliny and of Strabo, but Fée doubts its correctness. Media or Persia is in all probability the region of its original culture. Confirmation of this conclusion is found in the fact that the wild alfalfa of that region most closely resembles the cultivated.

Alfalfa is therefore the oldest plant, so far as known, to

be cultivated solely for forage. Furthermore, it is the only plant cultivated for such purpose by Asiatic peoples until modern times. Its culture in Italy in the days of the Roman Empire is referred to by Virgil, Columella and Varro, and it was doubtless introduced into Spain in imperial Roman days. In the sixteenth century, it was introduced into France and southern Germany and from thence to England at least as early as 1650.

The early American colonists made many attempts to cultivate the plant, but only in a few localities was any decided success achieved. Its rapid development in the United States dates from 1854, when it was introduced into California from Chile.

370. Origin of the common names. — The name alfalfa is of Arabian origin, adopted and modified by the Spanish. By different authorities the Arabian word is variously spelt, with or without the prefix *el* or *al*, thus, *fisfisat, isfast, elkasab, alfafa, alfasafat.* The Arabian designations are probably modifications of the Persian name *uspust, aspest* or *isfist.* The word alfalfa is now used almost exclusively in the United States.

In most countries, however, the name lucern is in common usage. According to some authorities the name is derived from the valley of Lucerna in northwestern Italy. De Candolle, however, considers it was probably derived from its local name in the south of France, *laouzerdo*, apparently a corruption of the Catalonian name *userdas.* Historical evidence indicates that the plant was introduced into France from Spain and not from Italy. The word *luzerne* was apparently first recorded in 1587 by Dalechamps who also gives the form *luzert.*

The name *medick* is derived directly from the Greek *Medicai* and Latin *Medica*, so called because introduced

into Greece from Media. Purple medick is ordinary
alfalfa, while yellow medick is sickle alfalfa, but the names
are rarely used. Black medick, however, is still often
used for *Medicago lupulina*, but yellow trefoil is a more
popular name. *Erba medica* is still an appellation of
alfalfa in Italy and the Spanish sometimes use *mielga* or
melga, perhaps corrupted forms of *Medica*.

371. Heat relations. — In climates of low humidity,
alfalfa seems able to withstand extreme summer temperatures under irrigation. No injury from heat has ever
been recorded in such climates as those of Arizona and
Punjab, India. It seems probable, therefore, that the
crop is not adaptatively limited in its heat relations.

High temperatures combined with even moderate
humidity are so injurious that the crop is nowhere successfully grown in humid subtropical or tropical regions.
This is partly due to the fact that such conditions are
favorable to many weedy plants which smother out the
alfalfa, but even if grown in cultivated rows, alfalfa
languishes under such climatic conditions.

372. Cold relations. — The minimum temperature that
alfalfa will withstand without injury is difficult to determine accurately, as it is affected by other factors, among
them variety, degree of dormancy, thickness of stand,
soil moisture and snow cover. These factors are further
discussed under winterkilling. In Europe, according to
Stebler, a temperature of $-13°$ Fahrenheit is injurious
only when the plants are unprotected by snow.

Brand and Waldron report the effects of winter cold
on 68 varieties and strains of alfalfa at Dickinson, North
Dakota, in the winter of 1908–1909, when a minimum of
$-31°$ Fahrenheit was reached. The seeds were planted
both in drilled rows and in hills in the spring of 1908,

and the resulting plants were not protected by snow during the coldest weather. The drilled rows suffered less than the hills.

Tabulated according to the geographical origin of the strains, the results are shown in the following table: —

AVERAGE MORTALITY OF REGIONAL STRAINS OF ALFALFA PLANTED IN HILLS AT DICKINSON, NORTH DAKOTA, 1908–1909

5 strains from South America	99.6%
2 strains from Africa	100.0%
2 strains from Russia	83.9%
5 strains from Germany	83.1%
5 strains from France	89.6%
1 strain from Italy	98.7%
1 strain from Spain	100.0%
4 strains from Arabia	100.0%
12 strains from Turkestan	72.3%
3 strains from Mongolia	33.5%
2 strains from Canada	45.4%
2 strains from Mexico	85.0%
18 strains from United States	83.3%
10 strains from Utah	90.4%
1 strain from Colorado	86.1%
1 strain from Kansas	84.8%
3 strains from Nebraska	76.4%
3 strains from Montana	65.4%
1 strain Grimm alfalfa, from Fargo, North Dakota .	2.8%
1 strain Grimm alfalfa, from Clearwater, Minnesota .	7.0%
1 strain Turkestan alfalfa, from Highmore, S. D. .	9.2%

While the mortality may not have been due to cold alone, the data clearly indicate great differences in cold resistance, as a rule correlated with the severity of the winter climate of the region whence the seed was secured.

Several of the same strains reported on had been sown broadcast in neighboring plots in the spring of 1907, and were exposed to the same conditions in the winter of 1908–1909. The mortality in these plots was very much less, in most cases not enough to injure the stand seriously. It is not clear to what extent this lessened mortality was due to the alfalfa being broadcasted and the plants therefore close together, and how far the greater age of the plants, and perhaps other factors, had a bearing on the results. The fact that the surviving stand varied considerably in different parts of the broadcasted plots indicates that other factors than low temperature were concerned.

The data clearly show, however, that a temperature of − 31° Fahrenheit in a region of comparatively low humidity is decidedly injurious to most varieties of alfalfa when growing in hills or rows and unprotected by snow. Even the most hardy cultivated sorts suffer a slight loss under such conditions.

Undoubtedly the highest degree of cold resistance is found in Siberian strains of sickle alfalfa. According to Hansen this occurs even farther northward than Yakutsk, latitude 62°, where a minimum temperature of − 83° Fahrenheit is recorded.

Extensive trials of alfalfa varieties were conducted at the Minnesota Experiment Station during six years, and data were kept on the loss due to winterkilling. The loss varied greatly in different winters and between different varieties in the same winter. In most cases Grimm alfalfa suffered the least loss. Turkestan proved very variable, a fact doubtless connected with the wide origin of the commercial seed. In one winter with a minimum temperature of − 17° Fahrenheit three strains of Turkestan alfalfa suffered no loss, while 14 strains of Grimm alfalfa lost from 15 to 23 per cent, a much higher loss than occurred in other winters with more severe cold.

373. Humidity relations. — Alfalfa is especially adapted to regions possessing a semi-arid climate, and in such areas succeeds well in nearly all types of soil, and through a wide range of normal annual temperatures. In moister climates, such as much of Europe and the eastern United States, success is rarely secured excepting where soil conditions are unusually favorable. In arid regions the plant will withstand great heat without injury, but a combination of heat and humidity is decidedly harmful. On this account, success with the crop in tropical or subtropical regions can be secured only where the climatic conditions are such as to render artificial irrigation necessary.

Even in temperate climates, wet weather is more injurious than drought. According to Stebler, little success is secured in Europe where the annual rainfall exceeds 32 to 36 inches. In the United States, however, marked success is obtained on certain soils in Mississippi and Alabama, where the annual rainfall exceeds 50 inches, but in general an excess of annual rainfall over 40 inches is decidedly unfavorable to the plant.

374. Soil relations. — Under semi-arid conditions of climate, alfalfa succeeds in most types of soil excepting those heavily charged with alkali. On account of its great root development, deep soils are especially suitable to alfalfa. Good drainage is also essential, as alfalfa roots will not grow in water-logged soils.

Under humid climatic conditions, alfalfa is especially intolerant of adverse soil conditions. In such climates, its culture is rarely successful, except on *deep, fairly fertile, well-drained* soils *rich in lime.* A few types of soil rich in potash, but poor in lime, have also been found suitable, but liming increases' the crop even in such soils.

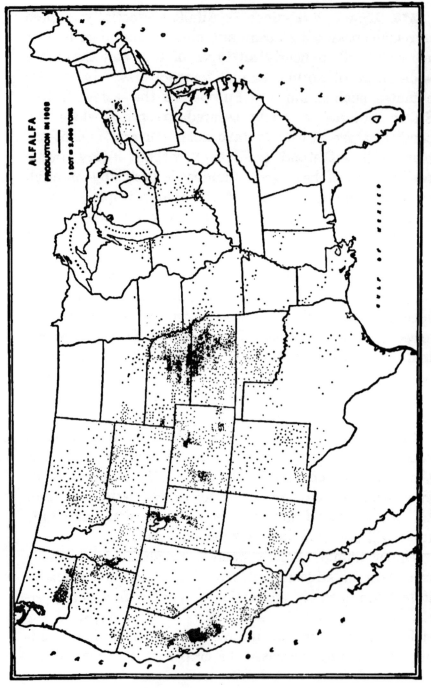

ALFALFA

PRODUCTION IN 1909

1 DOT = 2,000 TONS

FIG. 32. — Map of the United States showing production of alfalfa hay by tons in 1909. Each dot = 2000 tons.

375. Distribution of the alfalfa crop. — The regions in which alfalfa is prominent as a crop are those possessing the proper climatic conditions, or in lieu of this, unusually favorable soil conditions. Thus the crop is important in the western United States, the Mediterranean region, Australia, Argentina, Chile, Peru, South Africa and Central Asia because of favorable climate. Regions with

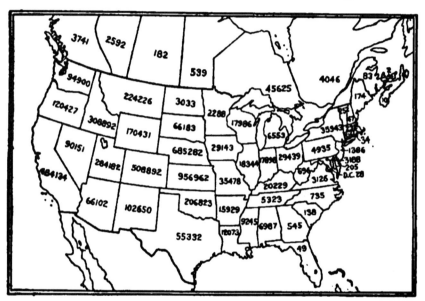

FIG. 33. — Map of the United States and Canada showing acreage of alfalfa. Figures = acres.

less favorable climate, but with an unusually favorable limestone soil occur in Mississippi, Alabama, New York, Ohio and other states and in portions of Europe.

The present northernmost limit of American culture is near the 51st parallel of latitude, in Assiniboia. In Colorado it is grown successfully at an altitude of 8637 feet, and one field 14 years old is recorded as being 7900 feet above sea level.

The accompanying map shows the distribution of the crop by acres in the United States and Canada.

376. Botanical varieties of alfalfa. — Wild alfalfas occur over much of central and western Asia, scattered through the southern half of Europe, and in the mountains of northern Africa. The wild plants are very variable, but some are so much like the cultivated that there is no reason to doubt the genetic origin of the latter.

Besides the ordinary cultivated form of alfalfa about 15 distinct varieties have been named by botanists. Only one of these has been of any particular economic importance, namely, variety *falcata* with yellow flowers and smooth sickle-shaped pods. The usefulness of this variety lies mainly in its hardiness and the valuable hybrids it makes with ordinary alfalfa.

377. Cultivated varieties of alfalfa. — At the present time, there are no established varieties of alfalfa that are even approximately pure strains. Every field, from whatever source, exhibits a widely diverse assemblage of individuals. Nevertheless, several of the commercial varieties or regional strains show combinations of characters by which they may be distinguished. Others, like Turkestan, can be differentiated from common alfalfa only by obscure differences in behavior.

The agronomically important varieties or strains of alfalfa include common or ordinary, Turkestan, Arabian, Peruvian, Siberian or sickle, and variegated (including sand lucern and Grimm).

Common or ordinary alfalfa. — Under this category is included the alfalfa ordinarily grown in Europe, the United States, Argentina and Australia. Most of the European seed imported into the United States is from Provence, France, but seed is also grown in Italy, Hungary and Germany. There is a growing tendency in the American seed trade to designate the state in which the seed is grown. Dryland alfalfa is ordinary alfalfa grown one or more generations under semi-arid conditions without irrigation. The seed is generally considered superior for dryland farming.

Turkestan alfalfa has.been imported into the United States since 1898. The seed can usually be distinguished by the weed seeds present, especially *Eruca sativa* and *Centaurea picris*. The plants are indistinguishable from ordinary alfalfa. The consensus of American opinion is that this variety is inferior in the humid eastern United States, but in the semi-arid regions has some superiority in drought and cold endurance. Under American conditions, Turkestan alfalfa produces but very small crops of seed. On this account, it is not increasing in importance notwithstanding the fact that most of imported alfalfa seed is from Turkestan.

Arabian alfalfa comes from the lower valley of the Euphrates. It is characterized by its hairiness, large leaflets, very rapid growth and relatively short life. The seeds, too, are decidedly larger than any other strain. It begins to grow and continues growth at a lower temperature than common alfalfa, which, together with its remarkably rapid growth, enables it to produce more cuttings in a season than any other variety. In the Imperial Valley of California, it has produced twelve cuttings in a season and in the Sacramento Valley of the same state, eight cuttings. Unfortunately it is short-lived, the stand becoming thin by the third year and but few plants surviving the fourth year.

Peruvian alfalfa. — This variety (*Medicago sativa* var. *polia* Brand) comes from the highlands of Peru. It is distinguished by the marked pubescence of its whole herbage, which gives it a somewhat bluish appearance;

its relatively coarse, very erect stems; its comparatively large leaflets. Physiologically it behaves much like Arabian alfalfa in that it begins to grow earlier in spring and continues growing later in fall than ordinary alfalfa. Partly on this account it is likely to be injured by severe cold. Its large size and rapid growth make it a valuable variety for California and Arizona.

Variegated alfalfa. — This term is applied to crosses between ordinary purple-flowered alfalfa and the yellow-flowered sickle alfalfa. In the cross, a great variety of flower colors appear — white, cream, yellow, bluish-green, smoky-green and purple. Variegated alfalfa is in some other respects intermediate between its parents. It is rather decumbent in habit, but has greater cold endurance than ordinary alfalfa. This is partly due to its tendency to produce rootstocks, a character inherited from its yellow-flowered parent.

Under the name sand lucern, variegated alfalfa has long been grown in Europe, especially Germany, where it enjoys the reputation of being superior for sandy soils. In the United States, sand lucern has given excellent results, being superior in both drought resistance and winter hardiness.

Grimm alfalfa is an acclimated strain of sand lucern brought to Minnesota from Wertheim, Germany, in 1857. In its half century of culture under severe climatic conditions, it has apparently gained additional winter hardiness through the elimination of the less hardy plants. At the present time, Grimm alfalfa seed is the most expensive on the market, being greatly in demand for sowing in states where the winter is very severe.

Yellow, sickle or *Siberian alfalfa* occurs wild throughout northern Europe and Siberia. The European form was formerly cultivated to a slight extent in Sweden and elsewhere in Europe. The yield, however, is small on account of its usually decumbent habit and the lack of aftermath, and the stems early become woody. The seed is expensive because it shatters readily.

Several forms from Siberia have been introduced into the United States in recent years, especially with the end in view of securing hardier alfalfas for Dakota, Montana, and other states with cold winters. Some of these Siberian strains are erect or nearly so, while others have a remarkable development of rootstocks. It is not unlikely that some of these may prove highly valuable, provided seed can be grown satisfactorily. In any case, they offer high promise for breeding work.

378. Importance of the varieties. — Thus far, regional or other varieties have been of relatively small importance. At least 95 per cent of the alfalfa of the United States may be called ordinary alfalfa. Most of the seed is either American grown, or imported from Turkestan. The Turkestan alfalfa is slightly more resistant to both cold and drought. Variegated alfalfa, especially the Grimm strain, is decidedly more cold resistant than ordinary alfalfa, and with cheaper seed will come into much larger use, especially in the northern tier of states. Peruvian alfalfa is more valuable than common alfalfa in the southwestern states, owing to its large size and rapid growth, but as yet it is not largely cultivated. Arabian alfalfa lasts only about two years, and in spite of its very rapid growth, this has militated against its use.

It is altogether likely that in the further development of alfalfa culture, improved varieties will occupy a more prominent place, especially such as are cold enduring or which produce large seed crops.

379. Influence of source of seed. — The general conclusion to be drawn from the available data concerning the influence of the source of the seed of alfalfa, is that the best results are as a rule to be secured from locally grown seed, provided there is no difference in variety involved. It may happen that a newly introduced variety or strain is superior not on account of source of the seed but because of inherently better qualities.

In places where alfalfa is grown, but which must depend on distant sources for seed, the question of the relative value of different regional strains becomes important. Elsewhere this factor is of minor consequence.

In Germany and France several investigators have compared the relative behavior of plots sown respectively with seed of American and of European alfalfa from different sources. In all the trials reported the yield of hay from the American seed was least. At Hohenheim, Germany, Kirchner found American alfalfa more subject to mildew than European. Provence-grown alfalfa seed is held in high regard throughout Europe, but comparative trials have not shown that it bears consistently heavier yields than other European grown seeds.

At three Danish experiment stations, the following results were secured with regional strains : —

Origin	1910	1911	1912
Hungarian	100	100	100
German	102	92	89
French	102	96	97
Italian	104	96	90
Russian	94	83	69
American	45	49	67

The amount of accurate data concerning the relative value in America of alfalfa seed from various sources is not large, but is supplemented by the experience of practical farmers. In the Eastern States French (Provence) seed has as a rule proven quite as satisfactory as western American seed, while Turkestan seed has given decidedly inferior results. In the West, excepting where the winters are very severe, Provence seed has also proven very satisfactory. California-grown seed is not held in high repute, even in that state, but there seems insufficient evidence to warrant this attitude. In general southern-grown seed is not favored in more northern regions, and the evidence is fairly conclusive that such strains are inferior in cold resistance.

380. Comparison of regional strains. — In recent years many experiment stations have tested the relative yielding capacities of alfalfa seed from different sources. This has been done more with the idea of determining whether any of the regional strains possess really different qualities as many of them come from countries where no considerable quantity of commercial seed is produced.

Practically all the imported commercial seed used in America is from Turkestan, so that the only source of seed problem which is at present of much concern, is the relative yielding capacity of Turkestan as compared with that from various American states.

The data thus far secured at most of the experiment stations do not admit of very clear deductions being drawn. Where the tests have been conducted longest the actual differences in yield are not very pronounced. The results shown in the following table were secured by planting the same bulked seed of the different strains reported upon : —

TABLE SHOWS YIELDS OF HAY IN POUNDS AN ACRE OF SEVERAL REGIONAL STRAINS OF ALFALFA GROWN AT VARIOUS EXPERIMENT STATIONS

Source of Seed	Indian Head Exp. Farm, Av. 2 Yr.	Lethbridge Exp. Farm, Av. 2 Yr.	Guelph, Ont., Av. 4 Yr.	Brandon Exp. Farm, Av. 2 Yr.	Brookings, S.D., Av. 4 Yr.	Dickinson, N.D., Av. 2 Yr.	Nebraska, Av. 5 Yr.	Highmore, S.D., Av. 3 Yr.
Canada	8,709			5,050				
Utah (irrigated)			6,800				9,980	
Utah (non-irrigated)	7,943		5,400		2,988	1,085	9,820	
Nebraska	7,473		8,300		3,160		11,820[1]	
Montana	6,294[1]	11,060	6,733	5,100	2,951[1]		11,500	2,405
Ohio	11,108							
Kansas		12,315	5,400		2,547	874	11,260	1,460
Texas			7,800[1]		3,045		11,000	
New York			7,800		3,008			
Colorado			6,000			1,121	11,040	
Grimm	5,589[2]	9,620		7,806		2,150[2]		960
Turkestan	5,825[1]	10,286	6,500	5,695[2]		1,646[2]	10,500	2,073[2]
Sand lucern	9,233[2]	9,895[2]		5,150		1,849[2]		
France	7,582[2]		6,800				10,140	

381. Important characteristics of alfalfa. — Alfalfa owes its high importance as a forage crop to a combination of characteristics, as follows : —

(1) its high nutritive value and palatability ;

(2) its large total yield where successful ;

(3) its drought resistance, due largely to its very deep roots ;

and (4) its long life.

Such a combination of desirable qualities has led to a vast amount of experimental investigations with alfalfa, perhaps more in the aggregate than has been devoted to any other forage plant.

[1] Average for seed from 2 sections of the state.
[2] Average for seed from 4 sources.
[3] Average for seed from 2 sources.

382. Life period. — The life period of the alfalfa plant varies according to conditions and variety. In the semi-arid regions of America, authenticated cases of fields twenty-five years old are recorded, and much longer ages are asserted. In the more humid East, fields rarely persist more than five years, largely owing to the ingress of weeds.

In Europe fields under ordinary conditions are reputed to last four to six years; under favorable conditions, nine to twelve years; and in exceptional cases, fifteen to twenty years, or very rarely thirty years.

Arabian alfalfa is a short-lived variety, few individuals persisting as much as four or five years even under favorable conditions.

Yellow or sickle alfalfa lives, according to Werner, six or eight years.

Variegated alfalfa is perhaps as long-lived as ordinary alfalfa, but records are lacking.

Alfalfa yields are heaviest from plots three years or more old, and tend to decline by the seventh year. Crud in France secured the heaviest yields in the third and fourth years followed by a gradual decline to the seventh year. Walz in Germany obtained maximum yields in the third, fourth, fifth and sixth years, a gradual diminution of the yield following in the next three years.

383. Roots. — The roots of alfalfa are remarkable for their length and the depth to which they penetrate the soil. Under ordinary conditions they will descend to a depth of 6 feet, and authentic instances are recorded where they have reached a depth of 15 feet. Less well-authenticated reports of roots 25 to 45 feet in length have been made, while Stebler and Schröter cite Bonnet's record of a tap root 66 feet long. In ordinary alfalfa the root maintains its tap character, the branches being usually much smaller than the main root which may become one inch in diameter, but rarely exceeds half this thickness. The crown which is just beneath the surface of the soil, becomes much branched and in old plants may give rise to as many as 100 ascending leafy branches. True rhizomes rarely occur in common alfalfa, though the crown may become branched 2 or 3 inches below the surface.

The root system of yellow or sickle alfalfa differs markedly from common alfalfa in producing abundant rhizomes. Not only this, but in some cases aërial branches arise directly from horizontal roots. Such roots may extend six feet or more, giving rise at intervals to aërial shoots.

Variegated alfalfa, in accord with its hybrid origin, possesses roots with intermediate characters. In many cases the roots promptly divide into several branches, and rootstock development also occurs in a large proportion of the plants. On account of this root branching, variegated alfalfa is less subject to heaving, and the deep crown and rootstocks protect the plant against severe winter cold.

Oliver has developed hybrids that under greenhouse conditions produce rootstocks luxuriantly, and suggests that such varieties will be especially valuable for pasturage.

Alfalfa will not thrive in water-logged soil, or, in the language of the farmer, will not withstand "wet feet." The probable reason for this is more likely due to insufficient air than to superabundance of moisture. Alfalfa will rarely succeed unless the water table is more than a foot from the surface.

On account of the deep roots, a friable subsoil is best

suited to alfalfa, though fair success can be secured where an impermeable layer occurs a foot or so beneath the surface. While alfalfa roots will penetrate a firm subsoil, they apparently possess no greater ability in this respect than most trees and shrubs.

The growth of the root on young plants is very rapid. Hays at the Minnesota Experiment Station found them to be 3 feet long in plants when 2 months old, and 6½ feet when 3 months old. Headden in Colorado reports roots 9 feet long on plants 9 months old.

Alfalfa roots have sometimes been reported as being destructive to drain tiling. Cook in Ohio records a case where the roots in a field seven years old had filled up thirty-two feet of three-inch drain tile placed three feet beneath the surface. It is very doubtful, however, whether alfalfa left only three years will in any way affect the tiles.

384. Relations to soil moisture. — Alfalfa roots will penetrate but a few inches deeper than the permanent water table. Further downward growth is probably mainly due to lack of air. It is on account of this moisture relation that alfalfa should be planted only on deep, well-drained soil, as other crops thrive better where the water table is shallow.

According to Fortier, alfalfa on irrigated land does not do well after the third year. He thinks this is due to the fact that the water table is kept too high during the spring and summer.

Alfalfa does not endure being covered by flood waters. During the growing season it may be destroyed if covered by water for twenty-four hours. When dormant, however, it will withstand a similar flooding for a week or more.

385. Seedlings. — Alfalfa seedlings are poorly adapted to cope with ordinary weeds because the initial growth is largely centered in root production. No exact study seems to have been made of the relative rate of growth in seedlings of roots and shoots. Porter at the Minnesota Experiment Station records that plants two months old had roots 3 feet long and tops 10 inches high; at five months the roots were 6½ feet long and the tops 16 inches high.

386. Rootstocks. — Common alfalfa rarely shows any trace of rootstocks. These are, however, well developed in some forms of sickle alfalfa, and remarkably so in *Medicago sativa Gaetula* from Tunis, in which they may reach a length of 3½ feet. They also appear commonly in the variegated hybrid alfalfas, and less so in Turkestan and Mongolian alfalfas, but appear to be absent in the Peruvian and Arabian forms.

Oliver has bred some hybrids remarkable for the extent to which they develop rootstocks, at least under greenhouse conditions. Some of the hybrids form a dense matted growth, a single plant covering a surface of several square feet, and presenting much the general appearance of white clover. The value of these for pasturage purposes is suggested.

Oakley has recently described some extraordinary examples of sickle alfalfa. These produce horizontal roots two to four feet long, which at intervals give rise to erect leafy shoots. These shoots may grow from as great a depth as twelve inches, and commonly arise from nodular swellings on the roots.

The development of rootstocks is greater when plants are grown isolated than when sown thickly. It seems also to be encouraged by partly covering the plants with soil. True rootstocks on alfalfa were first noted on variegated alfalfa in England in 1791 by Le Blanc, who states that he preferred this variety because of its greater ability to withstand cold and also to resist choking by grasses.

Under Colorado conditions, Blinn found that Arabian and North African strains of alfalfa, when planted in hills, suffered a loss of over one-half from winter-killing. Under the same conditions, strains from Mexico, Spain and South America also showed considerable loss, while Turkestan and Grimm alfalfa plants all survived. In connection with the last two varieties, the production of rootstocks is noted, and Blinn believes that winter hardiness is largely associated with this habit.

387. Shoots. — A well-developed alfalfa plant has from 20 to 50 erect or suberect leafy branched shoots, which usually grow to a height varying from 18 to 36 inches. The form of the leaflets, as well as the degree of leafiness, vary considerably. In different varieties the stem varies from very hairy to nearly smooth. It may be either green or purplish.

Under its natural conditions of environment — namely, a dry summer season — alfalfa produces but a single crop of stems, these drying as the seeds ripen. In a humid climate, however, a new crop of shoots begins to develop about the time the plant reaches full bloom, and this militates strongly against seed-production. In arid climates where irrigation is practiced, the development of the new shoots can be controlled by supplying or withholding water.

There seems to be no limit to the number of crops of shoots an alfalfa plant will produce under favorable conditions. Only when an unfavorable condition of cold or drought intervenes does growth cease.

Yellow or sickle alfalfa differs markedly from true alfalfa, in that the shoots are usually procumbent or prostrate, and a second crop is but rarely produced, correlated probably with the production of rootstocks.

Variegated alfalfa, at least in its commercial forms, behaves much like ordinary alfalfa, but the shoots are not so erect. In Germany, according to Werner, the new growth after cutting is less prompt than in common alfalfa, and the yield less.

Dillman found at Bellefourche, South Dakota, that a well-grown plant of alfalfa will produce in the first cutting 134 to 192 grams of hay.

388. Relative proportion of leaves, stems and roots. — Headden in Colorado has estimated the ratio of roots to tops to be as 1 : 1.3, based on the weights obtained from thirty-two plants. At the Delaware Experiment Station the roots and tops in one acre were determined respectively as 1980 and 2267 pounds. Ritthausen in Europe found the average percentage weight of leaves to stems in alfalfa hay to be 48 to 52. Cottrell in Kansas found an average relation of 45 parts leaves to 55 of stems. In very leafy plants, the proportion was 49 to 51; and in very stemmy individuals, 41 to 59.

The subject has been further studied at the Utah Experiment Station by Widtsoe, who determined the relative percentage of leaves, stems and flowers at nearly every stage of growth for the first, second and third cuttings. In the following table are shown the data obtained from the first and second cuttings made when the plants were in bloom. It will be noted that the percentage of leaves decreases as the plants grow older, and that the second crop is less stemmy than the first : —

TABLE SHOWING PERCENTAGE OF LEAVES, STEMS AND FLOW-
ERS IN DRY ALFALFA HARVESTED AT DIFFERENT STAGES.
UTAH EXPERIMENT STATION

FIRST CROP					SECOND CROP			
Date of Cutting	Condition of the Crop	% of Leaves	% of Stems	% of Flow-ers	Date of Cutting	% of Leaves	% of Stems	% of Flow-ers
June 22	Early bloom	38.4	58.8	2.8	July 14	43.7	54.6	1.7
June 29	Medium bloom	35.2	59.4	5.4	July 20	42.4	50.8	6.8
July 7	Full flower	33.9	59.8	6.3	July 27	36.8	55.6	7.6
July 20	Full flower	25.3	67.4	7.3	Aug. 3	35.1	51.6	13.3
July 27	Late bloom	22.7	67.3	10.0				

389. Seed-bed. — Young alfalfa plants are but poorly
adapted to compete with weeds, largely from the fact
that the early growth is devoted mainly to root extension.
On this account, a seed-bed as free as possible from weeds
is important, and it is also desirable that it be well settled
and moist. Such a seed-bed is best secured by fallowing
the land for six weeks or more before sowing. Or, where
the alfalfa is sown in the late summer or early fall, a clean
hoed crop, such as potatoes or tomatoes, may in some
states be harvested by the middle of August and leave the
land in excellent shape for alfalfa.

On land that is likely to drift, special care is necessary
to secure a stand of alfalfa. In such cases, nurse-crops
are seldom practicable on account of insufficient moisture.
Drifting, however, may be prevented by scattering straw
or coarse manure over the field, or the alfalfa may be sown
in the old stubble of corn or sorghum.

390. Inoculation. — Alfalfa will rarely grow to maturity unless the roots become noduled. Without the nodules the young plants grow but three to six inches high, gradually turn yellow and die. Natural inoculation is rare except in regions where alfalfa is grown extensively or where a few closely related plants have been growing, including melilotus, bur clover and yellow trefoil. The fact that the nodule germs of melilotus will inoculate alfalfa was first proven by Hopkins. There is no positive proof in the cases of bur clover and yellow trefoil, but field observations leave little doubt as to their efficacy.

The nodules, of alfalfa are small, club-shaped when simple, but often branched to resemble fingers. Rarely there are enough branches to form a globose mass. These nodules are all on the smaller roots, and are nearly always stripped off when a plant is pulled out of the ground.

391. Rate of seeding. — One pound of common alfalfa contains about 220,000 seeds. Therefore, each pound of alfalfa seed, if evenly sown on an acre of 43,560 square feet, would average over five seeds to the square foot. Alfalfa fields one year old rarely contain more than twenty plants to the square foot and older fields usually have less than ten. In the United States, the usual rate of seeding alfalfa to the acre is twenty pounds in the West and twenty-five to thirty pounds in the East. In Europe, the rate is variously given as twenty-five to thirty-five pounds to the acre. Fair stands of alfalfa have been secured in the West with one pound of seed to the acre, and good stands are not rarely obtained with five pounds an acre.

Westgate, on the basis of thorough inquiry into the practice of the best growers, recommends twenty-four to twenty-eight pounds an acre for the Atlantic and Southern States; twenty to twenty-four pounds for the region between the meridian of 98° and the Appalachian Mountains; five to fifteen pounds on unirrigated, semi-arid lands, depending on the amount of rainfall; fifteen pounds on irrigated lands.

Provided a good stand is secured, a low rate of seeding is just as satisfactory as a high rate. At Lethbridge, Alberta, alfalfa was seeded at the following rates on irrigated land: 5, 10, 15, 20, 25, 30 pounds an acre. The average yields for 3 years were, respectively, 10,273, 11,333, 11,426, 11,220, 10,875 and 11,394 pounds an acre.

392. Time of seeding. — Alfalfa is sown either in the spring or in late summer or early fall, depending on climatic and other conditions. In the irrigated lands of the West, spring seeding is most frequently practiced, but fall seeding is just as successful. On unirrigated lands in the West, the time is usually determined by the moisture conditions of the soil. In the Great Plains region, this is usually best in spring, while in the intermountain region, spring seeding on fallow land is a common practice. In states with very cold winters spring or early summer seeding is necessary, as fall-sown stands are likely to be winter-killed. Where the winters are not severe, and moisture conditions permit, late summer or early fall sowing is preferable. The sowing should be early enough to permit the alfalfa plants to become well rooted by winter; otherwise, serious losses may result from heaving; and late enough so that summer weeds — especially, crabgrass and pigeon-grass — will not seriously affect the stand. In the Northern States, winter-killing is the most serious difficulty in securing a stand of alfalfa, while southward, weeds become the principal factor. From an economic standpoint, fall sowing in the East is also preferable, as a good crop is secured the next season, while with spring sowing, very little alfalfa can be harvested the same season.

393. Method of seeding. — Alfalfa seeds germinate satisfactorily from all depths up to two inches under satisfactory conditions of moisture. At a greater depth all of the seedlings will not reach the surface. In field practice, the aim is to sow the seed from one-half to one inch deep in ordinary soils, but under droughty conditions or in sandy soils one and one-half inches is safer.

The seed is variously sown by hand or by using different types of seeders. A grain drill is the most economical implement to use where the planting is extensive. In this case the amount of seed sown may be regulated by the use of leather thongs to reduce the feed, or by mixing the seed with bran or other inert substance.

394. Nurse-crops. — The use of a nurse-crop for alfalfa is to be recommended only in regions or on soils where but little difficulty is experienced in securing a stand. It is doubtful whether a nurse-crop is ever beneficial to the alfalfa, but on the irrigated lands of the West, alfalfa may be sown with a nurse-crop, and a good stand usually secured. Spring-sown barley is used most often, as the nurse; oats less frequently. Barley draws less heavily on the soil moisture.

In the humid parts of the United States, occasional examples are found where success has been obtained by sowing alfalfa with spring oats or barley. This, however, involves sowing the alfalfa seed early in spring, an unfavorable time on account of weeds, besides increasing the chance of failure from drought. Seeding in fall with winter wheat, oats or rye postpones the sowing beyond the most favorable time to insure ample growth of the alfalfa before winter. In view of the care usually necessary to secure a stand of alfalfa in humid regions, the use of a nurse-crop under such conditions is inadvisable as a rule.

When, however, experience has shown that all the soil conditions are favorable, spring seeding with a nurse-crop gives good results. This is especially true in the northern tier of states and in Ontario. At the Ontario Agricultural College just as good results were secured with a nurse-crop of barley, seeding one bushel to the acre, as where no barley was used. In an experiment comparing wheat, barley and oats as nurse-crops, wheat was the best, but not much superior to barley, while oats was decidedly the poorest, all measured by the resulting yields of alfalfa for 2 years. In a few instances, successful stands of alfalfa have been secured by sowing between the rows of corn at the time of the last cultivation. Without very favorable moisture conditions, success with such sowing is problematical.

395. Clipping. — Some writers have recommended clipping young alfalfa, when three or four inches high, with the idea that this treatment would strengthen the subsequent growth in a manner analogous to the pruning of trees. The cases are, however, not comparable, inasmuch as there is no reserve store of food in the alfalfa plant, as there is in the branches of trees. Clipping is never justifiable unless weeds threaten to smother out the young alfalfa. Exact data are wanting to show the effect of clipping on yields. In one experiment at Pullman, Washington, the effects of clipping could easily be observed for two years, the clipped plot showing weaker growth.

At the Ohio Experiment Station, three plots of alfalfa were sown June 27. One of these was clipped September 9, when 12 to 18 inches high, and about 15 per cent in bloom;

the second, October 16, when the blossoms were mostly
dried up; the third was left uncut. In the spring the
unclipped plot started off with a noticeably stronger
growth than the others. It produced a yield in three
cuttings 522 pounds greater than the plot clipped October 16, and 1376 pounds greater than that clipped September 9. The September clipped plot was apparently
injured by the weed growth that took place after clipping.

At Lyngby, Denmark, the effect of cutting spring-sown
alfalfa the same year it was seeded was tested. It was
found that the first season's crop plus that of the second
season was not equal to that of the second year's crop
alone on plots that had not been cut the first year.

396. Winter-killing. — The injury or destruction of
alfalfa in winter is associated with various factors. Among
the most important are the variety; the actual minimum
temperature; the amount of snow cover; the thickness
of the stand; the amount of moisture in the soil; the
condition of dormancy; alternate freezing and thawing;
and particularly the condition of the plants at the beginning of winter.

The most cold-resistant varieties of alfalfa are Grimm
and strains of Turkestan and ordinary alfalfa which have
been grown under severe winter conditions, as in Montana and the Dakotas, for many years. In all these,
natural selection has eliminated the non-hardy individuals.

Injury to alfalfa by cold alone is rarely serious unless
the temperature falls to − 20° Fahrenheit or lower. In
North Dakota all but the most hardy varieties, when
planted in rows and not protected by snow, showed a
loss of 80 per cent or more in a winter where the minimum
temperature was − 31° Fahrenheit. In broadcasted
stands, however, the loss was much less. A thick stand

probably provides a somewhat higher soil temperature, and also reduces the percentage of soil moisture.

Alfalfa is, however, successfully grown in regions where a minimum of − 40° Fahrenheit, or even lower, is not uncommon, as in Minnesota, North Dakota and Montana. This is doubtless due in part to protection afforded by snow.

Young alfalfa is more often winter-killed by cold than older plants, but there are no accurate data as to their relative cold endurance. It sometimes happens that alfalfa — especially in low spots — becomes covered for a considerable period by a sheeting of ice. This usually kills the plants.

The degree of dormancy of the plants also affects their ability to resist cold. It is well known that fruit trees are much less likely to be injured by cold when the twigs have become fully hardened and dormant and remain so during the winter. In the irrigated regions, instances have occurred where a portion of the orchard was irrigated late in the season so that the trees did not become fully dormant. These were winter-killed when adjoining trees of the same variety not irrigated escaped injury. For the same reason, warm weather in late winter which starts growth in the trees is likely to be disastrous if followed by more cold. The behavior of alfalfa seems exactly comparable to that of fruit trees, in that dormant plants are much more resistant to cold and that high soil moisture tends to retard dormancy. Fortier cites the experience of a farmer at Chateau, Montana, who irrigated late in the fall a portion of a field of alfalfa two years old. This winter-killed, while the unirrigated portion was unharmed.

Peruvian and Arabian alfalfas are varieties which continue to grow at temperatures lower than that which induces dormancy in most varieties. This late production of tender shoots is probably the principal reason why these varieties succumb so easily to winter cold.

Alfalfa sometimes dies in very dry winters in Colorado and other western states apparently from lack of sufficient soil moisture. To remedy this, late fall irrigating would be necessary, though this involves an increased danger of injury by winter cold.

Young alfalfa is most frequently injured or destroyed by the heaving of the soil caused by alternate freezing and thawing. This results in the plants being raised out of the ground so that the young tap root may be exposed to a length of 2 to 5 inches. It is partly on this account that fall sowings should be early, as the larger the root development the less apt are the plants to be heaved. Heaving is especially likely to occur when the soil contains much moisture, and for this reason is far more common in clayey than in sandy soils.

Any conditions that do not permit the seedlings to make a good healthy growth before the beginning of winter, will tend to increase winter-killing. A top growth of 4 to 6 inches is considered good, but even more is desirable.

397. Time to cut for hay. — The important factors that determine the best time to cut alfalfa for hay are the effect on the succeeding cutting, and the relation of stage of maturity to feeding value. Both of these considerations are necessarily affected by the probability of good haying weather, as neither a somewhat superior quality or a lessened succeeding cutting would compensate for a loss or serious injury to the crop at hand.

The general practice in America is to cut for hay shortly after the first blossoms appear. After this time the stems become more woody, and the leaflets are more likely to fall off. In Europe, Stebler and Schröter recommend that it be cut some time before flowering.

In humid regions, alfalfa sometimes blooms but sparingly. In such climates the best rule is to cut for hay as soon as new shoots appear at the crown. If cutting is delayed longer, the new shoots are apt to be cut off, thus injuring the second crop. This difficulty does not arise during periods of drought, and in arid regions can be controlled by withholding irrigation.

Late cuttings may also be at the expense of total yield. At the Utah Experiment Station, three plots of alfalfa during five seasons were cut respectively when the first blossoms appeared; when in full bloom; and when half the blossoms had fallen. The first two plots produced three cuttings annually, the third but two, except one unusually favorable season when three were harvested. The average acre yields for the three plots were respectively, 4553, 3554 and 1776 pounds, or a relative proportion of 100 : 78 : 39.

At the Kansas Experiment Station, four plots of $\frac{1}{8}$ acre each duplicated were cut respectively when in first bloom, in one-tenth bloom, in one-half bloom and in full bloom. The respective acre yields for the first cutting were 1.36, 1.76, 1.81 and 2.04 tons; for the whole season, 4.69, 5.35, 4.52 and 5.99 tons. In this case the late cuttings gave both the greatest yield to the cutting and the largest total.

The question of the best time to cut alfalfa for hay has also been much studied from the viewpoint of chemical composition and digestibility. Thus, Willard, in Kansas, compared alfalfa hay cut at three stages — namely, when about 10 per cent in bloom; when about half in bloom; and in full bloom. The first mentioned was found " richer in ash, protein and fat than that produced by later cuttings, while the crude fiber and the nitrogen-free extract increase in percentage as the plant matures."

Harcourt, at the Ontario Agricultural College, concludes that " a much larger amount of digestible matter was obtained by cutting when the plants were about one-third in bloom than by cutting either two weeks earlier or two weeks later." Snyder and Hummel in Minnesota state that " alfalfa for hay should be cut when one-third of the blossoms have appeared because at this stage it will yield the largest amounts of the several nutrients in the most valuable forms." Widtsoe in Utah holds " that to insure a large yield of dry matter and the largest amounts of albuminoids, lucern should be cut not earlier than the period of medium bloom and not much later than the period of first full flower. This in most cases will be two or three weeks after the flower buds begin to appear. It will be a more serious error to cut too early than to cut too late." Headden in Colorado concludes from his investigations of alfalfa " that the best general-purpose hay is obtained by cutting it when it is in full bloom."

The object for which the hay is cut is also a factor to be considered. For horses it is generally held that alfalfa cut in full bloom is best, as earlier cuttings are too laxative. This conclusion is also reached by the Kansas Experiment Station, as the result of extensive horse feeding experiments. Horses, however, frequently eat only the alfalfa stems, leaving much of the leaves in the bottom of the manger.

Alfalfa straw or hay from ripe alfalfa must be fed

very cautiously. Werner states that it is dangerous to feed alfalfa hay containing ripe seeds to horses, as the seeds are apt to cause laryngeal trouble.

At the Ontario Agricultural College, a valuable cow died of stoppage of the bowels after being fed on ripened alfalfa. The ball of indigestible fiber found in the intestine was supposed to be formed from the alfalfa eaten. A sheep also was affected in a similar way, but recovered.

398. Number of cuttings. — The number of times alfalfa can be cut for hay depends mainly on the length of the season; secondly, on the moisture supply. Under the most favorable conditions, a cutting can be made every thirty days. As many as nine cuttings of ordinary alfalfa, and twelve of Arabian alfalfa have been secured in a year in the Imperial Valley, California. Over most of the irrigated region, from three to five cuttings are obtained. Without irrigation, frequently only one crop can be harvested in the drier states, but three cuttings are the rule wherever corn will mature and moisture conditions are favorable. At high altitudes in the Rocky Mountains where the season permits of but a single cutting of alfalfa, red clover is preferable, as it will make its growth in cooler weather.

399. Quality of different cuttings. — The first cutting of alfalfa is as a rule coarser than the later cuttings, and in some markets this has an effect on its price. From a chemical standpoint there is very little difference between the first and the later cuttings.

At the Utah Experiment Station alfalfa from three cuttings grown on light bench lands was fed to milch cows to determine their relative value in the production of butter fat. The opinion of dairymen in Utah is that the second cutting of alfalfa hay is far superior to the first cutting and somewhat better than the third cutting. The experiments were carried on two seasons with three lots of 5 dairy cows each, each lot being fed for 4 weeks with each cutting of hay after a preliminary feeding of 25 days. The cows both years ate most of the third crop, followed in order by the first and the second crops. The total amounts of butter fat produced were, respectively, 707, 687 and 675 pounds for the first, second and third cuttings in order. On the whole the experiment does not indicate any marked difference in feeding value of the three cuttings.

400. Irrigation. — A large proportion of the alfalfa grown in the United States and Canada is produced under irrigation in the semi-arid regions. The general practice of growers is to use far more water than is necessary. This is harmful, as in time it brings about a water-logged condition of the soil, which in itself is directly harmful to the alfalfa, but indirectly far more so, as it causes soluble alkali salts to rise and accumulate near the surface. On this account it is best to apply only as much water as will result in the production of satisfactory crops. This amount varies principally according to the character of the soil. To a less degree it is affected by the amount of evaporation and transpiration, these increasing with high temperature, dryness of the air and wind movements. The optimum amount of water required needs, therefore, to be determined in each locality by comparative plot trials.

401. Time to apply irrigating water. — In irrigation farming, alfalfa is practically always irrigated as soon as each crop is removed from the field. Additional irrigations are required in many places, the number depending on both soil and climatic conditions. The best guide is to

z

watch carefully the condition of the plants. When the water supply becomes too low, the growth is checked and the leaves become darker and duller in color than those of vigorously growing plants. The wilting of the leaves is also indicative of insufficient moisture, especially if it occur before or after the heat of midday. Fortier also recommends that the soil at a depth of about 6 inches be examined. If it will readily form a ball when pressed between the hands and retain its form, there is sufficient moisture present; but if the ball falls apart when the pressure is removed, irrigation is needed.

The number of irrigations a year when water is available varies from 4 in Montana to as many as 12 in Arizona and California. The number depends upon various factors, especially the depth and character of the soil, the depth of the water table, number of cuttings and such climatic factors as temperature, rainfall, humidity and wind movements.

In localities where water is abundant only in the spring and early summer, it is the common practice to water more freely and more frequently at that time, as this tends to lessen the amount needed later in the summer.

402. Winter irrigation. — In parts of the West, where the water supply happens to be abundant in winter and scant or even lacking in summer, fields are irrigated in winter when the plants are dormant. This is especially practical in regions where the winters are mild. The principal object is to conserve water which would otherwise be wasted, the soil retaining a large amount and thus lessening the water required during the summer. Even where no water is available in summer, one good cutting is in many places obtained as the result of winter irrigation. A second advantage is that winter-killing from excessive dryness of the soil is prevented. Where the winters are severe, however, too great an amount of soil moisture is conducive to winter-killing.

403. Relation of yield to water supply. — The actual water required in irrigating alfalfa depends largely on the permeability of the soil, but temperature, humidity and wind are also factors of importance. Fortier states that the larger number of western alfalfa fields are irrigated annually with 2.5 to 4.5 feet of water, but in quite a large number of cases the amount used would cover the field in depths ranging from 6 to 15 feet.

While larger yields are often obtained by using greater quantities of water, such use is wasteful and apt to be injurious to the land or to surrounding lands by causing waterlogging and the consequent rise of alkali.

Fortier secured the following results at the Montana Experiment Station : —

PLAT NUMBER	DEPTH OF IRRIGATION	DEPTH OF RAINFALL	TOTAL DEPTH	YIELD TO THE ACRE OF CURED ALFALFA
	Feet	Feet	Feet	Tons
1	0.5	0.7	1.20	4.61
2	0.0	0.7	0.70	1.95
3	1.0	0.7	1.70	4.42
4	1.5	0.7	2.20	3.75
5	2.0	0.7	2.70	6.35
6	2.5	0.7	3.20	7.20
7	3.0	0.7	3.70	7.68

The following yields are reported from the Utah Experiment Station, using different quantities of irrigation water : —

Inches of Water Applied	10.0	15.0	20.0	25.0	30.0	50.0
First Crop .	3567	3194	3759	3790	3326	3795
Second crop .	4077	2775	3193	3245	3338	4016
Third crop .	2240	1577	2145	2319	2176	3002
Total yield	9884	7546	9097	9354	8840	10813
Yield for each inch of irrigation water	988	503	455	374	295	216

(Quantities of water used are expressed in acre-inches. Yields of alfalfa are expressed in pounds to the acre.)

404. Care of an alfalfa field. — After a good stand of alfalfa has been secured, its subsequent treatment — apart from harvesting, and in dry regions, irrigating — should be mainly to hold weeds in check. The worst weeds that invade alfalfa fields are blue-grass in the north, and Bermuda-grass and crab-grass southward. Other weeds are held largely in check by the regular mowings, but the weedy grasses can be eradicated only by careful harrowing.

Blue-grass and Bermuda are both perennials, and gradually kill out the alfalfa as the grass sod extends. Usually this requires three or four years. Crab-grass grows most luxuriantly in moist hot weather, under which conditions alfalfa languishes, so that crab-grass often completely destroys an alfalfa field in the Southern States in a single season.

The best implement to destroy grass in alfalfa is the spike-tooth harrow, especially the form with broad chisel-shaped teeth. Where the ground is very hard, it is necessary first to use a disk harrow. This implement often splits up the crowns of the alfalfa plants, but this injury is ordinarily not serious. It certainly is not beneficial as some writers have claimed. The disk harrow alone is not effective against blue-grass, but needs to be followed with the spike-tooth.

When grass is troublesome, it is commonly recommended that alfalfa should be thoroughly harrowed after each cutting. By this means, the life of the field may be extended several years, at least in some localities.

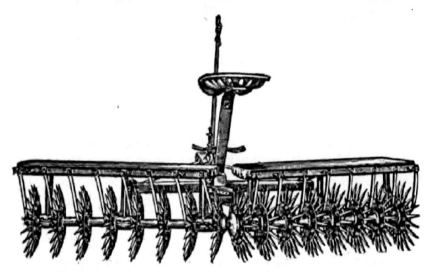

FIG. 34. — An implement for harrowing fields of alfalfa.

At the Kansas Experiment Station a plot disked every year for 3 years yielded at the average rate of 9922 pounds an acre, while one not disked gave a yield of 10,269 pounds.

405. Alfalfa in cultivated rows. — Alfalfa planted in rows has often been grown in an experimental way in humid regions where broadcasting is unsuccessful on account of weeds. Such a type of cultivation has never come into actual practice in such regions, mainly because other leguminous crops succeed in spite of weeds.

In some semi-arid regions, notably India and Algeria, alfalfa for hay is grown in this manner both with and without irrigation. In these countries, however, labor is much cheaper than in America.

Thus far the culture of alfalfa in rows in the United States has been mainly with the idea of producing seed crops. The success already attained leads to the belief that the method will come into wide use. The area particularly adapted to this method of seed-production is that east of the Rocky Mountains, where the annual rainfall lies between 14 and 25 inches, and west of the same mountains, where the precipitation is between 12 and 20 inches. Such conditions supply sufficient moisture if the alfalfa is planted thinly in rows 30 to 40 inches apart and cultivated frequently. Furthermore, it is under just such conditions of drought that seed setting is favored. Irrigable lands cannot be economically utilized in this manner, as they will produce 3 to 5 cuttings of hay from broadcasted alfalfa, while the unirrigable lands rarely produce more than one such cutting.

Fairchild has described an interesting method of alfalfa culture in Algeria, where the alfalfa is grown in double rows 40 inches apart, and every second year a crop of durum wheat is grown between the rows.

406. Alfalfa in mixtures. — Alfalfa is not commonly employed in grass mixtures, mainly because the especial peculiarity of the crop — namely, its ability to produce two or more cuttings — is thereby impaired.

In humid regions, alfalfa as a rule does not withstand the crowding of other grasses such as are usually employed in mixtures. It is not so well adapted for this purpose as is red clover.

In irrigated regions, especially at high altitudes, where

timothy is an important crop, the practice of growing it in mixture with alfalfa is increasing. This permits, in many places, the cutting of a second crop of hay, which is largely composed of alfalfa. Alfalfa as ordinarily cut is ready two weeks sooner than timothy, but additional maturity makes it better feed for horses. Furthermore, experience has shown that when mixed with timothy, the stems are more slender, and there is no objectionable woodiness.

407. Alfalfa in rotations. — On account of its long life, as well as the value of an established field, alfalfa is not much used in regular rotations. The almost universal custom is to retain a field in alfalfa as long as it continues to produce satisfactory crops. In Colorado, however, alfalfa is used in rotation with potatoes, the alfalfa commonly being sown with a nurse-crop of oats and usually allowed to stand two seasons.

In Europe the idea prevails that land should not again be sown to alfalfa until after a period of rest equal to the time the land was in alfalfa, or somewhat less if there is a deep and good subsoil. American experience has not as yet disclosed any need of such practice. It is, however, desirable, after a field of alfalfa has been plowed, to follow it with one intertilled crop and one of small grains, as this permits the land to be cleaned of weeds, and also secures the benefit of the fertilizing value of the alfalfa.

If alfalfa is again to be sown on the land, the intervening crops should be planned to permit alfalfa being sown at the best time. On farms where experience has shown that alfalfa can be successfully grown, it is most economically seeded after a cultivated crop that can be removed in time enough to sow the alfalfa. Among such crops are potatoes and sweet corn. Certain broadcasted crops will also leave the land in good shape for alfalfa, among them field peas and cowpeas.

408. Pasturing alfalfa. — Alfalfa may be pastured to all kinds of live stock, but this is rarely done in regions where the hay commands a good price, excepting when the field has become weedy. In the eastern United States pasturing will nearly always result in great injury to the stand of alfalfa, but in the West this difficulty is not so serious. It is best not to pasture alfalfa during the first two seasons, and even old fields cannot be pastured heavily without injuring the stand.

Hogs are most often employed in pasturing alfalfa and injure it less than other live stock. Where, however, the soil is loose, it is well to ring their noses to prevent rooting. Horses and sheep are most injurious to alfalfa plants, as they eat the young buds from the crowns. Both sheep and cattle are likely to become affected with bloat or hoven when upon alfalfa pasture. This danger is apparently lessened by not allowing the animals to go on the pasture when the alfalfa is wet with rain or dew. Neither should hungry cattle be turned in alfalfa so that they will gorge themselves, as this is particularly likely to cause bloat. The danger is always present, however, and so large that cautious farmers do not consider alfalfa a proper plant for pasturing valuable animals.

Fields of mixed alfalfa and grass are much better for pasturing cattle and sheep than alfalfa alone, as such a mixture is much less likely to cause bloating. Orchard-grass is well adapted to such a mixture in the more humid states; and brome-grass in the region west of the longitude 96° and north of the latitude 37°. Kentucky blue-grass should not be sown, as it tends to crowd out the alfalfa.

Eventually it invades many fields, and when this is the case the mixture makes fine pasturage.

Few data are available as to the carrying capacity of alfalfa pastures. In good alfalfa sections, a field will support an average of ten hogs to the acre throughout the grazing season. Fields should never be closely pastured to the end of the season, but the animals should be removed in time to allow a growth of 6 inches or more before the beginning of winter.

409. Use as a soiling crop. — Alfalfa is an excellent soiling crop, especially for dairy cows. Only one precaution needs to be taken; namely, not to cut the same field more often than it would be cut for hay, as otherwise the plants are greatly weakened and often succumb. Such an injurious result is not uncommonly seen in alfalfa near dairy barns, which, on account of its convenience, has been cut too frequently. No cases are on record of cut alfalfa ever having caused bloating.

410. Alfalfa silage. — Alfalfa alone has not given very satisfactory results as silage in the few tests reported. This method of preservation is rarely necessary in the West, where most of the alfalfa is grown. In the East, however, ensiling the crop would be a means of saving it during weather unfavorable for hay curing. One difficulty encountered in making good silage from alfalfa is to secure sufficiently dense packing to prevent spoiling. Chopping the alfalfa reduces the loss from this cause. Much additional investigation regarding the preservation of alfalfa as silage is needed.

At the Utah Experiment Station there was placed in one silo 14,165 pounds red clover, 4020 pounds sweet clover, 8620 pounds alfalfa and 3720 pounds Hungarian millet, a total of 30,525 pounds. The total silage taken out was 19,599 pounds, a loss of 35.7 per cent, and besides 7007 pounds were spoiled.   Neither the cut nor the whole alfalfa silage proved satisfactory in two years' trial.

411. Alfalfa meal. — In recent years, finely ground alfalfa has been placed on the market under the name of alfalfa meal.   The best quality of meal is bright pea green in color, as this indicates that it has been made from the best quality of hay.   The product is very convenient to use in mixed feeds, as there is practically no waste such as occurs with hay.   It usually commands a price about 25 per cent higher than prime alfalfa hay.

The ground material contains no more nutriment than hay of the same quality, and its digestibility is probably not increased materially.   The justification for its use lies in the convenience in feeding, and the avoidance of waste.

412. Seed production. — Alfalfa seed is rarely grown commercially except in semi-arid regions.   In humid regions, the production of seed is small except in seasons when drought prevails.   At the present time, about one-half of the commercial seed is grown on irrigated lands in regions of dry summers.   Moisture from rain or irrigation after the alfalfa plants are in bloom will stimulate new growth from the crown, which greatly reduces the seed yield.   When a seed crop is desired, irrigation is withheld until the seed has been harvested.   Usually the second crop of alfalfa is allowed to produce seed, but in the northernmost states of the West, it is necessarily the first crop, as the second will not mature, and in the Southwestern States the third crop is often preferred for seed.   ·

Various factors affect the amount of seed that alfalfa plants produce.   The most important are the thickness of stand, moisture supply, and conditions favorable for tripping.

Isolated plants of alfalfa produce most seed. West-gate compared isolated plants vegetatively propagated from the same mother plant. The plants that were farthest apart — namely, 18 by 39 inches — produced as many as 505 pods each, while those closest together — namely, 7 inches each way — produced a maximum of but 38 pods. The beneficial effect of isolation seems partly due to the increased sunlight received, as shaded plants produce but few pods. It is possible, too, that the heat of the sun favors tripping, as flowers can be tripped with a burning glass or by shading under a cage and then exposing to the hot sunshine.

Fig. 35. — A well-set cluster of alfalfa pods.

Abundant moisture lessens seed production, apparently mainly because it stimulates the growth of new sprouts. Too little moisture may also seriously reduce the seed yield, but alfalfa with its deep root system is not frequently subjected to this extreme. The subject is a difficult one for field experimentation, but needs much further study.

Tripping of the flowers (Par. 413) is doubtless an important factor, but more data and observations are needed, especially with reference to the relation of climatic factors to tripping. The relative importance of automatic tripping and insect tripping remains to be ascertained, but observations indicate that in some localities when tripping insects are rare, automatic tripping is probably the determining factor.

In all producing sections, the yield of seed varies greatly from season to season, but the factors actually involved are obscure. Maximum yields of 20 bushels to the acre have been reported, but 8 bushels is considered a large yield. Returns of from 2 to 5 bushels an acre represent the usual crop. In Europe the yield to the acre ranges from 300 to 700 pounds, according to different authorities.

In recent years, an increasing amount of alfalfa seed has been grown on unirrigated semi-arid lands. Such seed is considered preferable for dry land farming, and this is probably so, but there is no convincing experimental evidence of such superiority. In growing alfalfa for seed production on dry land, very thin stands are best, but there is an increasing tendency to plant it in rows about three feet wide with the plants about one foot apart in the rows. This permits of cultivation as frequently as may be desired.

The crop, if harvested for seed, should be cut as soon as most of the pods are ripe and the seeds yellow and hardened.

413. Pollination. — The structure of the alfalfa flower has a peculiar explosive mechanism which especially adapts it to being cross-pollinated by large bees, especially bumble bees. The filaments of the upper stamens forming the stamineal tube are under tension, but are held in a straight position in the keel by means of processes on the wings. The insertion of a toothpick into the nectary or the pressing downward of the keel will release these processes, when the stamineal column with the inclosed pistil recurves, violently striking the standard. This process is called " tripping." When a bee trips a flower, the pollen is scattered on its under side. If it then visits and trips another flower, it is quite likely to dust pollen from the first on the stigma of the second.

Numerous investigators have studied the process and have experimented in various ways with the flowers. These researches have shown that only in very rare cases will an alfalfa flower set seed without being tripped; that self-tripping takes place under certain conditions; that artificial tripping with self-pollination is hardly as efficacious as cross-pollination; that honey-bees are usually unable to trip the flowers, bumble bees and other large bees being the most efficient insects. Burkill's contention that the stigma must be ruptured or irritated by striking the standard or an insect does not hold true under American conditions. Cross-pollination results in the production of about 30 per cent more seeds to the pod than does self-pollination. It has not been definitely shown, however, that cross-pollinated seeds possess any superiority.

Under Western conditions, it is probable that more flowers are self-tripped than are tripped by insects, but more quantitative data on this point are needed.

414. Seeds. — Alfalfa seed may be adulterated with that of trefoil, sweet clover or bur clover. All of these resemble alfalfa seeds closely. The sweet clover can be detected easily by crushing a few seeds when the characteristic vanilla-like odor of the sweet clover will reveal its presence. A very small amount of sweet clover seed, up to 5 per cent, is sometimes present in American seed as an impurity,

Fig. 36. — Alfalfa seeds: *a*, individual seeds, showing variation in form; *b*, edge view of a seed, showing the scar; *c*, natural size of seeds.

but more than this is certainly an adulteration. To detect trefoil and bur clover seeds, careful examination is necessary. Very commonly both of these are added as adulterants, especially to European seed. Old alfalfa seed, as well as shriveled seed, has a dull reddish brown color.

Troublesome weeds that may be present in alfalfa are Canada thistle, dodder, curled dock, quack-grass, wild carrot and oxeye-daisy.

Good commercial seed may attain a purity of 98–99 per cent and a viability of 97–99 per cent. A bushel weighs from 60 to 63 pounds. One pound contains 182,000 to 237,000 seeds, an average of about 220,000. Usually a small per cent of the seed is hard, especially if the seed is new. Good seeds germinate within 6 days and mostly in 2 or 3 days.

415. Viability of seed. — Alfalfa seed retains its viability for many years, depending partly on the conditions of storage. Seed of the season does not germinate as well as that one year old.

The best alfalfa seed is characterized by its plumpness and a decidedly yellowish color. Dead seeds become reddish brown and are easily distinguished. Turkestan alfalfa seed is trampled out by animals, and may often be recognized by its dusty appearance and the presence of small pebbles.

In all alfalfa seed a varying percentage is " hard "; that is, does not absorb water and germinate promptly. There are no published data regarding the behavior of hard seeds in the soil, but the probability is that some of them remain dormant a long time and hence are practically worthless.

At the Colorado Experiment Station samples preserved in envelopes and vials for six years showed a range of germination of 66 to 92 per cent, and six years later the same samples, then twelve years old, still germinated 63 to 92.5 per cent. One sample germinated 72 per cent when ten years old and 63 per cent six years later.

Experiments in Austria showed a gradual decrease in germination from 94 per cent the first year to 54 per cent the eleventh year. Shriveled seed is inferior to plump seed, both in percentage of viability and in keeping qualities. It is probable, also, that the resultant plants are less vigorous.

416. Alfalfa improvement. — The wide diversity which exists both in wild and cultivated alfalfas has in recent years stimulated much interest in breeding to secure varieties especially adapted to certain purposes and to special localities. Among the improvements sought by various investigators along this line, the following may be enumerated : —

1. A higher degree of leafiness combined with erect stems, so as to produce more and better hay ;

2. Better seed production, especially if combined with good hay quality ;

3. Greater drought resistance ;

4. Greater cold resistance ;

5. Varieties that possess ability to produce seed under humid conditions, so that adapted strains may gradually be developed ;

6. Better pasture varieties, especially such as have rootstocks so as to withstand pasturing without injury ;

7. Disease resistance.

The characters enumerated are all possessed in varying degrees by different varieties. Especially promising for the breeder are hybrids between sickle alfalfa and true alfalfa, of both of which numerous forms exist. The greater hardiness and rootstock-producing tendency of the former, combined with the better seed-production and superior habit of the latter, are characters highly desirable to combine.

While breeders have already developed various promising improved alfalfas, none of these has yet become established commercially.

417. Breeding methods. — In connection with the improvement of alfalfa by breeding, certain special methods will be found useful. Due to the readiness with which natural crossing takes place, a large proportion of alfalfa plants are heterozygote; that is, do not breed true even when the seed is produced by bagged or caged flowers. On this account a progeny row of each selected plant should be grown from seed produced under bag to determine whether it will breed true to type.

For the rapid multiplication of a selected plant, two methods may be used: First, new plants can readily be produced either from cuttings, or, where rootstocks are present, by division; second, pure seed can be secured by growing the plants in cages to exclude insects, and tripping the flowers by pressure of the hand.

Increase plots of a selected strain must be grown at a considerable distance from any other alfalfa, otherwise crossing will be effected by bees.

418. Weeds. — In many places weeds constitute a serious drawback to alfalfa culture.

Kentucky blue-grass is probably most troublesome to established fields in Ontario and the Eastern States. Heavy liming so necessary for alfalfa also favors blue-grass, which usually appears by the second year, and unless restrained will kill out half of the alfalfa by the third or fourth year. In the northern part of the irrigated regions, blue-grass is also beginning to be troublesome in alfalfa. Blue-grass is best eradicated by means of a spring tooth harrow, especially one with broad pointed teeth. Care must be taken to subdue the blue-grass as soon as it begins to appear. The disk harrow is also commonly used, but this does not destroy the blue-grass as well as the spring tooth, though it may be used to precede the latter. Disking often splits the crowns of the alfalfa plant, and the opinion is growing that this is injurious rather than beneficial, as some writers have claimed.

Quack-grass (*Agropyron repens*), in Michigan, Vermont and other Eastern States, is a serious weed. Owing to its deep running rootstocks, it cannot be eradicated by harrowing, and thus continues to spread as long as the field remains in alfalfa.

Crab-grass (*Digitaria*) and foxtail or pigeon-grass (*Setaria*) are the worst alfalfa weeds in the Southern States. The former is troublesome as far north as Kansas and Maryland, and the latter still farther. Both are annuals and reseed in spite of any practical precaution. The plants are rather easily destroyed by harrowing, as they are annuals and lack the rootstocks characteristic of blue-grass. Humid weather especially favors crab-grass, while it injures alfalfa, which under such conditions may be smothered and practically destroyed.

Bermuda-grass is becoming an increasing menace in alfalfa fields in Arizona and California. In this region, Bermuda-grass produces an abundance of seed which reaches the alfalfa fields in irrigation water. Its eradication without plowing has not been accomplished. In Virginia, Bermuda-grass, even when abundant, has not proven to be troublesome in alfalfa.

Squirrel-tail (*Hordeum jubatum*), a grass native to the

2 A

Rocky Mountain region, is a troublesome weed in Colorado, Utah and other states. This grass matures before alfalfa, and the long bearded spikelets are very injurious to live stock. When squirrel-tail is very abundant, the first crop of alfalfa is rendered practically worthless. Such a crop is sometimes cut while very young before the squirrel-tail is mature enough to be objectionable to animals.

Wall-barley (*Hordeum murinum*) is a winter annual from the Mediterranean region abundant in California. Like squirrel-tail, it is very objectionable on account of its bearded glumes, but, before these are formed, provides good early pasturage. It is a common practice to burn this grass when dry. Where abundant, it may ruin the first crop of alfalfa.

419. Dodder or love-vine. — This parasite or weed is often very injurious in alfalfa fields. Alfalfa fields usually become infested by sowing dodder seed mixed in with alfalfa. The dodder seed germinates in the ground, and the young plantlets quickly twine about the alfalfa seedlings. Thereafter, they are parasitic on the alfalfa, absorbing their nourishment by means of sucker-like organs which penetrate the host. Dodder usually appears in alfalfa fields in small isolated spots which rapidly grow larger if the weed is not destroyed.

Four species of dodder have been found infesting alfalfa in the United States; namely, *Cuscuta planiflora, C. indecora, C. epithymum* and *C. arvensis*. The last named is native to America, infesting many kinds of herbaceous plants, while the other three are of Old World origin. *Cuscuta planiflora* is the most abundant and most injurious species on alfalfa in the West.

The best way to prevent this weed is to avoid planting

alfalfa seed containing dodder. The seeds of the latter can usually be detected by careful examination with a magnifier. In all the species the seeds are smaller than those of alfalfa, subglobose or somewhat angular, with a finely roughened, dull surface. The color may be grayish, yellowish or brownish.

Various methods of destroying patches of dodder in alfalfa fields have been suggested. A good plan is to cut the affected plants very close to the ground before the dodder sets seed. Burning the infested spots by means of straw or by spraying with kerosene is also effective.

If the whole field is affected, the best plan is to utilize it as pasture, especially for sheep, which eat the alfalfa close and

Fig. 37. — Dodder or love-vine growing on alfalfa.

thus check the dodder. If such a field be utilized for hay, some of the dodder seed will ripen and the field tend to become more infested every year.

When such a field is plowed up, it is best to grow other crops not subject to dodder, at least two years. Otherwise, there is likelihood of the alfalfa becoming infested by the dodder seed in the soil.

420. Diseases. — Alfalfa is subject to various fungous diseases, but it is exceptional for any of these to cause large damage, though the aggregate loss is considerable.

Root-rot (*Ozonium omnivorum*) occurs in Texas and Arizona, and attacks many other plants besides alfalfa. It appears on the roots as orange-colored threads. The attacked plant nearly always dies. The fungus gradually spreads to surrounding plants, which, with the rotting of the root, wilt and then die. Rarely a plant may survive by sending out new roots from near the crown. The circles of dead plants caused by this disease are characteristic.

Only indirect means of treatment can be used. The root-rot fungus thrives best in poorly ventilated soils, and further is not known to attack any monocotyledonous plant. The growing of such crops as corn, sorghum, the small grains and grasses, in rotation tends to free the land from the fungus.

At the Ohio Experiment Station a root-rot caused by *Fusarium roseum* has been found killing young alfalfa seedlings.

Bacillus tumefaciens, the organism of crown-gall on fruit trees, sometimes affects alfalfa, causing small irregular nodules on the roots and stems. Affected plants have been found in Kentucky, Maryland, Pennsylvania and Alabama. The affected plants are stunted somewhat, but no serious damage to fields has yet been traced to this organism.

Urophlyctis alfalfæ is a fungus that causes wart-like excrescences to appear near the crown, both on the larger roots and on the bases of the stems. The galls are usually small, but may become 3 or 4 inches in diameter. This disease was first observed in Ecuador, but has recently been found in Germany, England, California, Oregon and Arizona.

Bacterial stem-blight of alfalfa caused by *Pseudomonas medicaginis* has recently been described from Colorado and neighboring states. This disease attacks the stems primarily, usually causing a linear yellowish to blackish discoloration down one side of the stem through one or more internodes. Sometimes the disease extends to the crown, destroying the buds and eventually the plant. The disease is confined almost wholly to the first cutting, which may be seriously injured, but the subsequent cuttings are almost unaffected. Few plants are killed the first year, but thereafter the loss is greater so that in three or four years the stand may be ruined. Cutting the stubble very short in early spring as soon as the first damage is over has been recommended. This will remove any diseased portions which may infect the new growth, and besides removes the weakened frost-injured shoots which seem particularly liable to the disease. Hardy varieties which escape winter injury are likely to prove less subject to the disease. A very similar disease also occurs in Virginia and Maryland.

The leaves of alfalfa are attacked by various fungi. Most common is *Pseudopeziza medicaginis* which causes small dark brown spots on the leaves. When very abundant, there is considerable shedding of leaflets.

At the New Jersey Experiment Station comparative chemical analyses were made of healthy and diseased plants of the third cutting. The healthy plants showed 10 per cent more fat, 12 per cent more protein and 18 per cent more fiber than the diseased, and were richer in carbohydrates by 11 per cent.

Rust (*Uromyces striatus*) is another common leaf disease recognizable by forming small spots of reddish spores. *Macrosporium sarcinœforme* occurs frequently in the East, forming pale circular spots bearing scattered black spores.

Two mildews also occur occasionally, especially in the shade; namely, powdery mildew (*Erysiphe trifolii*) and downy mildew (*Peronospora trifolii*).

None of these leaf diseases has as yet proven to be of serious consequence.

Anthracnose (*Colletotrichum trifolii*) occurs on alfalfa in Virginia and Maryland, causing spots on both the stems and leaves. These are at first purplish, then brown. The stems are frequently girdled by the spot and then die, and the whole plant may succumb.

Alfalfa " yellows " is a disease of unknown cause. It occurs quite commonly in Virginia and other Eastern States. The leaves turn gradually to an orange-yellow color, and the plant then ceases growth. When this happens, it is best to cut the crop at once, even if but a few inches high. It has been suggested that the disease is probably related to the mosaic disease of tobacco, known to be transmitted by a species of aphis. A species of leaf-hopper seems to be constantly associated with alfalfa yellows.

421. Insects. — Insects have thus far not proved a serious menace to alfalfa culture in America, but locally and in occasional seasons a large amount of damage may be caused by grasshoppers or by caterpillars. The recently introduced alfalfa leaf weevil may, however, prove to be a serious factor to contend with.

Grasshoppers are the most injurious insects to alfalfa in the West at the present time, but the area of destruction varies from year to year, depending on the local abundance of the insects. The species that cause most damage are *Melanoplus differentialis* and *Melanoplus bivittatus*. They are more likely to be destructive in seasons when drought causes a shortage in natural food supply and in areas where the proportion of uncultivated land is large, as under these circumstances they congregate in the cultivated fields.

Two effective means of destroying these insects are by the use of the hopper-dozer and poisoned baits. The hopper-dozer is essentially a shallow pan with a vertical back one or two feet high. The pan contains water covered with a layer of kerosene. When this is dragged over the field, many of the insects jump directly into the pan or fall into it after striking the back.

Fig. 38. — Adult form of the alfalfa weevil (*Phytonomus posticus*): Adults clustering on and attacking a spray of alfalfa. (Slightly enlarged.)

The most effective poisoned bait is the Criddle mixture made by mixing one pound of paris green and one pound of salt in one-half barrel of *fresh* horse manure. Grasshoppers eat the bait very readily and are killed by the poison. Where grasshopper eggs are known to be abundant in an alfalfa field, many may be destroyed by disking in the fall or winter.

The alfalfa leaf weevil (*Phytonomus posticus*), a native

of Europe, appeared in Utah in 1904, and has now spread over a considerable portion of that state and south Idaho. The insect causes much damage by the larvæ eating the leaves of the first crop of alfalfa, and incidentally, by delaying the second crop, does not allow time enough for the third crop to mature.

The best method of control thus far devised is to cut the first crop and remove it from the field as soon as it shows signs of serious injury. The field should then be gone over with a spring tooth harrow and followed by thorough treatment with a heavy brush drag. The object is to destroy as many of the larvæ and pupæ as possible, partly by crushing, partly by burying in the dust, and partly by starving, as after thorough dragging the alfalfa stubble will be entirely bare of leaves. If the work has been well done, the second crop will be practically free from the weevil, and if done early enough, there will be ample time for the third crop to mature.

Several caterpillars cause more or less injury at times to alfalfa by eating the leaves. The most important are *Eurymus eurytheme* and *Autographa gamma californica*. The best practical remedy, if the caterpillars are abundant, is to cut the alfalfa as close to the ground as possible while the caterpillars are young, thus starving them and protecting the succeeding crop from injury. Close pasturing is also a means of preventing injury, as caterpillars rarely become abundant in fields thus utilized.

CHAPTER XVI

RED CLOVER

RED clover is the most important of all leguminous forage crops both on account of its high value as feed and from the fact that it can be so well employed in rotations. The last decade has witnessed a serious decline in the acreage grown in most of the eastern states, apparently due to an increasing difficulty in securing satisfactory stands.

422. Botany of red clover. — The plant occurs naturally in the greater part of Europe; in Algiers, northern Africa; and is found in Asia Minor, Armenia, Turkestan, southern Siberia and the Himalayas.

A large number of forms have been named by botanists, Ascherson and Graebner describing 30 varieties from middle Europe alone.

423. Agricultural history. — Red clover was not known as a crop by the ancient Greeks and Romans. It was apparently first cultivated in Media and south of the Caspian Sea, in the same general region where alfalfa was first domesticated. In Europe its use as an agricultural plant is comparatively modern, the first mention of its use as feed for cows being by Albertus Magnus in the thirteenth century. There are definite records of its cultivation in Italy in 1550, in Flanders in 1566, in France in 1583. From Flanders it was introduced into England in 1645, and shortly afterwards its culture was described in several books. Its use in Europe became extensive about the end of the eighteenth century.

It was probably introduced into the United States by the early English colonists, but the first published mention of its culture was by Jared Eliot, who wrote of its being grown in Massachusetts in 1747.

Fig. 39. — Red clover.

Its introduction into European agriculture had a profound effect in that clover soon came to be used in rotations in place of bare fallow. Its influence there on agriculture and civilization is stated by high authority to be greater than that of the potato, and much greater than that of any other forage plant. Clover not only increased the abundance of animal feed and therefore of manure, but also helped greatly by adding nitrogen to the soil directly.

It is now much cultivated not only in Europe and America, but also in Chile and New Zealand.

424. Importance and distribution. — Red clover is by far the most important leguminous crop grown in America. The area devoted to it is about five times as great as that to alfalfa. More exact comparisons are not possible, as clover is most commonly grown mixed with timothy, while alfalfa is mainly grown alone.

On the accompanying map is shown the acreage of all clovers in the United States and Canada in 1909. It will be noted that the crop becomes decidedly less important in the Southern States. This is also true of the semi-

Fig. 40. — Map showing acreage of red clover in the United States, 1909, and Canada, 1910.

arid states, except that in Colorado and Montana considerable red clover is grown in the mountain valleys at high altitudes.

In Norway it is grown as far north as latitude 69.2°. On the south coast of Alaska it succeeds fairly well, but it winter-kills in the interior.

425. Soil relations. — Red clover is not a particularly exacting crop in regard to its soil requirements, excepting that it be well drained. It succeeds better as a rule in clayey soils than in loams, and better in loams than in sandy soils. Tough clays are, however, very unfavorable, partly on account of their undrained condition. The best growth is secured on fertile clayey soils rich in lime. A good content of humus is also favorable. Deep soils are especially desirable, as this enables the plant to develop its extensive root system which may penetrate to a depth of over five feet.

Soil moisture conditions are most important for red clover. It will not thrive in sandy or gravelly soils that become droughty. It is especially intolerant of water-logged soil, and on this account is poorly adapted to growing under irrigation on poorly drained lands.

426. Climatic relations. — In a general way the climatic relations of red clover are shown by the map of its distribution, in which both the regions and the extent of its culture are indicated. It is distinctly a crop for humid regions without excessive summer or winter temperature.

No critical studies have been recorded of the cold resistance of red clover, but it is probably more hardy in this respect than alfalfa, as it endures well the winters of Nova Scotia, Maine and Minnesota. Seeds from northern-grown plants are preferred for regions of cold winters. Stebler and Schröter remark that dry cold is injurious in Switzerland in spring after growth has begun.

Regarding the heat tolerance of red clover, the data are even less definite. In the southernmost states the crop succeeds only if planted in the fall, and all of the plants usually disappear by the following August.

Humidity combined with moderate temperature is favorable to the plant, and dry atmospheric conditions are decidedly unfavorable. Combined with high temperature, humidity seems to be more injurious. Under such conditions, the Orel variety quickly shows signs of distress.

427. Effect of shade. — Red clover is often planted in orchards as a cover crop. It does not thrive very well in shaded places and mostly disappears after the first season. Stebler and Volkart report an experiment in which a mixture containing red clover was grown on two plots, one of them artificially shaded. These plots were observed six years and the percentage of clover plants determined each season, with the following results : —

	1903	1904	1905	1906	1907	1908
Not shaded .	38.7	22.3	4.7	0.2	0.8	23.2
Shaded . .	51.2	7.8	4.9	0.2	0.	0.1

428. Life period. — Red clover is commonly said to be a short-lived perennial. As a crop it is nearly always treated as a biennial over the principal area of its distribution in America. In the Southern States, it is often grown as a winter annual, as it does not as a rule survive the hot summers and such weeds as crab-grass. In the Pacific Northwest and northern Europe, red clover fields often yield satisfactorily for three years.

Individual plants of red clover may live six to nine years, but comparatively few live over three years. To some extent, the length of life period is a varietal character, both short- and long-lived strains being secured by selection. Pastured plants persist a long time and probably much longer than when not grazed. On the other hand, but few plants survive after a seed crop has been harvested from them.

429. Agricultural varieties. — Red clover is a very variable species, and in any field numerous forms may easily be selected. Many of these different forms are particularly prominent in the spring before the flowering branches appear. In speaking of varieties and strains, it must, therefore, be borne in mind that such are defined, not by the individuals being all alike, but only by possessing one or more characters in common. Two so-called varieties of red clover are distinguished in American agriculture : ordinary or medium, and mammoth or sapling. Other so-called varieties are usually named after the region in which they are produced and are better considered regional strains; such as, Chilean red clover, French red clover, etc., though in a few cases the plants are readily recognizable.

Ordinary or medium red clover, as grown in America, is distinguished by the fact that over most of the clover region it will produce both a hay crop and a seed crop the same season. If sown by itself, it produces satisfactory crops for only one season, but in grass mixtures, a good many of the plants live two years and some of them longer. Various characters to distinguish medium from mammoth red clover have been stated by authors, but none of them hold perfectly true. In the order of their trustworthiness, these characters may thus be contrasted :—

MEDIUM RED CLOVER	MAMMOTH RED CLOVER
Blooms two weeks earlier than timothy.	Blooms with timothy.
Stems hollow.	Stems solid.
Plants live two years.	Plants live three years or more.
Tap root branches little.	Tap root branches much.
Heads often in pairs.	Heads seldom in pairs.
Pedicels short, straight.	Pedicels longer, bent.

Mammoth red clover is also known as sapling clover, bull clover, pea-vine clover, perennial clover, and in Europe as cow-grass. Botanically it is known as *Trifolium pratense perenne* Host, but has erroneously been considered the same as zigzag clover (*Trifolium medium*), which is a distinct species, only very sparingly introduced into America. On account of its lateness, as well as its longer persistence, mammoth clover is preferable for mixing with timothy, as the blooming time of the two coincide. If sown alone, the yield is somewhat greater than the medium, as it usually grows taller. On this account, it is preferable where both a hay crop and a seed crop cannot be secured in the same season. Mammoth clover is preferred to medium for poor or sandy soils, as it is generally believed that it produces better crops under such circumstances.

The seed of mammoth clover is slightly larger than that of medium, but cannot be certainly distinguished. Genuine seed is scarce and commands a relatively high price. In Rhode Island, Card reports that it succeeds better than medium red on " acid " soils.

Regional strains of red clover are usually named from the region in which they are produced. Only a few of them differ markedly from the ordinary American strain. Orel or Russian clover has nearly smooth herbage, and, like mammoth, does not produce a second cutting. For the northern tier of states and Canada, it possesses considerable promise. Under Maryland conditions it suffers noticeably from the summer heat.

430. Comparison of regional strains. — Numerous comparative trials of red clovers from different sources have been made both in Europe and in America. In Europe, American red clover is objected to on account of its greater hairiness. The opinion prevails also that the yield is not as a rule as satisfactory, and that the plants are more subject to mildew. Werner states, however, that the value of the American seed under German conditions is not yet clear, in spite of the numerous field trials.

At the Wisconsin Experiment Station in 1901 American medium and mammoth both outyielded European strains from Hungary, England, Steirmark, Transylvania, Russia and Germany, though the hay of the European sorts was better in quality, owing to the plants being less hairy. In 1902 out of 16 American and European strains, the four highest yields were from American lots. In 1905 out of 22 American and 2 foreign strains, the largest yield, 2.2 tons an acre, was from the Orel strain from Russia.

At the Maine Experiment Station 29 regional strains of red clover were tested in 1902 on duplicate plots of one-eightieth acre. One plot of each was cut August 30, when the earliest was ready for cutting. The largest yields were obtained in the order given from plots with seed from Minnesota, Bohemia, Indiana, Wisconsin, Brittany and Ohio. In the following season the order of their excellence, arranged according to the total yield from two cuttings, was Indiana, Bohemia I, Russia, Bohemia II, Illinois, Indiana, Ohio.

A test of regional strains conducted coöperatively by the United States Department of Agriculture in 1905 gave the results shown in the accompanying table. In this series, Orel clover gave the highest total yield, as well as the highest at two of the stations. Orel clover yields, however, but one cutting, so the relative ranks of the varieties would undoubtedly be different if the total yields for the season were tabulated : —

TABLE SHOWING ACRE YIELDS OF THE FIRST CUTTING OF DIFFERENT REGIONAL STRAINS OF RED CLOVER AT FIVE STATIONS IN 1905

SOURCE OF SEED	OAKLAND, NEBRASKA	BIGSTONE, SOUTH DAKOTA	ST. ANTHONY PARK, MINNESOTA	FARGO, NORTH DAKOTA	GUELPH, ONTARIO	TOTAL
	lb.	lb.	lb.	lb.	lb.	lb.
Commercial seed (Western bulk)	5,700	4,400	4,320	5,220	3,633	23,273
Western Ohio	4,980	3,500	4,248	4,950	2,760	20,438
Northern Indiana	4,780	2,510	4,468	4,484	2,960	19,202
Southern Indiana	5,020	2,710	4,800	4,860	2,440	19,830
Illinois	4,990	3,990	4,068	4,830	2,720	20,598
Missouri	5,010	4,450	4,400	5,510	2,640	22,010
Iowa	3,950	4,130	4,120	3,960	2,320	18,480
Commercial seed (not inoculated)	5,750	3,998	4,420	4,680	3,520	22,368
Commercial seed (inoculated)	6,040	4,312	4,394	4,140	3,520	22,406
Michigan	5,570	4,400	4,109	3,750	2,240	20,069
Nebraska	3,590	4,500	4,308	5,080	2,720	20,198
Eastern Ohio	5,080	4,640	4,800	5,370	2,320	22,210
Kentucky	5,540	3,420	4,120	4,610	2,840	20,530
Tennessee	4,670	3,970	3,640	5,090	2,800	20,170
Kief, Russia	5,840	4,080	4,020	4,200	2,800	20,940
Orel, Russia	7,100	5,610	5,320	4,062	4,360	26,452
Mogileff, Russia	5,750	4,030	5,000	4,350	4,080	23,210
Courland	4,750	3,280	3,780	4,470	2,880	19,160
Wisconsin	4,950	2,970	3,760	4,380	2,960	19,020
Oregon	4,930	4,560	4,460	4,300	2,680	20,930
Pennsylvania	4,460	1,800	4,480	——	2,960	——
New York	——	2,400	——	——	3,640	——

431. Time of seeding. — The time of seeding red clover is determined largely by its relation to other crops in the rotation, and by climatic conditions. In the southernmost clover sections, fall sowing is necessary, as few plants are able to survive the summer after the hay is cut. In the northernmost places where it succeeds, spring sowing is usually necessary in order to avoid serious winter-killing. In the region of its most extensive culture, seeding may be done at any time from very early spring to early fall, or even in midwinter on the snow or frozen ground.

2 B

In the last-mentioned area, the seed is most commonly sown in spring on fall-sown grain, as the preparation of a special seedbed is thus rendered unnecessary. The actual time of thus seeding in grain is determined mainly by soil conditions. If the seed is broadcasted on the surface, the ideal soil condition is while the ground is still much cracked and honeycombed from alternate freezing and thawing in very early spring, as the seeds thus become covered.

Later spring sowing on grain, even with harrowing, or with a seed drill, is as a rule less desirable; the fall-grown grain is larger and the later started clover seedlings are less well able to withstand either the shading of the grain, or the drought of summer.

If sown alone, red clover may, in the region of its best development, be sown at any time from early spring until early autumn. Late fall plantings are undesirable, as the danger of winter injury is thereby increased.

At the Indiana Experiment Station, red clover was seeded in the middle of each month from April to September on well-prepared seed beds. Excellent stands were secured from the April, May and June seedings; good stands from those of August and September; while that of July was decidedly poor.

Crozier in Michigan obtained excellent stands by seeding in February, March, April and December. Sowings made in July, August, September and October succumbed to winter.

432. Rate of seeding. — Red clover contains about 250,000 seeds to the pound, varying from 207,000 in German seed to 297,000 in American. One pound of seed to an acre evenly scattered would be about 6 seeds to a square foot.

The usual rate of seeding red clover in America is 8 pounds to an acre. Different experiment stations recommend the following rates for their respective states: Wisconsin and North Dakota, 15 pounds; Oregon, 8 to 10 pounds; Louisiana and Kansas, 10 to 15 pounds.

In Europe the rate seems to be higher. Stebler and Volkart recommend 17 pounds an acre in Switzerland, and Glaerum in Norway found the optimum rate to be 25 pounds per acre.

433. Seedlings. — The first true leaf of red clover is compound, but consists of only one leaflet. This, however, is jointed on to the petiole in the same manner as the three leaflets of an ordinary leaf. The primary root is undivided and grows more rapidly than the stem. In contrast to the alfalfa primary root, that of red clover contracts as it grows older, resulting in the crown becoming deep-set. Nodules may appear on the roots by the time they are one week old.

434. Seeding with a nurse-crop. — Red clover is most frequently sown with some other crop, not because this is the best for the clover, but because it economizes labor. The seed may be sown in or with the following crops:—

1. In winter or spring on fall-sown wheat or rye.
2. In spring with wheat, barley or oats.
3. In corn at the last cultivation.
4. With rape or turnips in late summer.

If sown in spring on fall-sown grain, the clover seed may be broadcasted, preferably in early spring when the ground is still loose from frost action; or somewhat later in spring, the seed may be sown and the grain cross-harrowed.

Shepperd in North Dakota secured the best results by seeding with a disk grain-drill across the rows of wheat. This method is increasing in favor in other states.

In Ohio and neighboring states, Drake advocates scattering straw over fields of fall sown wheat in which it is planned to seed clover the following spring. A thin mulch of straw increases greatly the likelihood of a good " catch " of clover. The effect seems due to the straw keeping the soil surface moist and preventing packing and erosion, and perhaps also by supplying humus.

When the clover is seeded in spring with a small grain, barley is preferable to oats, as it does not make so dense a growth and thus injure the clover by shading. Where wheat can be planted in spring, it is preferable to either barley or oats. At the Minnesota Experiment Station, clover seeded with wheat yielded 4360 pounds an acre against 2360 pounds when seeded with oats.

Seeding in corn is becoming a common practice in the New England States. At the Massachusetts Experiment Station this method was used seventeen years without failure. In recent years, it has been the most satisfactory practice in Vermont, and has given good results in Minnesota. It has not been successful in Kansas.

Good stands of clover have been obtained in Tennessee by sowing in tobacco at the last cultivation about the end of July. Red clover may be sown in cotton stubble, but this is rarely practicable.

Sowing clover with two pounds of rape about the end of May gives good results in western Oregon. Sowing in July or August with turnips has proved satisfactory in the Eastern States.

At the South Dakota Station, excellent results were secured by sowing medium clover in early spring on brome-grass sod after thorough disking. The clover seed was sown at the rate of 10 to 12 pounds an acre. In one field the mixture yielded 5484 pounds of hay an acre of the mixture against 3294 for the brome alone; in another 9358 pounds to 2360 pounds.

Clover is sometimes sown in wheat or rye stubble. This is a frequent practice in Europe, especially if the spring-sown seed fails to catch. The same method gives excellent results in western Oregon if seeded in early September.

435. Seeding without a nurse-crop. — A stand of red clover is most likely to be secured when sown alone. This method is, however, seldom used unless all others prove unsatisfactory, as it involves special preparation of the land. In the South, such seeding must be in the fall, preferably about September 1; otherwise crab-grass and other weeds will destroy the clover. In the North, the seed may be sown on a well-prepared, firm seed-bed any time from early spring until fall. Late fall sowing is inadvisable, as winter-killing is likely to be excessive. Weeds are the principal menace to the success of spring seeding, but they may be controlled to some extent by occasionally clipping with the mower.

436. Depth of planting. — Clover seed should be planted shallow to get the best results, in no case more than an inch in clay soils and one and one-half inches in sandy soils.

At the Wisconsin Experiment Station less than one-half of the seeds germinated when covered with 1 inch of compacted garden soil, and less than one-fifth when covered with 2 inches. Shallow planting $\frac{1}{8}$ to $\frac{3}{4}$ of an inch in depth gave the best results and all very similar. The seeds planted $\frac{1}{8}$ to $\frac{3}{4}$ of an inch deep also germinated more promptly than those placed on the surface or those planted deeper. The longest rooted seedlings developed from the seeds planted $\frac{1}{4}$, $\frac{1}{2}$ and $\frac{3}{4}$ of an inch deep.

At the Michigan Experiment Station red clover was

seeded at various depths. The best germination was at a depth of 1 inch and none grew when planted 2 inches deep or more.

437. Winter-killing. — In soils composed of heavy clay or rich in humus, red clover is very apt to be uprooted and destroyed by the heaving of the soil in late winter or early spring. This is particularly likely to damage young clover seeded in the fall, but may injure that seeded the previous spring. A top dressing of coarse stable manure applied in fall will lessen greatly the liability to damage from this cause. If the roots be heaved out 1 inch or less, prompt rolling will be helpful. Very dry autumn weather sometimes weakens clover plants so that the winter mortality is increased.

According to Werner, red clover suffers from cold in Germany only on wet clay, limestone and humus soils during January in the coldest winters. Lund found that at Copenhagen in a severe winter American red clover was much more injured than was European.

438. Treatment of clover fields. — If clover be seeded in spring with a grain crop, there is usually no return the first season other than a little fall pasturage. Under very favorable conditions, however, a moderate crop of hay may be cut, or this may be allowed to mature for seed.

If the clover be seeded alone in spring on well-prepared land, a good cutting of hay is as a rule secured the same season, and in rare cases a second crop.

During the second season, the general practice is to cut the first crop for hay and the second for seed, after which most of the plants die.

439. Fertilizers. — Numerous fertilizer experiments on clover have been reported by American experiment stations. It is difficult, however, to generalize from them, but lime and barnyard manure both nearly always increase the yield, and phosphatic fertilizers are usually beneficial. The results with potash are negative in about half of the experiments reported.

Brooks in Massachusetts found no appreciable difference in the effect of potash when applied as muriate and as sulfate. Chemical analysis, however, showed in all cases a higher per cent of " nitrogen-free extract " in the clover fertilized with the sulfate of potash.

In New Jersey the use of superphosphates with other crops was quite beneficial in increasing the clover crop. Potash also was useful, but barnyard manure gave the best results of all. There was no residual effect from nitrate of soda, and land plaster was without effect.

At the Cornell Experiment Station pot experiments showed that clover was unable to obtain the phosphorus in ground rock phosphate, but was greatly benefited by acid phosphate, basic slag or bone black. These results agree with those of Kossovich in Russia.

At the West Virginia Experiment Station phosphatic fertilizers greatly benefited red clover, but potash did not increase the yield.

In southern Illinois, Hopkins secured an average increase of 1.14 tons hay to an acre by the use of 2000 pounds ground limestone and 1200 to 1500 pounds ground rock phosphate. " Accumulating evidence indicates that the increasing frequency of clover failure in the Illinois corn belt is due in many cases to deficiency in phosphorus."

Mooers at the Tennessee Experiment Station tested various fertilizers on a mixture of orchard-grass and red clover. " At the start all the plots had apparently about an equal stand of cover and of orchard-grass, but on the plots which received acid phosphate or a mixture of acid phosphate and potash salts the growth of clover predominated more and more as the season advanced. On the other hand, where the nitrate of soda was used alone or in a mixture with acid phosphate and potash the orchard-grass predominated; that is, the minerals enabled the clover to crowd the grass, while the nitrate of soda enabled the grass to crowd the clover."

440. Gypsum. — Gypsum was formerly much used for its favorable effect on clover, but in the United States now seems to be employed only in western Oregon. At the Oregon Experiment Station, increases in yield of from 20 to 200 per cent were secured. The rate of application varies from 40 to 200 pounds to an acre.

The cessation of the use of this substance in the Eastern States is perhaps largely the result of the increased use of lime. There is difference of opinion as to the action of gypsum, but it is generally agreed that it is ineffective on poor land.

441. Lime. — Lime has in general given an increased yield when applied to the soil before sowing red clover. Usual applications are 1000 to 2000 pounds of burned lime or twice as much of ground limestone to an acre.

Most investigators regard the litmus test as a fairly reliable indication that the soil needs lime, but in some cases this does not hold true. For example, at the Ohio Experiment Station clover grew normally on one soil and but poorly on two others, all of which reddened litmus paper. Lime alone did not benefit the first soil for clover but improved the crop on the last two, though it did not bring about a full yield.

442. Irrigation. — Clover is not much grown on irrigated lands, principally because alfalfa will yield far larger crops. In high mountain valleys, however, clover succeeds well under irrigation, notably in the Gallatin Valley, Montana, but similar success has been had in several Western States, either when sown alone or mixed with timothy.

King in Wisconsin tested irrigation on red clover. Where the plots were irrigated twice after the first cutting, the second cutting was over two tons to an acre as against one ton where not irrigated. Irrigation after the second cutting also increased greatly the fall pasturage. With an optimum amount of water, either rain or irrigation, King concludes that the clover crop may be double what is ordinarily secured.

443. Red clover in mixtures. — Much more red clover is sown in mixture with timothy than in any other way, approximately three-fourths of the total acreage being thus sown. The timothy is commonly sown with wheat in fall, and the clover added in the spring.

In this mixture the crop is mainly clover the season after sowing, but thereafter is mainly timothy. An objection to this mixture is that medium clover matures sooner than the timothy, but this may be avoided by using the mammoth variety. Red clover and alsike are also frequently sown together, especially where there is difficulty in securing a stand of the former.

Other grasses suitable to grow with red clover are orchard-grass and tall meadow oat-grass, but these mature somewhat sooner. In complex grass mixtures, which are more popular in Europe than in America, red clover should always be included.

444. Use in rotations. — The characteristics of red clover make it particularly well adapted to use in rotation with other crops. Various such rotations are possible, but only a few of the most important and their modifications need to be discussed.

1. *Corn, oats, wheat, clover, timothy.* — This five-year, five-crop rotation is the commonest one employed in the Central States. The timothy is seeded with the wheat in the fall, and the clover on the wheat in the spring. In the fourth year of the rotation the crop is largely clover, and in the fifth mainly timothy. Rye may be substituted for wheat in some places.

2. *Corn, oats, wheat, clover.* — Where the hay is not needed for live stock, the timothy may be omitted and the clover, preferably mammoth, grown for seed only, the straw and the stubble being plowed under. This is an excellent plan to follow on farms where it is not desired to keep live stock.

3. *Corn, wheat, clover.* — This rotation of three years and three crops is employed where wheat is sown in the spring. Rye, barley or oats may be used instead of the wheat, and any other cultivated crop in place of the corn.

4. *Corn, clover* or *corn, corn, clover.* — This is the simplest of all clover rotations, but probably brings the clover too frequently to secure the best results. The clover may be sown in the corn at its last cultivation, or in the spring in the stubble, or after preparing the land.

445. Effect of clover in rotations when only the stubble is turned under. — Red clover usually exercises a markedly beneficial influence on the crop that succeeds it, even where the clover has been cropped. This is ascribed mainly to the humus and nitrogen added to the soil by the roots and stubble.

At the Massachusetts Experiment Station, potatoes after clover stubble, on land that had not been fertilized for 16 years, the yield of potatoes was 95 per cent as great as on similar plots that had received a fair amount of fertilizer containing nitrogen each year. At the Rhode Island Experiment Station potatoes yielded 294.5 bushels after clover and 259.7 bushels after corn. At the Pennsylvania Experiment Station the fertility of the soil was fully maintained for 25 years on certain plots where clover was grown every fourth year in the rotation and only the stubble plowed under. No barnyard manure was used, but each alternate year 48 pounds of phosphoric acid and 100 pounds of potash per acre was added.

The results at the Ohio Experiment Station show that in general a good crop of clover will leave enough nitrogen in the roots and stubble for the succeeding crop, but the nitrogen supply cannot be maintained by clover alone even if planted every third year. At the Illinois Experiment Station the yield of corn grown continuously for 7 years averaged 35.7 bushels to an acre. In a rotation of corn, oats, clover, the average yield of corn for the 5 years immediately after clover was 55.1 bushels, and after clover cropped two years 46.8 bushels to an acre. At the Minnesota Experiment Station it was found that 6 pounds of red clover sown with wheat in continuous wheat culture increased the average yield of wheat for 10 years $3\frac{1}{4}$ bushels to an acre. The results at this station taken as a whole show that the nitrogen content of the soil is preserved if red clover is grown two years in a five-year rotation. At the Canebrake, Alabama, Experiment Station, oats yielded 52 bushels an acre after four-year-old clover stubble, while a yield of 54 bushels was obtained by using 200 pounds of nitrate of soda to an acre.

446. Volunteer crops. — A good stand of red clover is sometimes secured by the scattering of barnyard manure which happens to contain sufficient viable seed.

Volunteer crops may also be secured from fields when some of the seed has been lost in harvesting, or by allowing the seed to become shattered. Successful fields were obtained in this manner at the Louisiana Experiment Station and in Alabama.

To secure a stand in this manner is, however, very uncertain, and further, it is better to grow some other crop than to have clover follow clover.

447. Stage to cut. — If red clover be used as green feed, it is probably best cut before bloom. This method of feeding is more common in Europe than in America. European authorities nearly all agree that the clover for this purpose should be cut before blooming, as the digestibility is then highest, as well as the percentage composition of protein.

If cut for hay, different authorities recommend cutting in young bloom, in full bloom, and when the heads are half brown. The content of digestible nutrients is greatest in full bloom. Later cuttings, however, cure more easily than the early ones, and it is probable that better curing counterbalances largely the lower content of nutrients : —

TABLE SHOWING RELATION BETWEEN TIME OF CUTTING AND ACRE YIELD OF RED CLOVER IN POUNDS ON A WATER-FREE BASIS

STAGE WHEN CUT	ILLINOIS	PENNSYL-VANIA	CONNECTI-CUT
Just before bloom	——	——	1385
Full bloom	2526	3680	1401
Some heads dead	——	3420	——
Three-fourths heads dead . . .	2427	——	——
All heads dead	——	3361	——
Nearly out of bloom	——	——	1750
Nearly ripe	——	——	1523

A FIELD OF SUMAC SORGO IN TEXAS.

A FIELD OF RED CLOVER IN WASHINGTON STATE.

PLATE V.

448. Composition at different stages. — Several investigators have studied the composition of clover at different stages of its development. The total dry matter and the ash increase until maturity, though in some cases there is a slight decline after flowering, due to leaching. The highest percentage of protein is contained before blossoming, but the greatest total amount when the plants are in full bloom. The fatty substances show but little change in their relative amounts. The percentage of fiber increases quite rapidly after blooming. The percentage of carbohydrates shows little change, but is greatest during blooming.

The greatest total amount of digestible substance is about the time of full bloom. The highest percentage of nutritive substance is before bloom, and also the highest percentage of digestibility.

449. Number of cuttings. — Mammoth clover yields but a single cutting of mature hay, the second growth never becoming large enough to justify mowing. Orel red clover behaves in the same way.

Medium red clover, over much of the area best adapted to it, yields a heavy crop of hay at the first cutting, and later a second smaller cutting. Usually the second cutting is allowed to mature for seed.

Near the northern limit of clover culture but one crop of either hay or seed can be obtained.

In Louisiana, near the southern extreme of its successful culture, red clover is best sown in October, when two cuttings of hay, one in May and one in July, are usually secured.

European experiments have consistently shown a greater total yield of hay from two cuttings than from a greater number. Voelcker in Germany secured a less yield from

three and four cuttings than from two, and still less when
the clover was cut five and six times, but the smallest yield
of all when cut but once.   Weiske secured 3570 kilograms
to an hectare when cut twice, and only 3392 kilograms
when cut three times.   In another experiment in Germany,
clover was cut six times and yielded only 4678 pounds to
an acre against 9297 pounds when cut but twice.   It
is probable, therefore, that the total yield of red clover
is much less if pastured than if cut for hay.

450. Yields of hay. — The average yield of red clover
hay in the United States in 1909 was 1.29 tons to an
acre when sown alone and 1.27 tons to an acre mixed
with timothy.

At the Michigan Experiment Station red clover grown
continuously for 5 years from 1896 to 1900 averaged 3110
pounds hay to an acre.   In rotations the yields were
higher.   During the years 1906–7–8 clover grown continuously averaged 2430 pounds to an acre on one plot and
2240 pounds on another; in simple rotation with wheat
2520 pounds on one plot and 2457 pounds on another;
in a three-year rotation with wheat and corn, 2143 pounds
on one plot, 2683 pounds on another.

At the Rhode Island Experiment Station with very
heavy fertilizing red clover produced to an acre 6360 pounds
hay in the first cutting and 2760 pounds in the second.
At the North Dakota Experiment Station the average
hay yield to an acre of the first cutting for 7 years was 3547
pounds.   At the Ontario Agricultural College the average
hay yield to an acre for 6 years of the first cutting was 5900
pounds of medium red and 6620 pounds of mammoth.

451. Relation of green weight to hay weight. — Taking
the average water content of green clover at 72 per cent

and that of clover hay at 18 per cent, the ratio of green weight to hay weight would be approximately 3 to 1.

The available American field data show, however, a wide range of variation in the ratio both as to different places and as to different strains in the same place : —

TABLE SHOWING CORRESPONDING YIELDS OF RED CLOVER
GREEN AND DRY

GREEN WEIGHT	HAY	RATIO	PLACE AND AUTHORITY
Pounds	Pounds		
17461	4482	3.9	Penn. Exp. Sta.
17760	4808	3.7	Penn. Exp. Sta.
11020	3260	3.7	Wis. Exp. Sta. Bul. 121.
First cutting			
4620	1740	2.7	Wis. Exp. Sta. Bul. 121.
Second cutting			
20939	4335	4.8	Minn. Exp. Sta. (Bur. Pl. Ind. Bul. 95) average for 21 strains.
16474	2760	6.	Guelph, Canada (Bur. Pl. Ind. Bul. 95) average for 29 strains.
23280	2880	8.1	Guelph (Courland, Russia, strain).
20800	4360	4.8	Guelph (Orel, Russia, strain).

452. Feeding value. — But few feeding experiments have been recorded that show the feeding value of red clover compared with other hays. It is, however, generally recognized to be of high value.

At the Indiana Experiment Station clover and timothy were compared in fattening steers, using corn as a concentrate. The animals fed on clover consumed 1.41 pounds more hay each day and 3.06 pounds more corn. The actual gain and the cost of a hundredweight of gain was distinctly in favor of the clover. " Throughout the experiment the condition of the clover-fed steers was much better."

453. Comparative feeding value of the first and second crops of hay. — As the second crop of clover is but rarely cut for hay, the subject of the relative value of the hay of the two cuttings has received but little attention.

At the Tennessee Experiment Station the crop of red clover hay from the second cutting was found both less palatable and also less nutritious to steers. Comparative chemical analyses showed but very slight differences.

454. Soiling. — Red clover is an excellent green feed for milch cows. German experiments show that it produces more milk than an equivalent amount of hay.

Bloating seems never to occur when clover is fed in this manner, but it must be neither wet with dew or rain when cut, nor should it be wilted.

The acre yields of green matter from fields of red clover have been measured by several investigators. At the Pennsylvania Experiment Station, the first cutting yielded 17,461 pounds. At the Idaho Experiment Station yields of 12 tons from hill land and 18 tons from bottom were secured. Three cuttings at Agassiz, B. C., in one season, were, respectively, 14.5, 12.0 and 6.2 tons. At the Minnesota Experiment Station the average yield from 21 regional strains at the first cutting was 20,948 pounds.

Green feeding of clover is the usual mode of utilizing in many parts of Europe. It is usually cut shortly before the blossoms appear, as the nitrogen content is highest at this time, and there is but little fiber.

455. Pasturage. — Red clover makes an excellent pasture for all kinds of live stock, but care must be exercised with ruminants to avoid bloating (Par.101). As ordinarily grown in rotations, the crop furnishes some pasturage in the fall of the season it is planted, but it should not be grazed too closely, otherwise the danger of winter injury is increased. Where two crops of hay are harvested the second season, there may still be some pasturage produced, especially if soil moisture conditions are favorable. There is rarely much pasturage after a seed crop has been harvested.

456. Silage. — Red clover may be preserved as silage, especially when unfavorable weather makes haying impracticable. The results so far obtained with pure red clover thus preserved have not been entirely satisfactory. At the Canada Central Experimental Farm, clover silage was found on the basis of chemical analysis to be of less feeding value than green clover, but the silage was eaten with eagerness both when the clover was put in whole and when cut into lengths of 1 inch. At the Wisconsin Experiment Station clover silage varied greatly in quality, some samples being very good, others ill smelling.

At the Oregon Experiment Station, clover was ensiled when the first heads were beginning to discolor. The clover was run through a cutter and made good silage. There was no apparent need of additional water. At the Ohio Experiment Station clover silage was kept three years and was then eaten readily. The clover should be ensiled as rapidly as possible after mowing, first running it through a cutter to insure close packing.

457. Number of flowers and seeds to the head. — The number of flowers in a head of red clover averages about 85. At Ames, Iowa, Pammel reports that the number of flowers to a head varies apparently with soil conditions. On black loam the average for the first crop was 71.1 and for the second crop 98.1, or where underlaid with gravel, 101; on alluvial soil, third crop, 68.7. The maxi-

2 c

mum number found in any head was 140 for the first
crop, 150 for the second and 123 for the third.

The ovary of red clover contains two ovules, but of
these usually only one matures. Good heads contain
from 16 to 40 seeds each, the average being about 25. In
exceptional plants, both ovules may develop. Records
have been published of heads containing 90 to 130 seeds
each.

Beal in Michigan counted the seeds in 50 heads from
each of 6 plants, finding, respectively, 1260, 1275, 1640,
1485, 1820 and 2720 seeds.

Hopkins at the West Virginia Experiment Station
found that 122 red clover heads of the first crop contained
6042 seeds, an average of over 49 seeds per head.

Pammel has made numerous counts of seeds to the head
in Iowa. His results are tabulated as follows : —

RED CLOVER SEEDS TO THE HEAD — FIRST AND SECOND CROPS
IN IOWA

PLACE	SOIL	CROP	HEADS COUNTED	SEEDS PER HEAD
Ames . .	Clay loam	First	44	64.7
Idagrove . .	Black loess	First	50	1.82
Algona . .	Black loam	Second	28	80.4
Harlan . .	Black soil	Second	50	3.9
——	——	First	1242	25.99
——	——	Second	701	27.55
——	——	First	200	41.1
——	——	Second	200	43.7

The average number of seeds to a head is sometimes used
to estimate the probable yield of seed to an acre. If the
seeds average 25 to the head, and the stand is good, a
yield of one to two bushels to an acre may be expected.

458. Pollination and fecundation. — The flowers of red clover are especially adapted to being cross-pollinated by insects, especially bumble bees.

Müller records 39 species of insects that visit red clover flowers in Germany. One species of bumble bee secures the honey by biting through the base of the corolla. For Iowa, Pammel records 14 species, 8 of them being bumble bees. In Illinois, Robertson observed 20 species, five of them being bumble bees.

Plants screened from flying insects failed to set any seeds in the experiments conducted by Darwin in England, and this has been the common result secured by later experimenters. Some investigators have, however, found a few seeds produced by screened plants.

Frandsen in Sweden has recently made extensive studies regarding the matter. In 1910 out of numerous bagged and undisturbed flowers he secured no seed; when artificially self-pollinated, 0.1 per cent of the flowers set seed; when artificially pollinated by another flower of the same plant, 0.8 per cent; when artificially cross-pollinated, 46.1 per cent. In 1911 in similar experiments the percentage of seeds to flowers by the three methods was, respectively, 0 per cent, 0.1 per cent, 0.4 per cent and 42.3 per cent.

Waldron at Dickinson, North Dakota, found that 53.6 per cent of the heads produced seeds in the open and but 9 per cent when screened. When butterflies were placed in netting tents over red clover, only 2.4 per cent of the heads set seed, but when bumble bees were thus placed, 45.7 per cent of the heads produced seeds.

459. Seed-production. — Medium red clover seed is mainly produced in those regions where a crop of seed can be procured after one of hay has been harvested. In the northernmost regions of clover culture, only one crop can be secured, which may be either hay or seed. Mammoth clover does not produce much second growth, so that the hay crop must be sacrificed when a seed crop is desired.

Where two cuttings can be obtained, it is very rare that the first is ever cut for seed. The first crop does not as a rule seed heavily. Two reasons have been assigned in explanation — first, that pollinizing insects are not abundant enough; and second, the plants tend to produce new shoots from the base unless weather conditions are very dry. There are no experimental data recorded, however, as to the relative seed-yielding capacities of the first crop and the second crop, but in Iowa more seeds to a head have been found in the second crop than in the first.

Fig. 41. — Stages in the development of red clover seed. a and c, flower in prime and ripe; b and d, immature and mature seed vessel; e, mature seed.

Seed crops are not usually harvested until the second season, but sometimes a fair seed yield may be obtained from clover sown in spring, either on wheat or alone. This treatment is thought, however, to weaken the plants and materially lessen the growth the following season.

The best seed crops are obtained when the growth of the clover is not rank, and when dry, cloudless weather conditions prevail during the period of blooming and ripening. For the first reason, light soils are supposed to produce better seed crops than clays or clay loams, especially if the latter be moist so as to stimulate much vegetative growth. Pammel's investigations in Iowa did not, however, disclose any definite relations between the character of the soil and the number of seeds to a head. Sunshiny, warm days at blooming time insure a greater abundance of pollinizing insects, and these are absent in cold, wet weather.

Where the first crop is cut for hay, the time of cutting may affect markedly the subsequent seed crop. Clover hay is usually cut when the first heads turn brown, but the belief is general that the seed crop is apt to be better if the hay crop is cut a little before full bloom, as this makes the second growth stronger.

Where the season is not long enough to secure both a hay crop and a seed crop, as in the northern tier of states, it is a common practice to pasture the field or to clip it back in June, so as to bring the seed crop in September. It is claimed that by this means better yields of seed are obtained. Among the advantages supposed to be secured are: 1. A more even ripening of the crop; 2. A more favorable season for blooming and seed setting; 3. Lessening of injury by the clover midge and the clover chalcis; 4. A smaller growth, which is not likely to lodge and is more easily handled. Experimental data on this subject are lacking.

Prolonged rains at harvest time seem to be the cause of many of the seeds turning brown. Seeds that have turned brown with age do not germinate nearly as well as yellow or violet-tinged seeds.

460. Harvesting the seed crop. — Red clover for seed should be cut when the heads have all turned brown, and the seeds are firm and shining. Cutting in the soft dough stage results in shriveled seed. If the seeds are allowed to ripen, there is no loss by shattering, but the heads break off very easily. If the clover has become riper than stated, much loss of heads can be prevented by mowing in the early morning when wet with dew.

Mowing may be accomplished in several different ways. A self-rake reaper is very satisfactory. An ordinary mower with a bunching attachment (Fig. 42) that throws the bunches of clover to one side so that they may not be trampled upon, is also excellent. Heading machines which cut the straw high are sometimes used, and these are particularly desirable, as they economize labor and cut much less straw to be thrashed.

Fig. 42. — A bunching attachment on an ordinary mower.

Red clover is most commonly harvested, however, by mowing and then raking into windrows, using practically the same method as in harvesting hay.

In favorable weather the clover is ready to store or hull in about four days if cut in the late dough stage. The bunches should then be piled in cocks, or better, placed under cover. During unfavorable weather there is some danger of the seed sprouting if the clover is kept continuously damp.

In the principal seed-growing districts, special machines called clover hullers are used to thrash the seed and shell it from the pods. This can be done only when the straw is very dry.

461. Yields of seed. — The yield of seed to an acre for the main part of the clover area probably averages about

100 pounds, and rarely reaches 300 pounds. Yields have been reported by experiment stations, as follows: North Dakota, 46 to 146 pounds; Oregon, 175 to 250 pounds.

For the Willamette Valley, Oregon, Hunter reports the usual yield 4 to 6 bushels, and occasionally 7 to 9 bushels to an acre.

The average yield of seed in Wisconsin in 1905 was 1.84 bushels to an acre, but this was somewhat lower than usual. In northern Wisconsin, a maximum yield of 4¼ bushels to an acre is reported.

Werner gives the yields in Germany at 150 to 225 pounds to an acre.

462. Statistics of seed crop. — The total yield of clover seed in the United States in 1899 was 1,349,209 bushels valued at $5,359,578. In 1909 the corresponding figures were 1,025,816 bushels valued at $6,925,122. The principal seed-producing states in the order of the total yield produced were, in the latter year, Wisconsin, Ohio, Michigan, Illinois, Indiana, Missouri, Minnesota, Iowa, Oregon.

Clover seed has been an article of export from the United States since 1792.

463. Value of the straw. — The straw of red clover from which the seed has been thrashed possesses but little feeding value, and is both coarse and unpalatable. Usually much of its little feeding value is diminished by being rained upon. Animals will, however, eat some of the straw, and this, combined with its value for bedding, makes it worth saving.

Perhaps the best use to make of the straw is for bedding, but it is often scattered directly on the field.

464. Seed. — Seed of red clover (Fig. 43) is readily distinguished from similar leguminous seeds by its color, which is yellow or violet, or both combined. Old seeds become dull and brownish.

The seed may be adulterated with yellow trefoil; with old red clover seeds sometimes oiled and polished; and with small or shriveled seed obtained in screenings. Where cheaper foreign clover seed has been added to American seed it may be detected by the presence of certain weed seeds. A large proportion of small seeds indicates that these have been added.

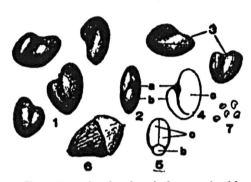

Fig. 43. — Seeds of red clover. **1**, side view and, **2**, edge view of seeds; **3**, the triangular form indicated; **4**, a seed cut lengthwise; **5**, a seed cut crosswise, showing the embryo; **a**, a seed scar; **b**, a stemlet (radicle) of the embryo; **c**, seed leaves (cotyledons) of the embryo; **6**, a pod of red clover; **7**, natural size of seeds.

The most objectionable weed seeds that may occur in red clover are dodder, Canada thistle, curled dock, buckhorn and oxeyedaisy.

The best commercial red clover seed may attain a purity of 99 per cent and a viability of 98 per cent. Good seeds germinate in from 2 to 6 days, excepting the " hard " seeds. The percentage of hard seeds is often 20 per cent and may reach 50 per cent in very fresh seeds.

The seed varies in weight from 60 to 63 pounds a bushel. One pound contains 279,000 seeds (Stebler), 232,000 seeds (Hunter), 200,000 to 240,000 seeds (Hunt).

The optimum temperature for germination was found by the Ontario Agricultural College to be 90° Fahrenheit. At 95° the vitality was distinctly impaired.

Hiltner and Kingel examined a sample of red clover seed that had been stored 8 years. It was separated into three lots: first, those which were apparently unchanged; second, those which were pale in color; and third, those which were brown and more or less shriveled. Of the first lot 10.5 per cent germinated and 81.9 per cent remained hard. In the other lots the germination ranged from 1.7 to 8.1 per cent. By scratching the seed coats of those that remained hard, it was found that nearly all were viable.

465. Color of seeds. — The seeds of red clover are either pure yellow or more or less completely tinged with violet, but never wholly violet. There is a popular belief that violet-tinged seed is superior in viability and vigor. This subject has received attention from various investigators.

Gernert in Illinois finds that white-flowered plants produce yellow seeds without trace of purple. Plants with dark red flowers yield invariably seeds much tinged with violet, while those with pink flowers in some cases produced yellow seeds. The violet color appears late, and may not show in prematurely gathered seeds. Five plants were selected, each with a different seed color; namely, pea; purple tint on yellow; reddish-purple on yellow; medium purple on yellow; dark purple on yellow. The progeny of each of these showed a wide range as regards seed color, indicating that the parent plants were heterozygote as regards seed color. The data suggest that the character is a Mendelian one, and that it is entirely feasible to isolate strains with violet-tinged seeds.

Früwirth in Austria concludes that there is a tendency for clover plants to produce seeds of one color. Thus one plant produced 160 deep yellow and 445 yellow seeds; another, 154 violet, 125 variegated, 58 deep yellow and 11 yellow seeds; a third, 177 deep yellow and 366 yellow seeds; a fourth, 131 variegated and 47 deep yellow seeds. Yellow seeds are more likely to breed true than violet-tinged seeds. In weight, violet seeds are heaviest, followed by variegated and yellow. He obtained a higher yield of air-dry substance in the crop from yellow seeds than from either violet or variegated, a result in accord with that of the Kentucky Experiment Station.

Card in Rhode Island analyzed plants grown from yellow seeds and from purple seeds, but found no difference in their nitrogen content.

466. Roots. — The roots of red clover penetrate to a maximum depth of about six feet, but ordinarily not more than four feet. Hays at the Minnesota Experiment Station found that the tap root was 7 inches long after 1 month, 2 feet after 2 months, and after five months 5½ feet. The lateral roots were a little deeper than the main root.

The greater part of the roots is in the top six inches of soil and according to all investigations about 95 per cent in the top 8 inches. Thus, John in Germany found the following vertical distribution : —

7.8 to 9.0 cm. deep	—	3760 kg. to a hectare.
15.7 to 18.3 cm. deep	—	338 kg. to a hectare.
27.4 to 28.8 cm. deep	—	196 kg. to a hectare.
36.6 to 39.2 cm. deep	—	78 kg. to a hectare.

At the Utah Experiment Station the weight of roots was estimated for each inch of depth in fields respectively 2 years old and 4 years old. The basis was the weight of roots obtained from an area 2 feet square : —

TABLE SHOWING WEIGHT OF RED CLOVER ROOTS TO AN ACRE
FOR EACH INCH OF DEPTH, UTAH EXPERIMENT STATION

DEPTH	4 YEARS OLD	2 YEARS OLD
Inches	Water-free	Water-free
1	1058.4	240.7
2	1248.5	449.3
3	1181.	433.9
4	1142.4	170.9
5	508.8	149.3
6	124.8	137.5
7	88.8	
8	66.3	
9	62.2	
10	50.4	
11	50.2	
12	48.5	
Total .	5630.3	1481.6

At the Minnesota Experiment Station, Snyder found in a square yard of earth that clover roots when water-free weighed: 122 grams just before the heads appeared; 320 grams in early bloom; and 916 grams in full bloom.

At the Delaware Experiment Station, Penny determined that the roots 8 inches deep weighed, air-dry, 1185 pounds, and the next 4 inches 27 pounds, the whole containing 33 pounds nitrogen. The tops weighed 2819 pounds.

At the Connecticut Experiment Station Woods estimated the roots 8 inches deep to contain 850 pounds, and those in the subsoil 48 pounds of dry matter. At Middletown, Connecticut, a crop was determined to have 1355 pounds of dry matter in the roots.

467. Shoots. — The main axis of the red clover is a rather deep-seated, short crown, from which arise a dense mass of basal leaves. From the axils of each of these, a secondary leafy aërial branch may arise, and these constitute the larger visible portion of the plants. Each secondary branch is terminated by a head of flowers, but commonly bears also tertiary branches each terminated by a head of flowers. One shoot may thus bear as high as 14 heads of flowers.

The height of the secondary branches varies with the fertility of the soil, but they seldom exceed 30 inches under field conditions. The number is usually from 10.to 20, but as many as 76 have been found on a single plant. After cutting, the branches die back as far as the lowest internodes.

In winter the hibernating shoots lie close to the ground.

Werner found that a well-grown plant with 108 leaves had a surface area of 712 square centimeters. Von Gahren in a similar examination found 875 square centimeters.

468. Proportion of roots to shoots. — Several investigators have determined the relative proportion of the different parts of the clover plant.

At the Arkansas Experiment Station single plants showed an average dry weight of two ounces for the tops and 2¼ ounces for the roots. Smith in Michigan examined plants of red clover at the end of September. Those sown the previous spring had 4.625 pounds of tops and .75 pound of roots, while those sown the year before in June had 1.5 pounds of tops to 1.44 pounds of roots, in each case weighed when fresh. King in Wisconsin estimated the green weight of the tops to an acre at 12,486 pounds and of the roots at 3120 pounds. The data used for the estimates were obtained by driving down a cylinder 12 inches in diameter and 30 inches long. Snyder in Minnesota estimated that an acre field yielding 4000 pounds of hay contained 1760 pounds of dry roots. At the Delaware Experiment Station the tops and roots to an acre were determined respectively at 2819 and 1212 pounds dry weight.

At the Central Experiment Farm, Canada, the roots were dug from areas 4 feet square and 9 inches deep on seven different plots. The estimated green weights to an acre are shown in the following table:—

ESTIMATED GREEN WEIGHT OF TOPS AND ROOTS TO AN ACRE, CANADA CENTRAL EXPERIMENT FARM

PLOTS	LEAVES AND STEMS	ROOTS	RATE OF SEEDING
	Pounds	Pounds	
1	5441	5105	4 pounds
2	6849	5147	4 pounds
3	6934	6047	4 pounds
4	8508	5785	4 pounds
5	7997	5615	4 pounds
6	7657	4349	4 pounds
7	10209	6296	14 pounds
Total . .	53595	38344	

469. Relative proportions of stems, leaves and flower heads. — Dietrich in Germany studied the relative percentage weights of leaves, stems and flower heads at different ages. The following results were secured:—

	MARCH 31 LEAVES FORMING	APRIL 26 STEMS FORMING	MAY 19 BUDS FORMING	JUNE 1 FIRST FLOWERS	JUNE 16 FULL BLOOM	FLOWER-ING FINISHED
	Per cent	Per cent	Per cent	Per cent	Per cent	Per cent
Leaves . . .	40	41	24	24	19	18
Leaf stalks .	60	29	14	12	11	10
Stems . . .	—	30	58	58	59	60
Flower heads	—	—	4	6	11	12

From these figures, clover hay should consist of about 60 per cent stems, 30 per cent leaves and 10 per cent flower heads.

470. Diseases. — Red clover is subject to a long list of fungous diseases, few of which are, however, a serious menace to its culture. Only the more important and more common ones are here mentioned.

The leaves may be affected by clover leaf-spot (*Pseudopeziza trifolii*); black spot (*Polythrincium trifolii*); powdery mildew (*Erysiphe polygoni*); downy mildew (*Peronospora trifoliorum*); and clover rust (*Uromyces striatus*). It is rare that any of these diseases causes much damage.

The roots are subject to a root rot (*Rhizoctonia violacea*).

The stems are sometimes injured by stem rot (*Sclerotinia trifoliorum*) which is easily recognizable by the large dark sclerotia formed. Clover anthracnose (*Colletotrichum trifolii*) is probably the most destructive disease that has attacked red clover in America. It appears as purplish spots on the stem which increase in size until the stem is girdled and thus killed. It is known to occur in Maryland, Virginia, Ohio, Tennessee and Alabama, and is probably much more widely spread. No direct means of control is known, but results secured at the Tennessee Experiment Station show that highly resistant strains may be secured by selection.

Two other anthracnoses, caused respectively by *Colletotrichum cereale* and *Gloeosporium trifolii*, are also found occasionally, but no serious damage by either has been reported.

471. Clover sickness. — This term is used to designate a condition or conditions which prevent the successful growing of red clover, at least continuously. This has long been recognized in Europe, where numerous explanations as to its cause have been advanced. The principal theories are: 1. The exhaustion of some necessary element from the soil, in particular lime, potash or phosphorus; 2. The formation or excretion by the clover plant of some deleterious substance; 3. Unfavorable physical condition of the soil, especially the subsoil; 4. Presence of disease-forming fungi or bacteria; 5. Injurious insects and other animals; 5. Depletion of humus content of the soil.

None of these theories has been proven, but it is not unlikely that there may be some truth in each of them.

Experience in Europe has shown that good clover may be grown on clover-sick soil if a sufficient interval of time elapse. In Germany this is usually four to six years, but on some soils a period of nine or even twelve years seems necessary.

It is not certain that the increasing difficulty in securing a stand of red clover in various parts of the United States is the same as the European clover sickness, but this seems highly probable. The evidence indicates that the trouble first became prominent in the Atlantic States and has been slowly extending westward. Even in regions where clover sickness is common, land that has long been uncultivated will often produce good crops of red clover for a few years. Alsike clover, however, grows readily on land "sick" to red clover, and in many places is now substituted for the red.

Soil acidity has recently been considered to be a cause of failure with red clover, but lime has not proven to be a remedy for the trouble. It has not yet been demonstrated that the European practice of planting red clover at long intervals will be equally successful in this country.

In England the question has been raised as to whether

land becomes sick to naturalized wild plants of red and white clover. Several experiments have shown that clover plants grown from cultivated seeds disappear largely in 1 year, while those from wild plants persist 3 to 5 years or more. One experiment with red clover resulted in the plants from cultivated seeds lasting but 2 years, while those grown from seed gathered in an old meadow lived 5 or 6 years.

472. Reduction of acreage probably due mainly to clover sickness.—The statistics of the thirteenth census of the United States, 1909, shows that a great decrease in the acreage of clovers has taken place since 1899, especially in the eastern part of the country. Every state east of the 95th degree of longitude, excepting Illinois, shows such a decrease.

The average decrease in the acreage of "clover" for the whole United States was 40 per cent. In certain states the decrease was much greater, being 88 per cent in New Jersey, 78 per cent in Pennsylvania and 65 per cent in Indiana. In the states immediately west of the Mississippi River the decrease was not so great, but is 30 per cent in Missouri, 23 per cent in Minnesota and 16 per cent in Iowa. In the states farther west the figures are of less interest, owing to the large acreage of new land brought under cultivation and the general preference for alfalfa.

While the significance of the figures is not wholly clear, the most probable explanation is that it is associated with the increasing difficulty in securing stands of red clover. The striking contrast in the figures for 1899 and 1909 may in part be due to unusual conditions in the latter year—but it does not appear from records that there was undue loss from winter-killing or other climatic causes in that year. The extent of the reduction in acreage is shown in the following table:—

TABLE SHOWING THE ACREAGE OF CLOVERS IN THE EASTERN
PART OF THE UNITED STATES IN 1899 AND 1909

| | CLOVER ACREAGE | | DECREASE PER CENT |
	1899	1909	
New England States . .	18,681	15,097	19
New York	103,155	87,267	15
New Jersey	57,635	6,893	88
Pennsylvania	293,683	64,372	78
Ohio	617,516	181,048	71
Indiana	776,810	271,697	65
Michigan	225,636	168,180	25
Iowa	148,720	125,751	16
Minnesota	74,669	57,358	23
Wisconsin	203,253	119,522	41
West Virginia	25,170	6,661	73
Maryland	67,375	26,545	60
Virginia	104,124	54,016	48
Missouri	377,228	262,263	30
United States	4,103,968	2,443,263	40

In Illinois the acreage in 1899 was 362,044, while in
1909 it was 427,957, an increase of over 18 per cent.

473. Insects. — There are five insects which cause rather
serious damage to red clover, one of them attacking the
root, one the foliage, one the hay, one the flower and one
the seed.

The clover root-borer (*Hylastinus obscurus*). — The
clover root-borer is easily recognized from the fact that
its larva burrows in the root, thus greatly injuring and
sometimes killing the plant. The damage is nearly always done in plants the second season, after the roots have
attained a considerable size. The only remedy suggested

2 D

is to plow under the clover immediately after the first crop of hay is cut. With the death of the plant the larvæ also die. If, however, the plowing is delayed until later, the larvæ may have attained their growth and will then develop into adults.

The clover-leaf weevil (Phytonomus punctatus). — This little beetle and its larvæ feed on the foliage of red clover in early spring. The damage is seldom serious, and in any event serves mainly to delay the maturing of the plant.

The clover-flower midge (Dasyneura leguminicola). — This little two-winged fly lays its eggs in the blossoms and the maggot injures the blossoms so that seeds are not formed. One method of control suggested is to cut the hay early, as this will destroy many of the larvæ before they have time to develop further. When clover is grown primarily for seed, sometimes the first crop is clipped so as to bring the blooming of the next crop later in the summer, in this way avoiding much injury by the midge.

FIG. 44. — Sketch showing the effect of the clover-seed chalcis fly. Calyx (a), seed capsule (b) and seeds (c and d). At c the mature insect is shown in the act of emerging.

The clover-seed chalcis fly (Brucho-phagus funebris). — This is a small, black, wasp-like insect whose larva develops in the clover seed, all of which is eaten excepting the hard shell. The work of this insect is conspicuous by the finding of hollow seeds, each containing a round hole through which the adult has emerged (Fig. 44). The only remedy suggested is pasturing the crop in early spring, or clipping the first crop so as to make the seed crop at a time when the fly is not abundant.

The clover-hay worm (Hypsopygia costalis). — This is the larva of a small, brown moth which feeds on the dry hay in storage. Most of the damage is usually done near the bottom of hay stacks or mows. To some extent, it may be prevented by salting the hay, especially near the bottom of the stack. Where hay is stacked in the field, the injury is much lessened by building the stacks on a foundation of logs, or other platform.

474. Improvement of red clover by breeding. — In recent years there has been much interest in the subject of breeding improved red clover. Individual plants differ greatly and this permits of selection for numerous distinctive characters. More or less work of this kind has been conducted at the experiment stations of Tennessee, Illinois, Iowa, Indiana and North Dakota and by the United States Department of Agriculture. In Europe similar breeding researches have been undertaken in Sweden, Denmark and Switzerland.

Breeding red clover presents difficulties in that cross-pollination is required and that, therefore, at least two individuals are necessary to start a strain. Furthermore, isolation is then required to prevent miscellaneous cross-pollination.

Mass selection is much simpler, especially where an unfavorable factor eliminates a large proportion of the population. In this way a strain resistant to anthracnose has been developed at the Tennessee Experiment Station.

Card in Rhode Island found that the nitrogen content of different individual plants ranged from 2.86 per cent to 4.62 per cent. This suggests the possibility of selecting strains with high protein content.

475. Disease-resistant strains. — There have been but few attempts made to secure strains of red clover immune to disease. Bain, at the Tennessee Experiment Station, has, however, thus bred a strain resistant to anthracnose (*Colletotrichum trifolii*) by selecting plants not affected by the disease. Apparently the same result was reached by Clarendon Davis, in northern Alabama, by merely saving the seed each year from the surviving plants. .

CHAPTER XVII

OTHER CLOVERS. — ALSIKE, HUNGARIAN, WHITE AND SWEET

THE genus *Trifolium* comprises a large list of species both annual and perennial, all of them confined to regions of temperate climate or at least temperate during the growing period. Red clover is by far the most important economic species, but where there is difficulty in growing this crop other species, especially alsike and white clover, are very valuable substitutes. The clover-like plants of the genus *Melilotus* are also useful and worthy of more attention than they have heretofore received.

ALSIKE CLOVER (*Trifolium hybridum*)

476. Botany of alsike. — The alsike clover is so named from a place in Sweden where it is much grown. It is also called Swedish clover. The scientific name was so given because Linnæus erroneously believed it to be a hybrid between red clover and white clover.

Alsike is native to the temperate portions of Europe and Asia and also occurs in Algiers. It is rare, however, in southern Europe. The plant is very variable, but only a few forms have received botanical names. Ascherson and Graebner consider that cultivated alsike is a subspecies (*Trifolium fistulosum* Gilibert), differing through long cultivation in having larger, less toothed leaves, larger heads and longer calyx teeth. Another subspecies

405

is *Trifolium elegans* Savi, with rose-colored flowers and other slight differences.

In recent years the improvement of alsike by selection has been undertaken at Svalöf and other places in Europe.

477. Agricultural history. — Alsike has long been cultivated in Sweden, probably as early as 1750. Its spread into other countries was, however, quite recent. In England and Scotland the first clear record is 1832.

Alsike seed was distributed in the United States by the Patent Office in 1854, but it was probably introduced earlier. The plant was called alsike in Scotland as early as 1832.

478. Adaptations. — Alsike clover is adapted to a wider range of both climatic and soil conditions than red clover, and nearly as great as that of white clover. It thrives especially well in cool climates with abundant moisture. It rarely winter-kills and often survives winter conditions that destroy red clover. On the whole it is, perhaps, as resistant to drought as red clover, but drought reduces its yield greatly. It endures both cold and heat better than red clover.

It is not particular as to soil, provided abundant moisture is available, thriving well on clay, clay loams, sandy loams and muck soils. Unlike most clovers, it will thrive even where the soil is waterlogged. On this account it is also well adapted to growing under irrigation.

Alsike is peculiar in that it will thrive where red clover culture has dwindled on account of " clover sickness "; a trouble that seems never to affect alsike, and which permits its frequent or almost continuous use on the same land.

479. Characteristics of alsike clover. — It is a long-lived perennial, fields enduring 4 to 6 years in good soil.

The stems are erect or ascending when crowded, but in isolated plants are spreading. The herbage is smooth and decidedly more leafy than red clover. The hay consists of about 60 per cent leaves and 40 per cent stems. Werner records 168 leaves on 8 branches, with a total flat surface of 504 square centimeters. Under favorable conditions it reaches a height of 2½ feet in the mass, but is usually less. On account of the dense growth the lower leaves are apt to decay, especially where growing in wet land. The root system is relatively shallow, and on this account the plant does not well withstand drought.

Hays at the Minnesota Experiment Station found that the tap root after one month was 9½ inches long and after two months more than 2 feet. It does not remain prominent as many of the secondary roots become as large. The mass of roots is greater at the same age than that of red clover.

The growth begins later in spring than red clover, and the blooming time is also somewhat later. Isolated plants often measure one foot in diameter, and in closely grazed pastures resemble white clover somewhat in habit.

480. Regional strains. — There is but very little difference in alsike, depending on the source from which seed is obtained, according to the results secured by Stebler and Volkart in Switzerland. Plots sown with American seed gave slightly better results the first year, but in the second year the results showed no definite superiority.

In extensive trials at the Danish Experiment Station the relative yields of regional strains were as follows: Swedish, 100; Rhine, 98; English, 97; German, 91; Canadian, 83; American, 80.

481. Importance. — Alsike clover has been growing in importance in America in recent years, mainly because it succeeds well on land that will no longer grow red clover on account of " clover sickness." Apart from this it is valuable for growing on land too wet for red clover and in mixed hay meadows because of its longer life.

No accurate statistical information is available, but alsike is probably most abundantly grown in the following states and provinces; namely, Ontario, Wisconsin, Michigan, Minnesota, Ohio, New York, Maryland, Virginia.

482. Culture. — The culture of alsike differs but little from that of red clover, and it may be used for the same purposes. Seed is sown alone or with a nurse-crop, either in fall or in spring. In Europe winter seeding is a common method. The rate of seeding is 8 to 12 pounds an acre, if seeded alone. Fields last well for two or three years and often for four or five years. Usually the second season gives the best yields.

Alsike is, however, best adapted to growing in mixtures, especially in low or wet soils. In mixtures the alsike is abundant for two years and then rapidly disappears.

483. Hay. — Alsike may be cut for hay over a longer period than red clover, as the main stems continue to grow with the production of new flowers. It is usually recommended to cut when in full bloom. Under favorable circumstances two cuttings are obtained, but the second is nearly always smaller than the first. If the cutting of the first crop is delayed, the second is reduced.

German records of hay yields are as follows: Pinckert, 4000 to 5600 pounds to an acre; Werner, 2600 to 4500 pounds; Schober, for the first cutting, 3000 pounds.

Yields on an acre are recorded by American experiment stations as follows: Pennsylvania, 3956 pounds; Kansas, 3110 pounds; Illinois, 2400 pounds; Michigan Upper Peninsula, 6800 pounds; Minnesota, 5860 pounds; Utah, 2780 pounds.

484. Seed-production. — Commercial seed of alsike clover is now produced mainly in Ontario, Wisconsin, Michigan, Ohio and Minnesota. It is also produced in most of the countries of northern Europe, but mainly for home consumption. Alsike usually yields less seed to the acre than either red clover or white clover.

The seed yields are best on land that is moderately dry. The plants are mowed when the heads are brown and the seed in the dough stage, as later cutting involves loss by shattering. If not cut till ripe, it should be mowed when moist with dew. Great care is necessary in curing. Usually the first crop is harvested as seed, as in most of the regions where seed is grown the second crop does not have time to ripen.

European seed yields are given by various authorities as ranging from 100 to 600 pounds to an acre, with about 300 pounds as the average.

In 9 coöperative trials in northern Wisconsin, the maximum yield was 6¼ bushels to an acre, and the average 3½ bushels.

485. Seed. — Alsike clover seed (Fig. 45) may be distinguished from most other clovers by its small, somewhat heart-shaped seeds, and from white clover by its green color.

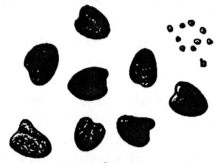

FIG. 45. — Alsike clover seeds. a, seeds showing variation in form and surface appearance, enlarged; b, natural size of seeds.

Old seeds turn brown. Old seeds and screenings are sometimes used as adulterants. Trefoil may be, and timothy is commonly, present as an impurity.

Good seed often attains a purity of 99 per cent and a

viability as high.   It will germinate in 2 to 6 days, excepting the hard seed, which is not as abundant as in red clover.   Any of the ordinary noxious weed seeds may occur in alsike as impurities, but the most dangerous is dodder.   The seed retains its viability well for two years, but then rapidly deteriorates.

A bushel of seed weighs 60 to 66 pounds.   One pound contains 700,000 to 718,000 seeds.

486. Value for pasturage. — Alsike clover is often used in pasture mixtures for low, wet lands and the aftermath of hay fields is also utilized by pasturing.   It is eagerly eaten by all farm animals, but with cattle and sheep the same precautions must be exercised to avoid bloating as with red clover and alfalfa.   In closely grazed pastures, the stems are commonly spreading or nearly prostrate.

Werner states that if fed green to horses, it is very laxative and results in much of the accompanying grain feed being voided undigested.

HUNGARIAN CLOVER (*Trifolium pannonicum*)

487. Hungarian clover is native from northern Italy to the Caucasus region of Asia Minor.   It is a deep-rooted, long-lived perennial having much the same general habits as red clover, but the whole herbage is more hairy, and the white or yellowish flowers are in large ovate heads.

Hungarian clover has been tested at many of the American experiment stations, and in most cases has grown quite as well as red clover.   It is not much cultivated in Europe, largely on account of the high cost of the seed, and for the same reason it has been tried only in an experimental way in America.   The seed can rarely be purchased for less than $1 to $1.25 a pound.

WHITE CLOVER (*Trifolium repens*)

488. Botany. — White clover is also known as Dutch clover and rarely as white trefoil. It is native throughout the temperate portion of Europe and Asia, while in Africa it occurs in the Azores.

Numerous botanical varieties have been named, but none of these have been of any agricultural importance. A variety with purple foliage is sometimes cultivated as an ornamental. The only really distinct agricultural variety is Ladino clover. Individual plants of white clover vary greatly so that it would be possible to secure numerous varieties by selection. Work of this kind has been undertaken at several places.

489. Description. — White clover is a long-lived but shallow-rooted perennial. It differs markedly from red and alsike clover in that the solid stems creep on the surface of the ground and root abundantly. On this account the growing point is seldom injured by mowing and grazing, and so the growth is not interrupted. When mowed, the hay consists entirely of leaves and flower stalks. The leaflets hold on much better in curing than do those of red clover. Single plants make a dense turf often a foot or more in diameter.

Hays at the Minnesota Experiment Station found the tap root after one month to be $4\frac{1}{2}$ inches long and with numerous side roots, and when two months old to be 2 feet long. At this time roots began to be found on the creeping branches. The tap root is said to die in one or two years.

Werner calculated the surface area of the leaves from 18 square centimeters, and found it to be 172 square centimeters.

490. Agricultural history. — White clover seems to have been first cultivated in Holland, where it forms an important element in the pasture lands. The harvesting of the seed for sowing began about 1759 in Holstein and in 1764 in England, but was apparently still earlier in Holland.

Jared Eliot mentions it in Massachusetts in 1747, and Kalm in his American travels a few years later found it common. Strickland, who traveled in the United States in 1794, writes as follows : —

"In every part of America, from New Hampshire to Carolina, from the sea to the mountains, the land, whether calcareous or argillaceous, whether wet or dry, whether worn out or retaining its original fertility, from the summit of the Alleghany ridge to the sandy plains of Virginia, is spontaneously covered with white clover, growing frequently with a luxuriance and perfection that art can rarely equal in Europe.

"I am told it is never met with far back in the woods, but immediately on their being cleared away, either by fire or otherwise, it takes possession of the ground; which should prove that it was natural to it; that the seed lies there, but cannot vegetate till the ground is cleared; but again I have been told, that by some tribes of Indians it is called 'white man's foot grass,' from an idea that wherever he has trodden, it grows; which should prove at least, that it had not been known in the country longer than the white man."

491. Adaptations. — White clover is adapted to moist soils in nearly the whole temperate zone. In America its range is quite as wide as that of redtop, occurring northward to the limits of agriculture, and southward nearly to the Gulf of Mexico. It thrives best in regions of cool, moist climates. In the South, it persists through the hot weather of summer and becomes an important element of the pastures in winter.

It will grow in any sort of soil, provided moisture is abundant, but it thrives best in loams and clay loams rich in humus, and fairly well drained.

Through all the moisture areas in America, it is so well adapted that it holds its own spontaneously, and in old pastures gradually becomes more abundant unless the soil is poor or droughty. From the fact that cattle avoid the flowers, spontaneous reseeding is continuous.

White clover also grows well in shady places and often makes up a considerable portion of the ground cover in orchards.

Phosphatic fertilizers have a marked effect on white clover and where these are applied, the growth of the clover is usually greatly stimulated. Potash fertilizers also have a similar but less marked effect.

492. Importance of white clover. — With the exception of blue-grass, and possibly Bermuda and redtop, white clover is the most important perennial pasture plant in America. It is nearly always an element in blue-grass pastures, but in the best blue-grass areas it is not abundant. Otherwise it is always an important element of mixed pastures, and in the cotton region is more important than blue-grass.

White clover is said not to be nearly as liable as red clover to cause bloating, but as it is usually mixed with grasses, this is rarely apt to occur. Under some conditions it causes horses to " slobber."

Apart from its use as pasture, white clover is very much used as an element in lawn mixtures.

493. Seeding. — White clover is rarely sown except in mixtures with other grasses, and after it is once established usually maintains itself indefinitely. The usual rate of pure seeding recommended is 9 to 13 pounds to an acre.

494. Yields. — White clover is so seldom grown pure as a hay crop that there are but scant data concerning its hay-yielding capacity.

Früwirth compared several strains both of ordinary and Ladino white clover in Austria in 1904 and 1905, with the following results, the weights being of the green clover : —

Strain	Yield to a Hectare — 1904	Yield to a Hectare — 1905	Total Yield
	Kilograms	Kilograms	Kgm.
Colossal Ladino (Hohenheim Seed)	39,239 4 cuttings	23,726 3 cuttings	62,965
Colossal Ladino (Hohenheim Seed)	43,476 4 cuttings	27,442 3 cuttings	70,918
Colossal Ladino from Italy	34,447 4 cuttings	29,214 3 cuttings	63,958
Carter's Common White Clover	23,098 3 cuttings	15,917 1 cutting	30,015
Carter's Giant White Clover	23,469 3 cuttings	15,158 1 cutting	38,627

Stebler and Volkart report an experiment in Switzerland in which white clover from various sources was grown in small plots. The Ladino clover plots were much injured by winter-killing. The others yielded hay at the following rates to a hectare in kilograms: English I, 5500; America, 5000; Bohemian I, 4750; Russian I, 4500; Bohemian II, 4250; Polish, 4000; Galician, 4000; Russian II, 3700; New Zealand, 3500; English II, 2500.

At the Danish Experiment Station various regional

strains were grown two years and gave comparative yields as follows: Danish, 100; Ladino, 94; Holland, 92; American, 89; Pomeranian, 86; English, 80; Silesian, 76; German, 73.

In England a number of experiments have shown that if seed gathered from wild white clover plants be sown, the plants will persist much longer than if seed of the cultivated plants be sown. The cultivated white clover disappears in one or two years, while the wild white clover persists much longer — at least three to five years. The explanation given is that the cultivated white clover is less resistant to the rigorous springs and perhaps also to " clover sickness."

Werner gives the hay yields to an acre in Germany as ranging from 1760 to 2640 pounds.

The only American hay yield reported seems to be the following: Pennsylvania Experiment Station, 4133 pounds to an acre.

495. Pollination. — White clover has long been valued as a honey plant. If the visits of insects are prevented, only about one-tenth as much seed is produced, according to Darwin's experiments in England.

Beal in Michigan secured only 5 seeds from covered heads, while 8 uncovered heads contained 236 seeds.

In an experiment by Cook, 10 heads covered to exclude insects set no seeds, while 10 heads in the open produced 541 seeds.

496. Seed-production. — Commercial seed of white clover is grown mainly in Europe (Bohemia, Poland, Russia, Germany, Holland, England), but some is produced in New Zealand. In America seed is produced in Ontario, Michigan, Wisconsin and western Washington. Ladino white clover seed comes wholly from Italy.

The yield of seed to an acre in Europe seems to vary greatly.   Werner gives it as 260 to 520 pounds; Schwerz, as 350 pounds; Sprengel, as 70 to 880 pounds; Krafft, 130 to 440 pounds.

Werner gives the average yield of straw as about 1000 pounds to an acre.

When white clover is tall enough, it may be cut with a mower, preferably with a buncher attachment.   If short, a light iron pan or a canvas is attached behind the mower and the cut clover removed by a helper with a pitch fork.

497. Seed. — White clover seed is very similar to that of alsike, but is slightly smaller and pale yellow, pinkish or pale brown in color.   It is seldom adulterated except with old seeds.

The purity should reach 98 per cent and the viability 99 per cent.   Good seeds germinate in 2 to 6 days.   The seed retains its viability well for two years and then gradually deteriorates.   It may contain any of the ordinary weed seeds as impurities.

A bushel weighs 60 to 63 pounds.   One pound contains 732,000 to 800,000 seeds.

498. Ladino white clover. — This variety grows to about twice the size of ordinary white clover.   In recent years various seedsmen have advertised it as Giant, Mammoth or Colossal White Clover.   Botanically this variety has been called *Trifolium repens latum* by McCarthy.

Ladino clover is abundantly cultivated on irrigated lands in Lombardy and derives its name from Lodi, where it was probably first developed.   In the subalpine Italian valleys it is cut four to five times, and under these conditions outyields alfalfa.   It is grown only on heavy lands

and is irrigated about every twelve days. According
to Früwirth the annual yield of hay in Italy is 7000 to
10,500 pounds to an acre. It is
usually sown with wheat, and the
fields are maintained from 2 to 7
years.

This variety is considerably
less cold-resistant than ordinary
white clover, and was badly injured by winter cold in Swiss
trials when ordinary white clover
was uninjured.

SWEET CLOVER (*Melilotus alba*)

499. Botany and description.
— Sweet clover (Fig. 46) is also
known by many other names,
among them Bokhara clover,
melilot, white melilot, sweet
melilot, Siberian melilot, bee
clover, honey clover and galy-
gumber. In the South it is now
commonly called *melilotus*. It is
native to temperate Europe and
Asia as far east as Tibet, but is
now spread over much of the
United States and Canada, and
also in the south temperate zone
of both hemispheres. Several varieties have been described by botanists.

Sweet clover is biennial in duration. The seedlings
appear in early spring under natural conditions and grow

FIG. 46. — Sweet clover.

2 E

rather slowly the first season, but by fall have reached a height of 3 to 4 feet, and a few of the plants will bloom, at least in the South.   By this time the root is large and fleshy and may extend to a depth of 6 feet.   The second season's growth begins quite early, two weeks before that of alfalfa, which at first it closely resembles.   The stems reach a height of 6 to 12 feet, and bear numerous white, sweet-scented flowers in narrow, erect racemes.   The mature pods are reticulated and each bears a single seed.   About the time the pods are well formed, the leaves begin to drop off.

Every part of the plant contains a bitter-tasting substance called cumarin, but which has a sweet, vanilla-like odor.   The young shoots contain but little cumarin, and so are quite readily eaten by sheep and cattle, but the older stems and leaves are decidedly better.   About the time sweet clover comes into bloom the stems rapidly become woody.   After fruiting the plants die.

Individual plants vary in their content of cumarin as well as in other characteristics, and some attempts have been made to improve the plant by selection, and particularly to secure a non-bitter variety.

500. Adaptations. — So far as climate is concerned, sweet clover is adapted to southern Canada and practically the whole of the United States, thriving equally well in semi-arid and in humid regions.

Its soil relations are likewise very wide, as sweet clover will grow in practically all types from cemented clays and gravels to poor sand.   It thrives best, however, on soils containing an abundance of lime.   Sweet clover, on account of its deep root system, is able to withstand drought nearly as well as alfalfa.   On the other hand, it can endure wet or poorly drained soils better than either red clover or alfalfa.

On account of its wide adaptations to both soils and climate, sweet clover is valuable to use in places where neither red clover nor alfalfa gives satisfactory results.

501. Agricultural history. — Sweet clover was probably first cultivated in western Asia in the same general region where alfalfa and red clover were first used in agriculture, but neither in Asia nor Europe has the culture of the plant ever been of much importance. It was introduced into North America at least as early as 1739, when it was found by Clayton in Virginia. It was recorded from New England in 1785. For 20 years or more it has been utilized on the black calcareous soils of Mississippi and Alabama, where it grows luxuriantly. In more recent times it has been grown in many other states.

It is a very aggressive plant, spreading along roads and railways and in irrigated sections along the ditches. Its spread has also been greatly increased by the habit of bee keepers of scattering seed in waste places so as to provide pasturage for bees.

On account of its tendency to spread, sweet clover has at times been feared as a weed, but it rarely causes any trouble in cultivated land.

502. Seeding. — Seeding may be done either by broadcasting or with a drill. Much of the seed is " hard " and does not germinate the first season. According to its viability, from 20 to 30 pounds of hulled seed should be used to an acre if broadcasted, or somewhat more if the seed is unhulled. Werner says the usual rate in Germany is 26 pounds, if broadcasted, and half this amount when drilled.

503. Securing a stand. — On account of the way sweet clover spreads as a weed in waste ground, it has commonly been supposed that it would be exceedingly easy to obtain a stand on cultivated land.   Numerous failures, however, show that this is not the case.   Westgate's investigations have led to the conclusion that the main requirement is a thoroughly firmed seed bed.   Another factor of importance is inoculation, as sweet clover seems just as likely as alfalfa to fail where the proper nodule organisms are absent.

Under natural conditions the pods of sweet clover fall on the ground in late summer and germinate in early spring, most of them remaining on the surface or being very shallowly embedded in the soil.   On cultivated land good stands may be secured either by sowing in early fall or in spring.

Fall seeding has the disadvantage that the root growth made the first season is not very large and consequently the plants the second season are not so vigorous.   Furthermore, the crop lasts but one growing season and not two, as is the case in spring planting.   Fall planting in rye is the common method in Germany according to Werner, but in this case the crop is used mainly as green manure and plowed under after one season.   This method has also been used occasionally with success in America, but sweet clover is nearly as apt to winter-kill if thus sown as is red clover.   At Arlington Farm, Virginia, sweet clover was sown at various dates but the best results were secured when sown in May and in October.

On the whole, spring seeding is to be preferred and this has generally proved satisfactory.

Lloyd thinks the best method for Ohio and Kentucky is to sow from January to March either on wheat or on bare ground, the former being the common practice in Kentucky.   In gullies the best method is to scatter sweet clover straw or ripe plants with the pods still attached.

504. Relative proportions of tops and roots of sweet clover. — Hopkins at the Illinois Experiment Station determined the total yield of tops and roots to a depth of 20 inches, when the plants were nearly mature, to be respectively 10,367 and 2410 pounds dry matter to an acre. 1809 pounds of the roots were in the first seven inches of soil and 601 pounds between 7 and 20 inches in depth. The tops contained 197 pounds of nitrogen and the roots 31 pounds.

505. Utilization. — Sweet clover may be utilized either as pasturage, hay or green manure, and has been used both for soiling and for silage.

While the herbage is bitter, it is much less so in early spring and most animals can be taught at this time to eat the plant. It may be thus used for all classes of farm animals, but is probably best for hogs and cattle. An acre of sweet clover will furnish pasturage through the season for about 20 young hogs, which apparently thrive quite as well as those on alfalfa or red clover. At the Iowa Experiment Station pigs made an average daily gain of 1.02 pounds on sweet clover as against 1.13 pounds on red clover pasturage. In pasturing cattle care must be taken to avoid bloating.

The use of sweet clover as a soiling crop is uncommon, but hogs eat it readily when thus fed. At the Ontario Experiment Station a yield of over 30 tons green matter to the acre was obtained.

Sweet clover is mostly used as hay and should be cut just as the first blossoms appear, or a little before, as the stems thereafter rapidly become woody. In curing, much of the cumarin volatilizes so that the hay loses much of its bitter taste.

If spring sown it is usually best to utilize sweet clover

by pasturing the first season, or a crop of hay may be cut. The second season it is best cut for hay or for seed, or both. Too close cutting with the mower is harmful, as new shoots appear only from the stems and not from the crown as in alfalfa.

Sweet clover is slightly more succulent than alfalfa and therefore a little more difficult to cure without undue loss of leaves. To avoid this the hay should be handled as little as possible, curing as much as possible in the windrows and then in small shocks.

Lloyd states that it has been utilized as silage by Ohio farmers, and thus fed to sheep and cattle with good results.

506. Advantages and disadvantages. — The chief disadvantages of sweet clover are : —

1. The cumarin content of the herbage, which makes animals avoid it until they have acquired a taste for its bitterness. On the other hand, this is said by some to be an advantage, as animals when first put in a pasture will not eat enough to cause bloating. 2. The rapidity with which the stems become woody, and the difficulty of curing.

On the other hand, sweet clover will thrive on soils where neither red clover nor alfalfa will succeed, and there can be little doubt that it will become much more utilized, especially for pasturage on poor sandy soils.

507. Yield. — Comparatively few data on the yields of sweet clover have been reported. In the North two cuttings may be secured the second year, both of hay or one of seed, while in the South three hay cuttings or two of hay and one of seed may be harvested. Tracy says that the three cuttings in the South will each average 1 to 2 tons an acre. At the Alabama (Canebrake) Substation the first season's spring-sown crop was at the rate of

5056 pounds of hay to an acre, and in the second season three cuttings gave 6320 pounds to an acre. On another plot the results were respectively 6672 and 7048 pounds to an acre.

At the Massachusetts Experiment Station, a plot seeded May 8 yielded September 9 at the rate of 2700 pounds of hay an acre. The next season it was cut on June 24 and September 22, yielding respectively 2727 and 1000 pounds an acre.

At the Utah Experiment Station a yield of 7700 pounds of hay an acre was obtained. At the Wyoming Experiment Station yields of 8960 pounds and 7500 pounds of hay to an acre were secured. At the Ontario Experimental Farm a yield of 61,300 pounds green matter an acre is recorded.

508. Seed-production. — Seed of sweet clover is produced both in Europe and in the United States. European commercial seed is always hulled. American seed is always in the hull and is produced in the South and in Kansas. On account of the limited demand until now the methods of seed-production have not been especially developed. The best yields of seed come from thin stands that have not been cut for hay, but satisfactory yields may be obtained from fields that have previously produced one cutting, or in the South two cuttings of hay. To avoid shattering the hard stems should be cut when damp, and cured in small shocks; or it may be cut with a binder. The time to cut is when about three-fourths of the pods have turned dark. In western Kansas it is sometimes harvested with a header and cured in medium-sized shocks. In the South the seed pods are usually removed by flailing, but in the West grain thrashers are now used. The yields in Kansas are said to be from 2 to 8 bushels to an acre.

509. Seed. — The seeds of sweet clover (Fig. 47) are yellowish brown, much like those of alfalfa, but the surface is duller and slightly uneven. By crushing, the vanilla-like odor of cumarin is evident, at once distin-

guishing it from all similar seeds except other species of *Melilotus*. Commercial seed usually has a high degree of purity and should approximate 100 per cent. The germination, however, is very variable on account of "hard" seed. In 22 southern-grown samples, the average

Fig. 47. — Seeds of sweet clover. **a,** seeds showing variation in form and size; **b,** natural size of seeds; **c,** a pod of sweet clover.

proportion of hard seed was 60 per cent, and in an equal number of northern-grown samples, 43 per cent. Imported seed showed but 12 per cent hard seeds in 28 samples. The probable explanation of the better quality of the European seed is that most of it was one year old or more. The seed is reported to have remained alive in some cases for 77 years. According to Werner, one pound contains 235,000 seeds.

510. Related species. — Various other species of *Melilotus* have been more or less utilized agriculturally, including *M. officinalis*, *M. indica*, *M. altissima*, *M. gracilis*, *M. speciosa* and *M. cœrulea*. The first two are abundantly and the third sparingly introduced into America. The last is really a species belonging to *Trigonella*.

Melilotus officinalis, official melilot, is a biennial yellow-flowered species. It is about two weeks earlier than

Bokhara clover, much less leafy and smaller in size, growing but 3 to 7 feet tall. It has spread over much the same territory as Bokhara clover. In New Jersey, it is becoming the dominant species. Some commercial seed is grown in Kentucky. It is from this species that cumarin was secured for medicinal use in olden times.

Melilotus indica (*Melilotus parviflora*), the " sour clover " of California and Arizona, is an annual species with small yellow flowers. It is called King Island melilot from the fact that it was introduced on King Island near Tasmania about 1906 and rapidly spread over the sandy lands of this island, resulting in the establishment of a great dairy industry.

In the United States, it is most common in the South, being abundant about Charleston, New Orleans and in southern California. In the citrus regions of California, it has been used in recent years as an orchard green manure crop, and commercial seed is now produced in that state.

CHAPTER XVIII

CRIMSON CLOVER AND OTHER ANNUALS

THE annual clovers and clover-like plants are much less important agriculturally than the perennials. They are variously used as hay, pasture and green manure crops. Their greatest use is as winter cover crops.

CRIMSON CLOVER (*Trifolium incarnatum*)

FIG. 48. — Crimson clover.

511. Botany. — Crimson clover (Fig. 48) is also known from the color of its flowers as scarlet, carnation and incarnate clover; also from its reputed origin as German, Italian and French clover.

The plant is native to southern Europe, occurring as far north as England. The wild plant (variety *Molinerii*) has yellow-white flowers, except one form in which they are rose-colored. The cultivated plant is taller, more vigorous and less hairy than the wild.

512. Agricultural history. — Crimson clover was probably first cultivated in southern France and adjacent Switzerland. It was cultivated in Germany as early as 1796. At the present time it is grown in France, Switzerland, northern Italy, Austria, the wine districts of Germany and in southern England. The earliest established record of its culture in the United States is 1818, when it was introduced by Bedingfield Hands of Chestertown, Pennsylvania, and distributed among his friends. It was widely distributed by the United States Patent Office in 1855, but its culture did not assume much importance till about 1880.

513. Description. — Crimson clover is an annual plant, reaching under favorable conditions a height of three feet. The root system penetrates at least as deep, as plants sown at the North Dakota Experiment Station in spring were found to have roots three feet deep by August 22. At the Delaware Experiment Station the tops and roots on an acre were determined to contain respectively 5372 and 413 pounds of dry matter. The stems are spreading or ascending where the plants are isolated, but more nearly erect where they are crowded. When sown in fall, the young plants are apt to be single stemmed. Well-grown plants from fall-sown seed may have as many as 20 stems and 50 or more flower spikes. The flower clusters are dense cylindric or slightly tapering spikes, $1\frac{1}{2}$ to 2 inches long, the flowers usually brilliant crimson, but rarely white, yellowish, rose or variegated.

514. Adaptations. — Crimson clover is normally a winter annual and is, therefore, primarily adapted to regions where the average minimum temperature is not fatal. In Germany Werner thinks this temperature is about 4° below zero Fahrenheit. By selective elimination, however, hardier strains can undoubtedly be secured, as J. H. Hale grew for a period of years in Connecticut a strain that he had thus selected. Ordinary crimson clover, however, usually winter-kills in the states north of New Jersey and west of the Alleghany Mountains.

Crimson clover has been successfully grown in Georgia, Alabama, Mississippi and Tennessee, but the prevailing dry autumns in these states make it difficult to secure a catch. In the moister region near the Gulf of Mexico, it succeeds well, but is little used.

In Oregon, Washington and British Columbia west of the Cascade Mountains, the conditions are also very favorable to crimson clover, but it has never been much used.

For fall sowing the important requisites are a mild winter climate and comparatively frequent rainfalls in late summer and early fall so that the plants can get well started.

As a spring-sown crop, crimson clover has succeeded in Michigan and North Dakota, but it is doubtful if it can compete with red and alsike clover used in this manner.

Crimson clover shows no very marked soil preferences, succeeding both on sandy and clayey soils, whether calcareous or not, so long as they are well drained. It does not succeed well on poor sandy soils and demands a good humus content for its best development. On muck soils it is said not to succeed well.

Crimson clover is well adapted to withstand shade, and so is often sown in orchards and with other crops.

Crimson clover apparently never has been troubled in America by " clover sickness," it having been sown on some farms continuously for at least ten years. Werner writes that in Germany it should not be again sown on the same ground until four to six years have elapsed.

515. Importance. — Crimson clover is grown in the United States mainly in New Jersey, Delaware, Maryland and Virginia, but its culture is increasing in the Carolinas.

In these states it is well adapted both to the sandy soils of the coastal area and the clayey soils of the Piedmont. Elsewhere in the United States it is but little grown. In the states above mentioned, the total area planted in 1909 was about 50,000 acres, basing this on the assumption that crimson clover was $\frac{2}{3}$ of the " clover " acreage in Delaware; $\frac{1}{4}$ in New Jersey, $\frac{1}{3}$ in Maryland, $\frac{1}{3}$ in Virginia and $\frac{1}{5}$ in North Carolina.

516. Variability and agricultural varieties. — Crimson clover is conspicuously variable in two respects; namely, the color of the corolla and the life period. In a single field of crimson clover, plants may be found with white, rose, crimson and variegated crimson and white flowers. As crimson clover is mainly self-pollinated, such varieties are easily selected and established.

At the present time European seedsmen offer five varieties; namely, extra early, ordinary, late and extra late crimson-flowered and late white-flowered.

517. Seeding. — The rate of seeding varies from 12 to 20 pounds to an acre, 15 pounds being the usual rate. One pound contains about 120,000 seeds, so that at the ordinary rate 45 seeds to the square foot are sown. In Europe the rate of seeding seems to be much higher, as Werner recommends 22 to 40 pounds if broadcasted, and 18 to 26 pounds if drilled.

Crimson clover is sown either by broadcasting or by drilling. Shallow seeding seems to be most satisfactory, but no critical experiments have been recorded. One inch depth in sandy soil and one-half inch in clay soils is probably a good general rule.

Home-grown seed in the hull is often sown by farmers, and the belief prevails that such seed is more likely to give a good stand than the hulled seed.

518. Time of sowing. — In the latitude of Maryland, crimson clover may be sown any time from midsummer until October. Midsummer sowings are apt to be injured by heat, and late sowings to be winter-killed. So far as temperature is concerned, the best time is probably late summer, which will permit about ten weeks' growth before the first frost. Ample moisture at the time of seeding and while the plants are young is quite as important as the temperature relations, and lack of timely rains results in more failures to secure stands than any other one cause. A common saying among farmers is that " crimson clover should be sown between showers."

In the Northern States and Canada, crimson clover may be sown in spring. Spring sowing is used to some extent in Europe and may be practicable for some purposes in America. A nurse-crop cannot be used with spring sowings, however, as the clover grows too rapidly.

519. Methods of sowing. — Crimson clover is sown in many different ways, whether grown primarily for hay, pasture or green manure. The principal methods are sowing alone ; sowing in an intertilled crop ; and sowing mixed with a small grain — wheat, rye, barley or winter oats for hay.

More crimson clover is probably sown in cultivated rows of corn than in any other way. This is commonly done by broadcasting at the time of the last cultivation of corn in Maryland, but farther south later sowing is more desirable to avoid injury to the crimson clover by hot summer weather. The clover matures early enough the next season so that the hay crop can be removed in time to plant corn again ; south of central Delaware the crimson clover may be harvested for seed and still leave time to grow a crop of corn.

In North Carolina successful stands of crimson clover have been secured by sowing in cotton in August, but it is difficult to cover the seeds without injuring the opened cotton. Among other intertilled crops in which crimson clover may be sown are soybeans, tobacco, cantaloupes and all vegetables except root crops, as the digging of these necessarily destroys much of the clover.

Crimson clover is most often sown alone, whether intended for use as green manure, hay or seed-production. In recent years it has been much grown in mixtures with wheat, oats, rye or barley. Sometimes only a small amount of the grain crop is added so as to prevent the clover from lodging, but more often a half seeding of the grain is used, and the resulting hay crop is much larger than that of clover alone. The common rate of seeding in such a mixture is 15 pounds of the clover seed and 30 pounds of the grain seed to the acre.

Crimson clover may be sown with buckwheat, in midsummer or even later, provided there is time for the buckwheat to mature before frost. The buckwheat must be seeded lightly, otherwise the clover may be destroyed by the dense shade. In place of buckwheat, cowpeas may be used, and either cut for hay before frost or allowed to remain on the ground.

520. Time to cut for hay. — Crimson clover should preferably be cut for hay just as soon as the lower flowers on the most advanced heads have faded. If cutting be delayed beyond this, the hairs on the calyx and elsewhere become hard and stiff, so that if the hay be fed to horses, the hairs are likely to form compact " hair-balls " in the intestines, which nearly always result in death. The danger is generally believed to be much lessened by feeding crimson clover mixed with other roughage, or by wetting the clover hay about 12 hours before feeding so that the hairs become soft. Such hair-balls rarely, if ever, form in cattle and sheep, so that late cut hay may be safely utilized as feed for such animals. If cut before bloom, the yield is much less and the curing more difficult.

521. Yields. — The yield of hay from crimson clover where the stand is good ranges from 1500 to 6000 pounds an acre, probably averaging about 2500 pounds.

Yields reported by experiment stations are as follows in pounds to an acre: Pennsylvania, 2154 to 5121; New Jersey, 2460 to 4600; South Carolina, 3600; Florida, about 4000; Alabama, 4057; Arizona, 145 to 570; Oregon, 13,340; Vermont, spring-sown, 4550; Michigan, spring-sown, 4400.

Mixtures usually yield more heavily. Thus, at the Alabama Experiment Station the following results were secured : —

Crimson clover seeded alone	2836 lb.
Crimson clover seeded in mixture : —	
Barley and crimson clover	3695 lb.
Wheat and crimson clover	3771 lb.
Oats and crimson clover	4228 lb.

522. Other uses of crimson clover. — Besides being used as a hay crop, crimson clover is extensively used for pasturage, to a slight extent for soiling and very much as a soil improver both in orchards and elsewhere.

Crimson clover will furnish a small amount of pasturage in fall, especially for hogs and calves. In the spring it comes on earlier than other clovers, and under the most favorable conditions may be grazed for a period of eight weeks. The usual precautions must be taken to avoid bloating.

Crimson clover may also be utilized as soiling, and will

furnish succulent green feed for a period of 2 to 5 weeks, especially if both early and late varieties be used.

As a green manure or cover crop, crimson clover is especially valuable because of the early date at which it can be plowed under, thus permitting corn and other crops to be planted in time.

Only two other legumes can be used in the same way and for the same purpose as crimson clover, — yellow trefoil and hairy vetch. Trefoil does not produce nearly so much herbage; while hairy vetch does not mature as early in spring, and the cost of seeding is considerably higher.

523. Seed-production. — Crimson clover is harvested for seed as soon as perfectly ripe. As the seeds shatter easily, it is best to mow early in the morning or when slightly moist, using either a mowing machine or a self-rake reaper. In drying, care is necessary to avoid loss by shattering, and to this end it is usually cured in small bunches. If the clover becomes wet from rain, the seed will sprout promptly, and this may be a source of serious loss. The unhulled seed may be secured by thrashing or by flailing.

To harvest seed for home use, there has long been used a device consisting essentially of a platform or box on the front of which is a comb, that may be raised or lowered, the whole mounted on wheels. This device is used when the seeds are ripe and dry. The most efficient of these combs is said to secure about 90 per cent of the seed.

The yield is said to average about 6 bushels to an acre. In Europe the yields are given as 250 to 450 pounds to an acre.

524. Seed. — Seed of crimson clover (Fig. 49) is larger and more rounded than most other clovers. Fresh seed

2 ғ

is shiny and somewhat pinkish in color.   Old seed becomes dull and brownish.   Rarely it may be adulterated

with red clover screenings, and sometimes there is considerable trefoil present.

Good, fresh commercial seed should be 99 per cent pure and have a viability of 98–99 per cent. It loses its viability rapidly, so that seed two years old is worth-

FIG. 49. — Seeds of crimson clover (enlarged and natural size).

less.   There is never much hard seed, and all the good seed should germinate in 2 to 6 days.

Troublesome weed seeds that may be present as impurities are Canada thistle, wild carrot, yellow dock, buckhorn and oxeye-daisy.

The legal weight of a bushel is 60 pounds, but it may weigh up to 63 pounds.   One pound contains 118,000 to 150,000 seeds.

SHAFTAL OR SCHABDAR (*Trifolium suaveolens*)

525. Shaftal or **Persian clover** is an annual, native to central Asia.   It is characterized by hollow stems, which lodge easily; smooth herbage; small heads of pink, very fragrant flowers; and pods inclosed in a much swollen calyx.

This clover is cultivated under irrigation in Persia and northwest India for forage.   In Europe it has been cultivated many years as an ornamental.   Seeds of it sometimes occur as an impurity in crimson clover seed from France, and thus occasional plants may be found in crimson clover fields.   Commercial seed in small quantities can be obtained in Persia.

While shaftal withstands the winter in Maryland when fall sown, its lodging habit makes it less desirable than crimson clover. It has given excellent results under irrigation in Arizona as a winter crop.

BERSEEM (*Trifolium alexandrinum*)

526. Berseem is an annual white-flowered clover, much cultivated in the valley of the Nile in lower Egypt, where about 1,500,000 acres are grown as a winter annual under irrigation. It is probably native to this region, but the species is not known in a wild state. There are three varieties grown: the Fachl, cut but once; the Saidi, cut twice; and the Muscowi, cut as many as four times.

. It was introduced into the United States in 1900 and widely tested. As it is destroyed when the temperature falls to about 18° F., it can be grown in most of the United States only as a summer annual. For that purpose it cannot compete with other clovers — especially red and alsike — as it does not yield as well and must be planted each season.

In the extreme southern portions of the United States, from California to Texas, berseem succeeds well enough under irrigation, but cannot compete with alfalfa. As a winter crop to grow in short rotations, it may eventually be utilized in this region.

The seed of berseem is cheap, but is likely to contain wild mustard seed as an impurity.

YELLOW TREFOIL (*Medicago lupulina*)

527. Yellow trefoil is also known as black medick and nonesuch, and rarely as hop clover, the last term being more properly applied to yellow-flowered clovers. Yellow trefoil has become rather notorious from the fact that its seed (Fig. 50) has been much used to adulterate alfalfa seed, but nevertheless the plant has some merit as a forage crop.   It is native to Europe and Asia, but has

become thoroughly established from Ontario to the Gulf of Mexico, and is also common on the Pacific Coast.   Its wide naturalization indicates its wide adaptation.

Fig. 50. — Seeds of yellow trefoil. a, seeds showing variation in form and size; b, natural size of seeds; c, oval form of trefoil seeds indicated; d, a pod of trefoil.

Of its wide value in Europe Stebler and Schröter write: " Although neither very productive nor persistent, still on many soils where red clover is not successful this plant becomes valuable because its fodder is so nutritive.   It is especially valuable in pastures.   Because of the diffuse stems and their spreading habit, yellow trefoil is usually sown in mixtures with clovers and grasses, and thus forms excellent pasturage.   As the plant itself only lasts for one or two years, it ought to be used in lays of short duration.   In mixtures on warm and favorable soils, it reaches maturity and propagates by sowing its own seeds."

The plant is normally an annual, but with perennating forms.   Its small size is the principal objection to its culture, but where it once becomes established, it makes a valuable addition to pastures, even on very poor soils. Planted thickly in late summer or early fall, the plants will make a dense mass of herbage 10 to 16 inches deep by the following May or June.   In this way it has much the same use as crimson clover, but it will withstand much greater cold, more even than red clover. Mixtures with crimson clover are very satisfactory, but probably do not increase the total yield. Under like conditions, yellow trefoil will probably not yield more than three-fourths as much as crimson clover, but with its wider range of adaptation and cheap seed should fill a niche in American agriculture. Difficulty in establishing trefoil may be expected until the ground has become inoculated for it.

Werner gives the average seed yield as 440 to 700 pounds an acre. The commercial supply has been scarce in recent years, perhaps because the practice of using it as an adulterant of alfalfa has greatly diminished.

BUR CLOVERS (*Medicago spp.*)

528. Bur clovers. — There are about 40 species of these plants native to the countries about the Mediterranean Sea. Most of these, probably all, are annuals, springing up in the fall, and maturing in early summer. They are all procumbent or prostrate plants when growing isolated, but if planted thickly, make a mass of herbage 8 to 18 inches deep. The species are distinguished largely by the burs or pods, which show a wide variation in size and form.

In America two species have thus far become used in agriculture; namely, the toothed bur clover (*Medicago hispida*) and the spotted bur clover (*Medicago arabica*), the former especially in California, the latter mainly in the Southern States.

Among the other species that are likely to become of importance are button clover (*Medicago orbicularis*) and snail clover (*Medicago scutellata*), both with large smooth pods.

Toothed bur clover. — Toothed bur clover is also known

as California bur clover, as it is especially abundant in that state. It was early introduced into California, where it has become widespread and proven valuable for pasturage both on cultivated and on range lands. The same species is also abundant in Argentina, Chile and Australia. The burs get caught in the fleece of sheep, and in recent years seed has been saved and cleaned in Europe from the rubbish taken out of wool.

While toothed bur clover is most abundant in California, it also occurs in Washington and Oregon, and to some extent in the Southern States. In the latter region it is not as well adapted as spotted bur clover, and instances are known where the toothed bur clover was winter-killed when the spotted was uninjured.

Toothed bur clover can hardly be called a cultivated crop, but where it persists it furnishes a large amount of pasturage, both on cultivated and on uncultivated land. Even after the burs are ripe and dry they are eaten eagerly by sheep. A considerable amount of bur clover seed is harvested incidentally with wheat in California, and from this source all of the American-grown seed is obtained.

There are several varieties of toothed bur clover, differing in the character of the fruits, two of them having spineless burs; namely, *confinis* with 3 coils, and *reticulata* with 5 coils to the pod.   .

Spotted bur clover. — Spotted bur clover differs from toothed bur clover in having a dark purple spot on each leaflet, and in the pods being beset with longer and softer bristles and the edges of the coils furrowed. A spineless variety, *inermis*, is also known.

Spotted bur clover is less abundant in California and more plentiful in the Southern States than toothed bur clover. This may be partly incidental to earlier introduction, but apparently spotted bur clover is better adapted to the conditions in the Southern States. It is quite certain that it is more resistant to winter cold, withstanding a temperature of about 15° F. without injury. Its area of usefulness extends from North Carolina to Arkansas and southward, both on sandy and clayey soils.

Bur clover may be sown any time from August to November. If the seed is hulled, it should be sown at the rate of 15 pounds an acre and harrowed in lightly. In the bur the seed weighs 10 pounds to the bushel, and two bushels should be sown to the acre, harrowing or brushing it in lightly. When sown in the bur, the resultant plants are nearly always abundantly noduled, but this is seldom the case when hulled seed is planted in new ground. Bur clover reseeds itself readily, even if the ground is plowed in late May or June for a summer crop, but it is never troublesome as a weed. Its use for winter pasturage in the South is increasing.

Commercial seed of spotted bur clover occurs as yet only in the bur and often contains much straw and other trash. The seeds are raked up from the ground after the plants have become thoroughly dry so that the pods readily detach.

DAKOTA VETCH (*Hosackia americana* or *Lotus americanus*)

529. Dakota vetch is a close relative of bird's-foot trefoil and has been called prairie bird's-foot trefoil. It is native to the western United States from Minnesota and Arkansas west to the Pacific. It is especially abundant in the Pacific States. The plant is a slender-stemmed, loosely branched annual, growing 12 to 24 inches high; leaves trifoliolate; flowers small, yellow and red; pods linear, pendent.

Dakota vetch has long been recognized by cattlemen as an excellent native forage plant and on this account was recommended for cultivation by the South Dakota Experiment Station in 1894. The plant and yield is so small, however, that the returns do not warrant its culture. A large percentage of the seed — at least of the California form — is hard and does not germinate.

CHAPTER XIX

PEAS AND PEA-LIKE PLANTS

Peas are grown more extensively for the seed than for the herbage. In mixed cultures, however, especially with oats, peas make an excellent quality of hay. The seeds are valuable both for human food and as feed for domestic animals. In contrast with the various kinds of beans, peas never cause digestive disturbances.

PEA (*Pisum sativum*)

530. Botany and history of the pea. — The pea is native to the Mediterranean region of southern Europe and north Africa, extending eastward to the Himalayas. Its culture is in all probability very ancient, seeds having been found in the remains of the lake dwellings in Switzerland. De Candolle, who considers the field pea distinct from the garden pea, inclines to the belief that the culture of the former is not ancient.

It is customary to distinguish agriculturally between the garden pea (*Pisum hortense*) and the field or Canada pea (*Pisum arvense*), but whatever distinguishing characteristics are used, there are all possible intergrades in the long series of cultivated varieties. In general the term field pea is restricted to those having somewhat angled, brown to black or marbled or speckled seeds, and colored flowers; garden pea, to those having white flowers and round yellow seeds. But several varieties are used both for vegetables and for forage.

A third group of varieties, the sugar peas (variety *saccharatum*), is distinguished by having broad, flat, tender pods, which are used as a vegetable after the manner of snap beans. Most of these have the pods green, but in one variety they are yellow.

531. Description. — The pea (Fig. 51) is an annual plant with hollow stems varying in length from 1½ to 10 feet, according to variety and conditions. The entire herbage is pale and glaucous. The stems are weak, usually decumbent at base and much inclined to lodge. The leaves are pinnate with 1 to 3 pairs of leaflets and one or more pairs of tendrils besides the tip of the rachis, by which the plant clings to supports. The stout, axillary peduncles each bear 1 to 3 flowers. The pods are green or rarely yellow.

Fig. 51. — Field pea.

The root system is rather shallow, not exceeding three feet, but nevertheless the pea is fairly resistant to drought.

532. Adaptations. — Field peas are adapted only to moderate temperatures; and while they will withstand heavy frosts, they quickly succumb to high temperatures, especially if combined with humidity. As their period of growth is short, — 60 to 100 days for hay, 80 to 120 days for seed, — they may be grown as summer crops in the North, winter crops in regions where the temperature rarely falls below freezing and spring or fall crops in intermediate areas. The non-adaptation of field peas to heat is frequently seen as far north as Maryland, where the crop is often severely injured by hot weather in May. Their preference for a cool growing season has led to their being much more extensively grown in Canada than in the United States.

Field peas are not particular in regard to humidity, thriving well both in humid and in semi-arid regions, but they succeed best in regions of moderate rainfall.

They do best on loams or clay loams, but will succeed on most soil types, if well drained. Like the majority of leguminous plants, they prefer an abundance of lime in the soil.

533. Importance. — Field peas are more important in Ontario, Michigan and Wisconsin than in any other states or provinces. To some extent they are grown in most of the northern tier of states in the Union and in all the southern provinces of Canada. In 1909, there were in Ontario, 258,461 acres; in Michigan, 94,932 acres; and in Wisconsin, 78,017 acres.

534. Agricultural varieties. — The varieties of field peas are very numerous, probably numbering over 100 and not including any of the more numerous sorts of garden peas.

Varieties differ in such characters as degree of earliness,

height, color of flowers, size of pods and especially in the
size, shape and color of the seeds. The seeds may be
either globose or more or less shrunken and angular. The
angular form is due to a higher sugar content and consequent greater shrinkage in drying. The color of the seeds
when of a single tint may be yellow, pea-green, brown or
black. Yellow or green seeds may be marbled with brown,
or speckled with blue-black or brown or both marbled and
speckled. The embryos are yellow in yellow seeds, and
green in green seeds.

The earliest varieties will mature seed in 73 days in
Canada, while the very late ones require 109 days.

Among the better known varieties are the following : —

Arthur. — This variety has round yellow seeds of
medium size. It is an early, productive variety which
originated at Ottawa, Canada. It is now one of the
most important varieties in Canada.

Golden Vine. — The Golden Vine, also called the French
June, is perhaps the most widely grown variety of field
pea in the United States. It is a medium-early pea, having a white blossom and small round cream-colored seeds,
and makes good yields of both forage and seed.

Marrowfat. — This name has been loosely applied to a
class of large cream-seeded varieties rather than to a
definite variety. This variety has a white blossom and
is medium to late, maturing about a week later than the
Golden Vine, and makes large quantities of forage with
fair yields of seed.

Canadian Beauty. — An early variety resembling Marrowfat, maturing at about the same time as the Golden Vine.
It makes a large growth of vine and fair yields of seed.

Blackeye Marrowfat. — The seeds of the Blackeye Marrowfat are similar in appearance to the regular Marrowfat

except for the black hilum. This variety matures a trifle
earlier than the Marrowfat and about five days later than
the Golden Vine.

Prussian Blue. — One of the " blue "-seeded forms of
the field pea, the seeds being round, smooth and bluish
green. This also has a white blossom and is rather late,
maturing about eleven days after the Golden Vine. It
makes good yields of both forage and seed.

Wisconsin Blue. — A " blue "-seeded form similar to the
Prussian Blue, but about four days later in maturing. In
yield of forage and seed it is about equal to the Prussian
Blue, but it has, perhaps, a trifle heavier growth of vine.

Early Britain. — The season of maturity of the Early
Britain is about the same as that of the Golden Vine.
The blossoms, however, are colored and the seeds large
and of a brown color. This variety, although not so well
known as the Golden Vine and the Marrowfat, is valuable
from both seed and forage standpoints.

As a result of extensive tests in Canada, the following
varieties proved in the order given the most satisfactory
for each province : —

For Ontario. — Arthur, Chancellor, Golden Vine, White
Marrowfat, Prussian Blue, Wisconsin Blue and English Grey.

For Manitoba. — Arthur, Chancellor, Golden Vine, English
Grey and Prussian Blue.

For Saskatchewan. — Arthur, Chancellor, Golden Vine and
Prussian Blue.

For Alberta. — English Grey, Arthur, Chancellor and Golden
Vine.

For British Columbia. — Chancellor, Arthur, Golden Vine
and Prussian Blue.

For Nova Scotia. — Arthur, White Marrowfat, Daniel
O'Rourke, Golden Vine and Prussian Blue.

For Prince Edward Island. — Arthur, Prussian Blue, White
Marrowfat and Golden Vine.

New varieties that have succeeded well in the western United States are Concordia from Sweden, with large, round, yellow seeds; Amraoti from India, with small, smooth, pale yellow seeds; Bangalia from India, with dull green, somewhat shrunken seeds; and Kaiser from Germany, with grayish seeds speckled with blue. The last named is very reliable and will withstand heat and humidity combined better than any other variety known.

535. Seeding. — Peas should be sown in temperate regions as early in the spring as danger from heavy frosts is over, and in tropical or subtropical regions as soon as the cool season begins, or at least in time to mature before very hot weather. In the Southern States it is sometimes possible to sow in fall and make a hay crop before winter. In the North fall preparation of the soil is desirable so that the peas may be sown in early spring. Where early and late seedings have been compared, the yield is usually highest from the early plantings and falls off quite rapidly in the later plantings.

The rate of seeding an acre varies from 1½ bushels for varieties with small seeds to 3 bushels for those with very large seeds.

The seed may be sown broadcast or drilled. The latter method is preferable on account of the more even germination. When broadcasted by hand, they may be plowed under lightly, or, if sown on freshly plowed soil, covered with a disk or drag harrow. In Ontario experiments extending over a period of more than 4 years, the yield of peas was slightly larger when the seed was drilled than when broadcasted, but in no case was the difference as great as 10 per cent.

The seed should be covered to a depth of 1½ to 3 inches, depending on the nature of the soil. At the Michigan

Experiment Station peas germinated best when planted 4 inches deep. Even when planted 8 inches deep, some of the plants emerged.

536. Development of the plant. — Stewart at the Utah Experiment Station has made a careful study of the composition of the Golden Vine pea at various stages of growth, when grown under irrigation. Some of his results are shown in the following table: —

Date and Stage of Cutting	Yield Dry Matter to the Acre	Percentage of Leaves Dry Weight	Protein	Percentage of Stalks	Percentage of Flowers and Pods
	Pounds	Per cent	Per cent	Per cent	Per cent
June 19 — 9 inches high	936	79	22.3	21	0
June 26 —	1628	76.6	26.1	23.4	0
July 3 —	2583	72.8	23.2	27.2	0
July 10 — early bloom	4997	67	26.7	27.8	5.2
July 17 —	4412	56.7	24.2	28.7	14.6
July 24 — pods filled	3496	48.6	20	19.7	31.7
July 31 — pods ripe	2658	40.9	22.2	17	42.1

537. Hay. — Field peas are usually cut for hay when the first pods are full grown but not yet filled, but cutting may be delayed until the leaves begin to turn yellow. This, however, will result in the hay containing many seeds.

At the Utah Experiment Station Golden Vine peas cut in bloom gave a larger yield to the acre than when cut late.

The yield of hay from peas alone probably averages less than 1 ton an acre. Partly on this account, and partly because of easier harvesting, they are nearly always sown mixed with oats when intended for hay.

At the Washington Experiment Station 7 varieties of field peas cut for hay gave an average yield of 5620 pounds an acre in 1909, while in 1910 the average of 11 varieties was 2730 pounds; at the Michigan Upper Peninsula Station the average hay yield an acre of 7 varieties was 4100 pounds, the best being Golden Vine with 5060 pounds; at the South Dakota Experiment Station two varieties yielded 1400 and 1520 pounds to the acre.

538. Peas and oats. — One of the oldest mixtures of a legume and non-legume for hay is peas and oats, both of which require much the same conditions, except that oats will withstand more cold. The advantage of the mixture is that the oats support the peas so that mowing is much easier. The rate of seeding is 1 to 2 bushels of peas and 1 to 2 bushels of oats to an acre.

At the Ontario Agricultural College the best results were secured with 2 bushels of peas and 1 bushel of oats, and the next best with 2 bushels of each to the acre. The average yield of peas and oats during 7 years was 12.08 tons green substance and 3.26 tons dry hay to the acre.

The crop is cut for hay when the oats are in the early dough stage, but both may be allowed to mature and the seeds separated after thrashing.

Other cereals are not quite as satisfactory as oats to grow with peas. Six-year average yields at the Ontario Agricultural College in green weight to the acre were as follows: peas and oats, 7.93 tons; peas and barley, 7.20 tons; peas, barley and oats, 7.07 tons; barley and oats, 6.78 tons; peas and wheat, 6.03 tons.

539. Pasture value. — Peas are sometimes utilized by pasturing to hogs or sheep. Shaw states that 1 acre of peas at the Minnesota Experiment Station furnished in 1895 pasture sufficient to feed 1 sheep for 345 days.

The pasturing of field peas to fatten lambs has become an important industry in the mountain valleys of Colorado. As a rule the peas are sown with a small quantity of wheat or oats to support the vines. The lambs or sheep are turned into the pea fields when the peas are mature and are fed upon them for 70 to 120 days. These pea-fattened lambs command a high price in the market.

540. Garden pea vines. — At canning factories where the green peas are separated from the vines by special machinery, the refuse vines are utilized as feed, being fed green, cured into hay or preserved as silage. It is sometimes made into silage by putting the green vines in large stacks, this being the common method at canneries. Pea-vine silage has proven to be a good feed for dairy cows as well as for beef cattle and sheep. In 1908, 96 canneries handled the pea vines grown in 66,959 acres, and about 60 per cent of the refuse vines were preserved as silage, the rest being fed green or cured into hay.

541. Irrigation. — Peas may be grown under irrigation, but it is doubtful if so short-lived a forage crop will prove desirable for this purpose.

At the Wyoming Experiment Station small plots were irrigated 1 to 7 times, using about 3 to 5 inches of water at an application. The yields of hay increased with the number of irrigations, the heaviest being 4.2 tons an acre from 7 applications, aggregating 23 inches of water.

For seed-production 4 irrigations, aggregating 20 inches, gave a yield of 34.75 bushels to the acre, much more than was obtained by using either more or fewer irrigations.

542. Seed-production. — Peas are usually harvested with an ordinary mower having an attachment in front of the knife so that the tangled vines are lifted up from the ground. Two men follow behind the mower and roll the

2 *o*

pea vines back in a row or in bunches, so as to be out of the way of the mower when the next swath is cut. Some machines have a platform behind the mower, from which the vines are thrown at short intervals in bunches.

From a small area the seed may be flailed, but usually grain thrashers are used. Precautions must be taken to avoid cracking too much of the seed; namely, by removing most of the teeth from the concaves, and by reducing the speed. If the crop is well cured, the seed thrashes out very easily.

Extensive work has been conducted at most of the Canadian Experimental Farms in testing field peas for grain production.

The average yield of the 12 best varieties tested for 6 to 8 years at 5 Canadian stations was 2141 pounds, somewhat over 35 bushels. At Ottawa the 12 best varieties averaged 2018 pounds to an acre; at Brandon, Manitoba, 2602 pounds; at Nappan, N. S., 1917 pounds; at Indian Head, Saskatchewan, 2253 pounds. The maximum yield reported is 85 bushels to an acre, a yield reached by the Mackay variety at Brandon, Manitoba, in 1904.

The average yield for Canada in 1909 was 19.34 bushels an acre and in 1910, 13.38 bushels.

In the table opposite are given the results of long-continued tests at 7 experimental farms in Canada.

At the Montana Experiment Station, the average yield of peas for 2 years of all varieties tested was 39.5 bushels, and at the Washington Experiment Station 7 varieties gave the following yields of seed to the acre: Potter, 23.7 bushels; Canadian Beauty, 23; White Marrowfat, 20.3; Early Britain, 21; Scotch, 20; Golden Vine, 18.7; Prussian Blue, 16.7.

543. Seed. — Peas germinate readily at low tempera-

AVERAGE YIELD OF PEAS AT 7 EXPERIMENTAL FARMS IN CANADA

VARIETY	GUELPH, ONT. 11 year average Grain bu. to an acre	GUELPH, ONT. 11 year average Straw tons to an acre	OTTAWA, ONT. 5 yr. av. bu.	NAPPAN, N.S. 5 yr. av. bu.	BRANDON, MANITOBA 5 yr. av. bu.	INDIAN HEAD, SASK. 5 yr. av. bu.	AGASSIZ, B.C. 5 yr. av. bu.	LACOMBE, ALBERTA 3 yr. av. bu.
Early Britain	37.7	1.36						
Potter	35.8	1.44						
New Canadian Beauty	32.6	1.43						
Blackeye Marrowfat	31.7	1.42	30.9	21	39.4	38.3	37.3	15.9
White-eye Marrowfat	31.4	1.53	36.2	26.2	32.8	36.1	42.1	15.2
Prussian Blue	28.2	1.55	40	20	40.4	43.5	37.6	18.7
Golden Vine	27.9	1.42	30.5	19	39.3	43	44.2	14.4
Multipliers	27.2	1.72						
Picton				27.9		39.9	42.4	17.1
Mackay					48.2	46.3	42.3	18
Chancellor								19.2

tures. The seed retains its viability well for 5 years and then quickly deteriorates. The legal weight of a bushel is 60 pounds, but a bushel may weigh as high as 68 pounds, or as low as 52 pounds.

Large seed is preferable to small seed of the same variety. In two-year trials at the Ontario Agricultural College the yield from the large seed averaged 26.2 bushels of peas and 1.14 tons of straw to an acre, while the small seed yielded 22.6 bushels of peas and 1.04 tons of straw.

544. Pea-weevil (*Laria pisorum* or *Bruchus pisorum*). — The most serious enemy of the pea, especially when grown for seed-production, is the pea-weevil. This insect lays its eggs in the very young pea pods, and the larva upon hatching burrows into the soft young seeds, only one larva entering each seed. The larvæ grow with the seed and remain therein until they become adult beetles. Normally the beetles do not emerge until spring, in fact usually being in the seed when planted; but if the seed is stored in a warm room, they emerge sooner. There is only one generation a year, and the insects do not multiply in the stored seeds.

Seed may be rid of weevils in two ways; namely, by fumigating with carbon bisulfide, so as to destroy the insects without injuring the seeds (Par. 625); or by keeping the seeds over one season in tight bags or other receptacles The beetles all emerge from the seeds and, being unable to escape, perish.

Where peas are grown each year, weevils tend to become increasingly abundant, and finally make it impossible to grow crops of satisfactory seed. If, however, their planting is suspended for 2 to 3 years, the weevils are nearly eradicated. The growing of peas for seed is practically limited to those regions where weevil injury is least. Weeviled seed shows greatly reduced germination, usually not over half of the seeds making plants.

In Ontario both grass-peas and chick-peas have been grown to some extent in place of field peas, as they are not attacked by the pea-weevil.

CHICK-PEA (*Cicer arietinum*)

545. The chick-pea is probably a native of western Asia. It was cultivated in ancient Greece and probably quite early in India. The plant has numerous other names, among them coffee bean, Idaho pea, Egyptian pea, Gipsy pea, garbanzo and Madras gram. At the present day its culture is important in India, Syria, Spain and Mexico, being grown mainly for the seeds, which are used as human food.

The plant is a branched annual, growing to a height of 1 to 2 feet; leaves odd-pinnate with 7 pairs of oval toothed leaflets; flowers small, white or pink, solitary; pods thin, inflated, less than 1 inch long, each having 1 or 2 seeds. The whole herbage is sparsely covered with glandular hairs which secrete an acid substance.

The varieties are numerous, differing in the size and shape of the seeds, and in Palestine, it is said, in their soil and seasonal adaptations. The variety grown in Spain and Mexico is that with the largest seeds, which are pale straw color.

In a general way the adaptations of the chick-pea are like those of the common garden pea, the plant requiring a cool season for its best growth.

It does not, however, withstand humidity as well as the garden pea, preferring a rather dry atmosphere. The crop is grown in winter in India, Spain, Mexico and to a slight extent in California. In the latter state it was uninjured by a temperature of 13° Fahrenheit.

As a spring-sown crop the chick-pea has done fairly well in Idaho, Washington, Colorado, Iowa and Ontario. At the Ontario Agricultural College it has produced an average annual yield of 35.6 bushels seed and 1 ton of straw to an acre, and the average yield obtained by 56 farmers was 19.8 bushels to an acre. In cold seasons, however, it does not thrive. The seeds are free from attack by the pea-weevil.

The hay or straw of the plant is not liked by animals on account of the acid secretion, which is said to be injurious both to cattle and horses. In any case its very small yield does not justify growing the plant for hay.

GRASS-PEA (*Lathyrus sativus*)

546. The grass-pea, vetchling or chickling vetch, is native to the Mediterranean region eastward to central Asia. Its culture, which is very ancient, probably began in the region south of the Caspian Sea. Seeds have been found in the ruins of Troy, in ancient Egyptian graves and with human remains of the stone age in Hungary. In the Old World the plant is more or less cultivated in India, western Asia and the south of Europe. The seeds are used as human food, but it is said that if eaten continuously they are likely to cause paralysis. This deleterious character is, however, probably restricted to the varieties with colored seeds.

The plant is an annual and has much the same adaptations as the pea, which in a general way it resembles. The stems are wing-margined and grow 2 to 3 feet high; the pinnate leaves have but a single pair of narrow lanceolate leaflets and tendrils at the tip; the long-peduncled

flowers are solitary and either white or blue; the pods are
4–5 seeded; the seeds are easily distinguished by being
wedge shaped. There are probably ten or more varieties,
distinguished most easily by the color of the flower and
the size and color of the seeds. The latter may be yellow,
brown or variously marbled and speckled.

The grass-pea does not grow as tall as the field pea,
but in yield of hay and grain it compares favorably. Its
value lies mainly in the fact that its seeds are never attacked by the pea-weevil and seed crops can therefore be
grown where weevils are too numerous for the field pea.

In America they have been grown mainly in Ontario,
but in small trials have been found to succeed in Iowa,
Texas, Washington and California, and probably will
thrive wherever the garden pea can be grown. At the
Ontario Agricultural College, a variety with white flowers
and yellow seeds has been extensively tested and has
given good results except in the cold wet seasons. The
average acre yield of seed for 7 years up to 1902 was 25.7
bushels and the maximum 43 bushels, yields but slightly
smaller than the best field peas. The average yield of
straw was 2.2 tons to an acre, as against 1.6 tons for the
Golden Vine pea. Grass-peas and common vetch were
also tested in comparison during 5 years, the average
green yield of the former being 6.7 tons to an acre
against 6.8 tons for the latter. In another series of
tests the average yield to an acre of green fodder was
grass-peas, 10 tons; common vetch, 8.93 tons; and
hairy vetch, 8.65 tons. More recent experience with
grass-peas has been less favorable.

The seeds of grass-peas have about the same feeding
value as field peas. A bushel weighs 64 pounds.

CHAPTER XX

VETCHES AND VETCH-LIKE PLANTS

THE term "vetch" has in common usage a rather loose application. Properly it refers to species of the botanical genus Vicia, but it is in the cases of some cultivated plants applied, to species in related groups of plants. Thus crown vetch is a species of Coronilla; kidney vetch is *Anthyllis vulneraria;* Dakota vetch is a species of Hosackia; and several of the vetchlings, species of Lathyrus, are sometimes called "vetch."

Botanists recognize about 120 kinds or species of Vicia, of which about 50 are annuals and most of the remainder perennials. In the United States, where about 20 wild kinds occur, they are commonly known as wild peas. Many of the species of vetch have been more or less extensively cultivated, and several others growing wild are utilized for hay or pasturage, or in a few cases the seeds are used for human food.

547. Kinds of vetches. — The cultivated vetches include the following: Common vetch, or tares (*Vicia sativa*); hairy, sand or Russian vetch (*Vicia villosa*); bitter vetch (*Vicia ervilia*); scarlet vetch (*Vicia fulgens*); purple vetch (*Vicia atropurpurea*); Narbonne vetch (*Vicia narbonnensis*); narrow-leaved vetch (*Vicia angustifolia*). Another species, *Vicia faba*, is extensively cultivated and has numerous varieties known as broad beans, Windsor beans,

456

sow beans, horse beans, and so on, but the name "vetch" is never used in referring to this crop. Only two kinds of vetches, namely, the common vetch and the hairy vetch, are much grown in the United States at present, but other species are likely to become of increasing importance. Thus bitter vetch is growing in favor as a cover crop in California, and scarlet, purple and woolly-podded vetches are all excellent, and with cheaper seed would certainly be largely grown.

548. Common vetch (*Vicia sativa*). — Common vetch, or tares, is strictly an annual, having much the same habit as the garden or English pea, but the stems are more slender and usually taller, growing 3 to 5 feet or more in length; leaves pinnate, with about seven pairs of leaflets and a terminal tendril; flowers violet-purple, rarely white and borne in pairs on a very short stalk; pods brown, each containing four or five seeds, which are gray or marbled in the commonest varieties. At maturity the pods readily coil and discharge the seeds.

Owing to the fact that the seed is grown largely in western Oregon, where it is usually fall sown, it has become known, also, as Oregon winter vetch. In contrast with hairy vetch, common vetch is also known as smooth vetch, and sometimes the name English vetch is applied to it. The gray-seeded variety of common vetch is the one most cultivated in the United States.

549. Botany and agricultural history. — Common vetch is native over much of Europe and western Asia. The species is very variable, and numerous botanical varieties have been named.

According to De Candolle, the earliest reference to its culture was by Cato about 60 B.C., when it was grown both for seed and for fodder.

Common vetch was grown in New York as early as 1794.

550. Adaptations. — Common vetch requires a cool growing season; the winter strains will withstand a temperature as low as 10° F. without injury, but zero weather results in much winter-killing. Vetch is therefore planted in the fall on the Pacific Coast and in the South. In the Northern States and Canada spring sowing is necessary. It languishes, however, under hot summer weather and is not adapted to the Central States.

It prefers a well-drained soil and will not thrive in poorly drained land. It does best in loams or sandy loams, though excellent crops are grown both on sandy and gravelly soils. On poor lands vetch is often used as a soil improver, and while the yield may not be large, to plant it is often good farm practice. On poor soils special care should be taken to provide thorough inoculation, as without it failures commonly result.

551. Importance. — Common vetch is important as a hay crop west of the Cascade Mountains in Oregon and Washington; as a winter green-manure crop in California; and as a hay crop in the Southern States. In the Northern States and Canada it is but little grown, hairy vetch being much better adapted.

In Europe, vetch is probably the most important annual legume grown for forage.

552. Agricultural varieties. — The cultivated varieties of common vetch are numerous and distinguished mainly by the size and color of the seeds. The most important variety has the seeds gray, marbled with a darker color. Of this there are two strains, distinguished in European agriculture as spring vetch and winter vetch. Pearl or white-seeded vetch has white seeds often used as human food. Sardinian vetch has the seeds brown; gray vetch is another name for the commonest variety with grayish seeds.

553. Culture. — The seed-bed for common vetch should be quite firm. For this reason it is a common practice in Oregon to broadcast the seed in wheat or oat stubble and then go over it with an ordinary disk harrow, or if the land is fairly loose the seed is simply sown in the stubble with a disk drill. This method gives satisfactory results, especially if the previous small-grain crop has been spring sown and if the vetch is sown quite early in the fall. If the planting is done later or if the previous grain crop was fall sown, the land is usually too compact, and thorough preparation of the soil is advantageous.

In the South special preparation of the soil before planting vetch is usually necessary. But few successes have thus far been noted by planting in cotton or other cultivated crop, but where the soil is thoroughly inoculated this method has given excellent results.

Common vetch seed may be sown either broadcast or by drilling. Broadcasting is the older method and perhaps still the most common, but the use of the drill has greatly increased in recent years, especially in Oregon.

Vetch may be sown alone or with one of the small grains as a supporting crop. To sow with grain has been and still is the commoner practice where the crop is grown mainly for hay, as the grain furnishes a support for the weak stems of the vetch and prevents lodging to a considerable extent. Oats are the favorite grain to use in combination with vetch, though rye, wheat and barley may be used. Oats are preferred, not only on account of the superior quality of oat hay, but from the fact that where a seed crop is grown the oat seed can be readily separated from the vetch seed, while there is greater difficulty with rye, wheat, or barley.

Where vetch is used mainly·as a green-manure crop, as in southern California, it is nearly always sown alone. In late years in Oregon the tendency has been to plant vetch alone when the crop is grown for seed. This change has been brought about as a result of the high prices charged for thrashing, the same price being charged for thrashing vetch and wheat or oats combined as for vetch alone.

554. Time of sowing. — Common vetch is usually sown in the fall, from September till as late as December. In western Oregon and western Washington most of it is seeded in October, but a growing tendency is to plant it in September, as the damage by winter-killing seems to be reduced. Pearl vetch, which is not winter hardy, is planted toward the end of March, and it is not uncommon to plant common vetch at the same time. Indeed, some dairy farmers plant it at various dates, so as to use it to feed green. Sown with oats about October 1, it is ready to feed about May 1; planted later, it·can be cut about June 1; and if early spring sowing in February or March is practiced, the vetch can be fed from June 15 to July 15. When cut early for soiling, a small second crop may be cut or used as pasture.

In southern California, when used for green-manuring purposes, common vetch is sown in September, so that it can be plowed under by March.

In the Southern States, oats and common vetch should always be sown in the fall, October being the best month, though the planting may be delayed till the middle of December. Early fall planting gives the best results for green manuring.

Where the winters are severe, common vetch must be planted in the spring, but it is not often grown. It succeeds wherever field peas do well, but the field peas are usually preferable.

555. Rate of seeding. — Common vetch if sown alone is perhaps most often seeded at the rate of 1 bushel (60 pounds) to the acre. This is sufficient to produce a perfect stand if there is no winter-killing. Thus, in Oregon, it is the common practice to sow 60 pounds of seed to the acre in the foothills where the drainage is good and the amount of winter-killing very small. If a mixture be sown, it varies from 30 pounds of vetch and 20 pounds of oats to double this combined quantity.

In the low-lying lands, where a certain amount of loss is likely from winter-killing, especially where soils become wet, a larger quantity of seed, namely, from 70 to 90 or even 120 pounds, is sown. If sown in combination with oats, 60 pounds of vetch and 40 pounds of oats are most commonly planted. The same rate of seeding is used as a rule whether the crop is grown for hay or for seed. Should the prospect be good for a high price for seed, the crop may be left to mature; otherwise it is cut for hay.

Some growers plant as high as 2 bushels of vetch to the acre when grown for seed alone. Such thick plantings stand up somewhat better, but it is doubtful whether any material gain results.

In California, when common vetch is planted as a green-manure crop, the usual rate of seeding is 60 pounds to the acre, but as low as 40 pounds are sometimes sown.

In the Southern States there is nearly as much variability in the seeding rate as in Oregon, but usually less seed is sown, about 40 or 45 pounds of vetch and 8 to 10 of oats.

556. Harvesting for hay. — Vetch should be cut for hay from the period of full bloom to formation of the first pods. It is commonly and satisfactorily cut with an ordinary mower with a swather attachment. After cutting, the vetch should be bunched with a horserake and then shocked with pitchforks. This handling should always be done before the vetch leaves are dry. It should be allowed to cure in the shocks several days, and, if possible, hay caps should be used, especially if rainy weather is feared. Where a swather is not used, the cutting is considerably more difficult. In either case it is the common practice to allow the vetch to lie one day before shocking.

It is sometimes desirable to pasture fall-sown vetch in the spring so as to bring the haying season somewhat later and also to prevent heavy lodging. This is quite commonly done in western Washington and western Oregon.

Common vetch yields from $1\frac{1}{2}$ to $3\frac{1}{2}$ tons of hay to an acre. An average yield in the Pacific States is $2\frac{1}{2}$ tons, and in the Southern States somewhat less.

557. Pasturing. — Common vetch is utilized by Oregon and Washington dairymen for pasturage during winter, spring and early summer. It is eagerly eaten by all farm live stock. As a general rule, the vetch is pastured only when the ground is dry, not only to avoid packing the soil but because both cattle and sheep are liable to bloat on vetch, especially in wet weather.

Even when vetch is grown primarily for hay or for seed, a limited amount of pasturing is often desirable, especially where the growth is unusually rank or where it is desirable to bring the harvest later. Hogs should not be used for this purpose, as they kill out many of the plants by biting them off below the crown. Sheep and calves do the least damage in pasturing vetch designed for a hay or seed crop.

558. Feeding value. — Common vetch is eagerly eaten by cows, hogs and sheep. Its high value for milk production has long been recognized in Europe. At the Oregon Experiment Station cows fed vetch hay for 45 days kept up their milk flow unimpaired. In a feeding test with steers fed for 42 days two animals fed vetch hay gained, respectively, 3.07 and 2.07 pounds a day, while two fed red-clover hay gained 2.56 and 2.16 pounds a day.

559. Rotations. — Common vetch is nearly always grown in rotation. Continuous cropping to vetch for seed production usually results in reduced yields after two or three years, according to Oregon experience. The effects of cutting the crop for hay seem to be far less marked, but, nevertheless, continuous cropping to vetch is unnecessary and undesirable.

In Oregon and Washington common vetch is usually grown after spring-sown oats. It is advantageously used also in rotation with potatoes or corn.

In the region about Augusta, Georgia, the most famous vetch-growing section in the South, the crop is mostly grown in rotation with Johnson-grass, this being especially true on valley lands where the Johnson-grass volunteers. Vetch, commonly mixed with oats or other small grain is usually planted in October on well-prepared land and harvested by the middle of May. After the vetch crop is removed, the Johnson-grass, more or less mixed with other grasses, begins to grow and commonly yields two hay cuttings during the season.

Where Johnson-grass does not permanently occupy the land it is not advisable to sow it, as it is extremely difficult to eradicate. In this case various summer crops can be grown in the rotation, such as sorghum, cowpeas, sorghum and cowpeas, soybeans, peanuts, etc.

Common vetch is not well adapted to rotating with cotton unless used merely as a green manure. The vetch cannot be harvested soon enough to permit the early planting of cotton, even when the seed is sown between the rows of cotton.

Common vetch is somewhat inclined to persist when once grown, especially where the winters are mild. Examples are known of its reseeding itself in pastures for five years. In cultivated fields it volunteers readily, which is especially objectionable in the wheat crop, owing to the difficulty of separating the vetch seed from the wheat. There is no danger of volunteer vetch unless a seed crop is grown or at least some of the seed allowed to ripen. In such cases, to avoid volunteer vetch, the best plan is to follow with a crop of vetch and oats for hay, pasturing the stubble, so that no seed is allowed to ripen. A cultivated crop should be grown the next season, and then the land can be planted to wheat without any danger of the vetch volunteering.

560. Fertilizers. — Information concerning the best fertilizers for common vetch is very limited. Barnyard manure is nearly always beneficial, and dairy farmers especially find it profitable to use on vetch fields.

In western Oregon, it is now a common practice to apply gypsum, or land plaster, and special machines are often used to apply it. It is commonly applied at the rate of 75 to 150 pounds to the acre. At the Oregon Experiment Station, 100 pounds of gypsum to the acre increased the yield from 7394 to 9031 pounds of hay to the acre.

In the South, a fertilizer containing phosphoric acid and potash is often used, a common rate of application being

200 pounds of acid phosphate and 100 pounds of muriate of potash to the acre.

561. Lime. — Vetches, like lupines, are injured by large applications of lime, but are not so sensitive to small amounts. Ulbricht in Germany found that in pot experiments the application of lime diminished the ability of the plant to assimilate phosphorus and nitrogen, but not potash.

Field experiments have given mixed results, but in general it appears clear that liming is not advisable for vetches.

562. Silage. — Vetch has been several times preserved as silage at the Oregon Experiment Station, where cattle preferred it to that made of red clover. Smith reports that it is also used for silage at a large dairy in South Carolina with entire satisfaction.

563. Seed-production. — Common vetch seed is produced in large quantities in the United States only in the Willamette Valley, Oregon. The methods of handling the seed crop vary, due partly to difference of opinion as to the best method, but more largely to the machinery possessed by the grower.

It is the general practice to cut vetch for seed as soon as the lower pods are fully ripe, at which time the upper pods will be fully formed and the plant will be carrying a maximum quantity of seed. Later cutting occasions more shattering of seed, while earlier cutting results in a considerable percentage of immature seed. In a few places, where but little seed is raised, the crop is cut with an ordinary mowing machine. Two men with pitchforks follow the mower and roll the vetch back from the uncut area so as to enable the machine to get through when cutting the next swath. Sometimes the first swath cut is rolled on the uncut vetch, and when the succeeding swath

2 H

is cut, the two are rolled back out of the way. This puts the vetch in larger swaths than the first-mentioned method and also somewhat reduces the loss from shattering. These two mower and pitchfork methods were formerly used generally, but now have been largely superseded by other methods.

An ordinary grain binder is used by some growers, especially when the vetch is short and therefore quite erect or when it is grown with a supporting crop, such as oats. When thus harvested, the crop is put in shocks similar to grain shocks and allowed to remain until thrashed.

The most common way of harvesting vetch at present is to use an ordinary mower with a swather attachment. The swather, which is attached to and behind the sickle bar, rolls the vetch in a swath to the outside and leaves the way clear to cut the next swath.

Whatever method is used in cutting, the vetch is put at once into shocks and remains till thrashed. The most important rule in the harvesting of vetch seed is to handle the crop rapidly and as little as possible when cut.

Common vetch varies considerably in the yield of seed to the acre. Five bushels is considered a low yield, and 20 to 25 bushel yields are near the maximum. The average acre yield is probably from 10 to 12 bushels.

564. Seed. — Common vetch seed has been extensively grown for some years in western Oregon, and practically all of this seed has been marketed on the Pacific Coast. Were it not for high freight rates, all of the seed required in the United States could be grown in this section. The price paid to the grower has varied greatly, the maximum being $1\frac{1}{2}$ cents a pound, but in 1909, owing to extraordinary conditions, he realized but one-half cent a pound, at which price the seed crop is not profitable.

Practically all of the common vetch seed used in the Southern States is from Europe. Its wholesale price at European ports is usually from 2 to 2½ cents a pound and the freight to American ports is about one-quarter of a cent a pound. The prices that American vetch seed growers obtain is practically controlled by the price of European seed.

Common vetch seed retains its vitality well for about three years, after which it rapidly deteriorates. Very

FIG. 52. — Seeds of common vetch (*Vicia sativa*). (Natural size.)

FIG. 53. — Seed scar of common vetch. (Enlarged.)

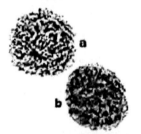

FIG. 54. Types of mottling of seeds of common vetch; a and b, from light and dark seeds, respectively. (Enlarged.)

fresh seed of common vetch does not germinate well. A large proportion of the seed is hard, and most of this probably does not germinate until the following season. One pound contains about 8000 seeds.

HAIRY VETCH (*Vicia villosa*)

565. Hairy vetch is also known as sand vetch, Russian vetch, Siberian vetch, and villose vetch. In the United States it has also come to be known as winter vetch, a term used in Europe wholly for a winter strain of common vetch. It is a winter annual, but often behaves as a biennial; stems slender, sometimes growing to a length of 12 feet, but on account of the weakness, the mass of plants seldom exceeds 4 feet in height; herbage hairy and somewhat silvery; leaflets narrow, 11 to 17; flowers blue-violet, rarely white, borne on a long stalk in dense one-sided clusters of about 30; pods pale colored, smooth, each containing two to eight small, globose, nearly black seeds.

The root system is richly branched and extends deep into the soil. At the Cornell station plants from seed sown July 10 had roots by November 10 which penetrated 3 feet 8 inches in tough clay. The young plants go largely to root development, so that the top growth is slow at first.

Fig. 55. — Hairy vetch.

At the Delaware Experiment Station the tops were estimated to produce 3064 and the roots 600 pounds dry weight to the acre.

566. Botany. — Hairy vetch is found wild in Russia, Germany and Hungary, in which countries it is apt to occur as a weed in grain fields. It was cultivated in England in 1815, in Scotland in 1833, and in Germany in 1857. Its first introduction into America was about 1847, but it obtained little prominence until 1886, when it was again introduced by the Department of Agriculture, since which time it has become more and more appreciated.

567. Climatic adaptations. — Hairy vetch is naturally adapted to cool temperate climates, under which conditions it behaves normally as a winter annual. The seeds ripen from July to September, germinate the same season, and the plant reaches maturity the next season. If planted in spring, the growth made is not nearly so large as if planted in fall. In the Northern States spring plantings may produce some flowers but rarely produce pods, the plants living over the winter and coming to maturity the second season. In the Southern States fall plantings are necessary, as hairy vetch will not withstand the heat of the summer. The cold resistance of the plants is very marked, hairy vetch rarely winter-killing in any of the states if well established in the fall. It is also markedly drought resistant, much more so than common vetch.

Perhaps correlated with its greater hardiness is the fact that hairy vetch makes much less growth in winter than common vetch and other species. On this account hairy vetch is not desirable as a green-manure crop to be plowed under in early spring.

568. Soil preferences. — Hairy vetch prefers sandy or sandy loam soils, especially such as are rich in lime. The plant will succeed, however, in a great variety of soils, doing well even on clays, provided they are well drained, but does not succeed on very wet soils. It is quite resistant to alkali, and will germinate in soils too alkaline for most legumes.

569. Rate of seeding. — Hairy vetch is not often sown alone, but when this is the case, the common American practice is to sow 40 to 60 pounds to the acre. No exact American experiments have been conducted to ascertain the most satisfactory rate in such seedings. In Europe, the seeding rates, according to Werner, are very much higher, 120 to 200 pounds to the acre when broadcast, 120 to 160 pounds when drilled.

On account of the weak stems of hairy vetch, the most common practice is to sow it with a supporting crop, usually one of the small grains — rye, wheat, oats or barley. In such mixtures a full seeding of the small grain is usual, and to this is added 20 to 25 pounds of hairy vetch.

At the Virginia Experiment Station the following results were secured from different mixtures: —

RATE OF SEEDING TO AN ACRE	PER CENT OF VETCH IN GREEN CROP	YIELD TO AN ACRE	
		Green Crop	Hay
		Tons	Tons
Vetch, 16 lb. — Oats, 25 lb. . . .	5.00	2.52	1.37
Vetch, 16 lb. — Oats, 37½ lb. . . .	4.57	2.60	1.57
Vetch, 16 lb. — Oats, 50 lb. . . .	2.00	2.52	1.47
Vetch, 32 lb. — Oats, 25 lb. . . .	9.03	1.80	.90
Vetch, 32 lb. — Oats, 37½ lb. . . .	4.94	2.15	1.25
Vetch, 32 lb. — Oats, 50 lb. . . .	1.86	2.35	1.45
Vetch, 48 lb. — Oats, 25 lb. . . .	12.68	1.67	.97
Vetch, 48 lb. — Oats, 37½ lb. . . .	5.35	1.75	1.00
Vetch, 48 lb. — Oats, 50 lb. . . .	1.76	2.12	1.25
Vetch, 0 lb. — Oats, 50 lb. . . .	——	2.25	1.32

570. Time of seeding. — Hairy vetch succeeds everywhere best if planted in the fall. However, in regions where soil moisture conditions are such as to render fall planting unsatisfactory, spring plantings often give good results, especially in the Northern and Western States. Spring seedings are, however, wholly unsatisfactory where the summer heat is great, as the plants quickly succumb under such conditions. The soil condition at the time of seeding is not a matter of vital importance, as if the ground is too dry, the seeds will remain a long time without germinating, and with comparatively little moisture the seedlings become well established.

Too late seedings are to be avoided. At the Virginia Experiment Station mixed seedings of hairy vetch 32 pounds and oats 50 pounds to an acre were made September 15, September 30, October 15 and October 30. The resultant hay yields were respectively 4200, 4500, 134 and 0 pounds to an acre.

571. Depth of seeding. — The seed of hairy vetch germinates very much like that of the field pea; that is, the cotyledons remain where planted, the plumule becoming much elongated. Largely on this account, hairy vetch seed may be sown quite deeply without any injury to the stand. Up to 4 inches in depth, no loss from deep planting occurs, and surface sowings are satisfactory, provided moisture conditions are good. Ordinarily, a depth of 1½ to 2 inches is to be recommended.

572. Inoculation. — Hairy vetch unless inoculated does not succeed. It is readily inoculated from both common vetch and narrow-leaved vetch, and doubtless by other vetches. According to Nobbe the pea and vetches readily inoculate each other. This idea prevails where vetches are most grown, but the evidence is not conclusive. The nodules are usually lobed and often in globose clusters.

573. Uses of the crop. — Hairy vetch may be fed either as hay, pasturage or silage. The greater part of the crop is fed as hay. Smith reports that a large dairy farm near Columbia, South Carolina, feeds it as silage with good results. As a pasture crop it is excellent for swine, sheep and cattle. It is sometimes pastured for a period while young, and then permitted to grow a crop of hay or seed. This has the advantage of making the second growth smaller, so that it does not lodge, which is especially desirable in seed-production. If the crop of hay is cut rather young, the aftermath furnishes good pasturage, or sometimes a second crop of hay.

574. Pollination. — Hairy vetch is much visited by bees, both honeybees and bumblebees. The structure of the flower is adapted to cross-pollination, and experiments in bagging the flowers to prevent visits of insects show that the latter are necessary for the formation of pods and seeds.

575. Harvesting for hay. — Hairy vetch is probably best cut for hay during the time that the first pods are full grown, but not filled out, but it is often cut when the plants are in full bloom. On account of the tangled mass of vines which hairy vetch makes, especially when grown alone, mowing is sometimes difficult. It may be cut with an ordinary mower, but a swather attachment is desirable. The curing is difficult on account of the tendency of the leaflets to dry before the stems. On this account, great care needs to be taken to avoid the loss of the leaves. Ordinarily hairy vetch is allowed to remain in the swath for one day and then shocked. With good weather, complete curing can be obtained in from five to eight days.

Hay of hairy vetch is palatable and as a rule readily eaten by animals. The yield of hay when grown alone ranges from 3000 to 5000 pounds or more to an acre. The acre yields actually reported by experiment stations are: Michigan, 4188; Colorado, 7000; Mississippi, broadcast, 3565, drilled in 30-inch rows, 2774; Alabama, 2540; Cornell, 6824; Pennsylvania, 1785; Idaho, 4600; Tennessee, 3200 to 6560.

Other stations have reported the yield green as follows in pounds to an acre: New Hampshire, 27,588; Colorado, 13,400; California, 32,760; Pennsylvania, 5250; Ontario Agricultural College, 20,400, average of 4 years; Massachusetts, 20,000.

576. Feeding value. — Little is definitely known of the value of hairy vetch, as but few feeding experiments are reported. Judged from chemical analyses alone its value would apparently be the highest of all legumes.

577. Use in rotations. — Hairy vetch is well adapted for use in a simple rotation with a summer crop, filling practically the same place in this respect as crimson clover, but hairy vetch is adapted to a much wider range of climatic conditions. As a winter crop, it can well be grown in rotation with such summer crops as sorghums, millets, late-planted corn, cowpeas and soybeans. In some southern states it is commonly grown in rotation with Johnson-grass. Johnson-grass sod is plowed in the fall, and the hairy vetch then planted usually with oats. The oat and vetch hay can then be cut in May, and following this, two crops of Johnson-grass hay can be secured. A fall plowing is not only necessary for the planting of the vetch and oats, but increases greatly the yield from the Johnson-grass. In the Northern States a crop of vetch hay can be cut early enough to grow a crop of millet hay the same season.

The practice of planting hairy vetch in corn at the last cultivation is increasing. The vetch is often more desirable than crimson clover from the fact that stands are much more easily obtained. In some instances mixtures of crimson clover and hairy vetch are being sown, partly because the mixture is a desirable one, and partly because a catch of vetch is often obtained when crimson clover fails.

578. Advantages and disadvantages. — The principal advantages of hairy vetch are its winter hardiness and drought resistance, and the fact that satisfactory crops, at least of hay, may be secured on nearly all types of soil. Its disadvantages are the fact that the cost of seed is usually too high, costing in recent years from 10 to 15 cents a pound, and the difficulty of mowing the tangled and often lodged mass of herbage. The problem of the cost of seed can easily be solved by most farmers by growing their own seed, but there is no good reason why the commercial cost of seed should be greater than 7 cents a pound. In feeding value and in effect on succeeding crops hairy vetch is comparable to other annual legumes. Another great advantage of hairy vetch up to the present day is that it is almost completely free from any serious insects or diseases. Occasionally fields are somewhat injured by mildew, but this damage is rarely important.

579. Growing seed. — Seed crops of hairy vetch can probably be grown in most parts of the United States. When grown for this purpose, it is rather better to plant with a small grain and to seed the vetch thinly. Much more vetch seed is also produced on poor soil than on rich soil. Where the stand of vetch in rye or other grain is thin, the crop is harvested as easily as if alone. On the other hand, if the vetch is too thick, the grain does not cut well with a binder, and often is lodged badly on account of the weight of the vetch plants. Most of the Russian

PLATE VI. — HAIRY VETCH AND RYE.

seed is that obtained incidentally from vetch occurring naturally in grain fields. When grown alone, hairy vetch should be harvested for seed as soon as the first pods are ripe, regardless of the fact that flowering takes place over a considerable period, and that many pods are green when the first are ripened.

The seeds of vetch are easily separated from wheat or rye by means of a spiral separator especially designed for the purpose. For local use, mixed seed of hairy vetch and a grain is sometimes sold as harvested, but usually, in such combinations, the proportion of grain to vetch seed is too large. Some farmers do not cut their vetch for hay until some of the seed has ripened and shattered. By this means a volunteer crop can be obtained year after year. The quality of the hay is injured, however, on account of late cutting. On fields of hairy vetch harvested for seed it usually happens that sufficient seed shatters to give a perfect stand.

The yields of seed vary greatly according to season. At the Ontario Agricultural College the maximum yield obtained was 21.2 bushels to an acre, but the average of 9 years was only 6.8 bushels. Yields recorded by experiment stations in bushels to an acre are: Washington, 14.7 and 5.5; South Dakota, 6.5; Colorado, 7.7; Wisconsin, 2.5; Mississippi, 5.57, 5.85, 7.4 and 10; Oregon, 10 bushels vetch and 30 bushels oats; Connecticut, 12 bushels vetch and 15 bushels rye.

580. Sources of seed. — Most of the seed used in the United States at the present time is obtained from Russia and eastern Germany. Larger quantities of it, however, are being grown in the United States each year, and undoubtedly sufficient for domestic use will soon be home-grown seed. European seed is frequently deficient in germination. Shamel reports experiments from Connecticut which seem to indicate that Connecticut-grown seed is considerably hardier than Russian seed. The experience at the Ontario Agricultural College shows clearly that acclimatized seed gives better results. The seed yield alone averaged 2.5 bushels more to an acre during 7 years from the acclimatized strain.

581. Seeds. — The seeds of hairy vetch are globose. Most of them appear black, but really are black marbled on an olive ground color. Rarely olive-colored seeds are found. When fresh, the surface appears velvety. They vary greatly in size, but one pound of an average sample contains from 70,000 to 80,000 seeds. Fresh seeds germinate well,

FIG. 56. — Seeds of hairy vetch (*Vicia villosa*). (Natural size.)

FIG. 57. — Seed scar of hairy vetch; a and b, forms showing the white, central slit of some scars. (Enlarged.)

usually over 90 per cent. Seeds a year old are characterized by a high percentage, 10 per cent to 40 per cent, of hard seeds which lie in the ground a long time without germinating. According to Hillman, the proportion of hard seeds diminishes in seeds older than one year.

Other vetch seeds, especially small seeds of common vetch, are used to adulterate hairy vetch. These can usually be detected by their grayish or mottled color. Hillman points out that hairy vetch seeds can be distinguished from any other vetch seed used as an adulterant by the shape of the hilum or seed scar. In hairy vetch this is narrowly elliptical in outline, almost equally broad at each end, while in other vetches it is lanceolate or wedge-shaped. Brown finds that the germ of hairy vetch seed is paler than other vetches used as adulterants. If any of the seeds when crushed disclose colors varying from dark fawn to reddish-orange, they are not hairy vetch.

OTHER VETCHES

582. Narrow-leaved vetch (*Vicia angustifolia*) is very nearly related to common vetch, but is distinguished by its narrower leaflets, smaller flowers, black pods and round, smaller seeds. It is much better adapted to the conditions of the eastern United States than common vetch, as it has become naturalized and thoroughly established from Georgia to Pennsylvania, and occurs even as far north as Nova Scotia. In Georgia it is highly appreciated in the vetch-growing sections and sometimes makes up a considerable portion of the hay. It maintains itself from year to year, as some seeds mature before common vetch is ready to cut for hay. On pastures it remains as a permanent element and is greatly valued. Seed is sometimes offered for sale, but is not available in quantity.

583. Purple vetch (*Vicia atropurpurea*) is a native of Europe cultivated to a slight extent in England, Germany, and France. It is an annual species with handsome red-purple flowers. Its adaptations are essentially those of common vetch.

It has proved to be very well adapted to western Oregon, where it has produced as good hay crops and better seed crops than common vetch. In California it has proven very satisfactory as a green-manure crop in citrus orchards, as it makes a heavy growth in the cool weather of winter.

In the Southern States it has also succeeded well, and with seed as cheap as common vetch will probably come into large use.

584. Woolly-pod vetch (*Vicia dasycarpa*) is native over much of Europe. It is very similar to hairy vetch in every respect, but the leaves are less pubescent, the fragrant flowers are purple, and the plant 2 to 3 weeks earlier. Agriculturally it can be used in exactly the same way as hairy vetch, but it makes better growth in cool weather, so that when mature the total yield is scarcely inferior.

585. Scarlet vetch (*Vicia fulgens*) is an annual, native to the Mediterranean region. It is cultivated to a small extent in France. Scarlet vetch is the most erect growing of the annual slender-stemmed vetches. It is characterized by its narrow leaflets and beautiful scarlet flowers in one-sided clusters. It is even less hardy than common vetch, but usually withstands the winters of the Pacific coast and the cotton states. Only rarely does it produce seed in large quantities, and the pods shatter readily, so that the seed is comparatively expensive. The plant is quite drought resistant, and from spring sowings has succeeded better in the semi-arid regions than any other vetch except the purple. It is very doubtful whether the seed of this vetch will ever be cheap enough to enable it to compete with other varieties.

586. Ervil or black bitter vetch (*Vicia ervilia*) was cultivated for fodder by the ancient Greeks and Romans, and seeds have been found in the ruins of ancient Troy. It still is a crop of some importance in Asiatic Turkey. The plant is apparently native to the region about the eastern end of the Mediterranean.

Unlike most other vetches, it is upright in habit, and without tendrils. The plants grow to a height of 2 to $2\frac{1}{2}$

feet. The seed habits are excellent, the plant producing numerous pods which shatter but little. Seed is grown so cheaply that it has been imported into England from Syria for stock feed.

The seeds, however, are said, like those of species of Lathyrus and Coronilla, to affect the nervous system and finally cause paralysis.

Ervil has succeeded admirably under California conditions when sown in the fall. The crop makes a good growth through the winter and for this reason is well adapted for use as a cover crop in orchards. To secure a good stand about 70 pounds of seed to an acre is needed.

At the Puyallup, Washington Station, five plots of ervil were planted in spring on clay uplands and yielded respectively 7.5, 21.5, and 37.7 bushels seed to an acre; one plot on alluvial clay yielded 36.6 bushels; and one on sandy loam 13.3 bushels to an acre.

587. Narbonne vetch (*Vicia narbonnensis*) is native to the Mediterranean region of Europe, Asia and Africa. In general appearance it is intermediate between common vetch and the horse bean, having tendrils like the former but resembling the latter in its thick foliage, which turns black in drying. By some writers it has been considered the wild original of the horse bean, but this view is not now held.

Its culture and requirements are essentially the same as those of common vetch, excepting that it requires more warmth for its best growth. It is cultivated for forage to a small extent in southern Europe, but under American conditions has found no place.

588. The horse bean (*Vicia faba*) in some of its varieties at least, is also known as tick bean, field bean, pigeon bean, broad bean, and Windsor bean. The last two names refer primarily to the large-seeded varieties used as human food, and the first four names to the smaller-seeded sorts used for animals. The culture of the horse bean antedates history, the seeds having been found in several places in remains of the stone age, as well as in ancient Egypt. What is apparently the wild original has been found in Algeria by Schweinfurth and by Trabut. The plant was abundantly cultivated in ancient Greece and other Mediterranean countries, and is important in Europe to-day, as well as in China, India, and Egypt. In warm countries it is grown as a winter crop, and in very cool regions as a summer crop.

The plant is a stout, erect annual, growing to a height of $2\frac{1}{2}$ to $4\frac{1}{2}$ feet; leaves pinnate with 2 or 3 pairs of leaflets, but no tendrils; flowers in short, axillary clusters of 2 to 4; corolla white and black. The stem is usually simple, but sometimes branched at the base.

The horse bean is adapted to a cool growing season, and will not endure heat. It is not particular in its soil requirements, except that it be well drained and rich in humus.

The cultivated varieties are very numerous, probably over 100 occurring in different parts of the world. They are distinguished mainly by the size, shape, and color of the seed. Most of them are adapted to spring planting, but a few varieties may be planted in fall in England.

In England and Germany they are mostly planted in early spring. The seed is sown broadcast, or preferably drilled, in rows 8 to 14 inches wide. The amount of seed to an acre depends on the size of the seed, which varies according to variety. With the common horse bean about 4 bushels to an acre is used, a bushel weighing about 56 pounds.

For green feed the plants are cut when in bloom; for

seed, when the lower pods turn black. The shocks are allowed to cure about two weeks before thrashing.

Horse beans have found but a small place in American agriculture. As a winter crop they succeed well in California, where they are grown to some extent as a vegetable, and have been used as a green-manure crop. On the north Pacific Coast, where climatic conditions are much like those of Europe, they also succeed well. The hardy winter varieties will usually survive the winter if planted in fall as far north as the District of Columbia. Farther south they have, in some seasons at least, given splendid results when thus planted, and would probably succeed generally. If planted in the spring, they suffer severely from hot summer weather, the herbage turning black. Even as far north as Ontario they suffer from heat, and after 15 years' experimental work at the Ontario Agricultural College, the conclusion is reached that the crop is not to be recommended, as the results are usually unsatisfactory. The best yield of seed, 29 bushels to an acre, was secured in an unusually cool season.

In Germany, the yield of green feed to an acre ranges from 14,000 to 20,000 pounds, and of seed from 25 to 50 bushels. When grown for green feed, horse beans are often mixed with peas or common vetch.

589. Bird or tufted vetch (*Vicia cracca*) is a perennial species native to Eurasia, also occurring naturally in North America from Newfoundland to New Jersey, west to Minnesota and perhaps to Washington. Bird vetch closely resembles hairy vetch, but the herbage is less pubescent. In Europe bird vetch occurs as a weed in grain fields, and the commercial seed is that separated from the grain. It is commonly mixed with that of *Vicia hirsuta* and *Vicia tetrasperma*.

21

The adaptations and culture of the plant are essentially the same as those of hairy vetch. At the Ontario Agricultural College it produced yields of green forage during 2 years of 2.2 and 3.9 tons to an acre, somewhat more than that produced by common vetch, but less than that of hairy vetch.

The native form is sometimes abundant in moist meadows in New England, but as it turns black in curing, is not always welcomed.

590. The Tangier pea (*Lathyrus tingitanus*) is an annual legume, native to North Africa, and similar in a general way to the garden sweet pea, but much more vigorous in growth. The flowers are deep red and smaller than the sweet pea. As an ornamental the Tangier pea has long been known. As a forage crop it was first grown and recommended by Trabut in Algeria.

It is adapted to about the same conditions as the sweet pea. In the North it must be planted in the spring; in the South and on the Pacific Coast, in the fall. In comparison with the vetches and other annual legumes used as winter green-manure crops in California, the Tangier pea has proved to be much more vigorous in growth and to choke out weeds perfectly. At the California Experiment Station a yield of 9 tons of hay to an acre in a single cutting has been recorded. Ordinarily, however, it will not yield nearly so large a crop as this.

Both in the Southern States and in western Oregon the Tangier pea has given very promising results.

The seed weighs 60 pounds to the bushel and is nearly as large as that of the field pea, though somewhat flattened. If broadcasted, about 45 pounds of seed to an acre is necessary; if drilled, 30 pounds is sufficient; very excellent stands have been secured by using only 12 pounds to the acre. On account of the enormous mass of rather stout stems which the Tangier pea produces, it is not advisable to plant with oats or barley. If, however, this is done, the amount of the seed should be reduced one-half.

In regard to the feed value of the Tangier pea there are but few data available. However, it is both palatable and nutritious, and no deleterious effects have been noted either in Algeria or in this country.

Seed is produced well both in western Oregon and in California, but the pods shatter easily. The principal difficulty is the production of seed cheaply enough so that the crop can

Fig. 58. — Tangier pea.

be used in competition with other vetches, and its final place in American agriculture will depend largely on this.

At the Puyallup, Washington, Station, Tangier peas gave in a small plot a yield of 72.4 bushels of seed to an acre.

As a spring-sown crop Tangier peas produced 2816 pounds hay to an acre at Dickinson, North Dakota, when field peas produced but 1780 pounds.

591. Flat-podded vetchling (*Lathyrus cicera*) is an annual, native to the Mediterranean region, at least in Europe. To a small extent it is cultivated as fodder in Spain, France, and Italy. Care must be taken in feeding, however, as the seeds, if eaten in quantity, have a dangerous effect.

The stems are weak; the leaves pale green with one pair of leaflets, the upper with a simple tendril; flowers red.

The flat-podded vetchling has made fine growth during several years at Chico, California, when planted in fall. It seems to possess no character, however, in which it is superior to common vetch, and it is not likely to be much grown. Planted at Arlington Farm, Virginia, in spring the plants languish with the summer heat and die without blooming.

592. Ochrus (*Lathyrus ochrus*) is an annual, native to the Mediterranean region, where it is cultivated to a slight extent for fodder, especially on the island of Crete and in Catalonia, Spain. From all other cultivated species of Lathyrus it is easily distinguished by the foliage, which consists mainly of the broadened petioles, only the upper leaves having 1 or 2 pairs of leaflets and a branched tendril. The solitary flowers are bright yellow.

Ochrus has grown very well in California when planted in fall. At Jackson, California, a small plot yielded at the rate of 30,855 pounds green weight to an acre. In plats at Chico, California, its behavior has not been consistent, some years being very good, other years very poor. At Puyallup, Washington, the average yield of seed from 3 plats was 8.7 bushels to an acre. The plant possesses no visible advantage over common vetch, and there is no apparent reason why it should be recommended.

593. Comparison of vetch species. — On the Pacific Coast all the vetch species are admirably adapted and in California a number of them have been tested as green-manure crops. In the data shown in the following table, it will be observed that the yield of hairy vetch is small if plowed under early, but if left to reach its maximum growth exceeds the other species. To a less degree common vetch shows the same lack of ability to grow in cool winter weather.

There is little to choose between the vetches in habit and feeding quality where they all succeed well. On this account preference is given mainly to those which have good seeding habits, and consequently cheaper seed: —

YIELDS TO AN ACRE OF DIFFERENT SPECIES OF VETCHES IN CALIFORNIA

Species	Chico	Chico	Southern California Substation	Berkeley
	Green Weight March 18, 1908	Green Weight March 16, 1909	Green Weight June 4, 1909	Green Weight
	Pounds	Pounds	Pounds	Pounds
Ervil	27,646	21,017	——	——
Purple vetch .	19,826	27,469	17,240	44,255
Woolly-pod vetch . . .	18,876	25,074	——	35,921
Hairy vetch .	11,616	5,880	32,670	——
Common vetch	7,623	2,831	25,410	51,152
Scarlet vetch .	——	——	18,150	——
Narbonne vetch	——	——	25,400	——
Horse bean .	10,890	21,130	——	68,970
Tangier pea .	13,794	12,840	——	34,485

OTHER LEGUMES

594. Fenugreek (*Trigonella fœnum-græcum*) is a native of the Mediterranean region of Europe, but extends to central Asia and north Africa. As a cultivated crop it is mainly grown in Turkey and India, and harvested principally for the seeds, but in India the very young plants are also used as a condiment. The seeds have a peculiar characteristic odor and possess definite medicinal qualities. Large quantities are imported into the United States to use in " condition powders " for horses.

Fenugreek is an erect plant with usually several stems from the same root. The leaves are clover-like, but the pods are long and pointed. The plant is remarkably free from insect enemies and diseases.

Fenugreek has thus far been found a useful plant in the United States only in California, where in Ventura and Orange counties it is now largely used as an orchard green-manure crop. The recognition of its value for this purpose dates back to 1903, when it was first distributed by the California Experiment Station. It is best adapted to the region near the seacoast, but has succeeded in all the citrus districts of the state.

The yield of green matter to an acre compares favorably with other legumes used for the purpose and the seed cost for an acre is very low. At Santa Paula, California, the green weight of fenugreek to an acre was estimated to be 11,745 pounds and common vetch 19,140 pounds; in the San Joaquin valley a yield of 15,518 pounds green fenugreek to an acre is recorded.

Fenugreek prefers loam soils but is not very exacting. In California the seed is sown either broadcast or drilled, using 30 pounds to the acre, if for a green-manure crop.

The usual time for seeding is September in southern California and October in northern California.

For seed production only 15 or 20 pounds to an acre is sown. The crop is cut with a mower when the pods are mature, cured in windrows, and thrashed with a grain thrasher. Some care is necessary in curing to avoid loss by shattering. The average yield of seed to an acre in the best seed district is 1500 pounds. The seed weighs 60 pounds to the bushel.

595. Lupines (*Lupinus spp.*). — Several annual species of lupine are much cultivated in southern and central Europe both as forage and green manure. The important species are white lupine (*Lupinus albus*), Egyptian lupine (*L. termis*), yellow lupine (*L. luteus*), and blue lupine (*L. angustifolius*).

All of these species are adapted to a cool growing season, and succeed best on sandy loams. They will not endure much lime in the soil nor an undrained subsoil. Light frosts are not injurious to the young seedlings.

Lupines are planted in early spring in northern countries, and in fall in regions where only light frosts occur. They are utilized as pasturage, green feed, or hay for sheep and goats, but other animals will not eat them on account of their bitter taste. The bitter substances can be removed from the hay by soaking in cold water, and when thus treated the hay is eaten by cows and horses. The seeds may be treated by boiling one hour and then washing 24 hours in running water. This treatment removes the bitter substances, but results in a loss of about one-sixth of the dry matter. The disembittered seeds furnish a rich proteid feed.

Lupines have often been tried in America but rarely make satisfactory growth. This may be partly due to lack of inoculation, but primarily because they cannot well endure the hot summer weather in the eastern United States.

Lupines have grown well in California when planted in the fall, and fair results have been obtained in Michigan, Massachusetts, Kentucky and Virginia when planted in the spring. At the California Foothill Station white lupines sown at the rate of 100, 150 and 200 pounds to an acre gave green yields of 1739, 2193 and 3819 pounds to an acre respectively. Ninety-five pounds of seed to an acre drilled gave a green yield of 3348 pounds to an acre, as compared to 3819 pounds obtained by broadcasting at the rate of 200 pounds to an acre. A sowing made October 22 yielded 4846 pounds of green herbage to an acre, much more than that from earlier and later seedings.

These yields are small compared with those secured in Europe. The average yield in Germany is given as 3600 pounds hay to an acre. Maximum yields in favorable seasons may reach 9000 pounds to an acre.

596. Serradella (*Ornithopus sativus*) is an annual legume native to the Spanish Peninsula and Morocco. It is cultivated for forage and green manure in Portugal, Spain, France, and Germany, in the last country beginning with 1842. In America it has thus far found no place. It has been tested in a small way at most of the experiment stations, but only at one has it been deemed worthy of recommendation. At the Massachusetts Experiment Station it yielded 10 to 12 tons green weight to an acre, containing 19 to 20 per cent water. It was there considered better than oats and vetch or cowpeas, and nearly as good as soybeans. At Guelph, Ontario, the yield of green forage was only 4.7 tons to an acre.

Serradella is a much-branched, slender-stemmed plant with pinnate leaves, a stout tap root, umbeled rose-colored flowers, and pods which break into joints, these constituting the commercial seed. Each joint is reticulated on the outside, but about one-fifth of these are empty. Well-grown plants of serradella reach a height of 2 feet.

Serradella is adapted primarily to moist sandy soils and a cool growing season. Unlike its effect on many other legumes, lime is not helpful but often deleterious to its growth. The young plants will withstand several degrees of frost in the spring, but not so much when in bloom.

In Europe serradella is sown in early spring, either alone on fall-sown rye or with spring-sown oats, using 40 to 60 pounds of seed to an acre. The seedlings grow very slowly at first, except the root. If sown alone, it may be cut for green feed by July. The first cutting of hay is made when the blooming has nearly ceased, and a second cutting can be made in the fall. The hay must be cured with great care, as the leaflets fall off easily. The average yield of hay in Germany is said by Werner to be 2500 to 5000 pounds to an acre.

Seed is harvested from the second cutting, and the yields are said to range from 350 to 1200 pounds to an acre.

Serradella may be found to be useful on moist sandy lands in the northernmost states and in Canada, and perhaps as a fall-sown crop in the extreme south. Many of the failures with this plant have doubtless been due to lack of inoculation.

597. Square-pod pea (*Lotus tetragonolobus*) is native to the countries bordering on the Mediterranean, where it has long been cultivated for the pods and seeds, which are used as human food. It is also grown to a small extent in England.

The plant is an annual with weak stems 12 to 18 inches long; leaves trifoliolate; flowers handsome, scarlet; pods dark colored with wings as broad as the body; seeds large, ovate, brownish.

The square-pod pea requires much the same conditions as the field pea, but is not so productive either of herbage or of seed.

At the California Experiment Station this pea produced on small plots yields of green herbage at the rates of 24 and 26 tons to an acre.

CHAPTER XXI

COWPEAS

THE cowpea is really not a pea at all but a bean, being indeed the one most commonly cultivated for human food in the Old World before the discovery of America. Its ease of culture and productivity have combined to make it popular in all the southern states.

598. Botanical origin. — The native home of the cowpea (*Vigna sinensis*) is doubtless Central Africa. Throughout much of that continent occurs a wild plant differing from the cultivated cowpea in having smaller seeds and dark pods which coil in ripening. Hybrids of this wild plant and the cowpea are readily obtained. Occasionally the wild plant is cultivated by African tribes, but ordinarily the cultivated plants are modified, having straw-colored pods and somewhat larger seeds. In no other region have wild cowpeas been found.

Cultivated varieties of cowpeas occur through Africa and over the southern half of Asia and the adjacent islands. The large number and great diversity of the varieties over this vast region indicate that its extended culture is very ancient. There is, however, no direct evidence on this point in the way of seeds from ancient temples or tombs.

599. Agricultural history. — In the old world, particularly Africa and Asia, as well as the Mediterranean region of Europe, the cowpea is of ancient cultivation for human food. It is without doubt the *phaseolus* of Pliny, Columella and other Roman writers, but this name became applied also to the kidney-bean following its introduction into Europe from America. In Italy, however, the black-eye cowpea is still called by the same name as kidney-beans, namely, *fagiolo*.

FIG. 59. — Cowpea.

The cowpea early became introduced into the West Indies and was well known in Carolina as early as 1775. Its culture had extended to Virginia by 1795, and was probably general early in the nineteenth century.

In the United States, the cowpea has always been grown mainly as a forage and restorative crop, but the seeds, particularly of the white or nearly white-seeded varieties, are commonly used as human food, especially in the South.

As early as 1822, several varieties are mentioned by American writers, one of which, with buff-colored seeds, was called the " Cow " pea. From this variety the name has become extended to the whole crop.

600. Adaptations. — The cowpea is adapted to almost

the same climatic conditions as corn. It requires, however, somewhat more heat, as corn will develop at least to the " roasting ear " stage in regions too cool for cowpeas. In drought resistance there is but slight difference, but that is in favor of the cowpea.

The cowpea is not particular as to soil except that it be well drained. It succeeds apparently quite as well on sandy soils as on heavy clays. Both in spring and in fall the leaves are injured by the least touch of frost, and a heavy frost is always fatal. Cowpeas withstand moderate shade, sufficiently so at least to be valuable to grow in orchards. In heavy shade they are usually much subject to mildew.

601. Importance. — The cowpea is the most important legume grown in the area where cotton is cultivated. The only statistics available are those which concern seed-production. There were harvested for seed in the Southern States 209,604 acres in 1909. This is probably only a small fraction of the entire acreage planted.

602. Uses of the crop. — The ancient use of cowpeas was as human food, and this is still the case in all Old World countries where the crop is grown. In the United States, varieties with white or nearly white seeds are mainly grown for this purpose, though seeds of any variety may be eaten. In California, blackeye cowpeas are grown primarily for the seeds, being adapted to drier soils than Lima beans.

Only in the United States are cowpeas grown mainly for forage and green manure. As forage, it is especially valuable because it will grow in all types of arable soil as a short summer crop, requiring but little attention, as it is able to smother most weeds, and producing most excellent forage either for hay or pasture. Incidentally, it is a splendid restorative crop, which has led to its being largely used purely for green manure.

603. Varietal distinctions. — The varieties of cowpea are very numerous. They are distinguished by various characters, those of agronomic importance being the habit, life-period, disease resistance and differences of pods and seeds.

On the pod and seed characters, three subspecies have been recognized, — namely, the catjang, with small erect pods and small subcylindric seeds; the asparagus bean, with very long inflated pods which in ripening collapse about the kidney-shaped seeds; and the cowpea, with pendent thick-walled pods which preserve their form, and containing variously shaped seeds.

In habit the unsupported plant may be *prostrate*, lying flat on the ground; *procumbent*, the mass two to four times as broad as high; *low, half-bushy*, the mass of vines once or twice as broad as high; *tall, half-bushy*, the mass taller than broad; *erect*, not at all vining and taller than broad. From a forage standpoint, the half-bushy varieties are most valuable, and when planted in corn or other supporting crop their vining habit asserts itself.

604. Life period. — The life period of the different varieties — that is, the time from germination till the plant is mature — is a matter of importance, especially toward the northern limit of the crop. The cowpea is *indeterminate* in growth — that is, under favorable conditions of moisture and temperature, it continues to grow indefinitely — and the conditions which favor excessive vegetative growth inhibit the formation of pods and seeds. In other words, the *fluctuating* variation of the cowpea is very great, and many writers have mistaken this for *hereditary* variation. On this account, some arbitrary stage of maturity needs to be selected in order to compare varieties. The dates that have been most used are when the first pod is ripe and when the majority of the pods are ripe, the latter date usually ten to fifteen days later than the former.

The length of the life period varies slightly according to season, but markedly depending on date of planting. Thus, at the Tennessee Experiment Station, Mooers found that the Whippoorwill cowpea varied in life period as follows: Planted April 15, 183 days; May 1, 168 days; May 15, 153 days; June 5, 132 days; June 17, 113 days; June 29, 101 days.

In general, *early* varieties of cowpea will mature their *first* pods in 70 to 90 days; *medium* varieties, in 90 to 100 days. Beyond this are all degrees of lateness, some tropical sorts not even coming to bloom under conditions in Virginia, Mississippi or northern Florida.

605. Pods and seeds. — The greatest variation in cowpeas occurs in the pods and seeds, characters of importance in distinguishing varieties. Considering only the true cowpeas — that is, excluding the catjangs and asparagus beans — they may be divided by their pod and seed characters into two groups; namely, kidney and crowder. Kidney cowpeas have their pods somewhat compressed, and reniform or subreniform seeds. Crowder cowpeas have thick-walled, terete pods, and globose, or, if much crowded, somewhat disk-form, seeds. The crowder varieties are not as numerous as the kidney, but nearly every color of seeds that occur in the latter may be found in the former. Cowpea pods are usually straw-colored, but in a few varieties are purple, and in a single known variety purple streaked.

The seeds closely resemble the common kidney-bean,

and there is quite as wide a range in the color of the testa. On uniformly colored seeds, the testa may be black, brown, purple, buff, maroon, pink, or white; or where more than one color is concerned, it may be speckled, usually blue speckles on a buff or brown background; or marbled, commonly brown on buff or on maroon; or both marbled and speckled. When the seed is not uniformly colored, the second color is concentrated about the eye or hilum in various forms, or else blotched in an irregular saddle-shaped area. White cowpeas may be *eyed* or *blotched* with any of the other colors, or the white may be exposed only on a small spot at the chalazal end of the seed. In all cowpeas, the germ is yellowish.

606. Correlations. — But few definite correlations of characters have been observed in cowpeas, and much breeding work is necessary before these can be considered proven. As in all annual legumes, earliness is nearly always associated with lessened growth. White-flowered cowpeas have their seeds white or mainly so, or coffee-colored. All other colors of seeds are associated with purple flowers. Purple coloration of the leaves or of the leaf-nodes is nearly always associated with purple flowers.

607. Important varieties. — Among the very numerous varieties of cowpeas, comparatively few are important either commercially or agronomically. Unfortunately, some of the commercial names are based wholly on the color of the seed, and thus comprise a number of distinct varieties under a single designation.

Whippoorwill. — Probably more than half of the acreage of cowpeas in the United States is devoted to this variety. It is easily distinguished by its subreniform seeds, which are buff marbled with brown. This variety

PLATE VII. — GROIT COWPEAS IN A BROADCASTED FIELD IN
VIRGINIA.

is also called Shinney and Speckled. It has been known in the United States for at least seventy years.

Iron. — This variety became known first from Barnwell County, South Carolina, in 1888. It is especially valuable on account of its immunity to rootknot and wilt. The seeds are rhomboid, buff in color, decidedly angular, and harder than most cowpeas. It is perhaps on this account that Iron volunteers to a greater extent than any other important variety, the hard seeds resisting decay. The Iron is not a heavy seed producer.

New Era. — Among well-known varieties, this is the most bushy in habit and earliest to mature, the first pods ripening in about seventy-five days. The seeds are easily recognizable, being small, rhomboidal, buff, thickly and evenly sprinkled with minute blue specks.

Groit. — This is a cross between Whippoorwill and New Era, the seeds sharing the coloration of both parents, apparently superimposed on each other. It is larger and more prolific than New Era, and on the whole the best forage cowpea for states north of the cotton belt.

Brabham. — This is a cross between Iron and Whippoorwill, having the immunity of the former, and being even more vigorous in growth than the latter. It is later than either parent, and in sandy soils very prolific.

Clay. — This name is given commercially to any buff-colored cowpea except Iron. There are several varieties with such seeds, differing much in earliness and habit, but most of them are quite viny. Those which mature their first pods in about 90 days make up most of the seed sold as Clay, while those which require 110 days or so probably constitute the variety which appears in agronomic literature as Wonderful or Unknown. None of the buff-seeded varieties except Iron possesses especial merit.

2 κ

Black. — Seedsmen sell all black-seeded cowpeas under this name, but there are several varieties. The most common are Early Black or Congo, maturing its first pods in about 70 days, and ordinary Black, requiring about 80 days. Both are decidedly viny, and somewhat sprawling. Black is nevertheless popular in some sections because the seeds do not decay readily after ripening, even if they lie on moist earth.

Red Ripper. — Commercially all cowpeas with maroon seeds are called Red Ripper, but there are at least eight varieties with maroon seeds more or less widely grown. In a general way, the maroon-seeded varieties closely resemble those with buff seeds, and none possesses outstanding merit.

Early Buff. — This is a new variety, the progeny of a single seed obtained from Leghorn, Italy, in 1907. It is a very prolific, half-bushy variety, maturing about two weeks earlier than New Era. The first pods ripen in about 65 days. It is the earliest variety of over 300 tested at Arlington Farm, Virginia, and should prove valuable at the northern limit of cowpea culture.

Blackeye. — Varieties of cowpeas having the seed white with a black spot at the hilum are mostly known as *Blackeye*, but among American varieties several possess such colored seeds. None of them has a bushy habit such as is desirable for forage, but blackeyed varieties are grown almost wholly for human food. It is probable that the total acreage of blackeyed varieties is exceeded by no other sort except Whippoorwill.

608. Rate and method of seeding. — Cowpeas, when planted alone, are sown broadcast, drilled, or in broad rows to be cultivated. When broadcasted, one or two bushels to an acre are planted; if drilled, five pecks to an acre is very satisfactory; while in three-foot rows, fifteen to twenty pounds is sufficient.

Formerly cowpeas were often planted in grain stubble without further preparation of the ground. This practice is now much less common, special preparation of the soil being the rule. On account of higher seed prices, as well as better yields of both hay and seed, planting in cultivated rows is becoming more popular. When thus planted, two or three cultivations are necessary.

At the Arkansas Experiment Station, six varieties of cowpeas were sown at rates varying from 6.25 pounds to 100 pounds to an acre. The highest average yield of hay was produced from 25 pounds of seed. The heaviest yields of hay varied to a considerable extent with the variety and amount of seed sown, ranging with the Whippoorwill from 12.5 pounds of seed to the Taylor from 100 pounds of seed. In another experiment with the same varieties, it was found that the best seed yields were secured by sowing not less than 12.5 nor more than 37.5 pounds to an acre.

At the North Carolina Experiment Station in a three years' test of different quantities of seed in $3\frac{1}{2}$ foot rows with the New Era variety the best yields of hay were secured by planting one-half bushel of seed to an acre.

609. Time of seeding. — Cowpeas should never be sown before the ground becomes well warmed. It is never advisable to sow them before corn planting time, and usually it is better to delay sowing at least two weeks later. After this time they can be sown whenever moisture conditions are favorable. The latest date for profitable sowing is about ninety days before the first killing frost.

Early sowings are unprofitable because the seed is apt to decay in the soil, but even if a perfect stand is secured,

the growth is very slow until hot weather comes. Thus,
Mooers at the Tennessee Experiment Station found that
Whippoorwill cowpeas sown April 15, May 1, May 15,
June 5, June 17, and June 29, all became fully mature at
about the same date; namely, the middle of October.
The earliest sowing required 183 days to mature, while
the latest needed but 101 days.

If grown primarily for hay, the time of planting should
be regulated so that the crop is ready to cut at the time
weather conditions are best. Through most of the cotton
region rains are less frequent in September and October
than earlier.

610. Inoculation. — It is rarely necessary to apply
bacteria for the production of the cowpea, as natural
inoculation is quite generally distributed throughout the
Southern States.

At the Michigan Experiment Station, investigations
were conducted to learn the influence of nodules on the
composition of the cowpea. The following table gives
the composition of the dry matter in the leaves, stems,
and roots of inoculated and not inoculated cowpeas : —

	Dry Matter Grams	Protein	Nitrogen	Ash	Phosphoric Acid	Potash
Inoculated :		Per Cent	Per Cent	Per Cent	Per Cent	Per Cent
Leaves . . .	220.61	27.08	4.33	16.38	.71	1.63
Stems . . .	220.21	17.93	2.87	12.40	.65	3.32
Roots . . .	171.15	5.61	.89	5.38	.62	1.32
Not inoculated						
Leaves . . .	238.41	21.52	3.48	18.30	.87	1.20
Stems . . .	315.44	10.47	1.67	9.73	.83	2.04
Roots . . .	62.75	12.34	1.97	8.57	.61	2.53

611. Number of cuttings. — Under favorable conditions, cowpea plants will sprout again from the base — indeed, this will take place indefinitely in a greenhouse plant, but the growth becomes greatly reduced. A second crop of hay, or at least considerable pasturage, is sometimes secured if good moisture conditions follow the first cutting, as happens not uncommonly near the Gulf coast. Ordinarily, however, but a single cutting of the crop can be made.

612. Hay. — Cowpeas should not be cut for hay until the first pods are ripe, and the cutting may be delayed until considerably later. After the pods begin to ripen, the leaflets are more likely to fall off, especially if the plants are attacked by leaf-spot or rust. Unless these diseases are serious, the cutting can be delayed until many of the pods are ripe. If these are promptly picked, a continuous succession of pods will be formed.

Cowpeas planted thickly, or even in three-foot rows, support each other so that they can be cut with an ordinary mower, to which it is desirable to add a bunching attachment. A self-rake reaper is also excellent to harvest cowpeas. The vining varieties like Clay, Black, and Red Ripper are less easily handled than the more bunchy varieties like Whippoorwill and New Era.

Cowpeas have rather succulent leaves and thick stems, so that they are not easily cured except in very favorable weather. Also the large leaflets are inclined to mat together. In hay making, it is common to use some type of shock supporter, as this greatly aids the final stages of curing. In curing, the especial points to guard against are permitting the leaves to become too dry in the swath before raking into windrows, as loss of leaves may result; and making the cocks too large, as the moist stems are apt to favor mildewing, especially of the pods. Even with favorable weather, quick curing is impossible owing to succulency of the stems and green pods. Should the hay be wetted by rain at any stage of curing, it should not be handled again until the surface is well dried.

Even when poorly cured — or indeed, moldy and decayed — cowpea hay is eaten by animals, a partial compensation for the difficulty of curing it satisfactorily.

It will be noted that the percentage of protein, and fat, as well as of the ash and fiber increases from first bloom until the pods are fully formed, while the carbohydrates decrease markedly. Chemical composition, therefore, agrees with other considerations in indicating that the best time to cut cowpeas for hay is when the first pods become mature. The fiber of the cowpea vines when mature is fairly strong and from time to time its use as a textile has been suggested.

In the following table is shown the composition of the cowpea at different stages of growth : —

TABLE SHOWING COMPOSITION OF COWPEA HAY AT DIFFERENT STAGES OF MATURITY. WATER-FREE

STAGE OF DEVELOPMENT	PROTEIN	FAT	FIBER	NITROGEN-FREE EXTRACT	ASH
	Per Cent	Per Cent	Per Cent	Per Cent	Per Cent
Full bloom	17.86	4.04	18.39	52.28	7.43
Pods forming	19.93	3.06	18.52	50.58	7.91
Pods formed	21.38	5.01	29.05	32.59	11.97

613. Hay yields. — The yield of cowpea hay ranges from one to three tons to the acre, varying according to variety, soil and weather conditions.

TABLE SHOWING ACRE YIELD IN POUNDS OF COWPEA HAY AT VARIOUS EXPERIMENT STATIONS

Variety	Alabama	Arkansas	Delaware	Georgia[1]	Indiana	Kansas	Mississippi	Missouri	New Jersey[1]	North Carolina
Whippoorwill	2720	3297	3850	16892	4476	5260	2880	3720	—	3424
Clay	2852	4872	3960	20664	4219	3880	2556	3660	16600	3688
Unknown	3143	3990	—	21730	—	—	2916	—	14000	5200
New Era	2310	2756	3620	—	3893	4280	2628	3660	14600	2727
Iron	2078	—	3700	—	4877	—	2160	3350	16200	3872
Red Ripper	3720	4230	—	25256	—	—	2350	4270	—	3339
Black	2239	2702	3190	21812	—	4460	2090	4420	11000	3175
Taylor	—	3041	3270	—	—	4940	2420	—	—	—
Large Blackeye	—	2803	—	16400	—	4340	2090	3290	15000	2560
Extra Early Blackeye	1416	1628	2650	—	2769	—	1369	3050	—	2602
Michigan Favorite	—	—	3450	—	4325	—	—	3350	13600	2400
Groit	—	—	—	—	—	—	—	3350	—	—

614. Feeding value. — The high feeding value of cowpea hay has long been recognized and it has been used extensively for all kinds of stock. It is particularly high in protein, and where properly cared for, furnishes one of the cheapest feeds for the modern farm.

Experiments in the feeding of cowpea hay in comparison with other feeds have been repeatedly made at various experiment stations throughout the country. The Tennessee Station found that 6 to 10 pounds of cowpea hay could be substituted for 3 to 5 pounds of cotton-seed meal in beef production. In the production of milk and butter this station reports that 1¼ pounds of chopped pea hay is equivalent to one pound of wheat bran, and 3 pounds of

[1] Green weight.

chopped pea hay to one pound of cotton-seed meal. In a comparison of cowpea hay with timothy hay for wintering yearlings, it was found that the steers made nearly 50 per cent better gains where the cowpea hay was used. In a three months' test at the North Carolina Experiment Station with two Percheron mares used as a team, the rations differed only in the use of 10 pounds of cowpea hay in one and the same quantity of wheat bran in the other. The horse fed bran just held its own, while the animal fed cowpea hay gained a little.

The high price of cowpea seed prevents its use as a feed, although its composition indicates that it is a richer feed than wheat bran. Excellent results were obtained by the Alabama Experiment Station by feeding cowpea seed to fattening hogs. More lean meat was found in the bodies of the pigs fed cowpeas than in those fed corn meal only. Cracked or split seeds, and also whole seeds have been fed to poultry with splendid results. Not only were the fowls kept in good condition, but a good production of eggs resulted, even in the winter months.

The straw obtained when cowpea seed is secured by running the vines through a thrashing machine is valuable as feed. Certain types of machines chop the straw so that it is in fine condition for feed. There is, however, lack of experimental data with regard to the feeding value of this straw. Reports from farmers and others who have fed the straw indicate that it is an excellent feed.

615. Cowpeas in broadcast mixtures. — To furnish support to the vines as well as to facilitate curing, cowpeas are often planted in combination with some other crop. When broadcasted or drilled, millet, sorghum, Johnson-grass, or soybeans may thus be used. The ideal mixture would be a stiff-stemmed easily curing grass that matures with the cowpea. Such a grass would prevent matting of the leaves, and otherwise promote aeration and drying of the shocks. None of the above-named plants quite fulfills these requirements. Millet of any variety matures earlier than the cowpea, and often is too small for support. Amber sorghum is excellent from the standpoint of size and time of maturity, but the juicy stems do not cure easily. Johnson-grass is excellent wherever it is not objectionable as a weed. The newly introduced Sudan-grass promises to be exactly what is needed. Soybeans help support the cowpeas, and with proper choice of variety, simultaneous maturity is easily secured, but the mixture does not cure much more easily than cowpeas alone.

In seeding such mixtures, enough seed should be used to secure a half stand, or better, of each. One bushel of cowpeas and half a bushel of Amber sorghum an acre gives excellent results; if millet is used, 15 to 20 pounds is sufficient. Johnson-grass seed is so poor in quality as a rule that at least a bushel should be used, with a bushel of cowpeas to an acre. Where a soybean-cowpea mixture is used, better results are usually secured if the former predominates, using one bushel of soybeans and one-half bushel of cowpeas to the acre.

616. Cowpea mixtures not broadcasted. — Cowpeas are very widely used for planting in between the rows of corn. When thus used, the seed is sown at the rate of about three pecks an acre after the last cultivation of the corn. Usually the crop is allowed to mature, and some of the pods picked, and the remainder of the crop is pastured. In some regions, however, the cowpeas are cut for hay after the corn has been harvested. If this is done, it is desirable to cut the corn stems close to the ground, as otherwise the stubble will interfere with a mower. Where the corn is not cut close to the ground, heavy wooden rakes are sometimes used to harvest cowpea vines.

Another method of sowing cowpeas in corn is to plant the seed close to the corn plants after the last cultivation of that crop. The cowpea vines then climb up the corn stalks and add materially to the amount of herbage. When the mixture is thus grown, it is usually preserved as silage. The cowpeas add considerably to the value of the silage, but also increase somewhat the difficulty of harvesting, as the vines bind the corn stalks together.

617. Growing cowpeas for seed. — The great bulk of the cowpea seed grown in the United States is hand-picked. When this is done, the vines should be picked over two times in order to secure the maximum yields. Hand-picking, however, necessarily means a high price for the seed.

The vines may be cut when half or more of the pods are ripe. The riper the pods, the more easy the curing, but the less valuable the residual straw for feed. The mowing is very satisfactorily done with a self-rake reaper. If this is not available, an ordinary mowing machine may be used, but it is very desirable to use with it a bunching attachment. Bean harvesters which cut the stems just beneath the surface of the ground are very satisfactory in sandy soils, but not in clay soils.

In thrashing cowpeas with an ordinary grain separator many of the seeds are cracked even when the speed of the cylinders is much reduced. The vines too are inclined to wrap about the cylinders, necessitating frequent stoppings. The use of sharpened teeth on the cylinders or concaves or both prevents this clogging, and also greatly reduces the percentage of seeds cracked.

618. Pollination. — The cowpea is completely self-fertile, flowers protected from insects setting pods normally.

Insect visitors are numerous, but they are attracted mainly to the extra-floral nectaries at the base of each flower. Natural cross-pollination is usually very rare, but in a few localities, as at the Michigan Experiment Station, occurs abundantly. This is probably due to bumblebees, but exact observations are lacking. Through such chance crosses the majority of American varieties of cowpeas have probably arisen.

619. Seed yield. — Varieties of cowpeas vary strikingly in their seed production, the bunch varieties usually yielding more seed than the trailing sorts. Moreover, the yield of seed with the same variety varies greatly from year to year, depending upon weather conditions and according to locality. In favorable seasons, good producing varieties yield from fifteen to thirty bushels to the acre, while in unfavorable seasons the same varieties may yield only five to ten bushels to the acre.

TABLE SHOWING ACRE YIELD OF COWPEA SEED AT VARIOUS
EXPERIMENT STATIONS

VARIETY	ALABAMA	ARKANSAS	DELAWARE	GEORGIA	INDIANA	KANSAS	MISSOURI	NORTH CAROLINA	SOUTH CAROLINA
	Bu.	Bu.	Bu.	Bu.	Bu.	Bu.	Bu.	Bu.	Bu.
Whippoorwill	12.4	25.6	13.2	25.3	18.3	11.5	14.0	11.7	13.8
Clay	10.8	9.8	6.6	34.3	5.3	10.9	14.4	7.0	13.3
Unknown	14.7	2.5		30.5				8.8	
New Era	22.0	39.9	15.6		14.0	12.4	14.0	11.9	24.2
Iron	14.9		7.4		6.3		17.5	9.9	9.3
Red Ripper	19.3	11.9		27.7			8.3	8.9	
Black	21.1	15.7	7.4	19.9		11.1	18.6		13.0
Taylor	23.6	19.9	4.9			11.9			11.5
Large Blackeye	17.0	23.6	5.6	31.3		12.7	14.8	9.8	21.7
Extra Early Blackeye	16.4	29.1	5.4		14.2		10.6	9.2	9.9
Michigan Favorite			8.2		19.3	11.2	11.4	7.9	
Groit			8.2				14.8		

620. Proportion of seed and hulls. — The method of gathering seed by hand, where the peas are planted in corn, is a very common practice throughout the South. Fields grown to cowpeas alone for seed-production are often hand picked. Generally the pods are picked at a price for each hundred pounds. From the results obtained at the Alabama and Arkansas Agricultural Experiment Stations, it appears that the proportion of seed and hulls varies according to the variety and locality.

TABLE SHOWING POUNDS OF COWPEA SEED IN 100 POUNDS OF PODS

Variety	Alabama	Arkansas	Variety	Alabama	Arkansas
Large White Crowder	83	75.0	Whippoorwill	73	67.3
Large Blackeye . .	77	71.2	New Era . .	73	61.8
Taylor	77	64.7	Red Ripper .	71	66.0
Ex. Early Blackeye	76	75.0	Wonderful .	70	
Black	76	63.2	Iron . . .	69	65.3
Lady	74	63.2	Clay . . .	67	58.3

621. Seeds. — Cowpea seed is usually considered to weigh 60 pounds to the bushel, but this varies considerably according to the variety. On the basis of 60 pounds, the number of seeds to the bushel has been calculated by Duggar, by Newman and by Morse. Duggar used the weight of 100 seeds as a basis, while Newman counted the number in one ounce, and Morse counted the number in three samples of one ounce each. The largest seeded varieties contain less than 100,000 seeds to the pound, while the smallest seeded catjangs contain five times as many. The common commercial varieties average about 150,000 seeds to the pound. The figures for standard and other varieties are shown in the following table : —

Cowpea Seeds, Number to the Ounce and Bushel and Weight of 100 Seeds of Different Varieties

Variety	Seeds in One Ounce		Weight of 100 Seeds	Seeds in 60 Pounds		
	Newman	Morse	Duggar	Duggar	Newman	Morse
			Grams			
Black Crowder .	—	102				97120
Taylor . . .	107	117	28.72	94634	102720	112320
Black	141	149	22.07	123153	135360	143040
Red Ripper . .	164	151	20.89	130110	157440	144960
Unknown . .	171	179	18.86	144117	164160	171840
Clay	165	181	17.86	151629	158400	173760
Whippoorwill	162	195	17.98	150621	155520	187200
Groit	—	202	.			193920
Iron	194	240			186240	230400
New Era . . .	223	278	11.49	236545	214080	266880
Catjang, 21295 D		324				311040
Catjang, 25144		491				471360

Small-seeded varieties like New Era are cheaper on account of the greater number of seeds, and because the percentage of broken seeds is usually less. This fact is becoming recognized by seedsmen, and therefore a slightly higher price is asked for small-seeded varieties. One bushel of New Era contains nearly 50 per cent more seeds than the same measure of Whippoorwill.

622. Viability. — Seed not properly cured or stored quickly loses its viability. For this reason a germination test is always advisable.

Good seed, especially of small-seeded varieties, may retain its viability for several years. The following table gives the germination of seed kept for various periods of time in a storeroom: —

VIABILITY OF COWPEA SEEDS OF STANDARD VARIETIES WHEN
4, 7 AND 10 YEARS OLD

VARIETY	SEED 4 YEARS OLD	SEED 7 YEARS OLD	SEED 10 YEARS OLD
	Per cent	Per cent	Per cent
Whippoorwill	96.0	93.5	79.5
New Era	73.0	61.0	18.0
Iron	60.5	17.5	14.5
Clay Crowder	42.0	42.0	9.0
Clay	38.0	8.0	1.5
Black	79.0	82.0	—
Taylor	50.0	26.5	0.0
Blackeye	22.0	3.5	0.0
Red Ripper	3.5	0.5	0.0
Groit	0.0	0.0	0.0
Michigan Favorite	0.0	0.0	0.0
Extra Early Blackeye . . .	0.0	0.0	0.0

Ordinarily, however, seed over two years old has lost much of its viability. Seeds which have been wetted or which are dead become duller and darker in color; therefore uniformly bright colored seeds should be selected.

623. Root system. — The root system of the cowpea is deep for an annual, there being a well-developed tap-root with a number of large branch roots. These roots spreading horizontally for a short distance, go deeply into the subsoil, thus enabling the plant to draw freely upon the minerals and water below the reach of the shallower-rooted crops.

At the Storrs Connecticut Experiment Station, an investigation was conducted upon the amount of stubble and roots, and distribution of the roots of the cowpea. The following table gives the amount of roots at different depths : —

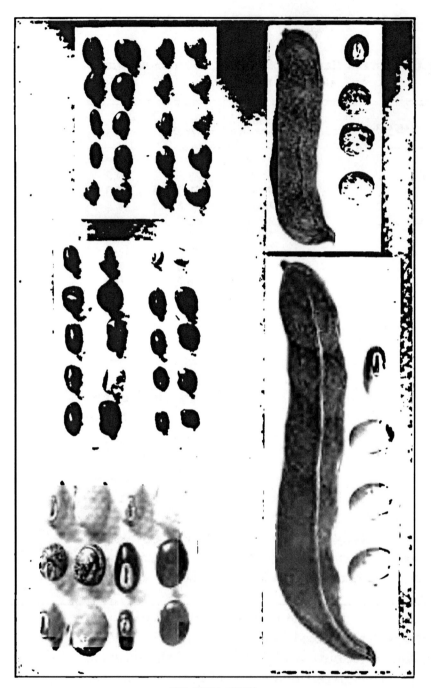

PLATE VIII.

Upper Left. SEEDS OF TEN VARIETIES OF SOYBEANS;
Center Left. SEEDS OF TEN VARIETIES OF COWPEAS;
Lower Left. SEEDS OF SIX VARIETIES OF VELVET-BEANS;
Upper Right. POD OF FLORIDA VELVET-BEAN;
Lower Right. POD OF YOKOHAMA BEAN.

Stubble and first 6 in. of roots	912 lb. an acre
Second 6 in. of roots (6–12 in.)	45 lb. an acre
Third 6 in. of roots (12–18 in.)	54 lb. an acre
Fourth 6 in. of roots (18–24 in.)	34 lb. an acre
Fifth 6 in. of roots (24–30 in.)	63 lb. an acre
Sixth 6 in. of roots (30–36 in.)	59 lb. an acre
Seventh 6 in. of roots (36–42 in.)	40 lb. an acre

At the Delaware Experiment Station, it was found that the cowpea did not have more than 10 per cent of the total weight in the roots.

624. Disease resistance. — In the United States, only two diseases of the cowpea can be considered serious; namely, rootknot, caused by the nematode (*Heterodera radicicola*); and wilt, caused by a *Fusarium* on the roots. The Iron variety — first found in Barnwell County, South Carolina, a region infested by these diseases — is almost perfectly immune to both. Orton has found that the immunizing character is transmitted to crosses. One such cross, the Brabham, whose parents are Iron and Whippoorwill, has become very popular in the Atlantic coastal region of the Southern States.

Several other diseases attack the cowpea, — among them rust (*Uromyces phaseoli*), white leaf-spot (*Amerosporium economicum*), red leaf-spot (*Cercospora cruenta*) and mildew (*Sphaerotheca sp.*). Most standard varieties of cowpeas are immune to rust, and the other diseases are rarely serious on the best varieties.

625. Insect enemies. — The leaves of cowpeas are more or less subject to attack by various insects, but this damage is seldom serious.

The seeds, however, are much subject to injury by two species of weevil (*Pachymerus chinensis* and *P. quadrimaculatus*) whose habits are practically identical. The weevil lays its eggs on the pods of the cowpea in the field or on the seeds when in storage.   The greatest amount of damage is done when the peas are in storage.   Each female lays as a rule 1 egg on a seed, but this does not deter other females from doing the same.   The larva upon hatching burrows into the seed, if necessary first penetrating the pod.   Under very favorable conditions the whole life cycle from egg to adult may take place in 18 days, but under ordinary conditions 30 days or more is required. Under indoor conditions at Washington, D.C., 6 or 7 broods occur in a year.   This rapid reproduction continues until all the peas are practically all destroyed.

Fumigation by carbon bisulfide is probably the best method of destroying the weevils in stored seeds.   The seeds are put in an airtight bin or other receptacle and fumigated 48 hours, using 2 to 3 pounds of carbon bisulfide for each 1000 cubic feet of space.   The bisulfide is poured in shallow pans or dishes on top of the seed, and as the gas volatilizes, it sinks between the seeds, as it is heavier than air.   When the fumigation is complete, the seed should be thoroughly aired, as otherwise the germination may be affected.

CHAPTER XXII

SOYBEANS

THE soybean is the most productive as regards seed of any legume adapted to temperate climates. This fact alone gives the crop a high potential importance and insures its greater agricultural development in America. At the present time the soybean is most largely grown for roughage, but the high value of the seed for human food, as well as animal feed and for oil, will in all probability result in its being more and more grown for the seed.

626. Agricultural history. — The soybean, or soja-bean, is a plant of ancient cultivation in Japan, China, Korea and Manchuria, and to a much less extent in northern India and in the highlands of Java. As grown in these countries, it is used mainly for human food, the beans being prepared in various ways. A large amount of the beans are utilized by first extracting the oil. In this case the bean cake is used both for cattle food and as a fertilizer.

The soybean was first cultivated in the United States in 1829, but it apparently attracted but little attention until 1854, when two varieties were brought back from Japan by the Perry expedition. Other varieties were introduced from time to time, among them the Mammoth, which was introduced previous to 1882. It is largely due to the introduction of this variety that the soybean has become an important crop in the United States, as a very large percentage of the acreage is still planted to this variety. Between the years 1900 and 1910, the United States Department of Agriculture introduced about 250 varieties from all portions of the Orient. In Europe a number of varieties were introduced by Haberlandt of Vienna in 1875, who experimented with them for a num-

Fig. 60. — Soybean.

ber of years. The crop, however, never obtained any great importance in Europe, but is cultivated to a limited extent, especially in France and Italy.

Beginning with 1908, large amounts of soybeans were exported from Manchuria to Europe and the United States. The beans were utilized for extracting the oil, which was used for various industrial purposes, and the bean cake was used as cattle food. This trade has had the effect of increasing interest in the soybean crop, especially from the standpoint of producing seed.

The total yield of seed in Manchuria during 1909 is estimated at 2,000,000 tons, of which over one-half is exported as seed, and three-fourths of the remainder as oil cake.

627. Botany. — The erect or nearly erect form of the soybean, as cultivated in Japan and Manchuria, is not known to grow wild. The nearest wild relative of the cultivated plant is a slender-stemmed vining plant with smaller flowers, pods and seeds. This has usually been considered a distinct species under the name of *Glycine ussuriensis*, and occurs wild in Japan, Manchuria and China. The Indian varieties of soybeans are quite intermediate between this wild plant and the Japanese and Manchurian varieties, being for the most part rather slender-stemmed, vining, small-flowered and small-seeded varieties. A critical study of an extensive series of varieties shows that all intergrades between the wild plant and the cultivated erect forms exist, so that there can be but little doubt that but one species is represented. The usual botanical designation for this species is *Glycine soja*, but under recent botanical codes it must be changed to *Soja max*. If two species are to be recognized, then both are cultivated, as some of the Indian varieties are much more like the wild soybean than they are like the erect Japanese varieties. The large number of varieties of the soybean and the great range of differences in these varieties indicate a very ancient cultivation.

The flowers of the soybean are small, white or purple, and borne on short axillary racemes, which usually bear eight to fifteen flowers in a cluster, but the number may be as high as thirty-five.

The pods of most varieties are compressed, though some are nearly terete, each bearing two or three seeds, or rarely four. The pods vary in length according to variety from three-quarters of an inch to three inches, and there may be considerable variation even on the same plant. The pods are commonly borne in clusters of three to five, in extreme cases as many as twelve. On single plants over 400 pods have been counted. The pods are gray or tawny or sometimes black. Gray pods always bear gray pubescence, while the tawny pods have tawny pubescence. Black pods may have either color as to pubescence.

The variation in the seeds of the soybean is very great. Some are nearly globose, others much flattened, but the great majority are elliptical in outline, the thickness less than the breadth. The largest seeded sorts contain about 2000 seeds to the pound, while the smallest seeded contain about 7000. The color of the testa shows the following range of colors: straw yellow, olive yellow, olive, green, brown and black. In a very few varieties, the testa may be bicolored. Among such combinations are green or yellow with a saddle of black, and brown and black in concentric bands. On heterozygote plants, the seeds are often irregularly two-colored, but these do not breed true. The embryo or germ may be either yellow or green. It is green in all the green-seeded varieties and in some of the black-seeded ones, in all others being yellow.

628. Description. — The soybean is an annual, and strictly determinate in growth; that is, the whole plant reaches maturity as the pods ripen, and no further growth takes place. Most of the cultivated varieties are erect and branching, the main axis being well defined. With few exceptions such varieties have decidedly stout stems. In other sorts the stems and branches are somewhat twining and weak, so that the plant is more or less procumbent. All intergrades between these types of growth exist, some sorts being slender-stemmed with the branches more or less twining. The height of the stem varies according to the variety from six inches to six feet. In general, the earliest varieties are the most dwarfed.

All soybeans are hairy plants, no smooth variety being

known. The hairiness occurs in two colors, grayish and tawny. The tawny pubescence is nearly always associated with dark-colored pods and usually with purple flowers.

The leaves of the soybean show large variation in size, shape and color. The leaflets are usually ovate-lanceolate, but in some varieties are narrowly lanceolate or almost linear. In broad-leaved varieties they may be nearly orbicular. With few exceptions the leaves of the soybeans begin to turn yellow as the pods ripen and usually all have fallen by the time the pods are mature. In a few sorts, however, the leaves persist and retain their green color even after all of the pods have ripened.

629. Soil adaptations. — Soybeans are not particular in their soil requirements. Even on poor soil they will make a satisfactory growth, provided they are inoculated, but on such soils the growth is rarely as good as is made by cowpeas. They succeed best on loams and clays, but the Mammoth variety also does admirably on sandy or silty soils. They are not sensitive to an excess of moisture, although they will not thrive in a soil where water stands for any considerable length of time. In marked contrast to their ability to grow on wet soils is the fact that the soybean is also decidedly drought resistant, much more so than cowpeas. Unfortunately, however, rabbits are very fond of the soybean, and in the semi-arid regions the danger of damage from these animals is a serious disadvantage.

630. Climatic adaptations. — In the United States, soybeans show almost exactly the same range of climatic adaptation as varieties of corn. Early varieties will mature northward wherever corn will mature. Southward, however, the soybean does not seem to be adapted to as extreme climatic conditions as the corn; for example, under Florida conditions, soybeans seldom grow normally. In southern Louisiana it is a common phenomenon for the Mammoth soybean to make a satisfactory growth, but the pods do not fill. Some very late varieties tested at Arlington Farm, Virginia, failed to bloom when killed by frost at the end of 150 days. Such varieties were mainly from the highlands of northern India, where a much longer growing season occurs.

Soybeans will withstand considerable frost, both when young and old. Some varieties will in the fall withstand temperatures as low as 27° Fahrenheit without serious injury to the leaves. If the pods are fairly well filled before a killing frost occurs, they will usually ripen satisfactorily.

631. Importance. — The soybean has been slowly but steadily increasing in importance in America during the past 20 years. Its relative importance is less than that of either the field pea or the cowpea.

632. Desirable characters in soybean varieties. — As the number of soybean varieties is very large, and as new sorts are easily secured by crossing, the most desirable characters, both for forage and for seed-production, need to be considered. In this crop as in others, yield is the most important single desideratum. Secondary considerations are habit, coarseness, ability to hold leaves, color of seed and ease of shattering.

An ideal variety for forage should be *erect; tall,* so that the pods are not too near the ground ; *slender,* but without tendency to lodge, so as to permit easy mowing ; *leafy* and with the ability to retain the leaves late ; *yellow-seeded,* as hogs will find such seeds as are shattered more readily ; *non-shattering,* a character more common in small-seeded than in larger-seeded varieties ; *disease resistant*, especially to nematodes and cowpea wilt, which seriously affect most varieties of the soybean.

For seed-production alone, percentage of oil content is second in importance to yield, and leafiness and ability to hold leaves of practically no concern. .

633. Commercial varieties. — At the present time about fifteen varieties of soybeans are handled commercially by seedsmen, the most important of which are Mammoth, Hollybrook, Haberlandt, Medium Yellow, Guelph, Ito San, Wilson and Peking.

Mammoth. — This is a tall late variety, under average conditions growing from three to five feet high, and strictly bushy in habit. At the present time probably two-thirds of the acreage of soybeans of the United States is devoted to this variety. On account of its lateness, it will not usually mature seed north of the District of Columbia and Kentucky. This variety was introduced prior to 1882, but there is no record as to its exact source. The seeds are yellow, one pound containing about 2100. The pubescence is gray, and the flowers are white.

Hollybrook. — The Hollybrook soybean matures 15 to 20 days earlier than the Mammoth. The plants are very compact, the pods being densely crowded. The pubescence is gray, but both white and red-flowered strains occur. The seeds are yellow, very much like Mammoth, 2100 weighing one pound. The plants seldom grow more than three feet high, and the pods cover the stems nearly to the ground. The Hollybrook was first introduced about 1904.

Haberlandt. — This variety matures about a week earlier than the Hollybrook. It is a more bushy and spreading plant, but grows to nearly the same height. It is a heavy yielder of seed, and also a good hay variety. The pubescence is tawny, and both purple-flowered and white-flowered strains occur. The seeds are straw yellow with a brown hilum, one pound containing about 2400. The Haberlandt variety was introduced from Pingyang, Korea, in 1901.

Medium Yellow. — This is an erect, bushy, heavy seeding variety growing 2½ to 3 feet high, and requiring about the same length of season as the Haberlandt. The pubescence is tawny, and the flowers either purple or white. The seeds are straw yellow with a pale hilum, one pound containing about 3500. This variety was introduced from central China in 1901. Some seedsmen advertise it under the name of Mongol.

Guelph. — This variety was introduced from Japan in 1889 by W. P. Brooks. It is also known under the names of Medium Green and Medium Early Green. The plants are stout and bushy, growing 1½ to 2 feet high. The pubescence is tawny, and the flowers purple. The whole seed, including both the coat and the germ, is green in color. One pound of seed contains about 2600. This variety has been much grown in the Northern States, as it requires only about 90 days to become fully mature.

Ito San. — This variety is also known as Japanese pea, Early White and Early Yellow. It was introduced from Japan by C. C. Georgeson in 1890, but apparently the same or a very similar variety was distributed by the United States Patent Office in 1853. It is a bushy variety growing 2 to 2½ feet high, with rather slender stems, and on this account, excellent for hay. It becomes fully mature in about one hundred days after planting. The pubescence is tawny, and the flowers purple. The seeds are rather small, straw yellow with a pale hilum, but with a brown speck near the micropyle, by which this variety may be certainly known. One pound contains about 3200 seeds. This variety has been much grown in the Northern States.

Wilson. — This variety was introduced from Newchwang, Manchuria, in 1906. It is a tall, slender variety, growing 3 to 4 feet high, with a few erect branches, and becoming fully mature in about 110 days. On account of its tall, slender height, it is readily harvested, and makes excellent hay, besides being a heavy seed producer. The pubescence is tawny, and the flowers either purple or white. The seeds are black, with a yellow germ, one pound containing about 2400 seeds.

Peking. — A variety introduced from Peking, China, in 1907. This variety is characterized by its dense bushiness, leafiness and slender stems, growing 2½ to 3 feet high, and becomes fully mature in about 120 days. The pubescence is tawny, the flowers white, the seeds black and much flattened, with a yellow germ. One pound contains about 6300 seeds. This variety is one of the most satisfactory of all, both for hay and seed production. It is rather remarkable among soybean varieties as being almost completely non-shattering.

634. Preparation of soil and cultivation. — The seed bed for soybeans should receive as thorough preparation as land for corn. This preparation should consist of deep plowing and subsequent working with disk and harrow until a firm seed bed, with the upper 2 or 3 inches loose and mellow, is secured.

Soybeans germinate in a very few days under proper soil conditions, and cultivation is begun as soon as the seedling plants appear. The cultivation should be shallow, and any good cultivator may be used. Soybeans require about the same number of cultivations as corn. Level cultivation is preferable, as the harvesting can be more easily done.

635. Rate of seeding. — The quantity of seed to be sown to the acre will vary somewhat according to the size of the seed and the use of the crop. With rows from 24 to 36 inches apart, from 20 to 30 pounds of seed to the acre is satisfactory. When sown broadcast for hay, from one to one and a half bushels of seed is required. Few rate of seeding experiments have been reported, but the following results were secured at the Ohio Agricultural Experiment Station : —

TABLE SHOWING ACRE YIELDS OF SOYBEAN HAY AND SEEDS
WHEN PLANTED AT DIFFERENT RATES

RATE OF SEEDING TO THE ACRE	WIDTH OF ROWS	YIELD TO THE ACRE					
		Hay			Thrashed Grain		
		1909	1910	1911	1909	1910	1911
Pounds	*Inches*	*Pounds*	*Pounds*	*Pounds*	*Bushels*	*Bushels*	*Bushels*
15	28	2480	2685	4510	10.66	18.91	35.58
30	28	3640	2775	4216	16.58	20.08	33.78
45	28	3760	3010	5040	17.33	21.00	38.40
60	28	3640	3345	4608	16.08	23.16	36.35
120	8	3080	4300	5393	12.66	15.42	33.86

636. Time of seeding. — Soybeans may be sown at any time after danger of severe frosts is over. The plants, however, grow slowly in cool weather and ordinarily there is no advantage in planting them earlier than corn, especially late varieties. In the cotton region, two crops of the early and medium varieties can be grown in a single season by planting the first early. With the very earliest varieties this can also be accomplished as far north as Maryland. Generally speaking, June 1 is about the best date for seeding.

637. Method of seeding. — The method of planting will depend on the purpose for which the soybeans are grown. Soybeans are grown either in cultivated rows or broadcasted. The former method is preferable in weedy land and usually gives larger yields of hay and practically always of seed. The general practice for seed-production is the row method, while for hay or soiling, drilling or broadcasting furnishes a forage of finer texture.

In Manchuria soybeans are usually planted in rows 17 inches wide, the plants about 2 inches apart in the row. With rows so close together, hand hoeing is necessary. In the United States the rows are most often 36 inches wide, so as to facilitate easy cultivation. This distance is not too much for large varieties like the Mammoth. In the low, poorly drained lands of eastern North Carolina, the rows are planted four feet apart and on raised beds, to facilitate drainage. For the smaller, earlier varieties, rows 18 inches apart give sufficient room for the plants to develop fully. The plants of different varieties range in height from one foot or less to five feet or more, so the optimum distance apart of rows is thus partly a matter of variety and partly one of the culture implement to be employed. For the larger varieties, three-foot rows are very satisfactory with plants 2 to 3 inches apart in the rows.

Soybeans may be drilled with an ordinary wheat drill, the width of the rows adjusted by covering the feed cups not in use. Corn planters are sometimes used in planting soybeans, as most of the modern planters have special plates for drilling beans.

638. Depth of planting. — The depth of planting soybean seed is very important, poor stands frequently resulting from too deep covering. The depth should not exceed two inches, since with shallow planting chance of failure due to formation of a soil crust is lessened. In a test under favorable conditions with the Mammoth and Peking varieties, 100 seeds each were planted respectively 1, 1½, 2, 2½, 3 and 4 inches deep. The percentages of plants reaching the surface one week after planting are shown in the table : —

GERMINATION OF SOYBEANS AT DIFFERENT DEPTHS OF PLANTING

VARIETY	PER CENT GERMINATION AT DIFFERENT DEPTHS					
	1 Inch	1½ Inches	2 Inches	2½ Inches	3 Inches	4 Inches
Mammoth .	100	93	98	95	92	84
Peking . . .	95	97	92	92	90	86

At the Tennessee Experiment Station, it was found that seed of the Ito San variety failed to reach the surface when planted 6 inches deep. At 5 inches the stand was very poor, but it was apparently perfect at any depth of planting between 1 and 4 inches.

639. Inoculation. — Natural inoculation now occurs quite generally throughout much of the soybean region in southern United States. In localities, however, where this crop has not been previously grown it is advisable to inoculate.

The inoculation of the soybean by means of artificial cultures has been found to be unusually difficult, the reasons for which are obscure. In soil supplied with nitrogen, the plants grow fairly well without nodules, and according to Kirchner nodules were not detected on European grown plants during the twenty years after the crop had been introduced.

Smith and Robinson at the Michigan Agricultural Experiment Station made observations on the influence of nodules on the roots upon the composition of the soybean. The conclusion of two years' work was that the nodules on the roots, in a fairly fertile soil, may not notably increase the yield, but do increase the relative and absolute

Fig. 61. — Roots of soybean, showing nodules.

amounts of nitrogen in the plants. In the following table is given the composition of the dry matter of leaves, stems and roots of inoculated and not inoculated soybeans :—

	DRY MATTER	PROTEIN	ASH	NITROGEN	PHOSPHORIC ACID	POTASH
	Grains	%	%	%	%	%
Inoculated :—						
Leaves . . .	205.98	22.71	11.26	3.63	.72	2.27
Stems . . .	284.37	11.54	7.02	1.85	.60	2.21
Roots . . .	55.2	5.72	7.14	.91	.40	1.29
Not inoculated :—						
Leaves . . .	198.92	17.89	13.86	2.86	.65	2.29
Stems . . .	247.48	8.35	7.36	1.33	.68	2.07
Roots . . .	49.00	6.60	12.08	1.05	.39	1.27

640. Life period. — The length of time required by the soybean plant from germination to maturity varies greatly with the variety and with the time of planting. Early plantings require a much longer time to mature than late plantings, but the same varieties do not behave consistently in this respect. With a single variety, Haberlandt found that the life period at Vienna, Austria, varied from 182 days when planted March 31 to 139 days if planted June 9, there being almost a perfectly regular gradation for intermediate planting.

Extensive experiments of this kind have been conducted by Mooers at the Tennessee Experiment Station. Some of his results are shown in the table: —

TABLE SHOWING RELATIONS BETWEEN DATE OF PLANTING AND LIFE PERIOD IN SOYBEAN

VARIETY	1907			1908		
	Date Planted	Date Harvested	Life Period Days	Date Planted	Date Harvested	Life Period Days
Mammoth	Apr. 3	Oct. 5	186	Apr. 2	Oct. 7	188
	Apr. 15	Oct. 5	173	Apr. 14	Oct. 7	179
	Apr. 30	Oct. 6	160	May 1	Oct. 7	159
	May 15	Oct. 9	146	May 15	Oct. 7	145
	June 5	Oct. 12	129	June 1	Oct. 7	128
	June 17	Oct. 22	127	June 17	Oct. 21	126
	June 29	Oct. 22	113	July 1	Oct. 21	112
	July 15	Oct. 28	105	July 17	Oct. 24	100
Ito San	Apr. 3	Aug. 9	114	Apr. 2	July 25	114
	Apr. 15	Aug. 9	106	Apr. 14	July 29	106
	Apr. 30	Aug. 9	96	May 1	Aug. 5	96
	May 15	Aug. 17	92	May 14	Aug. 15	92
	June 5	Sept. 3	87	June 1	Aug. 27	87
	June 17	Sept. 18	85	June 17	Sept. 10	85
	June 29	Sept. 18	80	July 1	Sept. 19	80
	July 15	Oct. 9	82	July 16	Oct. 6	82
	Aug. 6	Oct. 29	85	Aug. 1	Oct. 24	85

Ordinarily it is not advisable to sow soybeans until about the time for planting corn, as soybean plants grow but slowly during cool weather. Of 330 varieties grown at Arlington Farm, Virginia, 2 were classified as very early, maturing in 80 to 90 days; 12 as early, maturing in 90 to 100 days; 40 as medium early, maturing in 100 to 110 days; 76 as medium, maturing in 110 to 120 days; 85 as medium late, maturing in 120 to 130 days; 55 as late, maturing in 130 to 150 days, and 60 as very late, requiring more than 150 days.

On account of self-pollination, soybean varieties show but little variability. Of such important varieties as the Mammoth, Ito San and Guelph, which have been grown in the United States for many years, seed from different sources planted at the same place gave results which show that no change in the life period has taken place, whether the seed was grown in the North or in the South. In a few varieties, however, there is satisfactory evidence to show that the life period of a variety changes, becoming gradually shorter when grown northward, and gradually longer when grown southward.

641. Time to cut for hay. — Soybeans may be cut for hay at any time from the setting of the seed until the leaves begin to turn yellow. The crop is best fitted for hay when the pods are well formed. If allowed to stand much longer than this the stems rapidly become woody and the percentage of protein lower; and if left too long, there is much loss in leaves. In the development of the plant from bloom to maturity there is a marked increase in the percentage of fat, little change in that of carbohydrates, but a decided diminution in the percentage of protein. The following table shows the variation in the composition of soybean hay of the Mammoth variety at different stages of development: —

TABLE SHOWING CHEMICAL ANALYSES OF MAMMOTH SOYBEAN
HAY CUT AT FOUR DIFFERENT STAGES

STAGE WHEN CUT	WATER	PROTEIN	FAT	NITROGEN FREE EXTRACT	FIBER	ASH
Full bloom . . .	5.11	19.22	1.45	38.56	26.50	9.16
First pods . . .	5.35	12.72	1.06	42.50	30.82	7.55
Seed ½ grown . .	5.40	10.31	2.34	44.73	30.45	6.77
Seed full grown . .	5.30	15.94	7.83	38.76	25.97	6.20

642. Hay yields. — Yields of soybean hay range from 1
to 3 tons and occasionally 4 tons to the acre. The average
yield is about 2 tons to the acre : —

TABLE SHOWING YIELDS OF SOYBEAN HAY AT VARIOUS AMERI-
CAN EXPERIMENT STATIONS, IN POUNDS TO THE ACRE

VARIETY	DELAWARE	TENNESSEE	OHIO	KANSAS	VIRGINIA
Mammoth .		5660			5700
Hollybrook .	4500	5220			5900
Guelph . . .	4350	4560	1717		3260
Ito San . . .	3200	4340	1725	4739	5120
Haberlandt .	5800	5400		2431	
Med. Yellow .	4500	4560	1840	3595	4600
Wilson . . .	5200				
Peking . . .	4830				
Ebony . . .	3800		1860		
Cloud . . .	6100		2170		

643. Fertilizers. — On land of moderate fertility, commercial fertilizers do not seem to show marked results in
the yield of soybeans. On sandy soil or soils in poor condition, experiments show that a dressing of stable manure
or of acid phosphate and potash gives the best results.

At the Delaware Experiment Station, an application of 250 to 350 pounds to the acre of a mixture of 400 pounds of acid phosphate and 100 pounds of muriate of potash is recommended. Good results were obtained at the Tennessee Agricultural Experiment Station by using acid phosphate alone at the rate of 200 to 300 pounds to the acre. In using commercial fertilizer, it is well to apply broadcast before the soybeans are planted.

Lime as shown especially by Mooers' experiments in Tennessee almost invariably gives pronouncedly larger yields.

644. Soybean mixtures. — Soybeans are well adapted to planting in mixture with other farm crops. Results of experiments along this line indicate that a larger yield of hay can be secured and also a greater variety of forage. The chief advantage, perhaps, is in the varied ration.

Soybeans and corn. — Soybeans are more generally grown with corn than with any other crop. They may be planted in the same hills with corn, in alternate hills with the corn in the same row, in alternate rows of each or two rows of each. Rarely they are broadcasted in mixture. When soybeans are grown with corn by these methods, the crop may be fed on the land to hogs or harvested for silage. The early and medium varieties of soybeans may be planted in between the corn rows at the time of the last cultivation.

Soybeans and cowpeas. — A mixture of soybeans and cowpeas is more easily harvested and cured than cowpeas alone. In such mixtures, tall strong-growing varieties of soybeans are best as they tend to support the vining cowpeas. Care should be taken to select varieties of soybeans and cowpeas that mature about the same time. In sowing such a mixture, it is better to use a larger

2 м

proportion of soybeans. One bushel of soybeans to one-half bushel of cowpeas gives excellent results if broad-casted, but half this quantity is sufficient if planted in three-foot rows. The time for cutting for hay is determined primarily by the soybeans, as cowpeas can be cut for hay over a much longer period than the soybeans.

Soybeans and sorghums. — Soybeans may be grown very satisfactorily for hay or silage in a mixture with sorghum. The tall-growing vining varieties are best, and either Amber or Orange sorghum may be used. This mixture is most satisfactory in cultivated rows, as the sorghum is apt to choke out the soybeans when broad-casted, unless the sorghum is planted thinly.

Soybeans and Johnson-grass. — Johnson-grass as well as Sudan-grass is excellent for growing in mixtures with soybeans. Not only are better yields obtained with these mixtures but also the quality of the hay is improved. Twining varieties of soybeans have a distinct advantage for growing with these grasses.

Soybeans and millet. — Soybeans and millet are not to be recommended as a mixture. The millet matures too early for any of the good hay varieties of soybeans.

645. Silage. — Soybeans may be very satisfactorily used for silage, the best results being obtained when mixed with corn or sorghum. The soybeans may be grown either in combination with the corn or the sorghum, but it seems preferable to grow them separately and to mix them while cutting for the silo.

646. Rotations. — In the South soybeans are adapted to practically the same place in rotations as are cowpeas. In Tennessee and North Carolina, a soybean crop is often grown between two wheat crops, and in other parts of the South, between two oat crops. In such cases medium

early varieties are preferable. Where a whole season can
be devoted to soybeans in the South, two crops of early
varieties can be grown in place of one crop of a late variety.
Especially where seed-production is the object, much larger
yields can be obtained by this practice. In the North,
soybeans generally occupy the same place in rotation as
oats, the principal objection being that the harvesting of
the soybeans presses very closely on the seeding time for
wheat.

647. Feeding value of soybean hay. — At the Tennessee
Experiment Station, dairy cows were fed soybean hay in
comparison with alfalfa hay, and soybean straw in comparison with corn stover. Judging by the amount of milk
and butter fat obtained, the data show a slight superiority
of soybean hay alone over alfalfa hay alone. The
soybean straw alone produced 12 per cent more milk
and 14 per cent more butter fat than the corn stover
alone.

648. Seed-production. — The character of growth, the
uniform maturing habit of the soybean and the large
yield of grain recommend the plant for seed-production.
Tall varieties that do not branch nor bear pods close to
the ground are most desirable, as they are more easily
harvested.

When grown for grain alone, soybeans should be allowed
to develop fully. This stage of maturity is indicated in
the case of most varieties when all of the leaves have
fallen. The Guelph and a few varieties not on the market
retain the leaves late and much seed would be lost by
shattering if the harvesting were not done earlier. Soybeans may be also harvested for grain when the leaves first
begin to fall. If cut at this stage practically as much
seed is saved as when the plants are allowed to mature,

and the straw obtained is a much better feed. The plants should be allowed to become thoroughly dry after cutting. When ready to bunch and put into shocks, soybeans should be a little damp, as some shattering will occur if handled when very dry.

One of the chief difficulties in growing soybeans for seed has been the harvesting. The small early varieties can be harvested only with a mowing machine, or a bean harvester or by hand. For harvesting many of the later and more erect growing varieties, a mower with a bunching attachment or a self-rake reaper is better adapted. The self-binder has been found the most satisfactory machine to use with tall varieties.

Thrashing is most satisfactorily done in the field without previously stacking if conditions will permit. Soybeans may be thrashed with an ordinary grain separator if necessary adjustments are made, otherwise a large per cent of the beans will be cracked or split. The cylinder should be run at about one-half the speed used in thrashing grain, but at the same time maintaining the usual rate for the rest of the machine. Some of the concaves should be removed or a special set of thin concaves should be used. The ordinary wheat separators are now manufactured provided with a pea and bean hulling attachment which is said to do satisfactory work. Special pea and bean separators are now on the market which not only do clean hulling, but split none of the beans. Soybeans cannot be satisfactorily thrashed unless thoroughly dry, for when slightly damp the pods are tough, and much of the seed remains unthrashed.

Special care is required in storing soybean seed to prevent heating, which will ruin the beans as far as germination is concerned. The seed should be thoroughly dry when placed in storage or else placed where good ventilation is afforded and the seed not bulked together in large quantities. Under whatever conditions the seed may be stored, it should be examined occasionally to detect any tendency to heat. If signs of heating are found, the seed should be removed at once and spread out until perfectly dry.

649. Pollination. — The soybean flower is completely self-fertile, bagged plants setting pods as perfectly as those exposed. The flowers are much visited by bees, which seek principally the pollen, as the soybean flower secretes but little nectar. Pollination occurs even before the flower opens, but nevertheless occasional cross-pollinations occur where different varieties are grown in close proximity. Such natural hybrids can often be detected by the fact that the seeds of heterozygote plants present queer combinations of color, such as smoky green, smoky yellow, brown, and yellow and black banded. In the course of varietal trials at Arlington Farm, Virginia, extending over five years, many such natural hybrids were secured, and similar crosses occurred at the Kansas Experiment Station.

650. Seed yield. — With regard to the seed yield of the soybean, there is considerable variation in the figures given. When grown alone for seed, the best varieties under proper culture yield from 30 to 40 bushels of seed to the acre. A maximum yield of 50 bushels to the acre has been reported from North Carolina. According to various authorities, the yields in Manchuria range from about 1000 pounds to the acre on very poor soil up to about 1800 pounds to the acre on good soil.

In the United States, yields have been reported by various investigators as follows : —

TABLE SHOWING ACRE YIELD IN BUSHELS OF SOYBEAN SEED
AT VARIOUS EXPERIMENT STATIONS

VARIETY	ARLINGTON, VA.	TENNESSEE	KENTUCKY	DELAWARE	INDIANA	OHIO	ARKANSAS	VIRGINIA	GUELPH, ONTARIO
Mammoth	18.0	23.9					15.26		
Hollybrook	23.0	22.9	16.2	29.2		12.8	11.4		
Guelph	18.7	16.5		15.2		22.38		16.16	
Ito San	13.3	20.2	8.0	21.9		24.7		18.43	
Haberlandt	23.0	25.7	14.0	23.3				18.33	
Med. Yellow	23.2	25.9		26.9	18.1				17.2
Wilson	18.2		10.2	32.2	20.1				
Peking	23.4			32.7				15.00	
Ebony	15.7	25.0	10.0	25.2					
Chernie									23.5

651. Seeds. — Soybean seeds weigh about 60 pounds to the bushel and this weight is recognized as standard in most states. The size of the seeds varies greatly, as shown in the following table: —

TABLE SHOWING NUMBER OF SOYBEAN SEEDS TO THE POUND
AND TO THE BUSHEL IN TEN VARIETIES

VARIETY	NUMBER OF SEEDS		VARIETY	NUMBER OF SEEDS	
	One pound	One bushel		One pound	One bushel
Mammoth .	2144	128640	Ito San . .	3232	193920
Hollybrook .	2144	128640	Ebony . .	3240	194400
Haberlandt .	2400	144000	Med. Yellow	3552	213120
Wilson . . .	2400	144000	Wisconsin black . .	5104	306240
Guelph . . .	2624	157440	Peking . .	6388	383280

The seeds do not retain their viability well, and it is not advisable to sow seed two years old without previously testing. Unless care is exercised in properly curing and storing, soybean seeds are apt to heat and thus quickly have their viability destroyed. A small percentage of the seed will under favorable conditions retain its viability four or five years, and this has been found to vary according to variety, as shown in the table : —

VIABILITY OF SOYBEAN SEEDS

VARIETY	SEED COLOR	1 YEAR OLD	2 YEAR OLD	4 YEAR OLD
		Per cent	Per cent	Per cent
Shanghai	Black	99.0	93.0	43.5
Chernie	Black	94.0	76.5	46.5
Baird	Brown	97.0	88.0	24.5
Fairchild	Black	95.5	84.5	20.0
Jet	Black	92.5	60.0	19.5
Ebony	Black	94.0	71.5	4.0
Tashing	Green	90.5	81.5	3.0
Guelph	Green	97.5	86.5	1.5
Brownie	Brown	90.5	67.0	1.5
Ito San	Straw Yellow	100.0	83.0	2.5
Haberlandt . . .	Straw Yellow	76.0	2.5	0.0
Mammoth . . .	Straw Yellow	77.0	32.5	0.5

Weevils rarely injure soybean seeds, but under exceptional circumstances have been known to destroy them. This relative immunity to weevil injury is important, especially in the South.

652. Pests. — Soybeans are troubled by few serious enemies. On the whole, rabbits are most troublesome, as they are extravagantly fond of the herbage, and where they are abundant soybean culture is practically impossible. At the Tennessee Experimental Substation at Jackson, rabbit injury was much reduced by using scarecrows, to each of which a lantern was hung at night.

Rootknot caused by a nematode (*Heterodera radicicola*) often injures soybeans considerably, but more damage is caused by cowpea wilt, due to a *Fusarium*.

Caterpillars sometimes eat the leaves, but the loss from such insects is seldom serious.

On the whole it may be said that no insect or fungus pest has yet assumed any great economic importance in connection with the culture of the soybean.

653. Breeding. — The soybean lends itself readily to improvement, and considerable work in breeding is being carried on by the United States Department of Agriculture, the Tennessee Experiment Station and the Ohio Experiment Station.   The Ohio Station is testing individual plants in duplicate plant-row work in much the same way that it is testing ears of corn and is finding decided differences in yield of seed and forage, in tendency to shatter and in habits of growth.   The Tennessee Station is conducting selection work with a number of varieties and has found considerable variation in maturity, habit of growth and plant characters within the same varieties, so that several strains of the same variety are under test.   The United States Department of Agriculture has done a very considerable amount of work toward the improvement of the soybean by selection and hybridization.   The results of the breeding work thus far indicate that it is easily possible to improve the varieties now on the market.

654. Soybeans and cowpeas compared. — Inasmuch as soybeans are adapted to so nearly the same uses and same place in farm rotation as the cowpea, an agronomic comparison of the two crops has often been made.

The soybean is determinate in growth; that is, it reaches a definite size and matures. Nearly all varieties of cowpeas, on the other hand, are indeterminate, continuing growth until killed by frost. With the exception of a few varieties, the soybean does not vine, but grows erect or nearly erect. Cowpeas, on the other hand, are viny plants, and therefore more difficult to harvest. Soybeans mature all their pods at one time. Cowpeas continue to produce green pods as long as the plant lives.

Soybeans will withstand rather heavy frosts, both in the spring, when young, and in the fall, when nearly mature, while the same frosts are fatal to cowpeas. They are more drought resistant than cowpeas, and in a dry season will give much greater yields; they will also withstand excessive moisture much better.

For green manuring or soil improving, the cowpea is far more valuable than the soybean, as it will smother weeds much more successfully.

The value of the hay of the two plants is nearly the same. There is frequently doubt as to which is the more desirable to grow. On relatively poor soil or when broadcasted, cowpeas are always preferable. When cultivated, the soybean will yield the greater return, and if cut late, the hay is more easily cured.

For growing with corn or sorghum for hay or silage the cowpea is generally preferable to the soybean.

The feeding value of an acre of soybeans for beef cattle was found by the Tennessee Agricultural Experiment Station to be about 50 per cent greater than that of cowpeas grown on an adjoining acre. This was also approximately the difference in yield of the two crops.

As a grain producer the soybean is in every way preferable to the cowpea, as it produces larger yields of richer grain and can be harvested much more easily.

The soybean, therefore, is to be recommended above the cowpea where intensive rather than extensive farming is practicable and desirable.

CHAPTER XXIII

OTHER HOT–SEASON ANNUAL LEGUMES

THERE are numerous tropical and subtropical legumes well adapted to culture in the Southern States. None of these are of equal importance to the cowpea and the soybean, but several of them have high value for particular conditions. Among these are Japan clover, velvet-bean and beggar-weed. Others such as bonavist, guar, mung and related beans can hardly compete with the cowpea, although there is need of much further experimentation with these crops before their value can be clearly determined.

LESPEDEZA OR JAPAN CLOVER (*Lespedeza striata*)

655. Description. — Lespedeza or Japan clover is a native of eastern Asia, occurring in Japan, Korea, Manchuria, Mongolia and China. It is a summer annual with reddish, usually much-branched, wiry stems and numerous small, sessile, trifoliolate leaves. Over most of the area in which it occurs the plants are only 4 to 6 inches high, and isolated plants often make masses 6 to 12 inches across. Under very favorable conditions of soil and climate, the plants commonly grow 12 inches high, frequently reaching 18 inches and exceptionally 24 to 30 inches. In thin stands the plants are spreading, or even prostrate, but where dense are quite erect and not much branched.

The plants begin to appear rather late in spring, bloom

in late summer and mature their seeds in September and October. The small flowers are purple. Dodson found that a plant in good condition had 45.4 per cent of its weight in stems and the remainder in leaves and buds. As the plants get old, the lower leaves are shed more or less and the percentage of stem weight becomes higher. The roots are not deep, but Dodson estimated that the dry weight of the stubble and roots to 12 inches in depth is about one-third that of the hay removed. McCarthy at the North Carolina Experiment Station described a broad-leaved variety which showed " immense superiority " over the common sort.

656. Agricultural history. — Lespedeza was first found in the United States at Monticello, Georgia, by Thomas C. Porter in 1846, his specimens being still preserved. The plant seems to have already become common by the close of the Civil War, and perhaps was much spread by the movements of the cavalry during that conflict, as the seeds are not digested by horses. At the present time it occurs spontaneously in most of the area from central New Jersey west to central Kansas and south to the Gulf. Throughout all of this region it furnishes a portion of the summer pasturage, thriving even on the poorest soils. In the lower Mississippi valley, especially in Louisiana, Mississippi and Arkansas, it grows tall enough to cut for hay, and to a less extent this is the case in other southern states on rich lands.

There are no definite records as to when Lespedeza was first cut for hay, but about 1880 its culture was taken up and later strongly advocated by J. B. McGehee in Louisiana. Its status as a cultivated crop may be said to date from this time. Apparently it has never been cultivated in its native country.

657. Adaptations. — Lespedeza has spread naturally since its introduction into the United States over practically the whole area from southern New Jersey westward nearly to central Kansas and south to the Gulf of Mexico. It is only in the lower Mississippi valley that it grows large enough to cut for hay, elsewhere being valuable only for pasturage. It shows no marked preference for soils, occurring on every type, if well drained near the surface.

Lespedeza delights in heat and does not begin to grow in spring until warm weather. It does not withstand frost, but it rarely begins growth until all danger of frost is over. Its northern limit seems determined wholly by the length of the hot season necessary for it to mature seed.

658. Culture. — Lespedeza is best seeded in early spring, preferably February in Louisiana and Mississippi, but it may be sown up till April. From 15 to 25 pounds of seed is used to the acre. Where once land has grown Japan clover, it is rarely necessary to reseed it again if proper precautions be used. The seed, however, is quite cheap, and Lespedeza is being grown more and more in regular rotations.

It is most commonly sown perhaps with oats as a nurse-crop, sowing the Lespedeza with the oats in fall or better in early spring on the fall-sown oats. After the oats are harvested, a good crop of Lespedeza can be harvested the same season. It may thus occupy the land for two or more years, reseeding itself each year, or better, be succeeded by corn or cotton in a regular rotation.

The reseeding of the land to Lespedeza may be regulated in harvesting the crop. If cut when in bloom, the aftermath will ripen seed before frost, or strips of the

Lespedeza may be left between each swath for re-seeding.

If harvested for seed, enough will shatter to produce a good stand the next year.

Lespedeza is nearly always a spontaneous constituent of Bermuda-grass pastures, but if not present, should be sown. Redtop is another grass that makes a good mixture with it, the first crop being mainly redtop and the second Lespedeza.

659. Pasturage value. — Lespedeza is remarkable for its ability to grow in the very poorest of sandy or gravelly soils, but it makes far greater growth on rich calcareous loams or clay loams. If not too closely grazed, it maintains itself indefinitely where once established. It is a common element of the pastures throughout the area where it occurs except on wet lands. On poor thin soils it often occurs in dense pure growths. It endures shade fairly well, occurring abundantly in moderately open woodlands. In no sense can it be called a weed, as it is quickly destroyed by cultivation. The herbage is readily grazed by all farm animals, and will withstand very heavy pasturing. Like other clovers it sometimes causes mules and horses to " slobber," but it has never been known to cause bloating. Late spring frosts sometimes destroy it. Under close mowing, as on golf courses, it disappears after a few years because no seed is formed.

In the lower Mississippi valley, where it succeeds best, Lespedeza may be grazed until June and still make a hay crop, or cut in August and the aftermath used for pasture.

660. Hay. — Only in the lower Mississippi valley, where Lespedeza grows tall, is it much cut for hay. It is commonly harvested with an ordinary mowing machine, but is seldom cut for hay if less than 8 inches tall. The plants contain but little water, so the hay cures more readily than any other cultivated legume and nearly as easily as timothy.

Owing to the dense stands of Lespedeza and the solid stems, it weighs very heavy. If the stand is dense, a height of 8 or 9 inches will yield about 1 ton of hay to the acre; if 12 to 14 inches, approximately 2 tons; and when 24 to 30 inches high, 4 tons to the acre.

Probably the best time to cut Lespedeza for hay is when it is in full bloom, but as the weather conditions in the fall are usually better, it is mostly cut in October.

Dodson at the Louisiana Experiment Station compared Lespedeza hay protected from rain with that which had been subjected to various weather conditions, in two cases being rained upon twice. So far as chemical analyses show, practically no loss resulted, but rains do injure the appearance of the hay as well as its palatability.

661. Seed-production. — Seed of Lespedeza is mainly harvested in Louisiana. It is conveniently cut with a mowing machine having a bunching attachment. The cutting should take place when the seeds are ripe or nearly ripe, but the plants still green. Care is necessary in handling to avoid undue shattering, and the straw must be thoroughly dry before it is thrashed.

The seed crop produced by the dwarfer plants on poorer lands is often as large as that produced on better soils. Such a seed crop is best harvested by means of an iron pan attached behind the cutter bar of the mower, the top of the pan being covered by wires or a perforated sheet of galvanized iron to keep out trash. Sometimes such a pan is used in cutting tall Lespedeza, and in this way the best and ripest seed which otherwise would be lost is secured.

The yield of seed to the acre ranges from 5 to 12 bushels, and one bushel of clean, unhulled seed weighs about 25 pounds. One pound contains about 370,000 seeds.

FLORIDA VELVET BEAN (*Stizolobium deeringianum*)

662. Description and history. — The Florida velvet bean is a vigorous-growing bean-like vine, introduced into Florida previous to 1875. It is an annual, with much-branched twining stems, which under favorable conditions may attain a length of from 30 to 50 feet, usually growing to about half this length. The leaves are trifoliolate with large, membranaceous leaflets shorter than the petiole. The leaflets are ovate, the lateral ones oblique, and each is attached to a short pubescent stalk. The flowers are dark purple in long pendent racemes. The matured pods are about two inches long, turgid, somewhat constricted between the seeds, and covered with a soft, nearly black velvety pubescence. Each pod contains three to five, marbled brown and gray seeds.

The velvet bean will rarely mature its pods as far north as Washington, D.C. As the pods constitute the most valuable part of the plant, it is of importance only where these will become mature, which area includes Florida and the southern portions of Georgia, Alabama, Mississippi and Louisiana.

663. Utilization. — On account of the long vines and the tangled mass of herbage which it produces, the velvet bean is not a satisfactory hay plant, as it can be cut and cured only with great difficulty. On this account, it is utilized mainly as a pasturage, the stock being turned into the field in the fall after the pods have matured, as cattle will eat not only the pods but also the dry leaves which have fallen to the ground. It is fed mainly to cattle, but hogs also thrive upon it. Owing to the very viny nature of the plants, it is necessary to grow it in conjunction with some supporting crop; otherwise but a comparatively few pods are produced. Among the supporting crops that can be used are corn, pearl millet, and sorghums. Of these, corn is the best, especially the strong-growing varieties. Various methods of planting are used. When planted alone, the velvet bean should be planted after the ground has been thoroughly worked, so as to obtain one plant about every five feet each way. This requires about 12 pounds of seed to the acre. When planted with corn or other supporting crops, various plans are used. The beans may be planted in the same row with the corn, but under such conditions practically no corn is secured. Another method is to put the corn in successive rows and plant the velvet beans in the middle. Still another method is to plant two or three rows of corn to each row of velvet bean. The maximum yields of beans is secured where the plants are supported on poles or trellises, but this is not practicable where it is designed to pasture the crop.

664. Other species of Stizolobium. — Recent investigations have disclosed the fact that in the countries surrounding the Indian Ocean, there are numerous species of stizolobium closely related to the velvet bean. Most of these have been recently introduced and are being tested in comparison with the Florida velvet bean. Among the most important are the Lyon bean (*Stizolobium niveum*), differing from the Florida velvet bean in having white flowers and white seeds, and nearly smooth pods which, however, shatter readily when they become mature; the Chinese velvet bean, differing from the Lyon bean only in being much earlier, maturing its seeds as far north

2 N

as Washington, D.C., and the Yokohama bean (*Stizolobium hassjoo*) from Japan, the earliest and least vigorous of all the species, readily maturing its seeds as far north as Maryland and Kansas. Unfortunately the pods shatter quite readily and also rot where they lie in contact with the ground.

The most desirable type of the velvet bean would be one that is comparatively early, and relatively bushy in type, whose seeds would not shatter, and whose pods would not rot when lying in contact with the wet ground. At the Florida Experiment Station, hybrids have been made between the Florida velvet bean and the Lyon bean, which have given rise to numerous forms. From these, it seems very probable that much improved varieties will be secured, even if the ideal is not reached. Many of these hybrids resemble in some of their characteristics other species, and it is possible that all the species of cultivated stizolobiums are forms of a single species.

OTHER CROPS

665. Peanut (*Arachis hypogœa*). — The peanut is in all probability a native of South America. It is also known as ground nut, earth nut, goober, and pindar. The plant is cultivated primarily for its seeds for use as human food, but the herbage is nearly always saved for hay, and sometimes the whole crop is utilized by pasturing to hogs.

The peanut is adapted only to regions with long hot summers. In the United States it succeeds best south of 36°. The plant does well both on sandy and clay soils, but as the young pods must burrow into the ground to develop, peanuts are rarely planted except on sandy or silty soils. The principal producing states were, in order of their acreage in 1909, North Carolina, Georgia, Virginia, Florida and Alabama.

The varieties most cultivated are the following: Virginia Bunch, Virginia Runner, Tennessee Red, Valencia, and Spanish. All of these have decumbent branches except Spanish.

Peanuts are planted in late spring after the ground is thoroughly warmed. They are usually planted in rows 28 to 36 inches wide and 9 to 16 inches apart in the row, depending on the variety. The Spanish variety may be planted more closely than others, and on this account, as well as its erect habit, is practically the only one used where the entire crop is to be used for hay.

Peanuts are usually harvested by piling the vines in tall, narrow cocks about a stake with cross pieces near the base. When thoroughly cured, the nuts are removed and the straw used as fodder. The yield of fodder ranges from about 1500 to 3000 pounds or very rarely 4000 pounds to the acre.

If grown for forage, the same method is commonly used, but sometimes the tops are cut and cured for hay, and hogs then turned in the field to feed on the pods. As a hay plant the peanut cannot compete with the cowpea and the soybean, but as a crop to be pastured by hogs it has considerable importance.

Peanuts are not infrequently used as pasture to fatten hogs. From hogs thus fattened the famous Smithfield hams are made. Bennett, at the Arkansas Experiment Station, pastured pigs on peanuts and on chufas in comparison with penned animals fed corn. The pigs on peanuts showed a gain of $104\frac{1}{2}$ pounds a pig; on chufas 66 pounds; and on corn $112\frac{1}{2}$ pounds. Duggar, at the Alabama Experiment Station, found that one acre of peanuts would give pasturage for 1 month to about 25 pigs weighing 100 pounds each. In comparison with chufas, rape, cowpeas and sorghum, it was estimated that to make one pound of gain the pigs required in addition to the pasturage grain as follows: 1.77 pounds when on peanuts; 2.3 pounds when on chufas; 3.07 pounds when on cowpeas; 2.68 pounds when on rape; and 3.7 pounds when on sorghum.

666. Florida beggarweed (*Desmodium tortuosum* or *Meibomia tortuosa*). — Florida beggarweed is a native of the West Indies, but has been known in Florida at least since 1833. It is an erect annual with rather woody stalks from 3 to 10 feet high, bearing an abundant leafage above, and when in flower tipped with much-branched erect panicles, the ascending lateral branches being often 8 to 12 inches long. The seeds are borne in many-jointed prickly pods, which break apart at maturity and are carried about by sticking to the bodies of animals or the clothing of persons. The plant is hairy throughout, and has trifoliolate leaves, the obliquely rhomboid leaflets being from 2 to 4 inches long. Florida beggarweed is adapted only to the warmer parts of the Southern States, being grown especially on the sandy lands of the coastal plain from North Carolina to Texas. It is useful as a soil renovator and makes a fine quality of hay that is relished by all classes of farm stock. Beggarweed seems never to be attacked either by nematodes or root rot.

For a crop of seed, beggarweed should be sown at the rate of 5 or 6 pounds of clean seed to the acre. If grown for hay, from 8 to 10 pounds should be used. It should not be sown until the ground is warm and moist, and clean seed is preferable to the pods because of the more uniform germination and better stand which may be obtained.

If sown at the beginning of the summer rains, the seed need not be covered. It must not be covered too deeply, else the young plants will not be able to reach the surface. By sowing at the beginning of the summer two crops may be secured in Florida.

If cut for hay when the first flowers appear, the stubble will send up a second crop, which may be saved for seed, and enough seed will scatter to insure a crop next season. On very rich ground 4 cuttings in one season with a total yield of 4630 pounds to the acre were obtained at Charleston, South Carolina. The seed may also be scattered in the corn rows at the time of the last cultivation or at the beginning of the rains in June. Then, after the corn has been stripped or cut for fodder, the beggar-weed may be mown for hay or harvested for seed. The crop should be cut for hay when it is about 3 or 4 feet high, or at the beginning of the blooming period. If cut after full bloom, many of the lower leaves will have fallen and much of the best part of the crop will be lost.

Hulled seed is now commercial, being produced wholly in Florida.

667. The jackbean (*Canavalia ensiformis*). — The jackbean is a bushy, semi-erect annual plant, growing to a height of 2 to 4 feet. Its stems are rather coarse and become woody toward the base. The rather thickish leaves have a decidedly bitter taste. The flowers are purple, borne near the base of the stem, so that most of the pods hang low. When mature, the pods are hard and firm, 9 to 14 inches long, each containing 10 to 14 seeds. These are pure white, with a brown hilum. The plant will withstand much drought, and is remarkably free from insects and fungous diseases, but is affected by root-knot.

The jackbean is a native of the West Indies and the

adjacent mainland. In Jamaica, whence it first became well known, it is called the horse bean or the overlook bean. In this country it has been designated the Pearson bean, and recently the Wonder bean. Owing to confusion with the similar species cultivated in Japan, China and India, it has also been called the sword bean and the knife bean, but those names properly belong to the Asiatic species (*Canavalia gladiata*), used principally as a vegetable.

In the last 25 years, the jackbean has several times attracted attention on account of its vigorous growth and large yield of pods and seeds. It was extensively tested at the Mississippi Agricultural Experiment Station during the years 1890 to 1895. Under field conditions yields of 30 to 40 bushels of beans to the acre were obtained, even when grown on thin soil. Attempts were made to utilize these beans as feed for both beef and dairy cattle, but the beans were found to be both unpalatable and indigestible.

Seeds of the bean were distributed by P. Pearson, of Starkville, Mississippi, from which fact it became known as the Pearson bean. At the Texas Agricultural Experiment Station it produced 35 bushels to the acre. At the North Carolina Agricultural Experiment Station it produced an estimated yield of 40 bushels to the acre. It was also tested at the Louisiana Experiment Station. None of these stations regarded the bean as promising, but, so far as recorded, no attempt was made to utilize either the herbage or the seeds as forage. More recently the plant has been tested in Hawaii, and favorable reports as to its forage value have been published.

The value of the plant as forage is yet problematical. Its successful utilization as green feed in Hawaii encourages the belief that it may be found equally valuable in this country, especially in Texas and Oklahoma, where its great drought resistance gives it particular promise. There is also the probability that the jackbean may prove to be valuable for silage. Its coarse habit and heavy tonnage should adapt it well to this purpose.

The large yield of seed to the acre justifies further experiments to determine whether any means can be devised to utilize the seeds profitably as feed, which the work of the Mississippi Agricultural Experiment Station indicates is a difficult problem.

668. Mung bean (*Phaseolus aureus*). — The mung bean is native to southern Asia. It is probably a plant of very ancient culture, as it is grown by the natives throughout the southern half of Asia and the principal Malayan Islands as well as on the eastern coast of Africa. In these countries the mung bean is grown mainly for the seed which is an important article of human food, but in India the straw is also prized as forage for live stock.

The habit of the mung bean is very similar to that of the cowpea, but the plants are less viny and some are strictly bush. The adaptations of the plant are also practically identical with that of the cowpea. The plant was introduced into American agriculture as early as 1835 when it was known as the Chickasaw pea, and somewhat later it was called the Oregon pea under the erroneous idea that it came from that region. Notwithstanding its wide testing thus early in the Southern States and much testing in recent years with numerous varieties, the mung bean has not been able to find a place in American agriculture in competition with the cowpea. The reasons for this are mainly that the pods continue to be formed and ripen until frost, and they shatter very readily. In countries where labor is cheap and the pods are picked promptly as they ripen, this is not a serious objection to their culture.   The seeds also are very much attacked by the cowpea weevil, perhaps more so than any other legume seeds.

The culture of the mung bean is essentially the same as that of the cowpea, but it is preferable to plant in cultivated rows as the young plants do not compete with weeds as well as does the cowpea.   If cut for hay, this should be done as soon as the first pods begin to turn black in ripening.

The varieties are very numerous, differing in size, habit, earliness and the shape and color of the seeds. These are spherical in most varieties, green, brown or marbled.   The variety recently known as the Newman bean is undoubtedly the same as the old Chickasaw pea, and this variety has become spontaneous in portions of South Carolina.   The Newman bean is very late, strictly erect, reaching a height of 3½ feet and barely maturing seeds at Arlington Farm, Virginia.

669. Urd (*Phaseolus mungo*). — The urd is very closely related to the mung bean, but it differs in its procumbent habit, in its shorter, more hairy pods, and in its oblong green or mottled seeds which have a concave hilum.   The urd is probably native to India, in which country it is extensively grown for human food.   As a hay crop it is inferior to the mung bean on account of its procumbent habits which make it difficult to mow.   The largest and latest varieties, however, make a dense mass of herbage, a single plant covering an area 3 feet square and reaching a height of 20 to 30 inches.   One of these late varieties is used as a green-manure crop in the West Indies under the name of Woolly Pyrol.   There is hardly any likelihood of the urd becoming of agricultural value in the Southern States, as it can scarcely compete with the cowpea, except perhaps in Florida as a green-manure crop. Unfortunately, however, all of the varieties seem much subject to the attack of nematodes.

670. Moth bean (*Phaseolus aconitifolius*). — The moth-bean is an annual legume, native of India, where it is grown principally for its seeds, which are used as human food. In habit it forms mats 2 to 3 feet in diameter and 12 to 18 inches high, with very numerous viny branches, the lower ones lying prostrate on the ground. The leaves have three leaflets, each divided into 3 to 5 narrow segments. This bean has proved to be exceedingly well adapted to the conditions in northern Texas, where in many ways it is superior to the cowpea. The prostrate habit and immense amount of foliage enable it to cover the ground so completely that there is practically no evaporation of water from the soil. The very viny branches and the persistency with which the leaves are held make an unusually fine quality of hay, which stock of all kinds eat greedily. No difficulty has been found in mowing this plant if cultivated in rows, as is usually necessary in semi-arid regions, if the mower be started under the first plant.

The yield to the acre during the three years in which it was under trial averaged about 2 tons, fully equal to that of the cowpea. Under favorable conditions the pods are produced in large numbers and show no tendency to shatter. The roots are remarkably well provided with tubercles, indicating that the plant is a very efficient nitrogen gatherer. So far as can be ascertained in limited experience with it, it is somewhat more drought resistant than the cowpea, with which crop it will necessarily compete agriculturally. It seems reasonably certain that this plant will become of considerable use in southwestern Kansas, western Oklahoma and northern Texas. Where the rainfall is greater, comparative experiments indicate that the cowpea is distinctively preferable.

The methods employed in growing cowpeas are satisfactory for the moth bean. The crop should be planted in rows from 2½ to 3 feet apart, with plants every 2 to 3 inches. This requires from 5 to 6 pounds of seed to the acre. Owing to the thick mat of vines produced, the crop can be easily harvested with a mower by setting the cutter bar low. At least two cultivations should be given and the surface soil left as smooth as possible, so as to facilitate harvesting. The crop should not be harvested until it has made its maximum growth. The mass of green forage can best be cured in windrows and later hauled and stored without putting into cocks.

671. Adzuki bean (*Phaseolus angularis*). — The adzuki bean is probably native to eastern Asia, but the wild plant is not known. It is extensively cultivated in Manchuria, Korea and Japan, and is rarely found in the hill country of northern India. In Japan about 350,000 acres are grown annually. It is readily distinguished from the mung bean, to which it is closely related, by the pods and seeds. The seeds of this species are about the size of an average garden pea, but are oblong in shape, and red, cream, orange or mottled in color. The pods are mostly pale colored and smooth, resembling small cowpea pods, while those of the mung bean are dark colored, smaller, and hairy. This bean resembles an upright cowpea in its habits of growth, but the stems are not as large and hardly as woody. It is adapted to essentially the same conditions as the soybean.

In Japan and Manchuria the adzuki bean is grown

entirely for human food, and as a producer of seed it excels any other bean adapted to the region in which it will grow, excepting the soybean. On account of its heavy yield of seed it is likely to become of some importance in the United States, either for human food or for growing to feed animals. The plants are smaller than cowpeas or soybeans, so the yield of herbage is but moderate.

The adzuki bean does not compete satisfactorily with weeds and therefore must be planted in cultivated rows which may be from 18 inches to 3 feet apart, depending on the variety and the method of cultivation. The earliest varieties mature in about 90 days, while the latest varieties require 140 days.

672. Bonavist or hyacinth bean (*Dolichos lablab*). — This bean is probably a native of Africa, but has been cultivated since ancient, perhaps prehistoric, times in southern Asia, as well as in Africa. The ripe seeds, as well as the green pods, are used for human food.

The bonavist is an annual except in the tropics, where it may persist two years or more. In a general way it resembles the cowpea, but the stems are harder, and the plant more viny, but when supported, often grows to a height of 20 to 25 feet. The flowers are sweet scented and borne in panicles, 4 to 18 inches long; the much-compressed pods are shaped like a broad scimitar and the seeds have a conspicuous white caruncle extending one-third of their circumference.

The varieties are numerous, at least 30, and differ in earliness; color of foliage, green or purple; color of flowers, white, pink or purple; size, shape and color of the pods and seeds, the latter being white, reddish, black or speckled. The varieties with purple foliage are often grown as ornamentals. One variety with white, waxy pods is excellent as a vegetable.

The adaptations of the bonavist are practically identical with those of the cowpea, and it may be cultivated by identical methods. When grown in fields for hay, they have given very promising results in southern Kansas and northern Texas, being at least equal to cowpeas in yield and palatability. Some varieties are heavy seed producers, yielding about as much as cowpeas. The habit of all the varieties is very much more viny than cowpeas, in a general way being intermediate between cowpeas and velvet beans. When grown in Virginia with corn for silage or with sorghum for hay, they have outyielded cowpeas, the vines being much more rapid growers. There are two possible objections to them, however. The vines grow very much more rapidly than the cornstalks and tend to bind the rows of corn together, and there is also a much larger mass of herbage covering the ground than in the case of cowpeas, much of which cannot be saved in harvesting.

In Cuba this bean has been considered superior to the cowpea. Like many other legumes, however, the bonavist is susceptible both to the root-knot caused by nematodes and to wilt, although it is possible that varieties resistant to these diseases may be found, as has been the case with the cowpea. At the present time, however, the bonavist offers no particular promise throughout the cotton region except in Texas. In drought resistance it is at least equal to the cowpea and apparently somewhat superior. In all respects it will have to meet the cowpea in competition, and it still remains to be determined whether in any part of the country it will be sufficiently superior to the cowpea to warrant its general culture. The roots are remarkably well provided with tubercles; indeed, in this respect far surpassing the cowpea.

673. Guar (*Cyamopsis tetragonoloba*). — Guar is an annual, native of India, where it has long been cultivated to a limited extent. The plant is grown both for green forage and for the seed, which according to Duthie is used mainly to fatten cattle.

The plants are stiff and erect, simple stemmed or with comparatively few branches, and 3 to 6 feet high. The leaves are trifoliolate and angularly toothed. The small flowers are numerous in short erect axillary racemes. The pods are flat, 1½ to 2 inches long, and about 7-seeded.

Guar is adapted to about the same general conditions as the cowpea, but it does not ripen its seed in northern Virginia. It is especially characterized by its remarkable drought resistance. At Chico, California, a fine crop was produced without a drop of rain falling upon it from the time it was planted until nearly ready to harvest. During the whole season these plots showed no suffering whatever from the drought, which seriously affected adjoining plots of Kafir corn and sorghum. Similarly marked drought resistance was shown at San Antonio, Texas.

Guar is very prolific, a single plant grown at Chico producing 260 pods. The yield in India is stated to be about 13 bushels to the acre, but small plots in this country have shown a considerably greater yield.

There are many varieties, some of them with single stems; others branched from the base. The upright-growing varieties are preferable, at least from a seed-producing standpoint. Some of the varieties have much larger seeds than others, and on this account are more desirable.

In regard to its palatability to live stock, the evidence

is thus far somewhat conflicting. At the Oklahoma Experiment Station the cattle ate the straw readily after the seeds had been thrashed out, notwithstanding that it was decidedly coarse and the leaves had fallen. Most experimenters report that their mules and cows eat it as well as cowpeas. G. A. Schattenberg, of Boerne, Texas, found that his sheep ate it readily, and he regards it as an exceedingly valuable plant for pasture. A few experimenters have had less satisfactory experiences, in some cases the animals absolutely refusing to eat it. The mixed results would lead to the belief that most animals will acquire a taste for it, as animals commonly refuse a new forage at first. Its use in India certainly confirms this idea.

CHAPTER XXIV

MISCELLANEOUS PERENNIAL LEGUMES

THERE are parts of America to which none of the perennial clovers or alfalfa are well adapted and for which a good perennial legume is greatly to be desired. This need is greatest in the South. In Europe sainfoin, kidney vetch, and other perennials have been profitably employed, but none of these seems to possess much value for America. Among recently exploited crops of this class, kudzu is probably the most promising.

SAINFOIN (*Onobrychis viciæfolia*)

674. Description. — Sainfoin is also known as esparcet or esparsette. A synonym of its botanical name is *Onobrychis sativa* Lam. It occurs wild in most of the southern half of Europe and eastward to Lake Baikal. About twelve botanical varieties have been described from Europe, but none of these has come into agricultural use.

Sainfoin is a very long-lived, deep-rooted perennial. It is stated by Lawson that plants may live 100 years. The root may reach a diameter of 2 inches and extend to a depth of 20 feet or more. From the branched crown arise numerous stout, erect stems which reach a height of 1 to 2 feet. The leaves are odd-pinnate with 13 to 15 leaflets. The rose-colored (rarely white) flowers are in an erect, close raceme 2 to 5 inches long. The one-seeded pods are brown, indehiscent, lenticular and reticulated on the surface.

675. Agricultural history. — The culture of sainfoin probably dates back about 400 years. It was first cultivated in southern France, the first definite record according to Vianne being in 1582. Its culture was first described in 1629. It was grown in Germany in the seventeenth century, but not in Italy until the eighteenth century.

Its spread over Europe had a very marked effect inasmuch as it led to the profitable cultivation of much dry calcareous land, which before had been nearly valueless. Its culture has been largely restricted to chalky or other calcareous soils, particularly where subject to drought. In a general way, its distribution is nearly the same as that of the grape in Europe, but it does well in places too cool for grape culture.

Sainfoin has never attained any agricultural importance in America, though it has often been tested. It would seem, however, that on some calcareous soils its culture might become profitably established.

676. Culture. — Sainfoin is usually grown in pure cultures, the seed being sown at the rate of 120 to 150 pounds to the acre if drilled, more if broadcasted. Commercial seed is in the hull, and this germinates better than the hulled seed. The seed should be sown with a drill a half-inch or more deep, or else well harrowed after broadcasting. It is usually sown in spring with a nurse crop. Fall sowings are apt to winter-kill.

Usually but one cutting of hay is obtained each season, mowed during bloom, which lasts about one week. Under favorable conditions a second smaller cutting may be secured, but this as a rule is only half as large as the first, so that it is generally pastured. Sainfoin has never been known to cause bloating. The yield of hay varies from 1800 to 6000 pounds to the acre, on the average about 3000 pounds. The yield is as a rule best in the fourth year.

On poor soils fields are reported to last 15 to 22 years. On good soils, however, the better practice is to allow the fields to stand 4 to 7 years, and then not plant sainfoin again for an equal length of time, as soils become " sick " to sainfoin in a manner analogous to " clover sick " soils.

677. Seed. — Commercial seed of sainfoin is nearly always in the hull. Fresh seed should germinate 98 per cent and have a purity of 80 per cent. The seed loses its viability rapidly, so that after one year it is valueless. On this account the commercial seed is often very low in viability. After planting the seed is slow to germinate, requiring 2 to 3 weeks before it has all sprouted.

The seed is all grown in Europe, the average yield being stated as about 500 pounds to the acre.

678. American data. — Sainfoin has been tested in a small way at most of the American experiment stations, but nowhere on the continent has it become established as a crop. Long before the days of experiment stations, sainfoin had been frequently tested by farmers, and there are many references to it in early American agricultural literature. Fields have often been planted in the irrigated lands of the West, but neither under such conditions nor on the unirrigated lands has it yielded as heavily as alfalfa. Under irrigation the average yield for 2 years at the Utah Experiment Station was but 2000 pounds to the acre, much less than either red clover or alfalfa. Without irrigation but one early cutting was secured.

At the Ontario Agricultural College an average yield of 12 tons green matter to the acre has been secured from

2 o

spring sowings. In one case the plants survived in a plot for 8 to 10 years.

At the Central Experimental Farm, Ottawa, Canada, sainfoin has given the most favorable results reported in America. A plot sown May 14 was cut August 12 and yielded 3700 pounds hay to the acre; the next year it was cut twice, the yields being respectively 4200 and 5400 pounds of hay to the acre. During three years the annual yields in hay to the acre were respectively 7160, 9160 and 13,398 pounds. The yield in the third year was larger than that of any other of 18 hay crops, either single or in mixtures.

OTHER PERENNIAL LEGUMES

679. Sulla or Spanish sainfoin (*Hedysarum coronarium*) is a perennial legume native to the Mediterranean region of Europe and north Africa, where its culture is locally important in Spain, Sicily, Malta and southern France. Its culture was recorded in Italy in 1766, but it is probably still older. The plant has deep roots; ascending stems 1 to 3 feet long; pinnate leaves with 3 to 5 pairs of oval, obtuse, pale leaflets; flowers numerous in erect racemes; pods flattened, constricted between the circular joints.

The ordinary variety has red flowers and under favorable conditions grows 4 to 5 feet high. Another variety with white flowers grows less tall. In Algeria there is said to be a red-flowered, biennial variety.

Sulla is especially adapted to deep soils, especially if calcareous, but will grow on any deep, fertile, well-drained soils. It is commonly planted in the spring, and thus sown, will yield on dry soil one cutting the first season and thereafter two. Under irrigation three or more cuttings may be obtained.

The seed germinates poorly, much of it being hard, but

it is said that after immersing it 5 minutes in boiling water a germination of 95 per cent may be obtained. The seed costs about 25 cents per pound.

Fields are usually left 3 years or more and may yield as high as 5 tons of hay per season.

Fairly satisfactory results with sulla have been secured in southern Texas with irrigation, but under such conditions it cannot compete with alfalfa. At the Massachusetts Experiment Station it is said to have lived for several years.

680. Kudzu (*Pueraria thunbergiana*) is a woody, leguminous vine native to Japan. The leaves resemble in a general way those of the common bean, but they are larger and angularly lobed, besides being tougher in texture; the stems and leaf stalks are somewhat hairy. As far north as Maryland the vine will bloom, but only occasionally, and then late in the fall. The blossoms are dull purple-red in pendent racemes, but a white-flowered variety is said to occur in Japan. The pods are thin, very hairy and do not mature in the latitude of Washington, D.C.

Kudzu is remarkable for its very rapid growth during the warm weather of midsummer. It succeeds well in the humid eastern part of the United States, and will grow in almost any type of soil. It succeeds best, however, with an abundance of heat and moisture. Kudzu is a most excellent vine for arbors and porches, for which purpose it is grown in most of the southern cities, climbing to a height of 60 feet or more. It survives winter as far north as Nova Scotia.

Kudzu was probably first introduced in the United States in 1876, when it was grown at the Centennial Exposition in Philadelphia. It is only recently, however, that it has created interest as a forage crop, due largely to the work of C. E. Pleas of Chipley, Florida. Attracted by the remarkable luxuriance of the plant and the fact that horses and cows ate the leaves greedily, he cured some as hay and found it equally palatable to animals. He then planted a small field, probably the first of the kind ever planted in this country. Under field conditions kudzu sends out long prostrate branches which root at many of the joints And send up ascending twining branches to a height of 2 to 4 feet. Eventually these become separate plants as the prostrate stems usually die between the rooted joints. Such a field when full grown presents much the appearance of a thick field of cowpeas or soybeans. It can be readily cut with a mower, and the hay cures more readily than most legumes, as the leaves are less juicy. There is practically no shedding of the leaves in curing.

Some fields in northern Florida have yielded three cuttings of hay a season when well established, and yields of as high as 10 tons to the acre have been claimed. In other fields the total yield has been smaller than that of velvet beans. It seems probable that under favorable conditions kudzu will prove a very profitable crop, notwithstanding the fact that its perennial nature does not permit of growing a winter crop in rotation.

The seed of kudzu does not germinate very well, so that the plant is usually propagated by layers. A new field of kudzu is best established by the transplanting of well-rooted plants in very early spring. These should be planted about 10 feet apart each way, and the first season will pretty well cover the ground with prostrate runners. The second season a fair crop should be obtained, but the field will not produce best results till the third year. The planting should be done early in the spring, but in the extreme south may be done at any time during the winter. To avoid the loss of land the first season, corn may be planted after setting out the kudzu, and the two do not interfere with each other.

The culture of kudzu is still in an experimental stage, but for permanent hay fields, especially in the South, it is likely to become of considerable importance. Small experimental plots at the Kentucky and Alabama Experiment Stations, as well as at Arlington Farm, Virginia, have given promising results. At the Florida Experiment Station the plot yields have thus far not been as satisfactory as those of velvet beans.

681. Flat pea (*Lathyrus silvestris* var. *wagneri*) is a native of most of Europe and the Caucasus region of Asia. The cultivated variety was first domesticated by Wagner in 1862 from the Carpathian Mountains, Austria. The wild plant was unpalatable and the seeds very hard, but Wagner was able to improve the plant by selection in both these respects. Since 1878 the plant has been much discussed, and at times very extravagant claims made for it.

The plant is a long-lived perennial closely allied to the old perennial sweet pea of the gardens. The stems are wing-margined, weak and reclining without support, becoming 3 to 6 feet long; leaves with a single pair of lanceolate leaflets, and branched tendrils; flowers pink, 3 to 10 in a loose raceme.

It grows but slowly at first and usually does not bloom till the second year. In Germany the green plant is said to be eaten readily by horses and swine.

The flat pea has been tested at many of the American experiment stations, but by none has the plant been commended nor has it won for itself a place in American agriculture. When once established it may persist for years. At the Michigan Experiment Station one acre yielded in its second year two cuttings; the first cutting, June 29, weighed 23,997 pounds green and 5431 pounds dry; the second cutting, September 16, weighed 17,188 pounds green and 3636 pounds dry — a total yield of 20.5 tons of green matter and 4.5 tons dry hay. Cattle ate the green forage readily.

At the Vermont Experiment Station the second year's crop was 6¾ tons green matter or 1¾ tons hay to the acre, and the third year's crop fully as large.

At the Pennsylvania Experiment Station, flat peas gave in two years an average yield to the acre of 17,700 pounds green herbage of 3700 pounds of hay, but the crop is not recommended, because of the difficulty of securing a stand, and its unpalatability.

The flat pea has nowhere in America attained any definite status as a field crop, but where a long-lived perennial legume is needed in the Northern States, probably no other species is better adapted to the purpose.

682. Kidney vetch (*Anthyllis vulneraria*) is native to much of temperate Europe, Asia and North Africa. It was first brought into cultivation in Prussia about 1859. Two varieties are cultivated, one with pale yellow and the other with reddish flowers, but otherwise they scarcely differ.

The plant is a perennial with roots 3 feet or more long. The basal leaves are simple, but the cauline are pinnate. The stems are stout and erect, not at all viny as in the true vetches, to which it is not closely related.

Kidney vetch is most important on sandy and calcareous soils in North Germany, but is grown to some extent in other European countries. It is especially valuable where clover and other legumes do not thrive. In all respects it is cultivated much like red clover, being sown in Germany in fall with a grain crop. The plants grow so slowly that there is but little fall pasturage after the grain crop is removed. Thereafter it yields moderate hay crops for two years; if pastured, it lasts 3 to 4 years. Usually but one hay crop a year can be obtained, and the aftermath is very small. Kidney vetch is, however, rarely sown alone but in mixtures, and is better adapted for pastures than for meadows. Both as pasturage and as hay, kidney vetch is more readily eaten by sheep than by other animals. It seems never to cause bloating.

The harvesting of the seed is rather difficult, as, if cut too green, it will not thrash out, and if too ripe, it shatters much. The plants usually die after seed harvest. The seed yield varies from 350 to 700 pounds an acre. A bushel weighs 60 to 64 pounds, and one pound contains 126,000 to 182,000 seeds, according to Stebler.

Kidney vetch is usually sown in mixtures, but if sown alone 20 pounds of seed an acre is used. Werner says that the yield of hay on calcareous sand is 5000 to 9000 pounds an acre; on good sandy soil, 3500 to 5000 pounds; and on poor sandy soils, 1800 to 2500 pounds; or on the average about 4000 pounds to the acre.

Kidney vetch has not proved of any particular value under American conditions. The plant is not rarely found in ballast grounds, but nowhere has it become really naturalized. It has been tested in a small way at many American Experiment Stations, but none have recommended it as being promising.

At the Utah Experiment Station it gave a yield of only 1150 pounds of hay to the acre. At the Ontario Agricultural College the average yield for 2 years was 2.6 tons green matter to the acre.

683. Goat's rue (*Galega officinalis*) is native from southeast Europe to Persia, and came into agricultural use in Germany in the latter part of the eighteenth century. It seems never to have been much grown, and is not now important except in special localities. Goat's rue has succeeded well in small trials at many places in the United States, but has never come into agricultural use.

The plant is a deep-rooted perennial with abundant stout stems three to four feet high, each terminated by a raceme of pale violet flowers, but white-flowered and rose-flowered varieties occur. The leaves are numerous and pinnately compound.

Two cuttings are obtained under favorable conditions in Europe, and this has also been the experience at Arlington Farm, Virginia. The plant is too coarse to make good hay, and so is used mainly for soiling. In good soil, the yield of green substance is said to equal that of alfalfa. It is usually sown in spring, and is best grown in cultivated rows, never in mixtures. The seeds are rather large, one pound containing 62,000, and 22 pounds an acre is the rate of seeding. The Utah Experiment Station records yields of 4490 pounds of hay to the acre.

One instance in France is recorded where 54 sheep died and 84 were badly affected from eating goat's rue. In further tests it was found that 7 pounds of the plant would kill a sheep.

684. Bird's-foot trefoil (*Lotus corniculatus*) is native to much of temperate Europe and Asia. It is a low-growing perennial with a stout root and bearing numerous slender, ascending or spreading branches 6 to 18 inches long. The leaves bear five small leaflets. The bright yellow, showy flowers are in umbels of 2 to 6.

In northern Europe bird's-foot trefoil is considered

a valuable constituent in pasture lands, and is sometimes sown in hay mixtures, but it is too small to be of much value for such purpose.

Bird's-foot trefoil has succeeded well enough in trials in nearly all the humid portions of the United States, except the extreme south, but its growth is too small to warrant its cultivation, and it has not shown any aggressiveness in becoming established. It is nowhere really naturalized in North America.

The seed weighs 60 pounds to the bushel and 11 pounds to the acre is seeded, if sown alone. It is expensive to harvest, and this has perhaps prevented the greater use of the plant.

Two varieties of *Lotus corniculatus* are also utilized agriculturally and sold by seedsmen; namely, var. *tenuifolius* with narrow leaves, and var. *villosus* with pubescent foliage. Another species, *Lotus uliginosus*, is also offered by seedsmen, and not infrequently under the name *villosus*, according to Stebler.

685. Astragalus falcatus is native to the Caucasus region and utilized to a small extent in Europe for forage, especially in Russia and France. It is a deep-rooted, long-lived perennial; leaves pinnate with 15 to 20 pairs of leaflets; flowers yellowish in a spike-like panicle. This species is very hardy and probably will withstand as severe conditions as alfalfa. In France it is said not to be able to compete with alfalfa on good soil, but to be valuable on poor, dry lands. It begins its growth very early in spring, and in France may be cut three times. It is mostly fed green, and animals eat it readily.

This astragalus has grown well at Arlington Farm, Virginia; Pullman, Washington; and Akron, Colorado. Well-grown plants become a foot or more in diameter and 2 to

2½ feet high.   The commercial seed is not high priced, but much of it is " hard " and does not germinate.   The crop is worthy of further investigation in connection with dry farming.

686. Furze (*Ulex europæus*). — Furze or gorse is a spiny leguminous shrub native to northern Europe. The leaves are very small, and with the twigs are evergreen. The handsome yellow blossoms are much ike those of the Scotch broom.

Furze has never been cultivated for forage in America, but it has become established in places along the New England coast, and on the Pacific coast in Washington and British Columbia.   Its adaptation to these regions may in time lead to its utilization for forage.

In Europe it is planted more or less on sandy or rocky land, and the crops either cut and fed green in winter, or browsed with sheep and cattle.   Where cultivated it is cut every year, as the year-old branches become quite woody.

CHAPTER XXV

MISCELLANEOUS HERBS USED AS FORAGE

APART from the grasses and legumes few plants are worth cultivating for forage and none of these is of high importance. Those discussed in this chapter are the best known.

687. Mexican clover (*Richardsonia scabra*) is wrongly named, as it is not clover at all, but belongs to the family *Rubiaceæ*. In Florida and other Southern States it is commonly called purslane or " pusley." Mexican clover is native to Mexico, and now extends along the Gulf coast and throughout Florida. In the latter region there is some question as to whether it is truly native, as it is found almost entirely in cultivated land.

Mexican clover is an annual plant much branched from the base, the weak decumbent stems reaching a length of 1 to 2 feet; leaves opposite, simple, entire; flowers small, pinkish, crowded into close heads.

Mexican clover is a summer annual springing up in cultivated land in spring after the manner of crab-grass. It is especially abundant in sandy land, springing up after cultivation has ceased in hoed crops, or after early crops have been removed. Under favorable conditions it makes a dense mass of herbage 1 foot to nearly 2 feet deep. The plant is rather succulent and not easily cured into hay, but when well cured is readily eaten by farm animals.

The maximum yield of hay is probably about 2 tons to the acre.

Mexican clover may also be used for pasturage, and is readily eaten by most farm animals.

Seed is produced in abundance and can easily be saved, but there is no commercial demand, as the plant when once established volunteers year after year indefinitely. Strictly speaking, it is not a cultivated plant at all, but a useful weed comparable in this respect to crab-grass and bur clover. In the United States it is adapted only to Florida and a relatively narrow region westward to Texas. It succeeds best on sandy soils.

688. Prickly pear (*Opuntia spp.*). — These " pears " are all natives to America. Some of the larger species which grow to a height of from 3 to 6 feet or more and which have flat, oblong or circular joints, have long been utilized for forage. Some of these species, especially those which are nearly spineless, were long ago introduced into northern Africa, where they are grown quite extensively, not only for the fruit but as feed for camels and bullocks. In Texas they have been used as forage, especially during periods of drought, for 50 years or more. In recent years their cultivation for forage has received considerable attention in the United States.

In the United States the larger species of *Opuntia* are well adapted only to southern Texas and California and portions of Arizona and New Mexico. They will withstand a temperature as low as 20° Fahrenheit for a short time, but where the temperature often falls lower their culture is not advisable. The spiny species especially endure periods of drought remarkably well, but to obtain a satisfactory growth under cultivation a good supply of moisture is necessary. The root is comparatively shallow, and without a good supply of soil moisture the growth is exceedingly slow. Prickly pears are like other plants, in that the best growth is secured on the best soils, although the plants will make some growth on any type of soil so long as it is well drained and there is sufficient moisture for growth. All of the species thrive best in regions where there is a season of low moisture supply during which the plants become semi-dormant.

Prickly pears may be propagated either by seed or by plant joints. Propagation by seed is, however, more costly and a longer time must elapse before the plants can be harvested. Griffiths finds that there is considerable difference between plants of the same species grown from seed and propagated from cuttings. The latter tend to be tree-like, while the former are headed on the ground and without distinct trunks. In propagating vegetatively, single joints 1 to 3 years old should be used, as younger joints are not as certain and do not start off as vigorously as the older ones. Old trunks which have lost their joint character are also satisfactory. It is preferable to cut the joints below the articulation. In planting, the best plan is to have the joint covered ½ to ⅔ of its length. In plantings thus far made the plants have been put 3 feet apart in rows 6 feet wide, but with the larger sorts 8-foot rows are probably more advantageous. When thus planted they can be easily cultivated, and better results are secured by cultivating fields often enough to maintain a good tilth and destroy weeds.

The prickly pears can be harvested and fed at any time of the year. Cattle, however, do not like the young joints and there is therefore considerable waste in harvesting the plants while growth is active. In California it has been found inadvisable to harvest them in winter from December to March, as during the cool season the remaining portion of the stem is likely to rot instead of healing over.

Under moderately favorable conditions yields of 20 to 25 tons of green matter to the acre may be obtained.

Prickly pears are readily eaten by cattle, hogs, sheep and goats. The spineless ones may be fed directly, but the spiny sorts require preliminary treatment. The spines may be removed by singeing either with a brush fire or by means of a gasoline torch, or the plants may be chopped into pieces and piled into heaps when the spines become softened so that they do not trouble animals, or the whole plant may be steamed in vats. The feeding value is low, as from 80 to 90 per cent or more of the plant consists of water. Nevertheless, very satisfactory results have been obtained in using prickly pears as roughage feed for dairy and beef cattle as well as for hogs, sheep and goats.

Under Texas conditions some of the spiny sorts have given more satisfactory results than the spineless ones. The latter are more subject to damage by rabbits.

689. Sunflower (*Helianthus annuus*). — The sunflower is native to the western United States, where the wild form often occupies extensive areas. It is an annual with a stout, erect, usually simple stem which becomes woody; alternate ovate petioled leaves; and one or more large half-nodding heads with a black disk and numerous golden-yellow rays. Under cultivation numerous varieties have been developed, some with all the flowers ligulate. The agriculturally valuable sorts are those which produce a single large head, which may be 8 to 12 inches in diameter.

Sunflowers are grown extensively in Russia for the seeds, which are used both for poultry feed and for oil production. In America their culture has not been large, partly from the fact that there are several insects that live naturally in the seeds.

The plants are cultivated much after the manner of corn in rows 28 to 36 inches wide, with the plants a foot apart in the rows.

Sometimes sunflowers are grown thickly and cut for fodder, but the woody nature of the plants makes them undesirable for this purpose.

At the New Hampshire Experiment Station three varieties gave the following yields of heads to the acre: Russian, 23,958 pounds; White Russian, 19,360 pounds; and Grey, 20,812 pounds.

In Ontario they have been grown to some extent as a forage crop, the heads being put into silos with corn. There seems, however, to be no economy in this practice. At the Ontario Agricultural College three varieties have been grown continuously for a period of years, the resulting yield data being as follows: —

VARIETIES	AVERAGE DIAMETER OF 25 HEADS (10 yrs.)	AVERAGE HEIGHT (13 yrs.)	AVERAGE YIELD TO THE ACRE		
			Heads (13 yrs.)	Whole Crop (13 yrs.)	Grain (12 yrs.)
	Inches	*Inches*	*Tons*	*Tons*	*Bushels*
Mammoth Russian	7.29	100	5.97	18.05	74.7
White Beauty . .	7.38	87	5.60	16.18	74.4
Black Giant . .	7.08	107	6.32	22.36	72.0

According to the last census, the total area of cultivated sunflowers in the United States was 4731 acres, which yielded 63,677 bushels of seed. Illinois, with 3979 acres, produced most of the crop; namely, 49,064 bushels.

690. Spurrey (*Spergula sativa*). — Cultivated spurrey has been much confused with the very similar corn spurrey (*Spergula arvensis*). The latter is generally introduced in America as a rather harmless weed in cultivated soil. Common spurrey was cultivated for forage in Europe in 1566 and probably much earlier.

Spurrey is much employed as a catch crop and for green manure on sandy lands in north central Europe, especially France, Belgium, Holland, Germany, Denmark and Russia. It is adapted to a moist, cool growing season, and under such conditions will produce a crop of green fodder 12 to 14 inches high in 7 or 8 weeks. Three crops may thus be grown on the same piece of land in a season, the first being sown as soon as danger of frost is over; or one crop may be grown after a crop of winter grain is harvested and before another is planted. It is often sown with a grain crop in spring, and after it has grown in the stubble, used as pasture. If sown alone, it is cut when in bloom and fed green or cured into hay, the latter being rather difficult, as the plant is quite succulent. The value of spurrey for sandy lands in Europe is so great that some writers have called it the " clover of sandy soils."

Spurrey has often been tested in America, beginning with 1853, but thus far it has been but little used. One crop can be grown in early spring and another in fall if the frosts are not too early. The plant languishes, however, in our hot midsummers, to which it is not adapted. Young plants do not withstand frost, but when well grown ordinary frosts are not injurious.

The most extensive investigations were those conducted on the sandy Jack pine land of Michigan. The results reported were very promising, but the culture of the crop does not seem to have become established. At Grayling,

Michigan, seed yields of 8 to 12 bushels an acre were secured. There is likelihood, however, that spurrey may in time be a useful plant in America on very sandy lands in the Northern States, when economic conditions will justify their development. On better lands it is not likely ever to be used.

In Germany the hay yields are said to be about 6000 pounds and the seed yields 450 to 600 pounds an acre. The straw is nearly as good feed as the hay.

Spurrey has sometimes been condemned as a weed, but such references belong to corn spurrey and not to the cultivated plant. The seed is small, one pound containing 1,350,000. The usual rate of seeding is 15 to 20 pounds to the acre.

Another species, the Giant Spurrey (*Spergula maxima*), has also been cultivated since 1841. This is a larger plant with larger seeds, 740,000 weighing one pound. It reaches its growth in 10 to 12 weeks and ripens its seed in 16 weeks. Unlike common spurrey, this species is adapted to heavier soils rich in lime, and its culture is of much less importance. At the Michigan Upper Peninsula Station, it was sown July 28 and cut September 10, giving a yield of about 3.5 tons hay to the acre.

691. Yarrow (*Achillea millefolium*), in some of its numerous forms, is native throughout the north temperate zone. The plant has the strong odor of chamomile, but cattle and sheep eat it when young. It is a long-lived, deep-rooted perennial; leaves pinnately divided into very fine, numerous segments; heads numerous, small, white-rayed, in a dense flat umbel.

Yarrow will grow in any type of soil if well drained and, because of its persistence, has been used in pasture mixtures for poor, hilly lands in Europe. It will withstand

2 P

heavy trampling and close grazing, and if kept closely clipped on lawns, makes a fine turf. The seed is very small, one pound containing 1,667,000 seeds.

At the Ontario Agricultural College it gave a yield to the acre of 3.5 tons green matter or .9 tons of hay.

692. Sachaline (*Polygonum sachalinense*) is a native of the island of Saghalien. It was introduced into cultivation in 1869 as an ornamental and has been used for this purpose ever since. In 1893 it was considered in France to possess some value as forage, and in the succeeding years was much advertised and extravagant claims made for it.

The plant is a stout perennial herb, spreading by rootstocks, and growing to a height of 6 to 10 feet; the leaves are heart-shaped, and the greenish flowers inconspicuous. Well-established plants produce an abundance of herbage, and this is eaten readily by all farm animals. The habit of the plant adapts it better to green feeding and possibly silage than for dry fodder. In Germany it is said to yield 8 to 16 tons green matter to the acre.

The difficulty with sachaline as a forage crop is that it is troublesome to start, hard stemmed, and does not yield more than corn or sorghum. Its rootstock habit makes it rather difficult to destroy promptly, but it is never troublesome as a weed. Its only practicable use would seem to be to furnish an abundance of green feed from a small area without planting each year.

Sachaline was tested at many of the American experiment stations, but has not commended itself as worthy of culture except as an ornamental. Plants may be started either by seeds or propagated by rootstocks.

693. Burnet (*Sanguisorba minor*) is a native of Europe. It was first cultivated in England about 1760 as a pasture plant, and since that time has been used in England and France. It is a deep-rooted perennial that withstands heavy pasturing, and in England continues to grow during most of the winter. For these reasons it is commonly used in pasture mixtures, especially on poor, dry hills where the soil is calcareous.

On good land, plants will grow 2 feet high, and under such conditions yield as much as 6 tons of green matter to the acre. Burnet is, however, not well adapted to such use.

In America burnet has not yet been found sufficiently valuable to justify cultivation. It has been tested at many experiment stations, but mostly in small plots and not as a pasture plant. From the fact that it has become spontaneous in New England, it may be worthy of more attention as a pasture plant for that region.

At the Utah Experiment Station a small plot yielded hay at the rate of 1567 pounds to the acre.

694. Buckhorn (*Plantago lanceolata*), or narrow-leaved plantain, is a native of Europe, but has become a common weed nearly everywhere in America, having been introduced as an impurity in grass and clover seeds. It is a long-lived perennial which maintains itself firmly on any soil so long as it is well drained. On this account buckhorn has been used more or less in Europe in pasture mixtures for poor hill lands, and to some extent has also been included in hay mixtures. In America it is commonly looked upon as a troublesome weed, especially in alfalfa and red clover. The herbage, however, is readily grazed upon by sheep and cattle and eaten when cured into hay. As a pasture plant it is apparently deserving of more consideration than it has received, especially for thin, stony soils. It is probably never necessary to sow buckhorn, as more or less seed is usually mixed with grass and clover seeds, and where once established the plant spreads abundantly by its seed. While the plant is justly condemned as a troublesome weed in lawns and elsewhere, its value for pasturage should not be overlooked.

695. Prickly comfrey (*Symphytum asperrimum*) is a perennial herb native to the Caucasus region. The plant has a large taproot 8 or 9 feet deep; stems 2 to 4 feet high; leaves oblong, large, rough, sometimes a foot or more long; flowers tubular, bright-blue, nodding in one-sided clusters. The plant is hardy, withstanding the winters in Ontario and succeeding well in most of the United States.

It was introduced into England as early as 1801 as an ornamental, and beginning with 1830 has from time to time been praised as a forage plant, especially to furnish green feed for hogs, sheep and cows.

The seed of prickly comfrey is not very satisfactory, so the plant is usually propagated by divisions of the crown or by sections of the taproot. On rich soil with intensive cultivation prickly comfrey may be cut green from 3 to 6 times in a season, and the yield is said to range from 10 to 50 tons of green matter to the acre. The plants are long-lived and are said to produce abundantly for 15 to 20 years.

The plant has been tested by a number of experiment stations, but has never come into much use in America. Yields have been reported by various American experiment stations in green matter to the acre as follows:—

Ontario Agricultural College, 9¾ tons in 4 cuttings; New York (Geneva), 14 to 16 tons; Vermont, 46 tons; North Carolina, 6½ to 17½ tons; Wisconsin, 33½ tons.

Even with these large yields comfrey can hardly compete

with other forage crops. At the Wisconsin Experiment Station the yield of dry matter to the acre for red clover was 23 per cent greater than that of comfrey. At the New York Experiment Station alfalfa yielded 16 tons of green matter as compared to 14 tons by prickly comfrey. At the Pennsylvania Experiment Station the yield of digestible matter by prickly comfrey was considerably less than that produced by either Kafir corn or cowpeas.

The value of prickly comfrey would seem to be restricted entirely to that of a soilage crop where a large amount of green matter is to be grown on a limited acreage, but even in this respect it is surpassed by other crops. As a silage crop it has been used somewhat, but the product is said to be disagreeable in odor. Animals are somewhat averse to eating comfrey at first, either green or preserved, but soon acquire a taste for it.

696. Australian saltbush (*Atriplex semibaccata*). — This plant is native to alkali lands in Australia, where it has long been recognized as a valuable natural forage for sheep. It was introduced into the United States in the hope that it would be profitable as a crop to grow on lands too alkaline for ordinary crops. This hope, however, has not been realized, and about all that is cultivated are a few fields to supply the small demand for seed which still persists from the advertising the plant received. In southern California the Australian saltbush has become naturalized and moderately aggressive in a few places, but elsewhere it has not shown this trait.

After *Atriplex semibaccata* was introduced, many other species from Australia and South Africa were tested. Many of them grow well and some are quite ornamental, but none of them has come into use as a crop.

On the whole, the introduced species of *Atriplex* are

little, if any, superior to the numerous native species that grow on the alkaline lands of the West. None of the species yet introduced has shown any tendency to spread and become aggressive, except the European *Atriplex hastata* L. in the Columbia Basin.

CHAPTER XXVI

ROOT CROPS AND OTHER COMPARABLE FORAGES

Root crops were all developed primarily for use as human food and are still mainly grown for this purpose. They are similarly useful, however, as rich feed for domestic animals, and where they can be grown more cheaply than grain are important for such use.

697. Root crops. — This general phrase is used somewhat loosely in agronomic literature. In the broadest sense it includes all plants whose roots, tubers, bulbs or other underground vegetative parts are utilized. More generally, tubers, such as potatoes, and bulbs, such as onions, are excluded. As usually employed the term includes primarily beets or mangels, rutabagas, turnips and carrots. Some other roots used as forage are cassava, artichokes, sweet potatoes and chufas, but these are adapted to warmer climates. In a looser usage rape, kale and cabbage have been included with " root crops." The German term *hackfrüchte* or " hoe crops " is even less definite, including not only ordinary root crops, but pumpkins, cabbage and kale.

All of the root crops used for forage are also used as vegetables for human food, but the varieties grown for forage are the larger, coarser ones which produce correspondingly heavier yields.

583

Root crops for forage comprise in America but a small portion of the root crops grown. Much the larger part of the " root " crop is grown for vegetables and the acreage of beets for sugar is far greater than that of roots for forage.

The portion of the plant harvested in " root " crops is truly a thickened root in cassava, chufas and sweet potatoes. In beets, carrots, rutabagas and turnips, it is partly root and partly stem which merge insensibly together.

A root crop may replace any other cultivated crop in a rotation. As a rule four or more years should elapse before the same or a related root crop is grown on the same piece of land, as otherwise the damage by insects and disease is apt to be large.

698. Importance of root crops. — Root crops for forage are extensively grown for stock feed in northern Europe, especially Great Britain, Ireland, Germany, Denmark and Scandinavia. In America they have thus far been grown mainly in Canada. In the United States they are nowhere important, but according to the thirteenth census are most largely grown in the states of California, Colorado, Utah, New Mexico, Wisconsin, Washington, Oregon, Michigan and New York in order. The large use of forage roots in the first four states is probably associated with beet culture for sugar.

On the accompanying map is shown the number of acres of roots for forage in each state, according to the Thirteenth United States Census, and in each province according to the Fifth Canadian Census.

In a general way the lack of importance of root crops in the United States is correlated with the extensive culture of corn, which supplies a cheap grain feed for live stock. In northern localities, on the Pacific Coast and at high altitudes where corn or other equally cheap grain cannot be grown, root crops furnish the most satisfactory substitute. One pound of dry matter in root crops is considered about equal in feeding value to one pound of grain.

Perhaps the principal reason why root crops are not grown where corn or grain sorghums can be produced is the large amount of hand labor required by the former.

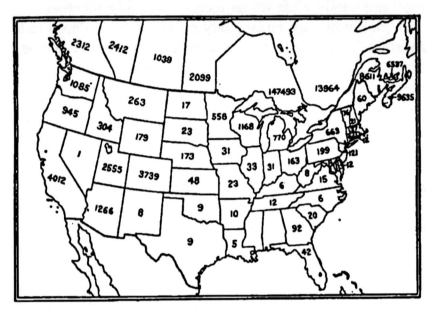

FIG. 62. — Root crops 1909–1910. Figures = acres.

If such be the explanation, root crops are likely to become more important as population becomes denser. At the Cornell Experiment Station the average cost for four years of producing one acre of mangels was $77.28 as contrasted with $40.77 for corn. The cost per pound of dry matter was low enough to be a profitable substitute for part of the grain rations.

699. Kinds of root crops. — The most important root crops grown for forage are mangels and sugar beets (*Beta* *vulgaris*), rutabaga (*Brassica campestris*), turnip (*Brassica rapa*), carrot (*Daucus carota*) and parsnip (*Pastinaca sativa*). These are all cultivated as vegetables; their culture on a large scale is by essentially the same methods. All of these root crops are best adapted to regions with a cool growing season, and hence their culture is most important northward. Southward the mangel and the turnip are grown more successfully than the others.

All of these root crops require a fertile, loamy soil to secure the largest yields. They are nearly always grown in rows wide enough to permit of easy cultivation. The culture of most of them, however, involves considerable hand labor, especially in thinning the rows.

700. Comparison of various root crops. — Inasmuch as mangels, sugar beets, rutabagas, turnips, carrots and parsnips are all adapted to very closely the same conditions, the problem arises as to which is to be preferred. In Great Britain more than 3 times as many rutabagas are grown as mangels, while in Germany, the reverse is the case. In Canada the acreage of mangels in 1910 was 53,576 against 76,488 for rutabagas and turnips.

In feeding value these roots apparently stand in the following order, sugar beets highest, followed by parsnips, mangels, rutabagas, carrots, turnips, but the differences are small.

The yields of mangels and rutabagas are decidedly greater than other roots, so the latter are grown more for special purposes or for variety. At the Ontario Agricultural College, the average yields to the acre for 26 years have been 27,600 pounds mangels, 25,740 pounds rutabagas and 20,760 pounds carrots. The yields at five different stations are compiled in the accompanying table : —

Comparative Acre' Yields of Different Root and Similar Crops at Experiment Stations.

Experiment Station or Farm	Mangels	Sugar Mangels	Sugar Beets	Carrots	Rutabagas	Hybrid Turnips	Turnips	Kohl-rabi	Cabbage	Parsnips
	Tons	*Tons*	*Tons*	*Tons*	*Tons*	*Tons*	*Tons*	*Tons*	*Tons*	*Tons*
Cornell, New York — 5-year averages:										
Green weight	39.7	28.1	28.3	18.5	26.3	27.1	16.8	23.4	36.4	8.3
Dry weight	4.2	3.2	4.0	2.2	2.5	2.6	1.8	2.3	2.3	1.9
Guelph, Ontario — 5-year averages 5 varieties	32.2		26.4	30.1	21.8		23.3 (4 vars.)	19.3 (2 vars. 7 yr.)	25.6 (4 vars.)	11 (4 vars.)
Ottawa, Ontario — 5-year averages 5 varieties	34.2		21.4 (3 vars.)	23.9	29					
Agassi, B.C. — 5-year averages 5 varieties	21.1		13.9 (3 vars.)	29.2 (4 vars.)	26		25.9			
Nappan, N.S. — 5-year averages 5 varieties	27.8		13.2 (3 vars.)	16.5	29.6					

The relation of roots to corn and other crops, as secured in Maine, show that even in the Northern States corn may outyield any root crop : —

SUMMARY OF AVERAGE YIELDS OF FODDER AND ROOT CROPS FOR 1890 AND 1891, MAINE EXPERIMENT STATION

CROP	ACRE YIELD OF CROP AS HARVESTED	ACRE YIELD OF DRY MATTER	ACRE YIELD OF DIGESTIBLE DRY MATTER
	Pounds	*Pounds*	*Pounds*
Southern corn	39,645	5,580	3,850
Rutabagas	31,695	3,415	2,978
Hungarian grass	18,910	4,680	2,967
Sugar beets	17,645	2,590	2,447
English flat turnips	28,500	2,559	2,375
Field corn (flint)	21,690	3,110	2,208
Sweet corn	18,260	2,671	1,870
Mangel-wurzels	15,375	1,613	1,266
Peas (seed)	1,665	1,415	1,231
Timothy hay (assumed crop)	4,000	3,500	2,065

701. Roots compared with corn and sorghum. — At the Michigan Experiment Station the yield of various root crops, both green and dry, was compared with those of corn and sorghum.

COMPARATIVE ACRE YIELDS OF ROOT CROPS, CORN AND SORGHUM AT THE MICHIGAN EXPERIMENT STATION

CROP	GREEN WEIGHT TO THE ACRE	DRY WEIGHT TO THE ACRE
	Pounds	*Pounds*
Carrots	28,836	3,322
Long red mangels	25,616	3,381
Tankard mangels	21,744	2,111
Rutabagas	31,028	3,742
Sugar beets	28,320	5,347
Corn	29,684	8,656
Sorghum	38,676	7,700

These results agree with those obtained by many other experimenters; namely, that where corn or sorghum will grow well, they will produce larger yields of dry matter than root crops.

RAPE (*Brassica napus*)

702. Rape is a native of temperate Europe. The wild plant is an annual, but the cultivated form may be either annual or biennial. The former is grown only for the seed, from which oil is extracted; and the latter mainly for forage. Like the other Brassicas it is best adapted to a cool growing season, and for heavy yields rich, moist soil is required.

There are several varieties of rape, but the Dwarf Essex is practically the only one grown for forage. Another variety, the Dwarf Victoria, is nearly as good, but in long-continued trials at the Ontario Agricultural College proved somewhat inferior.

703. Importance. — Rape is not an important forage crop in North America, but deserves far more attention than it has received. It is especially valuable for furnishing good feed in autumn and early winter when little other green feed is available. If thus utilized, it conserves the stock of hay and silage for winter use.

704. Seeding. — Rape may be sown in the North from May 1 to about the end of July. In Canada June 15 is about the best date. In the South fall sowing is most satisfactory. The seed should be planted about one-half inch deep, as with deeper planting the stand is likely to be very imperfect. At the Ontario Agricultural College large seed gave decidedly better yields than either medium or small seeds.

When rape is sown alone, the seed bed should be well

prepared. Three methods of seeding may be used; namely, in cultivated rows, in drill rows and broadcasted. If planted in rows to be cultivated, the rows should be as close as possible to permit of easy cultivation; 24 to 28 inches is the usual width of the rows, but they may be as narrow as 18 inches, or as wide as 36 inches. In 24-inch rows, 2 pounds of seed an acre is sufficient, and more than 3 pounds should not be used.

When planted in close rows with a grain drill, 4 pounds of seed an acre is used. If broadcasted, the same or a slightly larger amount is necessary. Too dense seeding causes crowding and consequently smaller growth.

At the Ontario Experimental Farm seed was drilled at various rates to the acre from 1.2 to 186.6 pounds. The lightest seeding gave the best results, but up to 6 pounds there was no great difference. The highest yield in the series was 18.5 tons and the lowest 14.1 tons. At the Tennessee Experiment Station rape was seeded March 31, April 16, April 30, May 14, June 15 and July. The last two seedings were failures. The others yielded respectively 8.5, 7.0, 6.0 and 3.9 tons green crop to the acre.

705. Place in rotations. — In the North rape is best adapted as a catch crop to come after oats or other spring-seeded grain. In the South it may take the place of crimson clover or fall-sown grain.

Where rape does well, it makes a dense growth which tends to smother out many weeds, and the subsequent close pasturing will destroy many of the remainder.

706. Sowing with another crop. — Rape is sometimes sown in spring with or in a crop of grain, such as wheat, oats or rye. One method is to broadcast the rape when the grain is two or three inches high, covering the seed by harrowing afterwards. Under favorable conditions a good stand of rape is obtained, which in a few weeks after harvesting the grain is ready for pasturing. At the Iowa Experiment Station rape was sown with oats in spring, but it grew large enough to interfere somewhat with the harvesting of the oat crop.

Sowing rape in corn at the last cultivation is frequently practiced, and where there is sufficient moisture for both crops, good results are obtained.

In Oregon rape is sometimes sown in spring with red clover, and the crops pastured in fall and early winter.

707. Utilization. — Rape is commonly utilized by pasturing to sheep or hogs. Cattle eat it readily, but destroy a considerable proportion by trampling. The loss from this cause is less where the rape is grown in rows, as the animals tend to follow the rows. Animals feeding on rape consume larger amounts of salt than usual, so that this should be freely supplied. It seems to prevent too great a purging effect which rape often produces. Most animals have to acquire a taste for rape before they will eat it readily. Care must be taken to avoid bloating.

Rape may also be used as a soiling crop. If fed to milch cows, it should be just after milking, as otherwise it may taint the milk. At the Michigan Experiment Station rape was preserved in a silo and the product was readily eaten by cows.

708. Carrying capacity of rape pastures. — Under favorable conditions rape is ready to pasture in 8 to 10 weeks after seeding. On this account it is often sown as a catch crop.

At the Ontario Agricultural College in 1890, 54 acres of rape were fed upon by 537 sheep and lambs and 18 head of steers for 59 days, and several acres were left unconsumed. In 1891, 666 lambs fed on 40 acres for over 2 months.

Craig states that an acre of good rape will carry 30 hogs for 2 months.

709. Yields. — Yields of rape range from 5 to 30 tons an acre green weight. The average yield on the experimental plots at Guelph, Ontario, for 6 years was 20.1 tons and the maximum 27.7 tons. Yields ·to the acre reported from other experiment stations are: New Hampshire, 50 tons; Wyoming, 14.6 tons; North Dakota, 5.5, 6.5, 14 and 5.2 tons for four years in succession; Florida, 16.59 tons; Michigan, 6.46 tons.

The average yield of a good field of rape is probably about 10 tons an acre.

710. Insects. — Rape, like all plants of the cabbage tribe, is much subject to the attacks of numerous insects, and this factor tends to restrict its culture as a field crop to regions where the growing season is cool. The most troublesome insects are the *Cabbage Aphis* (*Aphis brassicæ*), a small plant louse which often swarms on the plants in enormous numbers; the *Cabbage-worm* (*Pieris rapæ*), a smooth, green caterpillar that feeds on the leaves; the *Harlequin Plant-bug* (*Murgantia histrionica*), a handsome insect which sometimes attacks the leaves in enormous numbers and the *Root-maggot* (*Anthomyia brassicæ*), a small white grub which feeds on the roots near the surface.

KALE (*Brassica oleracea*)

711. The varieties of kale used for forage are the coarse-growing sorts, especially the one known as Thousand-headed. This is much grown in England and France as a soiling crop, and has been found admirably adapted to the north Pacific Coast, in Ontario, and in New England. The plants grow to a height of 3 to 5 feet or more and produce larger yields of succulent forage, which can be fed from October to April in regions where the winters are mild. Kale is usually fed to dairy cows, but to avoid tainting the milk, it should be fed just after milking, 25 to 40 pounds a day, in two feeds. The kale may be fed fresh or allowed to wilt before feeding, but it should not be cut more than four or five days before it is fed, nor should it be thrown in heaps, as it heats readily. Kale should not be fed while it is frozen. On the approach of freezing weather a supply sufficient to last several days should be placed in the barn.

Kale may be grown by planting the seeds in hills 2.5 to 3 feet apart and then thinning to one plant. It is better, however, to start the plants in a seed bed and then transplant. The seed should be sown as early in spring as conditions will permit, and the young plants transplanted to well-prepared land when 3 or 4 inches high. The transplanting is commonly done by dropping the plants into furrows at the proper distance apart so that the next furrow will cover the roots, but not the tops. The land is then rolled and any " misses " are later planted by hand.

Kale does not seed until the second year, and on the Pacific Coast the plants survive the winter. As the plants vary considerably, it is advisable to select the best plants. At the Puyallup, Washington, Substation, a yield of 1800 pounds of seed to an acre is reported.

Thousand-headed kale produced an average yield for 6 years of 19.1 tons an acre at the Ontario Agricultural College. At the New Hampshire Experiment Station a yield of 47,432 pounds to the acre was secured.

Another variety of kale called marrow cabbage, which has thick fleshy stems, has given very promising results in western Washington. This variety is differ-

2 Q

ent from marrow-stem kale, also used as a forage plant.

712. Diseases. — Kale, like other plants of the cabbage

VARIETIES OF RAPE, CABBAGE, KALE, ETC., AS FARM CROPS

VARIETIES	HEIGHT		GREEN FODDER TO THE ACRE	
	1910	Average, 6 yr., 1905-1910	1910	Average, 6 yr., 1905-1910
	Ins.	*Ins.*	*Tons*	*Tons*
Sutton Earliest Drumhead cabbage	20	18	25.2	27.3
Thousand-headed kale . . .	32	35	21.3	25.4
Sutton Giant Drumhead cabbage	21	21	21.2	25.2
Sutton Earliest Sheepfold cabbage	19	18	21.8	24.1
Large-seeded Umbrella rape .	32	28	25.7	22.7
Sutton Best of All Savoy cabbage	19	18	20.5	22.1
Large-seeded Common rape .	30	30	20.4	21.8
Dwarf Victoria rape	25	29	19.6	21.5
Marrow collards	28	24	19.2	21.5
Buckbee Wonderful Dwarf Bonanza rape	32	30	23.8	21.4
Dwarf Essex rape	24	29	20.1	21.2
Large-seeded White-flowering rape	29	30	22.3	20.8
Purple-sprouting boroccoli .	30	31	19.0	20.5
Hardy Curled kale	28	28	20.0	20.4
Jersey kale	34	33	19.5	20.2
Cabbage-leafed rape . . .	32	32	16.9	19.6
Brussels sprouts	25	25	16.0	16.3
New Chinese mustard . . .	50	60	12.8	14.8
Bloomsdale large-leafed mustard	50	58	12.4	14.5
White mustard	46	55	12.4	13.5
German rape	11	17	9.6	5.9

family, may be attacked by various diseases. One of the most common is club-root, or " finger and toe disease," caused by the myxomycete *Plasmodiophora brassicæ.* This causes the roots to become greatly enlarged and malformed. There is no direct remedy, and the organism causing the disease will live in the ground several years. Rotation is the best means of control.

713. Yields of kale, cabbage and other brassicaceous plants. — The relative yields of various brassicaceous plants other than root crops is well shown by the long-continued tests at the Ontario Agricultural College. In these trials the different varieties of cabbage taken together outyield any of the related groups ; namely, rape, kale, collards and similar plants.

JERUSALEM ARTICHOKE (*Helianthus tuberosus*)

714. The Jerusalem artichoke or topinambur is a native of America from Ontario to Saskatchewan south to Georgia and Arkansas. It was cultivated by the Indians for the edible tubers, and was early introduced into Europe. The artichoke is a sunflower with medium-sized heads, subcordate petioled leaves, and clustered tuberous roots. There are several varieties, distinguished by the color of the tubers, — white, yellow or red, — and by the shape of the leaves, either narrow or broad.

Artichokes seem to be less cultivated now than formerly, and are apparently relatively more important in Europe than in America. They are cultivated much after the manner of potatoes, the tubers being planted in hills 20 inches apart each way, or better, in rows 24 to 30 inches wide. The crop is permitted to grow until the plants are killed by frost. Artichokes are valuable as forage chiefly for hogs, and they are usually harvested by turning these animals in the field. The tubers keep in the ground all winter and usually enough of them are left by the hogs to make a new crop. Indeed, it is this weedy propensity of the artichoke that has militated much against its culture.

The yield of tubers to the acre ranges from 4 to 18 tons, but in western Washington records of 20 to 39 tons to the acre are reported.

CHUFA (*Cyperus esculentus*)

715. The chufa is apparently native in the subtropical regions of both hemispheres, but its culture originated in Mediterranean countries. It is a sedge-like plant with creeping rootstocks which produce small sweet tubers rarely over 1 inch in diameter. The tubers are eaten as human food or pastured to hogs.

The plant is propagated by the tubers, which are planted in spring in rows wide enough to be cultivated, placing the tubers about one foot apart in the rows. In the South they are sometimes planted in corn at the last cultivation. One peck of tubers is needed to plant an acre, and it is better to soak them a few days before planting.

Chufas are grown mainly in the Southern States. Practically all the " seed " is produced in Georgia, the product in 1909 of 481 acres being 12,531 bushels. The yields seem to vary greatly. At the Arkansas Experiment Station the product was estimated at 6992 pounds to the acre. At the Alabama Experiment Station the number of tubers in 8 hills were counted and found to average 568. The yield to the acre was determined as 172 bushels green or 115.24 bushels dry. At the Ontario Agricultural College the yield averaged 22.8 bushels an acre. One bushel weighs 44 pounds.

At the Arkansas Experiment Station one-fourth acre of chufas pastured by hogs was estimated to produce 138 pounds of pork. At the Alabama Experiment Station it was calculated that an acre of chufas pastured to hogs produced 307 pounds of pork.

CASSAVA (*Manihot utilissima*)

716. Cassava is a tropical plant probably native to Brazil. It is now cultivated in all parts of the tropics, mainly as a source of human food, and also as a basis for the manufacture of tapioca. Its culture is probably more important in Java than in any other country.

Cassava is a bushy, branched, woody-based herb commonly growing 4 to 10 feet in height. The leaves are palmately divided into 3 to 11 divisions which are oblanceolate, or rarely lanceolate, and from 5 to 10 inches long and about 1 inch wide. The flowers are polygamo-diœcious, that is, some are staminate, some pistillate and some perfect. Usually flowers on one plant are primarily pistillate and those on another primarily staminate. The fleshy, starchy roots grow in clusters of 4 to 8 to each plant, the largest being 3 to 4 feet in length and 2 to 3 inches in diameter, a single cluster weighing usually 5 to 10 pounds, but sometimes 20 to 30 pounds.

Cassava is adapted in the United States only to Florida and the southern portions of Georgia, Alabama, Mississippi, Louisiana, the coastal region of Texas and California. The plant requires abundant moisture during the growing season and preferably a sandy loam soil. The plants will grow well in clay soils, but the cost of harvesting the roots then becomes excessive.

The varieties of cassava are very numerous, but are usually put into two groups, namely, the sweet and the bitter, the latter containing more or less hydrocyanic acid in the roots and therefore poisonous. Under certain favorable conditions of soil and climate it seems that all cassavas tend to become sweet, and under unfavorable conditions there is a tendency for them to become bitter.

Cassava has been cultivated to a slight extent in Florida for at least 50 years, primarily for the manufacture of starch. It has also been employed to some extent to furnish root forage for live stock. Cultivated in this way, however, it is probably not as advantageous on the whole as sweet potatoes.

Cassava is commonly propagated by means of portions of the roots or portions of the stems which are stored in a dry place during winter and protected against damage by frost. The plants can also be propagated by means of seeds, but this results in great variation and besides the plants will not make as large growth in the same time. Seed canes are usually cut in pieces 4 to 8 inches in length and planted after all danger of frost is over. They are usually planted 4 feet apart each way.

One great trouble with cassava is the difficulty, at least under Florida conditions, of securing a perfect stand, as many of the canes rot or otherwise become weakened and do not produce plants. On this account the yields are very variable, the maximum being perhaps 20 tons to the acre.

The culture of cassava has never been very important in the United States and has greatly decreased in the last 20 years.

INDEX

THE following pages contain advertisements of a few of the Macmillan books on kindred subjects.

The Corn Crops

By E. G. MONTGOMERY

(Rural Text-book Series)

Cloth, 347 pages, index, ill., 12mo, $1.60 net

A valuable handbook on maize, kafirs and sorghum crops, including the grain sorghums, the sweet sorghums for syrup or forage and the broom corns. Adapted to both elementary and advanced classes of readers, as the theoretical principles of physiology, of production as related to climate and soils, and of the adaptation of the plant to the environment are separated from the practical treatment of cultural methods. These methods of cultivation may, therefore, be understood by the beginning student in school or college and by the busy farmer, without a previous study of the theoretical portions of the book.

Southern Field Crops

By Professor J. F. DUGGAR

Illustrated, cloth, 12mo, $1.75 net

This work has been prepared with special reference to the needs of high schools and colleges of the Southern States. In a systematic, yet simple manner it discusses each of the important field crops of the South.

Cotton and corn receive most extended treatment. Briefer space is devoted to oats, wheat, rice, the sorghums, sweet potatoes, cassava, peanuts, sugar cane and tobacco.

THE MACMILLAN COMPANY
Publishers   64-66 Fifth Avenue   New York

Manures and Fertilizers

By H. J. WHEELER, Ph.D., D.Sc.

Formerly Director of the Rhode Island Experiment Station
(Rural Text-book Series)

Illustrated. Cloth, 12mo, $1.60 net

The clear and unusually full discussion of the practical utilization of manures and fertilizers of all kinds, and of their relations to the plant and to the soil, makes this book not only an excellent text for college students, but also one which will be generally welcomed by all up-to-date agriculturists. All the animal manures, litter and waste nitrogenous materials of every sort are discussed. A helpful feature for the student is the extended treatment of the availability of organic nitrogen and of the organisms contained in barnyard manure which give rise to the various fermentations taking place therein. The well-known and also the new, nitrogenous manures, such as calcium cyanamid and calcium nitrate, are considered in detail. The chapters devoted to the potash salts, phosphates, lime, magnesia, soda, gypsum, iron and manganese are exceptionally complete, and chlorin, sulfur, silica, carbon disulfid, toluene and other substances exerting catalytic and other effects are described. Much of the material in this book, which will be new to students and other readers, has suggested itself to the author in the course of twenty-two years of continuous research.

Farm Management

By G. F. WARREN

(Rural Text-book Series)

Illustrated. 12mo, $1.75 net

This book teaches the necessity of efficient farm organization and management so as to secure the farmer the best crops at the lowest price. Professor Warren shows the way to such efficiency and thoroughly discusses the more important phases of farm management from the selection and purchase of the farm to the marketing of its products.

THE MACMILLAN COMPANY

Publishers   64-66 Fifth Avenue   New York

Principles of Soil Management

By Dr. T. L. LYON and Professor E. O. FIPPIN

(Rural Text-book Series)

Cloth, Ill., 12mo, $1.75 net

The volume is a complete and comprehensive study of everything relating to soils and soil management. The material is arranged under three general heads of (1) the soil as a medium for root development, (2) the soil as a reservoir for water and (3) plant nutrients of the soil.

"As a book indispensable to the teacher of agriculture, the intelligent farmer and student of farming, this is recommended."—*School Journal.*

". . . explicit and clear, and will undoubtedly prove a valuable reference book for all students of soils." — *Industrialist.*

"Complicated questions of farm management and conservation of lands are described with care, but, at the same time, with a lucidity which will gain for the book an entrance into homes of many practical farmers." — *Philadelphia North American.*

"An exhaustive and carefully prepared volume." — *Suburban Life.*

"It is one of the best books yet produced for college work on the study of soils." — *School Review.*

Plant Physiology with special reference to Plant Production

By Dr. B. M. DUGGAR

Ill., dec. cloth, 12mo, $1.60 net

In this book the author discusses the life relations of plants and crops from a fundamental point of view. The important physiological activities of the plan are demonstrated experimentally, and the practices of the crop-grower are reviewed from this standpoint. Some of the special topics that are considered are as follows: The relation of the plant and the crop to water; the relation to soil nutrients, stimulants and inhibiting agents; the relation to light and air; the relation to heat and cold; the relation to the disease environment.

THE MACMILLAN COMPANY

Publishers   64-66 Fifth Avenue   New York